The Sociology of Healthcare

A Reader for Health Professionals

Edited by

Sarah Earle and Gayle Letherby

palgrave
macmillan

First published 2008 by
PALGRAVE MACMILLAN
Houndmills, Basingstoke, Hampshire RG21 6XS and
175 Fifth Avenue, New York, N.Y. 10010
Companies and representatives throughout the world

PALGRAVE MACMILLAN is the global academic imprint of the Palgrave Macmillan division of St. Martin's Press, LLC and of Palgrave Macmillan Ltd. Macmillan® is a registered trademark in the United States, United Kingdom and other countries. Palgrave is a registered trademark in the European Union and other countries.

ISBN-13: 9–781–4039–4080–3 paperback
ISBN-10: 1–4039–4080–0 paperback

This book is printed on paper suitable for recycling and made from fully managed and sustained forest sources. Logging, pulping and manufacturing processes are expected to conform to the environmental regulations of the country of origin.

A catalogue record for this book is available from the British Library.

10   9   8   7   6   5   4   3   2   1
17   16   15   14   13   12   11   10   09   08

Printed in China

DEDICATION
For Charles Anthony Sharp

Contents

Acknowledgements

The editors and publishers wish to thank the following for permission to reprint copyright material:

PART I

Polity Press for pp. 11–20 of Annandale, *The Sociology of Health and Medicine*, copyright © Polity Press, 1998; Routledge for P. Abott, C. Wallace and M. Tyler, *An Introduction to Sociology: Feminist Perspectives*, 3rd edn, copyright © Routledge 2006; Hodder Education for D. Armstrong, *Outline of Sociology as Applied to Medicine*, 5th edn, Arnold 2003, copyright © David Armstrong, reproduced by permission of Edward Arnold; Sage for P. Atkinson, *Medical Talk and Medical Work: The Liturgy of the Clinic*, copyright © Sage 1995; Oxford University Press for C. Wright Mills, *The Sociological Imagination*, copyright © Oxford University Press, Inc 1999

PART II

Sage for K.F. Punch, *Introduction to Social Research: Quantitative and Qualitative Approaches*, copyright © Sage 1998; Sage for Sara Mallinson, Jennie Popay, Eva Elliot, Sharon Bennett, Lisa Bostock, Anthony Gatrell, Carol Thomas and Gareth Williams, 'Historical data for health inequalities: a research note', *Sociology*, 37:4 (2003) 771–80, copyright © Sage 2003; Sage for N. Fox, 'Practice based evidence: towards collaborative and transgressive research', *Sociology*, 37:1 (2003), 81–102, copyright © Sage 2003; The University of Surrey for B. Humphries, 'From critical thought to emancipatory action', *Sociological Research Online*, 2:1 (1997), copyright © University of Surrey 1997; Routledge for H. Roberts, 'Answering back: the role of respondents in women' health research', in H. Roberts (ed.) *Women's Health Matters*, copyright © Routledge 1992; The University of Surrey for C. Truman, 'Ethics and the ruling relations of research', *Sociological Research Online*, 8:1 (2003), copyright © University of Surrey 2003.

PART III

Baywood Publishing co., Inc for R. Crawford, 'You are dangerous to your health: the ideology and politics of victim blaming', *International Journal of Health Services*, 7:4 (1977) 663–80, copyright © Baywood Publishing Co., Inc 1977; Open University Press for Heather Joshi, Richard D. Wiggins, Mel Bartley, Richard Mitchell, Simon Gleave and Kevin Lynch, 'Putting health inequalities on the map', in H. Graham (ed.) *Understanding Health Inequalities*, copyright © Open University Press 2000; Elsevier for K. Backett–Milburn, S. Cunningham–Burley, and J. Davis, 'Contrasting lives, contrasting views? Understandings of health inequalities from children in differing social circumstances', *Social Science and Medicine*, 57 (2003) 613–23, copyright © Elsevier 2003; Palgrave Macmillan for L. Doyal, *What Makes Women Sick*, copyright © Palgrave Macmillan 1995; Polity Press for M. Bartley, *Health Inequality: An Introduction to Theories, Concepts and Methods*, copyright © Polity Press 2004

PART IV

Sage for D. Lupton, *Medicine as Culture: Illness, Disease and the Body in Western Culture*, copyright © Sage 2003; Taylor and Francis for P. Conrad and H. Jacobson, 'Enhancing biology: cosmetic surgery and breast augmentation', S. J. Williams, L. Burke and G. Bendelow (eds) *Debating Biology*, copyright © Taylor and Francis 2003; Sage Publications, Inc for A. Chapple and S. Ziebland, 'The role of humour for men with testicular cancer', *Qualitative Health Research*, 14:8, 1123 39, copyright © Sage Publications, Inc 2001; Taylor and Francis for S. Tierney, 'A reluctance to be defined "disabled": how can the social model of disability enhance understanding of anorexia?', *Disability and Society*, 16:5 (2001), copyright © Taylor and Francis; Sage Publications, Inc for I. Shaw, 'Dirty work patients and revolving doors', *Qualitative Health Research*, 14:8, copyright © Sage Publications, Inc 2004; Blackwell Publishing Ltd for B. Hunter, 'Emotion work in midwifery: a review of current knowledge', *Journal of Advanced Nursing*, 34:4 (2001) 436–44, copyright © Blackwell Publishing Ltd, 2001.

PART V

The University of Chicago Press for E. Freidson, *Profession of Medicine: A Study of the Sociology of Applied Knowledge*', copyright © University of Chicago Press, 1988 [1970]; Elsevier for M. Kelner, B. Wellman, H. Boon and S. Walsh, 'Responses of established healthcare to the professionalisation of complementary and alternative medicine in Ontario', *Social Science and Medicine*, 59:5, copyright © Elsevier

(2004); University of Toronto Press, Inc for T. L. Adams, 'Feminization of profession', *Canadian Journal of Sociology*, 30:1, copyright © University of Toronto Press, Inc, www.utpjournals.com (2005); Blackwell Publishing Ltd for S. Timmons and J. Tanner, 'A disputed occupational boundary', *Sociology of Health and Illness*, 26:5, copyright © Blackwell Publishing Ltd 2004; Palgrave Macmillan for A. Campbell, 'Cutting out motherhood', in S. Earle and G. Letherby (eds) *Gender, Identity and Reproduction: Social Perspectives*, copyright © Palgrave Macmillan 2003; Sage Publications, Inc for A. Broom 'Virtually He@lthy: the Impact of Internet use on disease experience and the doctor–patient relationship', *Qualitative Health Research*, 15:3, copyright © Sage Publications, Inc.

About the Editors

Sarah Earle is Lecturer in Health and Social Care at the Open University. Her research focuses on the sociology of reproduction and sexuality. She has worked within higher education for over 15 years and has a special interest in sociology as applied to health and healthcare education. She is Convenor of the British Sociological Association's Human Reproduction Study Group and Chair of the Open University's Birth and Death Research Group.

Gayle Letherby is Professor of Sociology at the University of Plymouth. Her research and writing interests are eclectic and include issues of method, methodology and epistemology; reproductive and non/parental identity (including pregnancy loss, infertility and involuntary childlessness, teenage pregnancy and young parenthood) and gender and health.

Thinking Sociologically about Health and Healthcare

Sarah Earle and Gayle Letherby

Sociology is a social science concerned, very broadly, with the study of human societies; and, indeed, it has been described as the 'science of society'. It is a relatively new discipline that originated in the early nineteenth Century and is one that consists of a range of perspectives, or ways of looking at the world; for this reason, sociology can be described as multi-paradigmatic. The sociology of health and healthcare has a much more recent history. It had its origins in the 1950s, although it did not really grow as a sub-discipline until the 1960s and 1970s. The sociology of health and healthcare, like sociology itself, is a broad church, encompassing a multiplicity of ways of thinking about the social world. The variety of subject areas that interest sociologists working within this sub-discipline are also diverse, ranging from the sociology of reproduction to the sociology of dying, death and disposal, the sociology of emotions, the sociology of the professions, the sociology of chronic illness and the sociology of organisations – to name just a few. In fact, it could be argued that it is possible to have a 'sociology of' just about any aspect of health and healthcare.

There are already numerous books on the sociology of health, illness and healthcare. So, you may ask, why another? Broadly, there are two reasons. Firstly, the majority of books of this type assume that the reader knows a considerable amount about sociology, and very little about health and illness, or healthcare. This book has been written specifically for healthcare professionals and, therefore, assumes the very opposite! However, although the book can be used by those for whom sociology is completely new, some of the readings will also challenge those who are more familiar with the discipline, at either pre- or post-registration levels. Secondly, the majority of similar books offer a collection of articles with little, or no, commentary on them and little effort is made to show where, when or how sociology can contribute to professional practice. It is our aim in this book to demonstrate how sociology can be usefully applied to health and healthcare and how it can be of use to the reflective practitioner.

The social sciences, including sociology, now play a part in the curricula of all the health professions in the UK, and elsewhere. However, over recent years there has been considerable interest and debate in this development. In particular, debates have focused on whether sociology should be included in the curricula of these professions and, if so, what role the discipline should play. The debate has been particularly lively in relation to the nursing curriculum. For example, Hannah Cooke (1993) and Sam Porter (1996; 1997) have both argued in favour of teaching sociology to nurses and indeed, in this context, Cooke has described sociology as an 'emancipatory discipline' (p. 125). In contrast, Keith Sharp (1994; 1995; 1996) has argued strongly against teaching sociology to nurses, as he believes that it cannot inform professional practice and, in fact, given its multi-paradigmatic nature, can actually be unhelpful. This debate has also been explored and extended elsewhere within nursing (for example, see Mullholland, 1997; Allen, 2001; Denny and Earle, 2005). The role of sociology within healthcare education has also been considered in relation to the training of doctors (Friedson, 1970; Guidotti, 1998), midwives (Symonds and Hunt, 1996; Kent 2000), and other professions allied to medicine (Jones *et al.*, 1998; Earle 2001).

There is no scope to rehearse all of these debates here. Nonetheless, this book seeks to show that the study of sociology as an intellectual discipline can be both challenging and rewarding for healthcare professionals. C. Wright Mills (1959) developed the concept of 'the sociological imagination' to show that it was necessary to look beyond common sense in order to make sense of society. He argued that the personal is influenced by social, political and economic factors and explained this by stating that 'private troubles' were often, in fact, 'public issues' (see Reading 5). In relation to health, illness and healthcare, it is easy to see how the problems sometimes faced by patients, carers or practitioners – which are often individual concerns – can often be better understood when placed into a wider context that takes into account the social, cultural and economic context that shapes and maintains such problems, and within which such problems are experienced. Another of our aims in editing the collection of readings in this book is to demonstrate how the substantive subject matter of the sociology of health and healthcare – with its broad-ranging interest in a variety of health matters and experiences – can offer a wealth of insight into the issues that concern practitioners working in different professions, within different settings and with a diverse range of patients or clients.

This reader focuses on a range of theoretical, methodological and conceptual themes and the main body of the book is organised into five discrete parts. The readings have been organised so as to develop key ideas and/or to set up debates between different perspectives or approaches within the sociology of health and healthcare. For example, the first part introduces you, very generally, to theoretical perspectives on the sociology of health and illness, the second part considers methodological approaches to researching health, the third examines inequalities in health, and so on. It would, therefore, make a lot of sense to work through this book chronologically, reading each part of the book in turn. Or, at least, it would make sense to work, chronologically, through the readings within discrete parts. However, this is not the only way in which you could use this book and, indeed, it would also work well if you were to adopt a 'pick-and-mix' approach, dipping into the readings that are most relevant to your own interests or professional needs at any particular time.

We provide a commentary on every reading, as well as an introduction to each section. The purpose of these commentaries is to facilitate a way into the reading that does not assume prior knowledge or expertise in either sociology or the sociology of health and healthcare. We would hope that this book will provide the stimulus to encourage further scholarship, and that the readings presented here will provide a springboard for this. To this aim, at the end of each reading there is a section giving annotated suggestions of books, book chapters, journals and articles on other interesting work in the area. After each reading you will also find several study questions and/or activities. Some of these questions and activities will encourage you to reflect critically on what you have read; others will encourage you to make connections between different readings within that part of the book, or across different parts. Many questions/activities will explicitly enable you to apply sociological concepts to your own practice. Overall then, if you use the book as we intend it to be used, it will encourage you to reflect critically on your own professional practice and on other aspects of health and healthcare.

Sociology provides a way of thinking about human society, as well as offers a methodological toolbox with which to explore it. In other words, this reader seeks to show how sociology can provide healthcare professionals with a conceptual and methodological framework to make better sense of health and healthcare. Some of the readings presented here have, over time, become classics within the sociology of health and healthcare. However, not all of the readings fall into this category. Many are far more recent and have been chosen for one, or more, of the following three reasons: (1) they reflect topical concerns; (2) they demonstrate sociological breadth and/or (3) they are relevant to a broad range of practice areas. Some of the readings are broad ranging and others are more immediately relevant to specific professional interests and occupations. What all the readings and associated commentaries have in common is a concern with the conceptual, theoretical and/or political issues relevant to the sociology of health and healthcare. Whatever your occupation and wherever you work, thinking sociologically about your own practice and that of others will enrich your professional role and enhance inter-professional working. The majority of readings focus on the United Kingdom, but others draw on work that has been carried out either in, or on, other countries in Europe, Australia, Canada or the United States.

The sociology of health and healthcare is a relatively new area of study, but there is an enormous, and growing, body of literature on the subject. As such, it has really not been possible to provide a 'definitive', or even a comprehensive, set of readings. The readings are intended to provide a theoretical, conceptual and methodological map of the sociology of health and healthcare that can be applied, by the reader, to their own practice. However, the selections presented here are as much a reflection of the literature, as they are a reflection of our own particular interests – as editors - and our own way of making sense of the social world. As with any similar endeavour, there is always a chance that we have offended by not choosing something that someone else would have chosen in our place. Given the limitations of space, there are some notable omissions and our favourites will not be shared by all.

In sum, we hope that you find the readings in this book interesting and that they will serve as a catalyst for further reading and reflection on the sociology of health and healthcare.

REFERENCES

D. Allen, 'Review article: nursing and sociology: an uneasy marriage?' *Sociology of Health & Illness*, 23:3 (2001) 386–96.

H. Cooke, 'Why teach sociology?' *Nurse Education Today*, 13:3 (1993) 210–17.

E. Denny and S. Earle, *Sociology for Nurses* (Oxford: Polity, 2005).

S. Earle, 'Teaching Sociology within the Speech and Language Therapy Curriculum', *Education for Health*, 14:3 (2001) 383–91.

E. Friedson, *Profession of Medicine: A Study of the Sociology of Applied Knowledge* (London: University of Chicago Press, 1988 [1970]).

T. L. Guidotti, 'An Alternative Medical Curriculum for Changing Times', *Education for Health*, 11:4 (1998) 233–42.

D. Jones, S. E. E. Blaire, T. Hartery and R. K. Jones (eds) *Sociology & Occupational Therapy* (London: Churchill Livingstone, 1988).

J. Kent, *Social Perspectives on Pregnancy and Childbirth for Midwives, Nurses and the Caring Professions* (Buckingham: OUP, 2000).

C. Wright Mills, *The Sociological Imagination* (Oxford: Oxford University Press, 1959).

J. Mullholland, 'Assimilating sociology: critical reflections on the "Sociology in nursing" debate', *Journal of Advanced Nursing*, 25 (1997) 844–52.

S. Porter, 'Why teach sociology? A contribution to the debate', *Nurse Education Today*, 16:3 (1996) 170–4.

S. Porter, 'Sociology and the nursing curriculum: a further comment', *Journal of Advanced Nursing*, 26:1 (1997) 214–18.

K. Sharp, 'Sociology and the nursing curriculum: a note of caution', *Journal of Advanced Nursing*, 20 (1994) 391–5.

K. Sharp, 'Sociology in nurse education: help or hindrance?' *Nursing Times*, 91:20 (1995) 34–5.

K. Sharp, 'Sociology and the Nursing Curriculum: A Response to Sam Porter', *Journal of Advanced Nursing*, 26 (1996) 1–4.

A. Symonds and S. C. Hunt, *The Midwife and Society: Perspectives, Policies and Practice* (London: Macmillan, 1996).

Sociological Perspectives on Health and Healthcare

Introduction

In this, the first part of the reader, we introduce you to some of the sociological concepts and theories that are of particular concern when studying the sociological aspects of health and illness, and experiences of healthcare. We could have selected the readings in this part with the view of guiding you through a 'grand tour' of theories and theorists: starting with the founders of the discipline – Karl Marx, Max Weber and Emile Durkheim – and following this with historical and contemporary critique and development. Alternatively, we could have included only readings that provide an introduction to, or outline of, the sociology of health. We have taken neither of these approaches. Instead, we have included a mixture of readings; some that focus on particular theoretical and/or political approaches, some that introduce sociological concepts, some that claim a special place for sociology in intellectual thinking and others that critique previous sociological works.

Anyone who has ever heard of sociology will almost certainly have heard some of the criticisms levied at the discipline. Sociology is sometimes described as 'soft', as 'just common sense', or as 'trivial'. Ironically, it is also criticised for being 'full of jargon', 'too theoretical' and 'obsessed with data'. What is particularly interesting and useful about sociology is that it has relevance for us all as it challenges the taken-for-granted and asks questions about aspects of all of our lives. Arguably, this is what leads to the criticisms, as sociology both confirms and disturbs what we think we know about the world in which we live. So as Peter Berger (1967, pp. 32–3) argues:

> The fascination of sociology lies in the fact that its perspective makes us see in a new light the very world in which we have lived all our lives.

1

There are five readings in this part of the book and after reading them we hope that you will begin to see the relevance of, and be fascinated by, the sociological exploration and the explanation of health. The first reading is by Ellen Annandale who outlines some sociological explanations of health, and some of the sociological critiques of healthcare. Annandale focuses on some of the earliest sociological considerations of health – and some of the most recent – so this reading will provide you with an interesting, if partial, historical view of the discipline. From this you will see how sociological research and writing responds to societal change. In Reading 2, Pamela Abbott, Claire Wallace and Melissa Tyler consider the specific contribution of feminist sociology to understanding health and healthcare. They look at the relationship between women, health and reproduction and consider the positives and negatives of the medicalisation of experiences such as birth control, pregnancy, childbirth and infertility; experiences in the past were considered to be subject to individual biological capabilities. Both the next two readings – Reading 3 by David Armstrong and Reading 4 by Paul Atkinson – are concerned with the social aspects, and experiences, of medicine. As such, Armstrong and Atkinson each consider the relationships within medical settings, for example, the doctor/patient relationship. In addition, Armstrong is concerned about the problems with defining a disease, and Atkinson, with anthropological as well as sociological issues relating to healthcare settings. Finally, Reading 5 is an extract from C. Wright Mills' (1959) classic text *The Sociological Imagination*, already mentioned in the general introduction to the reader. Thinking sociologically about health and healthcare, we include this here for several reasons. Firstly, to provide an example of how to think sociologically. Secondly, to demonstrate the usefulness of thinking sociologically in relation to 'healthy' and 'unhealthy' behaviours, relationships between dentists and their clients, differences between health in the United Kingdom and health in developing countries, and so on. And, thirdly, to introduce you to sociological thinking before you go on to read the next part of the book that focuses on issues of method, methodology and epistemology within sociology.

REFERENCES

P. L. Berger, *Invitation to Sociology: A Humanist Perspective* (Harmondsworth: Penguin, 1967).

C. Wright Mills, *The Sociological Imagination* (Oxford: Oxford University Press, 1959).

Reading 1

The Political Economy of Health and Healthcare

Ellen Annandale

By outlining some of the earliest sociological explanations of health and illness, and sociological critiques of healthcare, Ellen Annandale's discussion demonstrates sociology's concern to move beyond individual explanations, towards a social analysis of health, illness and healthcare. Taken from one chapter in a whole book concerned with the sociology of health and illness, in this reading Annandale considers the origins and current relevance of the political economy perspective as relevant to health, illness and healthcare systems. The roots of this approach lie generally in Marxist thinking, and specifically, in Freidrich Engels' *The Condition of the Working Class in England*, which was first published in 1845. Engels argued that health and healthcare could be understood only in relation to the political and economic framework. Illness, then, is socially produced under capitalism and the healthcare service itself becomes part of the capitalist system. Having outlined the main argument of the political economy approach, Annandale goes on to consider two ways in which capitalism operates in the search for profit in the field of health and healthcare today. Her first example is the manufacture of the silicone breast implant, which she provides as an example of body modification. For her second example she considers how the focus on lifestyle, in a time that some have called late capitalism, leads to a stress on individual responsibility for health. Through these two examples Annandale introduces some of the criticisms of the political economy approach. She also briefly considers the argument suggested by some contemporary theorists that it is through an analysis of 'risk' and not class (and other differences such as gender and 'race') that we can best understand individual experiences of health and healthcare.

Although this is only a short reading, many of the issues that Annandale explores are considered by other authors in this reader. For example see

Section III for several articles on inequalities and diversity in health and healthcare and see Section IV (especially Reading 18) for some further examples of body commodification/modification.

THE POLITICAL ECONOMY PERSPECTIVE

By the 1970s a clear agenda had been set for medical sociology: to liberate contemporary understandings of health and medicine from the political straitjacket of the biomedical model. The roots of the political economy approach lie in Engels' *The Condition of the Working Class in England* (1993 [1845]). Engels analysed the aetiology and distribution of typhoid, tuberculosis, scrofula and rickets in the population and concluded that, since they had a direct association with the relations of production under capitalism, medical intervention alone was insufficient for the eradication of disease. Out of these beginnings, the political economy approach has built a profound criticism of the social production of ill health under capitalism. The central tenet is that there is a contradiction between the pursuit of health and the pursuit of profit (Doyal, 1979). Medicine is enmeshed in the constant search for profit by finance and industrial capitalists, itself both contributing to and bolstered by the capitalist system and girded by the activities of the state. Crucially, this tripartite relationship operates in the interests of capitalism (largely) in the interests of medicine, but definitely not in the interests of the health of the population.

It should be apparent that from this perspective there is little to be gained by attempting to understand health and healthcare by reference to the activities of individuals or to the institution of medicine; they must be placed within a broader political and economic framework. McKinlay sets this framework up nicely through the analogy of the game. He argues that

> one can conceive of medical care-related activities as the game among a group of highly trained players, carefully selected for the affinity of their interests with the requirements of capitalist institutions, which is watched by a vast number of spectators (involving all of the people some of the time and, increasingly, some of the people all the time). And surrounding this game itself, with its interested public, is the capitalistic state (setting the rules by which the game ought to be played before the public), the presence of which ensures the legitimacy of the game and guarantees, through resources derived from spectators, that the prerogatives and interests of the park (finance and industrial capital) are always protected and advanced. (1977: 464–5)

Capital invades all areas of life (home, work, leisure time) creating health-related problems such as unemployment, pollution and stress in the unmitigated search for profits. Social services grow to meet this demand and medicine takes on the impossible task of solving problems that are outside its control (Navarro, 1986).

So, although the profession of medicine is a target of criticism from the political economy perspective, since historically it can be seen to have actively sought a position of dominance, it is not the ultimate culprit since its power is delegated by capital. Capital operates in the field of health in the same way that it does in all other areas of society: 'invading, exploiting, and ultimately despoiling any field of endeavour – with no necessary humane commitment to it – in order to seize and carry away an acceptable level of profit' (McKinlay, 1977: 461). McKinlay (1984) refers to a logic of capital accumulation in healthcare which operates in cycles as follows: (1) competition forces capitalists to expand their output and sales (irrespective of the use-values of the commodities that are produced); (2) this generates profit, which (3) needs to be reinvested (in new ventures and in research); (4) profit must be realized on these new ventures; (5) there is a search for new buyers and new markets, often using deceptive advertising and the creation of a commodity-fetishist culture; (6) foreign markets are also captured; (7) profits are reinvested, returning us to the beginning of the cycle. These forces underpin the operation of formal and informal healthcare, and also circumscribe our definitions of health and illness.

Political economists have explored the range of ways in which capital operates in the search for profit in the field of health and healthcare, supported by the state and mediated by medicine. Here we will look at just two broad areas for illustration. First of all, we will consider the commodification of the body, taking the manufacture of silicone breast implants as our example. The second illustration will be the way in which the lifestyle politics of 'late capitalism' foster an ideology of health which stresses individual responsibility.

CAPITAL AND THE COMMODIFICATION OF THE BODY

The process of industrialization, from the early development of manufacturing capital through to the high-technology industries of the late twentieth century, carries risks to health of various kinds from exposure to chemical toxins, to the E. coli outbreak and BSE crisis, to dangers in the construction trade, and the stresses and strains experienced by chief executive and shop-floor worker alike. For some commentators (e.g. Hart, 1982) it is this wider process of industrialization, rather than in capitalist variant, which is at fault. Yet political economists insist that there is an inevitable contradiction between safety and the pursuit of profit. Women's current struggle for compensation for the side-effects of silicone breast implants provides a good illustration of this. In 1963 Dow Corning (a subsidiary of Dow Chemical Company) began manufacturing a breast implant consisting of a semi-permeable envelope of silicone elastomer filled with silicone gel. The silicone gel was deemed to be inert, so if a rupture occurred the gel would not migrate or be harmful to body tissue. However, since the 1970s a minority of surgeons became concerned with the transgression of silicone across the envelope of the implant (often called gel-bleed) and began to press manufacturers and the US Federal Drugs Agency (FDA) for a moratorium on production. According to Jenny (1994) and others, this pressure went unheeded for far too long as plastic surgeons and manufacturers convinced the FDA that silicone implants were safe.

Approximately one million women had implants for cosmetic reasons and for reconstruction after surgery for breast cancer and other conditions during the 1980s and early 1990s. Levy (1994) estimates that this includes between 30,000 and 50,000 women in the United Kingdom (about 60 per cent of these implants were done after surgery for breast cancer). By 1994, 36,000 women had reported injuries (such as implant ruptures) and were seeking damages (Tran, 1995). Two major risks to health have now been identified. First of all, silicone gel bleeds into the body from the envelope and has been linked to serious diseases such as systemic sclerosis, lupus and other auto-immune and neurological conditions (many of these conditions may have a latency period of thirty years). The second problem is encapsulation, which occurs as the body reacts to the presence of silicone by developing a hard encircling capsule of fibrous tissue around the implant. In addition to these two problems, since silicone gel is radio-opaque, radiographers can have difficulty visualizing breast tissue behind the implant, which hampers the early detection of breast cancers. Several women have died as a result of the side-effects of silicone implants and a great many more live with chronic illnesses which seriously impair their lives. In August 1997 a state jury in Louisiana found that the Dow Chemical Company had knowingly deceived women by hiding information about silicone and health risks. In 1992 the FDA had banned all but their limited use in the US (in the UK the Department of Health has taken the stance that more evidence is needed before it can be concluded that they are unsafe, although at the time of writing in the summer of 1997 a new review looks imminent). Dow Corning and other manufacturers have stopped manufacturing implants, but still insist that they are safe.

During the 1980s Dow Corning (the major manufacturer) settled a number of US lawsuits out of court with confidentiality clauses attached and court protection of all findings and medical records. In 1988 Mariann Hopkins filed a lawsuit and resolved not to settle despite an offer of $1.8 million to do so. The jury ruled in her favour to the tune of $7.3 million and Dow Corning was found guilty of fraud and malice. The case opened up the floodgates to litigation, prompting Dow Corning to settle $4.225 billion in 1993 on a class action suit. In such a suit the claims and rights of many people (currently estimated at approximately 400,000 women world-wide) are decided in a single court proceeding on a 'no win no fee' basis. There are a number of benefits of opting into a class action suit, not the least being that there is no need to prove that current illness postdates the claimant's first implant. On the down side, it is rumoured that the very large number of women in the class action means that payouts may be considerably smaller than those that could be achieved in a successful individual lawsuit. Moreover, while in the class action Dow Corning and other manufactures can continue to deny liability (it is a 'business decision' to settle cases), in separate lawsuits they can be held accountable. However, in an individual case in the US a woman would need to prove cause, and such suits have had a chequered success rate to date. Tran (1995) reports that 1,500 women have opted out of the class settlement to date to pursue separate actions. According to a spokesperson for Dow Corning 'we have consistently said that we cannot both fund the global settlement [class action] and afford large numbers of law suits outside the settlement' (quoted in Tran, 1995: 3). In May 1995 Dow Corning filed for bankruptcy protection.

Particular technologies are, then, implicated in health risks, but these risks are exacerbated by the search for profit, with medicine operating as a lucrative site for capital. In brief, capitalism despoils both health and healthcare.

The political economy perspective has been subject to strong criticism on a number of counts. For example, several commentators (Hart, 1982, 1985; Reidy, 1984) argue that it fails to recognize health gains – such as the increases in living standards and in longevity – that have accompanied capitalist development. In response political economists – Navarro (1985a, 1985b) in particular – have pointed to the contradictions of capitalism and the possibility for (short-term) working-class gains. In addition, many sociologists within this tradition are themselves actively engaged in activities to effect reform from *within* the capitalist system. (For example, Navarro (1994) was centrally involved in defining health policy for Jesse Jackson's Rainbow Coalition in the late 1980s and was a member of Hillary Clinton's National Healthcare Reform Task Force.) To argue that improvements in mortality undermine the political economy position in particular seems to miss the mark since the concern is with *relative* differentials in morbidity and mortality between social classes.... Concerns about the ability of individuals and social groups to effect social change within the Marxist political economy perspective, however, carry more weight. While Navarro has consistently emphasized the role of working-class praxis in the struggle for health and healthcare under capitalism, this has often been framed at a fairly high level of generality drawing upon limited examples, leaving the complex relationship between structure and agency largely unarticulated. Gerhardt (1989: 331) raises the question of whether 'individuals are seen as anything but docile members of a pervasive social order'. Even Waitzkin's (1991) work on the micro-politics of healthcare, which explores the ways in which apparently humanistic and unproblematic encounters between doctors and patients mask assumptions which encourage conformity with the dominant expectations of capitalism (such as the work ethic), leaving the structural problems which foster ill health unchallenged, seems to overstate the influence of medical ideology on patients, or at least fails to explore the possibility that patients do not accept the doctors' view of their problem uncritically.

DISORGANIZED CAPITALISM: A NEW POLITICAL ECONOMY OF HEALTH?

Although the criticisms that have been raised deserve ongoing consideration, their immediacy as *particular* issues for debate is tempered by the weightier general question of the current status of Marxist social theory itself. Bluntly put, if Marxism is dead, what implications does this have for the political economy of health? For many, events of the early 1990s in the former Soviet Union and eastern Europe signal not only the end of communism, but also a death blow to Marxism, which is seen to have come to an 'end' itself (Makdisi et al., 1996: ix). For example, Lash and Urry (1994: 1) begin their exploration of the nature of late capitalism in a deliberately provocative tone, by asking: is 'any writer more dated, more of a "dinosaur", than Marx?' Certainly, the industrial capitalism that Marx described no longer exists, as the extraction of surplus for profit has shifted from the production of commodities with a relatively stable use-value to satisfy fairly easily defined needs, to a phase of what Lash and Urry call 'disorganized capitalism' where use-values are destabilized as capitalism becomes at once increasingly fragmented, flexible and international in form. In concrete terms, we have seen a radical shift from an economy in which people transform raw material into mass-market goods, to a flexible economy based on the production of knowledge and information. The old order where the 'capitalist core was characterised by a set of producer networks clustered around a heavy-industrial hub of the motor, chemicals, electrical and steel industries' and where 'finance, services and distribution functions were either subordinate to, or driven by, industrial production' has given way to a new cluster of information, communication and other industries (Lash and Urry, 1994: 17).

While – as has been the case for Marxism ever since the nineteenth century – conflicting interpretations abound, for many commentators what we are witnessing rather than the *end* of capitalism, is its *revitalization* as new arenas of exploitation open up quite unlike any that have gone before. As Landry and MacLean (1993: xii) put it, now 'the market is "in" everything and nothing is incapable of being commodified'. Modernity, therefore, has not been superseded, but, in the words of Lash and Urry, radically exaggerated. Individuals live in a world that has a runaway character, subject to a veritable barrage of information and new goods, many of which are more important for the status that they confer than for their use-value – status symbols, such as designer labels, for example, having more importance than the basic use of the product. Lash and Urry (1994: 3) argue that the flows and accumulations of images and symbols of disorganized capitalism do not 'just lead to increasing meaninglessness', rather, they encourage the development of a new *critical reflexivity*, or sense of freedom to act, on the part of individuals, which is itself a *precondition* of capital accumulation through consumption. For a large part of society – the professional–managerial classes and the skilled working class – this means a new empowerment, as traditional structures like social class and the family recede to be replaced by a new ability to make consumer choices; for others there is spiralling downward mobility into the de-industrialized spaces of the impacted ghetto (in the shift of manufacturing from the cities to the suburban and ex-urban locations).

Capitalism, then, is still with us and the issue that we must wrestle with is not its demise, but its revitalization in new forms. For some, Marx's social theory is still relevant to this task, while for others it has lost its usefulness and new conceptualizations are needed. For example, Giddens (1994: 87) contends that Marxist politics provide no solution to new risks associated with 'the driving expansionism of capitalistic enterprise'. To date, with just a few exceptions, sociologists of health and medicine have remained relatively quiet on these issues. However, it is possible for us to follow their implications through to a number of key areas of interest such as inequalities in health, the restructuring of healthcare provision, and the experience of illness.... Here we will briefly take up recent theoretical work on reflexivity, risk and health in late modernity.

REFLEXIVITY AND RISK, AND HEALTH IN LATE MODERNITY

Modern society, it has been argued, is a 'risk society' which puts the phenomenon of health centre-stage. Concern now is no longer simply that economic hazards undermine health, but that environmental risks to health threaten the very existence of society as 'everywhere and eternally' they 'penetrate the economic and political system' (Beck, 1992: 83). In this new social environment, risk is increasingly opened to the public gaze and new political forms emerge. Power is decentralized from the state into the specialized division of labour which Beck refers to as 'techno-economic subpolitics'. Modes of living in risk society are very much tied to the sub-politics of medicine, that is, the broad arena of medical industries and health institutions. Medicine, defined in this way, employs a market strategy which profits from risk. Beck claims that

> in more and more fields of action a **reality** defined and thoroughly structured by medicine is becoming the prerequisite of thought and action ... not only is the spiral of medical formation and decision-making twisted deeper and deeper into the ... reality of the risk society, but an **insatiable appetite for medicine** is produced, a permanently expanding market for the services of the medical profession whose ramifications echo into the distant depths. (1992: 211)

This means that risks to health *themselves* become an economic factor as new markets are generated for products such as filters for pollutants and vitamin complexes to enhance nutrition in an age of chemically infused fast foods. Science itself turns towards the definition and management of the very risks which it itself produces. The boom industry of cosmetic surgery, on which $300 million and rising are spent every year in the USA (Davis, 1995), epitomizes Beck's medical sub-politics. As we have seen in the discussion of silicone breast implants, the health risks that it generates can be enormous, yet the decision to undergo cosmetic surgery is itself part and parcel of the emergence of the self as a 'reflexive project'. Giddens in particular stresses that under conditions of high modernity, the body is 'reflectively mobilised' becoming a 'phenomenon of choices and options' (1991: 8). As the 'visible aspect of the self', the body is not passive but needs to be monitored by individuals as they balance opportunities and risks, virtually forced to design their own bodies, and to do so under conditions of considerable uncertainty. Anorexia, Giddens claims, is symptomatic of the negative effects of what he calls manufactured uncertainty on everyday life: 'deciding what to eat', he writes, 'is also deciding "how to be" in respect to the body – and for individuals subject to specific social tension, particularly young women, the iron self-discipline of anorexia results' (1994: 82). In wider terms, of course, the billion-dollar diet industry also epitomizes the new forms of capitalist enterprise that have emerged over recent decades.

In the opinion of both Giddens and Beck, the global conditions of late modernity invite us to reconsider the nature of individual experience which, it is argued, is no longer bound by class, gender and 'race', but exposed to new social parameters of risk and uncertainty which cross-cut traditional social divisions. To be sure, these divisions still have *relevance* for people, but they are no longer, in a straightforward way, the units from which experience derives. Risks to health of various kinds, ranging from nuclear catastrophe to mysterious viral infections, contaminated foods, and stresses from unemployment and unhappy marriages, must be dealt with reflexively as the individual increasingly stands alone, looking for security in the face of uncertainty and an implosion of knowledge-systems. While arguably reflexivity might increase 'health awareness' – indeed this is a plank of contemporary health promotion – being forced to make choices by accessing an array of expert information, under conditions of uncertainty, can create considerable anxiety. How does the individual cope?... at this point it may be useful to take one illustration, that of prenatal diagnosis. Katz Rothman's (1988) study of prenatal diagnosis vividly demonstrates the stresses that women experience in a social climate of risk that values knowledge and making informed choices. Women's reasons for refusing amniocentesis (taking amniotic fluid from the uterus to test for genetic abnormalities), which may centre around a commitment to the foetus/baby, feelings of safety (will the baby be 'normal'?), a sense of late, or the unacceptability of abortion, are difficult to justify in a world which values the information and 'choice' that an amniocentesis result ostensibly provides. Katz Rothman shows that, far from providing choice and control, amniocentesis creates a 'tentative pregnancy'; fearful of a 'bad result', women cannot embrace their pregnancy, maintaining an emotional distance from the baby/foetus and denying or not letting themselves really feel foetal movements until the test result is available.

As Crawford (1984) has discussed very well, capitalist ideology is refracted through health beliefs, be this through the promotion and consumption of new medical technologies such as amniocentesis or silicone breast implants, or through diet stuffs and exercise programmes. In many ways foreshadowing the work of Giddens, Beck and others, he points out that 'when macro-conditions that affect health appear out of control, self-control over the considerable range of personal behaviours that also affect health is an only remaining option' (1984: 74). The burden of responsibility is placed squarely upon the individual, breaking the connection between good health and the demand for public services in the process. Yet an economy built on 'responsibility' and *selfcontrol* alone – profitable though it may be (the diet industry, health clubs) – is ruinous to late capitalism. Consequently it exists alongside the economic mandate to *consume* market-offered goods, as immediate gratification is portrayed as a source of stress reduction and emotional and physical well-being.

This introductory discussion of the political economy perspective has highlighted its status as a theory in transition. Buffeted by the significant challenges to its Marxist foundations and by the restructuring of capitalism ... within the field of the sociology of health and medicine it has yet to re-establish a truly firm theoretical foundation in an era of significant social change....

REFERENCES

Beck, U. (1992) *Risk Society*. London: Sage.
Crawford, R. (1984) A cultural account of 'health': control, release, and the social body. In J. McKinlay (ed.), *Issues in the Political Economy of Health Care*, London: Tavistock, 60–103.
Davis, K. (1995) *Reshaping the Female Body: The Dilemma of Cosmetic Surgery*. London: Routledge.
Doyal, L. (1979) *The Political Economy of Health*. Boston: South End Press.
Engels, F. (1993 [1845]) *The Condition of the Working Class in England*. Oxford: Oxford University Press.
Gerhardt, U. (1989) *Ideas about Illness*. Basingstoke: Macmillan.
Giddens, A. (1991) *Modernity and Self Identity*. Cambridge: Polity Press.
—— (1994) *Beyond Left and Right: The Future of Radical Politics*. Cambridge: Polity Press.
Hart, N. (1982) Is capitalism bad for your health? *British Journal of Sociology*, 33, 435–43.
—— (1985) *The Sociology of Health and Medicine*. Ormskirk, Lancs.: Causeway Books.
Katz Rothman, B. (1988) *The Tentative Pregnancy*. London: Pandora.
Landry, D. and MacLean, G. (1993) *Materialist Feminisms*. Oxford: Blackwell.
Lash, S. and Urry, J. (1994) *Economies of Signs and Space*. London: Sage.
Levy, R. (1994) Silicone litigation. *Solicitors Journal*, 25 November, 1214–15.
McKinlay, J. (1977) The business of good doctoring or doctoring as good business: reflections on Freidson's view of the medical game. *International Journal of Health Services*, 7, 459–83.
—— (ed.) (1984) *Issues in the Political Economy of Health Care*. London: Tavistock.
Makdisi, S., Caserino, C. and Kark, R. (1996) Preface and Introduction. Marxism, communism and history: a reintroduction. In S. Makdisi, C. Caserino, and R. Kark (eds), *Marxism Beyond Marxism*. London: Routledge, ix–x, 1–13.
Navarro, V. (1985a) US Marxist scholarship in the analysis of health and medicine. *Social Science and Medicine*, 15, 525–45.
—— (1985b) Double standards in the analysis of Marxist scholarship: a reply to Reidy's critique of my work. *Social Science and Medicine*, 20, 441–51.
—— (1986) *Crisis, Health and Medicine*. London: Tavistock.
—— (1994) *The Politics of Health Policy: The US Reforms 1980–1994*. Oxford: Blackwell.
Reidy, A. (1984) Marxist functionalism in medicine: a critique of the work of Vicente Navarro on health and medicine. *Social Science and Medicine*, 19, 897–910.
Tran, M. (1995) Breast implant firm files for bankruptcy. *Guardian*, 16 May, 3.
Waitzkin, H. (1991) *The Politics of Medical Encounters*. New Haven: Yale University Press.

Source: E. Annandale, *The Sociology of Health and Medicine: A Critical Introduction* (Cambridge: Polity Press, 1998).

Study Questions and Activities

1. From the perspective of the political economy approach, why is illness inevitable under capitalism? Consider the 'logic of capital accumulation' (McKinlay 1977 cited by Annandale) in relation to your own area of practice. Explain whether you agree or disagree with this theory.
2. Do the work of Giddens (1991) and Beck (1992) challenge or add to the political economy perspective?
3. In what ways is the self a 'reflexive project'?
4. Who do you think has benefited most from the manufacture of the silicone breast implant?

————————————————— **Further Reading** —————————————————

In addition to the book from which this reading is taken, Ellen Annandale has written several other books that you will find interesting and useful: *Gender Inequalities in Health* (edited with K. Hunt Buckingham: Open University Press, 2000); *The Sociology of Medical Knowledge, Medical Work and Healthcare* (edited with M. Elston and L. Prior, London: Blackwell, 2004) and *Feminist Theory and the Sociology of Health and Illness* (London: Routledge, 2002). There are lots of other books that provide overviews of the sociology of health. See, for example: M. Bury, *Health and Illness in a Changing Society* (London: Routledge, 1997); S. Nettleton, *Sociology of Health and Illness* (Cambridge: Polity Press, 1995) and M. Stacey, *The Sociology of Health and Healing* (London: Macmillan, 1988). If you would like to follow up some of the arguments that Annandale introduces, look for Freidrich Engels' *The Condition of the Working Class in England* (Oxford: Oxford University Press, 1999 [1845]); Ivan Illich's *Limits to Medicine: Medical Nemesis: The Expropriation of Health* (London: M. Boyars, 1995); Anthony Giddens' *Modernity and Self-Identity. Self and Society in the Late Modern Age* (Cambridge: Polity Press, 1991); Ulrich Beck's *Risk Society: Towards a New Modernity* (London: Sage, 1991); Barbara Adam, Ulrich Beck and Joost Van Loon's *The Risk Society and Beyond: Critical Issues for Social Theory* (London: Sage, 2000).

If you think you would like to read more about sociology and what sociologists are interested in, as well as about health and healthcare, try an introductory book. There are several of these – examples include: A. Giddens, *Sociology*, 5th edn (Cambridge: Polity Press, 2006); I. Marsh and M. Keating (eds) *Sociology: Making Sense of Society*, 3rd edn (Harlow: Pearson, 2006) and the text from which the next reading is taken.

The Medicalisation of Reproduction

Pamela Abbott, Claire Wallace and Melissa Tyler

In this reading, Pamela Abbott, Claire Wallace and Melissa Tyler consider two distinct but linked issues, both with reference to women's health. They begin by considering iatrogenic medicine – treatment that causes more harm than good – focusing mostly on the issue of female contraception. They follow on from this by considering the relationship between medicine and reproduction. As Abbott and colleagues argue, many women have benefited from the development of modern forms of contraception and from developments in the care of pregnant and birthing women and reproductive technologies that assist conception. However, the associated medicalisation of reproduction has also led to increased medical management of both women's bodies and their reproductive choices. This reading then provides examples of how an individual's choices and experiences are socially controlled by the healthcare system, and how the social norms that doctors and other healthcare professionals operate within are affected by wider societal norms and values.

As Abbott and her colleagues point out, medicine is involved in three areas of reproduction: contraception, pregnancy and childbirth, and reproductive technologies designed to enable women who could not otherwise do so to become pregnant. Here the attention is given to the history of medical advancements in these areas and to the challenges to these developments from within and outside of the medical profession. Abbott and colleagues provide a feminist sociological critique of medicalisation in general and reproductive medicine in particular. Of course, feminist sociologists are interested in other areas of health, illness and healthcare as you will discover as you continue working through this reader.

LATROGENIC MEDICINE

Some medical intervention, it is suggested, is iatrogenic – that is, it causes more harm than good; the treatment actually causes more symptoms and side effects than the original illness. We have already mentioned the side effects of hormone replacement therapy, prescribed for menopausal women. Another good example is the use of a particular drug to treat arthritis. Some patients who were prescribed the drug, which relieves the pain of arthritis, ended up with poor health as a result of the so-called 'side effects' of the drug, such as an inability to tolerate daylight. However, with women's health there is greater concern because some drugs or treatments that are prescribed on a routine basis, not to treat illness but to prevent unwanted pregnancies, have been found to be iatrogenic. The 'coil', for example, has been found to cause extensive menstrual bleeding and low back pain in some women. However, the main cause for concern has been the contraceptive pill, the most reliable method of contraception available to most women.

The pill was introduced into the US in 1960 and has subsequently been used by millions of women throughout the world. It was seen as an effective, modern and scientifically respectable method for controlling fertility and was freely prescribed by doctors to women of childbearing age. However, by the mid-1960s it began to be suspected that there was a link between the pill and cancer of the cervix and circulatory (heart) diseases. Attempts to assess the validity of this suspicion uncovered serious deficiencies in the testing of contraceptive drugs. It was found that they had not been tested on women for the whole period of the reproductive cycle, so that the possible effects of taking the pill for twenty or thirty years were unknown. A study by the Royal College of General Practitioners in 1974 found that the risk of dying from circulatory disease was five times greater for women taking the oral contraceptive pill than for others. Women who were over 35 years old who had been taking the pill for five or more years and who smoked were found to be at the greatest risk. The pill has also been found to have a number of side effects – depression, a loss of libido (sex drive), headaches, nausea and excessive weight gain – but there has been little research into these. Furthermore, the subjective experiences and feelings of women have often been dismissed as irrelevant or 'not real' by medical men. Indeed, research indicates that GPs strongly prefer the pill, especially for young women, and the medical profession seem to have few doubts about its safety (Reid, 1985) and feel that women are unnecessarily worried about it (Tindall, 1987). Similarly, there is medical confidence in Depo-Provera and the IUD (see Wilson, 1985; Guillebaud and Low, 1987; and an editorial in *The Lancet*, 28 March 1992). However, in the United States most drug companies ceased researching, developing and manufacturing contraceptive drugs nearly fifteen years ago because of the escalating costs of testing the product and the high price of the insurance needed to protect them against lawsuits from those damaged by their products (Lincoln and Kaeser, 1988).

It has by now, and as a result of availability of such devices as the pill and the coil, become generally accepted that it should be women who take the responsibility for birth control precautions, and it is women who suffer the serious consequences if contraception fails. (This has changed to some small extent, however, with the AIDS risk and the emphasis on using condoms and barrier cream. However, these are less effective as a prevention of pregnancy than they are in preventing the spread of HIV and other infections.)

It seems unlikely that what are often referred to as the 'side effects' of female contraception would be so readily ignored if men were the users. It would be interesting to know how many men would be prepared to use the intra-penile device (IPD) described by Dr Sophie Merkin:

> The newest development in male contraception was unveiled recently at the American Women's Center. Dr Sophie Merkin of the Merkin Clinic announced the preliminary findings of a study conducted on 763 unsuspecting male undergraduates at a large mid-Western university. In her report, Dr Merkin stated that the new contraceptive – the IPD – was a breakthrough in male contraception. It will be marketed under the trade name Umbrelly.
>
> The IPD (intra-penile device) resembles a tightly rolled umbrella which is inserted through the head of the penis and pushed into the scrotum with a plunger-like device. Occasionally there is a perforation of the scrotum, but this is disregarded as the male has few nerve-endings in this area of his body. The underside of the umbrella contains a spermicidal jelly, hence the name Umbrelly.
>
> Experiments on 1000 white whales from the continental shelf (whose sexual apparatus is said to be closest to man's) proved the IPD to be 100% effective in preventing the production of sperm and eminently satisfactory to the female whale since it does not interfere with her rutting pleasure.
>
> Dr Merkin declared the Umbrelly to be statistically safe for the human male. She reported that of the 763 undergraduates tested with the device only two died of scrotal infection, only twenty developed swelling of the testicles and only thirteen were too depressed to have an erection. She stated that common complaints ranged from cramping and bleeding to acute abdominal pains. She emphasised that these symptoms were merely indications that the man's body had not yet adjusted to the device. Hopefully the symptoms would disappear within a year. One complication caused by the IPD and briefly mentioned by Dr Merkin was the incidence of massive scrotal infection necessitating the surgical removal of the testicles. 'But this is a rare case,' said Dr Merkin, 'too rare to be statistically important.' She and other distinguished members of the Women's College of Surgeons agreed that the benefits far out-weighed the risk to any individual man.
>
> (From *Outcome* magazine, the *East Bay Men's Center newsletter*, and *The Periodical Lunch* published by Andrew Rock, Ann Arbor, Michigan, USA)

This is of course a spoof – no such device has actually been invented. The account was published to illustrate the fact that most men would not be expected to suffer what many women experience with an IUD, such as heavy bleeding, backache and vaginal infections. Indeed, any development at all in this direction is highly unlikely, given that little attempt has been made to develop and market new methods of contraception for men (Bruce, 1987).

While it may be true that women choose what method of contraception to use their choice is limited by what is available. Modern methods do enable a woman to have control over her own fertility, rather than relying on her partner or risking having an abortion after conception, but her choice is limited by decisions that have already been made by drug company executives, doctors, researchers and others about which methods will be developed and made available. Further, given that most methods have their own problems, the choice is often a negative one. Women choose the method that affects them least – so one may choose the pill because the IUD caused excessive bleeding, while another may make the reverse decision because the pill resulted in excessive weight gain. Medical control of many of the newer methods of birth control means that women are dependent on their doctors for advice, and doctors are generally inadequately trained in this area. Most women will have to make a judgement based on what their doctors tell them, and doctors often become resentful if female patients question their advice or reveal that they are knowledgeable in the area. Doctors frequently expect patients to accept that they know best. Yet they rarely talk to their female patients about birth control in detail and are inclined to dismiss subjective experience and base their advice on what they regard as sound scientific judgement. (A further restriction of women's ability to choose which method of contraception to use is the preference of their partners. Pollack (1985), for example, found that many men preferred their partners to use the pill rather than spoil their pleasure and use a condom.)

Nevertheless, doctors' non-medical values do influence the decisions they make about sterilisation and abortion, for example (and about the issue of less drastic means of contraception – see Hawkes, 1995). While white middle-class women have been demanding the right to choose to be sterilised or to have an abortion, working-class and Black women have pointed out that they have often been pressurised into having an abortion or being sterilised against their inclinations. On the other hand, Rose Shapiro has suggested that:

> The need of family planning organisations and doctors to prevent pregnancy is so powerful that it manifests itself almost as an irrational fear. The impression given is that accidental pregnancy is the worst thing that could ever happen to women and that abortion is an absolute disaster.
>
> (Shapiro, 1987, p. 41)

However, in other parts of the world abortion has been the main or only form of contraception available to women. Lesley Doyal (1995) indicates that, worldwide, abortion ranks fourth after female sterilisation, IUDs and contraceptive pills as a method of contraception. In Russia and other transitional societies abortion has been seen as the main form of contraception (United Nations, 2003).

While many women have undoubtedly benefited from the development of modern forms of contraception and these have enabled women to avoid unwanted pregnancies, they have nevertheless extended medical and social control over women. The worldwide market for contraceptive pills and devices is worth billions of dollars, and it is in the interests of multinational companies to encourage the medical profession to prescribe and women to use high-tech contraception. Women's ability to control their own fertility has been restricted and heavily controlled by the medical profession and the multinational pharmaceutical companies....

WOMEN, MEDICINE AND REPRODUCTION

As Lesley Doyal has pointed out,

> If women are to maximise their health and their autonomy they must be able to determine the nature of their reproductive lives ... they must be able to control their own fertility without risking unpleasant or dangerous side effects and they must be able to pass safely through pregnancy and childbirth.
>
> (Doyal, 1995, p. 93)

Medicine is involved in three areas of reproduction:

1. contraception – the prevention of unwanted pregnancy;
2. pregnancy and childbirth; and
3. reproductive technologies designed to enable women who could not otherwise do so to become pregnant.

While feminists have been critical of medical intervention in these areas, it is nevertheless important to recognise that there have been positive aspects to this intervention. In the nineteenth and early twentieth centuries women did face extreme hazard in childbirth, and many, including upper-class women, had severe complications and long-term ill health as a result of pregnancy and childbirth, including prolapse of the uterus and irreparable pelvic tears. Medical advances have made pregnancy and childbirth a much less hazardous process for both the mother and the child. Medicine cannot take all the credit – improved diet, hygienic conditions and a general rise in the standard of living have all played an important role in reducing maternal and infant mortality and morbidity. Nonetheless, credit is due.

However, medical dominance in these areas of women's lives means that women are controlled to a large extent by medical men, and they rely on doctors for advice and information. For example, pregnant women are treated 'as if' something is going to go wrong – women are required to make regular ante-natal visits and are often subject to medical pressure to have their babies in hospital, where doctors control the management of labour and childbirth. As Ann Oakley (1987) argues, motherhood has become a medicalised domain.

The key point is not that medical intervention has played no role in making pregnancy and childbirth safer, but that doctors have taken over total control of the management of pregnant women, so that women are unable to make informed decisions about their lives. This came out clearly in the case of Wendy Savage, the consultant obstetrician who was suspended on a charge of incompetence (of which she was eventually cleared) after a campaign by her male colleagues, who objected to the ways in which she practised (see Savage, 1986). During the campaign to clear her and the subsequent inquiry it became evident that the key issues surrounded how pregnancy and childbirth were to be managed. Savage argued that women should be allowed to make informed choices during pregnancy and childbirth, that ante-natal care should be provided in clinics near women's homes and that they should be allowed to give birth at home if they wanted to do so. The role of the doctor was to assist women, not to control them and make decisions for them.

Feminists have argued not only that women often do not feel in control during pregnancy and childbirth, but also that there is little evidence to support the view that technological intervention in childbirth is beneficial for mother and/or child. Ann Oakley (1982), reporting on research carried out in 1975, found that 69 per cent of first-time mothers did not feel in control of themselves and what was going on in labour. She also quotes research carried out in Wales, finding that the increased use of induction (artificial starting of labour) did not reduce perinatal mortality (death of the baby in the first two months of life), but did increase the number of low birth-weight babies. Induction carries risks to both maternal and foetal health – for example, the tearing of the perineum in the mother and an increased likelihood of a forceps-assisted birth with its associated risks. There has also been an increase in the use of Caesarean section without clear evidence that this has improved the health of babies or mothers. Other routine procedures such as foetal heart monitoring and routine episiotomy (cutting the perineum to prevent tearing) are also of doubtful benefit.

Feminists have suggested that women and doctors have very different views about pregnancy and childbirth. During pregnancy, they suggest, the mother is seen by doctors as a life-support system for the foetus, and the emphasis is on the needs and health of the baby rather than those of the mother. Doctors regard themselves as the experts on childbirth and pregnancy. Medical practice is based on the assumption that doctors have access to a scientific body of knowledge about childbirth, but doctors deal mainly with illness and they tend to treat pregnancy as if it were a sickness. This means that they are more interested in the pathological than the normal, in using technology, and in women taking medical advice.

Graham and Oakley (1981) argue that while doctors see pregnancy as a medical problem, women see it as a natural phenomenon. While for the doctor pregnancy and childbirth are medical events starting with diagnosis and ending with discharge from medical supervision, for women they are parts of a process which has to be integrated with other social roles. They are accompanied by a change in status, to mother, with the obligations that this imposes permanently and comprehensively on a woman's life. While for medical men the success of pregnancy and childbirth is measured by low perinatal and maternal mortality rates and low incidence of certain kinds of morbidity, and a 'successful' outcome is a healthy mother and baby in the immediate post-birth period, for the mother success is measured by a healthy baby, a satisfactory personal experience of labour and delivery, the establishment of a satisfactory relationship with the baby and integrating the demands of motherhood into her lifestyle. While the doctor sees himself as the expert, possessing superior knowledge and therefore in control, the mother sees herself as knowledgeable about pregnancy, as perceptive about the sensations of her body and its needs. However, the mothers in Graham and Oakley's research felt they were not in control. Pregnant women spoke of problems in communicating with their doctors, of not being able to ask questions, and of being treated as ignorant. They also disliked being seen by different doctors at each visit and complained that they felt like battery hens – as just one unimportant item in a factory production system.

While feminists have argued that doctors have medicalised childbirth and in the process taken away control from women, they have also pointed to medical control in other areas of reproduction. Doctors control the most effective means of birth control – the pill, the coil, the cap and sterilisation. Women have to seek medical advice to be able to use these methods of controlling their fertility. The 1968 Abortion Reform law made abortion on medical grounds legal and more freely available, but the decision as to whether a woman can have an abortion is made by doctors. Doctors also control the new reproductive technologies concerned with helping women to conceive and have children. Doctors often refuse sterilisation or abortion to young married women while single women and women from ethnic minority groups are positively encouraged to have abortions. Doctors also decide which women should have access to reproductive technology, and the decision is often based on moral rather than medical judgement. (Many health authorities in the UK routinely refer applications for NHS assistance with reproduction to their Ethics Committees when these are from lesbian couples, but not necessarily from heterosexual ones, for instance.) Also, access to reproductive technology and abortion is mediated by ability to pay; NHS provision is greatly outstripped by demand, so many women are forced to turn to private practitioners. This option, however, is available only to those with money. Scientific and medical advances in the area of reproduction have on the one hand given women the possibility of deciding if, when and under what conditions they will have children. On the other hand, however, the dominance of so much of reproductive technology by the medical profession and the state has permitted doctors to have even greater control over women's lives.

The development of *in vitro* fertilisation in the late 1970s, which was seen as a 'miracle cure', has led feminists more recently to turn their attention to what are commonly described as the 'new' reproductive technologies – the medicalisation of infertility. These include not only technologies that make it possible to extend parenthood to people who have been unable to realise their wish to have a child, but also techniques that can be used to diagnose genetic or chromosomal abnormalities *in utero* and which at the same time enable the sex of the child to be determined. Feminists and disability activists have raised concerns about the ethical issues raised by these developments (Hughes, 2000). Traditionally, childlessness has been seen as a punishment or a sign of divine disfavour – the stigma of being barren. IVF offer infertile couples hope (although many of those treated do not conceive). However, medicalised reproductive genetics treat the body as a machine and there is a disjuncture between women exercising agency and the medical imperative to produce a perfect baby (Ettore, 2002).

While some feminists have been concerned about the availability of the services on the NHS and the ways in which access to them is controlled by the medical profession, others have raised questions about the impact that they will have on women's lives. Access to infertility treatment is restricted and a majority of infertile women who undergo techniques such as IVF still do not have a child – 90 per cent of treated women do not have a baby. Some have suggested that the new technologies will be used by men to control and exploit women even further. Amniocentesis, it is argued, will be and has been used to determine the sex of the unborn foetus and force women to have an abortion if the foetus is not of the desired sex – generally male – while it is very difficult for a single woman to get IVF treatment, reinforcing the patriarchal ideology of the heterosexual nuclear family. (Indeed, there is evidence that new technologies are used to determine sex in India, where male children are valued over female ones – see Therborn, 2004.)

Other feminists (e.g. Michele Stanworth, 1987) have suggested a more cautious approach. While recognising the strong desire of some women to have children and the ways in which they will be assisted by the new technologies, Stanworth suggests that insufficient attention has been paid to questions of safety, women's health and their ability to make informed decisions. Also, it is necessary to recognise that there is a range of reproductive technologies – not just the various 'new' techniques that have been the focus of public attention. While many of these techniques are flawed and their safety questionable, nevertheless they provide an indisputable resource on which women draw according to their priorities. What is necessary is for women to be better informed about these technologies so that they can make better informed decisions. While science may be seen as helping women, the control over it is often not in their hands, but those of doctors.

These issues can be illustrated by reference to ultrasound – a method of enabling doctors and patients to see an image of the foetus on the screen. Doctors use it to detect abnormalities and to date conception exactly (women's knowledge of when they became pregnant is regarded as unreliable, and some women cannot give an exact date for the first day of their last period, which is used to date conception). Women gain great benefit from seeing their own baby in this way (Petchesky, 1987), but, Ann Oakley (1987) has pointed out that it is not entirely certain that the procedure is completely safe – it may cause some risk to the health of the mother and/or the foetus....

REFERENCES

Bruce, J. (1987) 'Users Perspectives on Contraceptive Technology and Delivery Systems: Highlighting Some Feminist Issues', *Technology in Society*. 9: 359–383.

Doyal, L. (1995) *What Makes Women Sick*. London: Macmillan.

Ettore, E. (2002) 'Reproductive Genetics, Gender and the Body: "Please, Doctor, may I have a normal baby?", in S. Nettleton and V. Gustaffson (eds) *The Sociology of Health and Illness Reader*. Cambridge: Polity.

Graham, H. and Oakley, A. (1981) 'Competing Ideologies of Reproduction: Medical and Maternal Perspectives on Pregnancy', in H. Roberts (ed.) *Women, Health and Reproduction*. London: Routledge and Kegan Paul.

Guillebaud, J. and Low, B. (1987) 'Contraception', in A. McPherson (ed.) *Women's Problems in General Practice*. Oxford: Oxford University Press.

Hawkes, G. (1995) 'Responsibility and Irresponsibility: Young Women and Family Planning', *Sociology*. 29(2): 257–273.

Hughes, B. (2000) 'Medicine and the Aesthetic Invalidation of Disabled People', *Disability and Society*. 15(4): 555–568.

Lincoln, R. and Kaeser, L. (1988) 'Whatever Happened to the Contraceptive Revolution?', *Family Planning Perspectives*. 20: 20–24.

Oakley, A. (1982) *Subject Women*. London: Fontana.

Oakley, A. (1987) 'From Walking Wombs to Test-Tube Babies', in M. Stanworth (ed.) *Reproductive Technologies*. Cambridge: Polity.

Petchesky, R.P. (1987) 'Foetal Images: The Power of Visual Culture in the Politics of Reproduction', in M. Stanworth (ed.) *Reproductive Technologies*. Cambridge: Polity.

Pollack, S. (1985) 'Sex and the Contraceptive Act', in H. Holmans (ed.) *The Sexual Politics of Reproduction*. Aldershot: Gower.

Reid, K. (1985) 'Choice of Method', in N. Loudon (ed.) *Handbook of Family Planning*. Edinburgh: Churchill.

Savage, W. (1986) *A Savage Enquiry*. London: Virago.

Shapiro, R. (1987) *Contraception: A Practical and Political Guide*. London: Virago.

Stanworth, M. (ed.) (1987) *Reproductive Technologies: Gender, Motherhood and Medicine*. Cambridge: Polity.

Therborn, G. (2004) *Between Sex and Power: Family in the World 1900–2000*. London: Routledge.

Tindall, V.R. (1987) *Jeffcoate's Principles of Gynaecology*. Fifth edition. London: Butterworth.

United Nations (2003) *World Youth Report*. Vienna: United Nations.

Wilson, E.S. (1985) 'Ingestible Contraceptives', in N. Loudon (ed.) *Handbook of Family Planning*. Edinburgh: Churchill.

Source: P. Abbott, C. Wallace and M. Tyler, *An Introduction to Sociology: Feminist Perspectives*, 3rd edn (London: Routledge, 2006).

Study Questions and Activities

1. With specific reference to your own professional experience, what other examples of iatrogenic medicine can you think of?
2. In what ways is medical 'success' in relation to pregnancy and childbirth at odds with women's self-defined needs and feelings? With reference to any other area of healthcare, outline the costs and benefits of medicalisation.
3. Do the new reproductive technologies provide 'miracle solutions'?
4. Find the book from which this reading is taken. Read the chapter entitled *Health, Illness and Caring*. Also read the chapter entitled *Introduction: Feminism and the Sociological Imagination*. What specific contribution does feminism bring to a sociological understanding of health, illness, health and healthcare?

——————————————— **Further Reading** ———————————————

If this reading has stimulated your interest in women's health, you will enjoy Reading 15, *Gender and Women's Health* by Lesley Doyal, and the subsequent suggested further reading. For more on women and reproduction, the following is a small selection of the large amount of literature available: H. Roberts (ed.) *Women, Health and Reproduction* (London: Routledge and Kegan Paul, 1981); A. Oakley, *Women Confined: Towards a Sociology of Childbirth* (Oxford: Martin Robertson, 1980); B. Katz Rothman, *The Tentative Pregnancy: Amniocentesis and the Sexual Politics of Motherhood* (London: Pandora/Harper Collins, 1986); M. Stanworth, *Reproductive Technologies: Gender, Motherhood and Medicine* (Cambridge: Polity Press, 1987); and E. Ettorre, *Reproductive Genetics, Gender and the Body* (London: Routledge, 2002). It is important, however, not to think of reproduction as just 'women's business', a point which we argue in our edited book S. Earle and G. Letherby, *Gender, Identity and Reproduction: Social Perspectives* (Houndmills: Palgrave, 2003). One specific example of a piece of work focusing on men's relationship to reproduction is M. C. Mason, *Male Infertility: Men Talking* (London: Routledge, 1993). Indeed, despite stereotypes to the contrary, feminists are interested in men's experiences as well as women's, which you will discover if you do any further reading in this and related areas. For more general texts on feminist sociology look at, for example: L. Stanley and S. Wise, *Breaking Out Again: Feminist Ontology and Epistemology* (Buckingham: Open University Press, 1993); M. Evans (ed.) *The Woman Question*, 2nd edn (London: Sage, 1994); J. Evans, *Feminist Theory Today: An Introduction to Second Wave Feminism* (London: Sage, 1995); M. Evans, *Introducing Contemporary Feminist Thought* (Cambridge: Polity Press, 1997); and S. Delamont, *Feminist Sociology* (London: Sage, 2003).

The Social Role of Medicine

David Armstrong

Following on from Readings 1 and 2, this reading provides further evidence of the social role of medicine. Through a consideration of definitions of disease and of the role of the doctor, David Armstrong argues that medicine is influential in the social construction of reality, and argues that it is an instrument of social control. With reference to definitions of disease, Armstrong shows how disease is defined in terms of socially defined understandings of the normal and the abnormal, and how medicine reflects and informs social values through disease diagnoses. Following this, he considers the relationship between biological and socio-political definitions of disease. Next, Armstrong turns his attention to the doctor/patient encounter. He argues that the medical encounter is an institution of social control, and the doctor is an agent of social control. Through an examination of the four expectations and obligations of the 'sick role' – (1) the patient is temporarily excused normal social roles; (2) the patient is not held responsible for his/her illness; (3) the patient must want to get better and (4) the patient must co-operate with the doctor – Armstrong demonstrates social control in practice. He concludes by suggesting that not only can sociology explain the place and significance of medicine in society but, in turn, any society in any historical period can be studied through the lens of its medical system.

Put simply, ... because all knowledge of the natural world (physics, chemistry, biology etc.) emerges from within a certain social context, then, to a greater or lesser extent, that knowledge will be marked by the particular form of the society in which it arose. A good example is the argument that Darwin's theory of evolution – which involved seeing a natural world dominated by competing species – could not have arisen outside of a class-ridden, capitalist Victorian society. Indeed, further evidence for the importance of the social milieu to the emergence of ideas is afforded by the fact that Wallace, quite independently, was only a few weeks behind Darwin in devising a theory of evolution.

By examining the nature of disease and the role of the doctor as social phenomena, this ... chapter applies this sociological approach (often dubbed the social construction of reality) to medicine (Berger and Luckmann 1967).

DEFINING DISEASE

In any discussion of what constitutes good health, the concept of disease has an important part to play. However, knowledge of the nature and characteristics of disease is peculiar to the medical profession and is usually couched in biological terms. Patients claim to be ill, doctors decide whether they have a disease or not. Yet although doctors rarely have any problem in describing the characteristics of specific diseases, there does seem to be some difficulty in defining what 'disease' as a general concept actually is.

One approach is to break the term 'disease' down into its historical constituent parts, dis-ease. Dis-ease, however, places the definition of disease firmly with the patient and becomes synonymous with the lay concept of illness. This is unsatisfactory, as it ignores three factors:

1. the claim of the medical profession to an exclusive skill in identifying disease quite independently of whether the patient feels ill or not;
2. the 'objective' status usually afforded disease, as against the more subjective experience of the patient;
3. the existence of pre-symptomatic diseases that do not immediately cause dis-ease.

Another approach is to view disease as a 'real' biological phenomenon; this is the traditional medical view. The problem with this approach is threefold:

1. though the characteristics of specific diseases have been identified, as has been pointed out, there is no such agreement on what disease, as a group noun, actually is;
2. great numbers of 'conditions' for which there is no known biological basis, e.g. most psychiatric diseases, are not encompassed within the definition;
3. the non-disease state, by these criteria, is also a biological phenomenon: how is pathology to be separated from physiology?

Although most diseases undoubtedly can be expressed in biological terms, these are not sufficient to explain the nature of disease per se. An alternative approach to the problem is to start from the idea of what is normal, as its definition plays such a crucial role in identifying health and disease.

NORMALITY IN MEDICINE

Put simply, medicine divides bodily functions and processes into two types, physiological and pathological – vision is physiological, blindness is pathological; the growth of epidermal cells is physiological, the growth of cancer cells is pathological – one is normal whereas the other is abnormal. But how is it that medicine knows whether a cell on a microscope slide is normal or abnormal? How does medicine know – with such authority – what is normal? The problem is that the word normal has two meanings.

Statistical

In this sense normal is the 'usual'. It may be given by the average or it may be described by some measure of central tendency.

Does medicine simply rely on numerical occurrences for its definition of normal? It might at first seem so, but there are three difficulties.

1. Statistics can provide no hard and fast boundary between normal and abnormal. They can tell which measurement is more or less normal but not the point at which it becomes 'abnormal'. This problem may not arise in conditions in which the difference between normal and abnormal is clearly distinct, but most physiological and biochemical parameters are continuously distributed and the exact cut-off point where normal variation becomes pathology is difficult to establish, e.g. diabetes, hypertension etc.
2. There are so-called pathological phenomena or processes that are statistically normal in some populations. For example, in Western countries, it is actually abnormal to have atheroma-free arteries, though such a condition is viewed as healthier than the presence of atheroma.
3. There are many 'abnormal' or 'unusual' biological states and processes in which it would seem absurd to suggest that the patient was diseased. An unusual eye colour, high IQ, long hair etc. might all be (biologically) abnormal but still be construed as 'normal variations' rather than diseases.

Thus, the statistical notion of the normal cannot of itself determine which biological parameters are to be considered as potential bases of disease.

Social or Ideal

In this sense the normal is that which prevalent social values hold to be acceptable or desirable. This social definition of normality has various advantages over the purely statistical.

The socially acceptable or desirable is very often equivalent to the statistically common. Thus the concept embraces many of those diseases that apparently exist because of their unusualness in the sense of being statistically abnormal. Moreover, because the socially acceptable may vary for different communities, this definition will accommodate variation in the ascription of disease across social groups. For example, the slowing in psychomotor performance with old age, though a decline from the pattern of youth, is still normal in view of social expectations.

If normality is defined by reference to what is socially acceptable, disease becomes a phenomenon that leads to (or may lead to) undesirable social consequences. (The fact that patients are not held to be responsible for their diseases tends to separate disease off from other states, such as crime, that lead to consequences that are similarly socially undesirable.) For many years, congenital hyperbilirubinaemia (Gilbert's disease) was viewed as a disease – and was treated – until it was noticed that it had no deleterious effects. It was then renamed as a normal variation. In this way, reference to social disadvantage fixes the boundary between normality and abnormality among continuously distributed variables. A blood pressure or a blood sugar level is pathological when it may lead to potentially undesirable consequences for the patient. Difficulty in drawing that boundary reflects the unknown implications of an apparently small rise in blood pressure or blood sugar.

Psychiatric disease, which could not be accounted for by exclusively biological notions of disease, is no longer a problem if a social definition is used. The patient who claims to have two identities contravenes our basic assumptions that people only have one: this break with (our) rationality means the patient is diseased. Or the patient who campaigns against the government in a state in which political dissent and criticism are irrational (in that they contravene the dominant culture) is similarly held to be mentally ill. The question is not whether such people are 'really' diseased or not, but whether the social criteria by which the disease is established are justified.

A social definition clarifies the debate about whether or not certain 'abnormalities' are to be classified as diseases. Is sickle-cell trait a disease? Only in so far as it confers no advantage on patients or their progeny in a non-malarial country. Is homosexuality a disease? It depends on whether the condition is viewed socially as an abnormality or as a normal variation: conflict over its disease status merely reflects the lack of consensus in a society over its social acceptability. Can dyslexia ('word blindness') exist as a disease in a pre-literate society? No, because it confers no social disadvantage.

Use of social criteria to define disease also explains the frequently experienced difficulty of distinguishing between involution and pathology in old age. It is well established that various physiological or involutionary changes occur with age, in particular degeneration of various tissues. Degeneration of tissues, however, is also a characteristic of pathology. In short, disease and involution manifest themselves in similar changes: so how are they to be distinguished?

Whereas biologically these two phenomena are inseparable, they can be socially defined by reference to expectations of old age. Roughly, if the change is expected it is involution, if it is unexpected it is pathology. Of course, our expectations can vary over time and place, but in general our current perceptions of what old age *should* be like – perhaps mobility and a full life or perhaps slowing and withdrawal – will define the limits of the pathology of the aged as against what is to be construed as 'natural' bodily changes. Sedgewick (1973) pointed out that a fungus growing on wheat is a disease of the wheat only because we want to eat the wheat; if we wished to eat the fungus, it would not be a disease.

In summary, although it is obvious that social values inform political beliefs or legal statutes, it is perhaps less apparent that in its very subject matter medicine codifies these same social imperatives. The 'physiological' and the 'pathological' of medicine are only meaningful in a social context that separates the normal from the abnormal. If every time a doctor diagnoses a disease (pathology), a social norm is manipulated, then medicine, as described below, has a very important social role. The fact that, unlike in the law or politics, the codification of social values in medicine remains for the most part concealed has further implications for the authority and social purpose of medicine.

THE BIOLOGICAL BASIS OF DISEASE

The reader who [holds] a firm view of the essentially biological character of disease and the doctor's role may feel somewhat confused: surely, it might be argued, diseases are biological and medicine can be practised without playing with politics? The answer is that this claim is correct but incomplete. Whether or not a particular biological change in the body is socially construed as a disease does not detract from the biological character of the change. For example, during menstruation various biological changes occur in the body, but these are held to be normal. Pneumonia, of course, can kill you, but so can crossing the road or living to a ripe old age. Indeed, it is a matter of (social) judgement whether it is pneumonia that kills or the infecting organism that gained entry to the lungs or the poor nutrition that allows it to be fatal or the cardiac arrest when the heart finally stops. Disease and death are treated as 'facts' by medicine, but they involve social judgement and social labels.

In effect, a disease such as pneumonia can be identified (though not ultimately defined) by the presence of certain biological phenomena, such as raised temperature, distinctive chest sounds, shortness of breath, leucocytosis etc. Diagnosis becomes a process of 'pattern recognition' of the biological correlates of disease; moreover, the biological character of the disease enables treatment to be appropriately directed. A doctor, therefore, need not be aware of the social basis of disease to practise medicine, though this does not mean that medicine is other than a social enterprise.

An analogous situation might be that of architects, who look at buildings through their social eye – what is it used for, what are its aesthetics etc. – but require knowledge of the physical properties of the materials used to construct it. Whether a building is a house, a palace or a cathedral is a social judgement and ultimately cannot be made from the number and quality of materials used to build it. Bricks and mortar only make a building when they are put together with a social purpose. The important point is not that buildings – and, by analogy, diseases – are exclusively either social or physical/biological phenomena, rather they can be described in either way. Sometimes the biological basis of the disease may be of paramount importance, especially when biological/pharmacological treatments are available, but equally it can be useful to view disease as a social phenomenon for the light it can throw on the role of medicine in society.

THE DOCTOR AS AGENT OF SOCIAL CONTROL

Because disease labels encode social evaluations, the encounter between doctor and patient becomes a fundamentally social phenomenon. The patient presented problem; this represents a personal assessment by the patient that something is or may be 'abnormal'. The doctor then determines whether a disease is present or not. As argued above, each disease label carries a social judgement, so that the diagnostic process involves juxtaposing a social judgement against a personal one. In effect, medicine is performing a social function as well as its more obvious therapeutic one. Specifically, the evaluation of personal deviance in terms of social values means that medicine is intimately involved in maintaining social consensus and coherence. In this role of arbiter of social values, medicine therefore acts as what has been called an institution of social control and the doctor as an agent of social control (Zola 1972). By constantly reaffirming the boundaries of social normality, the doctor serves as a support for the maintenance of social order.

The Professions

A social control function is not unique to medicine: it has been, and still is, carried out by other occupational groups....

Medicine too, ... can be seen to be upholding social values and, to a certain extent, social behaviour (though the latter is gaining more emphasis).

For example, take the problem arising from a patient requesting that treatment be withheld in a terminal illness. These situations present dilemmas for the doctor because there is a conflict of social values. On the one hand, the general view in our society is that death is an undesirable outcome. (Again, it is worth noting that death is a social event as well as a biological one. In certain situations in various communities – the old in a nomadic tribe, the martyr, the political prisoner who starves himself – death may be seen as a desirable end because it serves to reinforce the integrity or social goals of community.) In Western society, strenuous attempts will often be made to maintain life, though even these may vary from country to country and from culture to culture....

On the other hand, freedom from pain and suffering and the right of patients as individuals to have some say in their future are, like the undesirability of death, widely held social values. Thus when the patient wants to die, it falls on the doctor to resolve the conflict between the importance of human life and of personal autonomy. In some situations drugs can relieve the pain, and the patient's right to a part in the decision can be reduced if it is believed that, because of the imminence of death, he or she is not 'rational'. (Because the desire to die offends fundamental social values, it is easy to label it as 'irrational'.) The dilemma arises for the doctor when there is a certainty that the patient 'really' does want to die. Then the doctor must act as the arbiter of social values, as an agent of social control.

To argue that medicine is engaged in 'social control' is not to say that doctors are some sort of secret policemen. All it means is that medicine, like many other apparently innocuous social activities such as bringing up children, reading a textbook, going to school, watching television etc., controls aspects of knowledge and ideas that support the existing social order.

The Sick Role

Once it is established that medicine is an institution of social control, many other aspects of the sociology of medicine tend to fall into place. The 'sick role', for example ... can ... be seen in context (Parsons 1951). The four expectations and obligations really only make sense if viewed in their relationship to medicine's social role.

The patient is temporarily excused normal social roles

The power to legitimate sickness absence is vested in the medical profession and provides an essential element in social control in that commitment to normal responsibilities such as work is a central value of our society.

The patient is not held responsible for his illness

The ascription of responsibility is an important factor in differentiating a medical from a legal problem. Law holds miscreants responsible for their actions, whereas medicine does not. For example, whether murderers are to be viewed as criminals to be punished by prison or patients to be treated in a psychiatric hospital depends on whether or not they were responsible for their actions. Similarly, if a shoplifter can establish that, due to some hormonal imbalance (e.g. during the menopause) she was not responsible for her act of theft, she becomes a medical rather than a legal problem.

In many ways it is somewhat arbitrary whether people are held responsible for their actions or not. Ultimately, it is underpinned by a philosophical debate over freewill and determinism rather than a dispute that can be settled with recourse to 'evidence'. The boundary between medicine and law is, therefore, often blurred and it is open to medicine to invade areas of human conduct traditionally maintained by legal mechanisms. Indeed, it has been claimed that medicine is increasingly intruding into new areas of human conduct and using its powerful social position to legislate on appropriate and inappropriate behaviour. In part this has been the result of medicine taking over the role of other agencies such as the Church and the Law; it is also the result of medicine extending its definition of health problems to include more and more psychological and social aspects....

Not being held responsible for illness is one of the benefits that medicine can confer on the patient. Unlike many other agencies, there is apparently no need for the patient to feel guilt or failure at having to consult a doctor. This undoubtedly helps explain why many 'problems of living' are brought to the doctor rather than to other professionals (such as social workers, marriage guidance counsellors, housing officers etc.), because the latter may be seen to hold patients, at least in part, responsible for their actions or current situation.

However, as mentioned above, the denial of responsibility is always somewhat arbitrary and it is quite possible to 'blame' patients for having disease. Cigarette smokers who present with lung cancer or coronary heart disease could be held to be partly responsible for their predicament if they knew beforehand of the dangers of smoking yet still continued.

On the other hand, if patients are held responsible for their health, this may encourage them to take preventive action. Prevention, it is argued, now rests with individuals, who must change unhealthy behaviour patterns if they are to avoid ill-health. (The emphasis on personal responsibility for health is also, of course, a political issue, as it makes important assumptions about the control people can exert over their own lives in contemporary society.) There is therefore a stress on personal responsibility in the language of disease prevention. A by-product of the success of this approach, however, might be a decreasing inclination to consult the doctor for these 'preventable' diseases because of the blame and guilt attached to them.

This problem can be seen in those medical problems that already have a measure of responsibility attached to them. These range from people who attempt suicide who, inasmuch as they are directly responsible for their condition, often seem to receive less sympathy from medical staff (though if they are 'really' ill with, say, severe depression, attitudes might change), to the guilt surrounding sexually transmitted diseases for which the patient can be held responsible. In the latter, the feelings of guilt are catered for by anonymity during treatment, while strenuous attempts are made publicly to 'de-stigmatize' the disease so that help will be sought early.

The patient must want to get well/The patient must co-operate with the doctor

Both of these obligations serve to uphold the legitimacy of the social control functions of medicine while at the same time ensuring that they are effective. Just as defendants must recognize the authority of the court (otherwise they are in contempt), so the patient must defer to the authority of the doctor. Failure to do so involves removal of the benefits of the sick role such that the patient is not considered ill so much as a 'malingerer'.

MEDICINE AND SOCIETY

... Sociology can, ... explain the place of medicine in society, its role and its effects.

Medicine, however, in its turn, can provide an important window into society. Medicine – its diseases, its practitioners, its organization – reflects the society in which it exists, so that any society in any historical period can be studied through how it approaches health and illness. Medicine reflects what is normal and abnormal, what is acceptable and unacceptable; medicine reflects the wider society in the illnesses it must address and in the forms of inequality with which it must grapple. Medicine also mediates between the broader aspects of society, the 'out there' parts, and the individual person or patient. In this way, medicine enables the ever-changing nature of human identity – biological, psychological, social – to be studied and better understood. The relationship between medicine and sociology is certainly not one way. The future of medicine in its various forms can only be analysed in the context of a society of which it is part and with which it has reciprocal relations.

BIBLIOGRAPHY

Berger P, Luckmann T. *The social construction of reality*. Penguin, London, 1967.
Parsons T. *The social system*. Free Press, New York, 1951.
Sedgewick P. Mental illness *is* illness. *Salmagundi* 1973; 20:196–224.
Zola I. Medicine as an institution of social control. *Sociological Review* 1972; 20: 487–504.

Source: D. Armstrong, *Outline of Sociology as Applied to Medicine*, 5th edn (London: Arnold, 2003).

Study Questions and Activities

1. David Armstrong refers to statistical and 'ideal' measures of normality – what are the problems with these in relation to definitions of disease?
2. Armstrong argues that medical encounters, like other social encounters, are instruments of social control. He cites bringing up children, reading a text book, going to school, and watching television as other social encounters (amongst others) that support the existing social order. Take one of these encounters and give examples of how this might happen. Think back to a medical encounter

---

continued

that you have experienced (either as practitioner or patient/client) and consider how dominant social norms were reproduced.

3. What do you understand by the term 'sick role'?

4. How would you define your own health state? Can you envisage any changes in your life that might result in a change in the way you define your own health as good, not so good, or bad?

5. Armstrong argues that, through medicine, we can understand the norms and values of society. Thinking historically and cross-culturally provide some examples of this.

————————————————— **Further Reading** —————————————————

This reading is taken from a book devoted to sociology as applied to medicine. It is an accessible, introductory text the whole of which you might find interesting (in addition to those already suggested after Reading 1). If you are interested in medicine as surveillance you should look for an article written by David Armstrong in 1995: 'The rise of surveillance medicine' (published in the journal *Sociology of Health and Illness*, 17:3, 393–404). Michel Foucault's work has been extremely influential in this area, so also try to find *The Birth of the Clinic: An Archaeology of Medical Perception* (London: Tavistock, 1973). See, also, P. Pinell, 'Modern medicine and the civilising process', *Sociology of Health and Illness*, 18:1 (1996) 1–16. Interesting pieces on the definitions and meanings of disease include: S. Sontag, *Illness as Metaphor* (London: Penguin, 1979) and B. M. Hoffmann and H. M. Eriksen, 'The concept of disease: ethical challenges and relevance to dentistry and dental education', *European Journal of Dental Education*, 5:1 (2001) 2–8. For more of Talcott Parson's work see *The Social System* (New York: Free Press, 1951) and for a different perspective on the relationship between illness and identity, see Erving Goffman's *Stigma: Studies in Spoiled Identity* (London: Penguin, 1963). For more on doctor/patient relationships, see Kathy Davis' *Paternalism under the Microscope* (Norwood, NJ: Albex, 1988) and Jocelyn Cornwell's *Hard-Earned Lives: Accounts of Health and Illness from East London* (London: Routledge, 1984). There is also a volume of literature on nurse–patient relationships. For a classic piece on this, see C. May, 'Research on nurse–patient relationships: problems of theory, problems of practice', *Journal of Advanced Nursing*, 15:3 (1990) 307–15. You might also want to look for some of Carl May's more recently published work on relationships between patients and practitioners.

The Sociological Construction of Medicine

Paul Atkinson

Reading 4 can be read as a critique of the large body of work that focuses on doctor/patient relationships (including that which we have presented in Reading 3). Paul Atkinson begins by outlining some of the reasons why the relationships between doctors and patients are so interesting to sociologists and other social scientists. He notes that sociologists are generally critical of medical encounters, as they are impersonal and depersonalising, even though at the same time researchers and writers recognise that doctors must behave in this way in order to get the job done. Atkinson suggests that whilst this specific relationship has been somewhat over-researched, other medical relationships – for example, relationships between doctors, and between clinicians and non-clinical specialists – have received comparatively little attention. There is little or no sociological consideration, Atkinson argues, of much of what he calls the 'back regions' of medical institutions: the laboratories within hospitals, the morgue, the medical classrooms. Thus, his argument continues, sociological and anthropological literature is deficient in its explanation of how medical science is produced and reproduced. The result of this, Atkinson insists, is an over-simplified representation of medicine as a social domain.

THE CONSTRUCTION OF THE CLINIC

The social-scientific literature on medical work and medical encounters is characterized by a very marked bias in its coverage. It has been a feature of this intellectual domain since its emergence. A good deal of sociological analysis has been carried out on medical encounters. Social interaction in medical settings has become one of the most consistently studied topics in micro-sociology (ten Have, 1989). The reasons are not hard to find. The clinic provides a rich source of focused encounters, in which the exchange of information between the parties is of major importance. The medical encounter has been taken as a microcosm for the complex division of labour and its interactional consequences in modern society. It readily provides a localized manifestation of the differential distribution of knowledge within that division of labour.

An inspection of the relevant research literature reveals consistent biases in the microsociology of medical encounters. Again, they reflect some of medical sociology's taken-for-granted assumptions concerning what is self-evidently social. Interpersonal encounters in medical settings are overwhelmingly represented as 'doctor–patient' interactions. The social encounter in and of the clinic is, therefore the *consultation*. Over the past decades we have accumulated a substantial corpus of data and interpretation concerning doctor–patient interactions.

Doctor–patient interaction lends itself to contemporary investigation from a number of points of view. Sociologists, anthropologists and linguists have increasingly come to recognize the significance of spoken action. The analysis of talk by conversation analysts or discourse analysts has already proved one of the most important and fruitful areas for micro-sociological work. The accomplishment of the medical consultation is readily approached as the collaborative task of two parties – doctor and patient. In common with other focused encounters that have proved popular – such as school lessons (for example, Mehan, 1979) or courtrooms (for example, Atkinson and Drew, 1979) – the medical consultation has certain in-built advantages for the would-be analyst. First, the talk itself is focused and consequential. Whatever the merits and advantages of studying mundane discourse, there is a certain inherent interest in the form and content of medical consultations.

One reason for that is the *political* character with which it may be endowed. Again, like the classroom recitation, the medical encounter is essentially asymmetric. It may thus be addressed as the micro-social play of power. The doctor and his or her patient confront one another with different resources of cultural capital. Whatever the everyday status of the patient, he or she is – by definition – a lay participant in the medical consultation. Likewise, whatever his or her actual competence and skill (however defined and measured), the medical practitioner is by definition 'expert' within the consultation. It may therefore be assumed by many sociological analyses that the consultation encapsulates the wider social system or cultural cleavage that divides the professional from the lay. The micro-sociology or discourse analysis of the consultation all too readily recapitulates the construction of medicine as other. The encounter may be represented as the coming together not just of two social actors, but of two contrasting cultures – hence emphasizing not just the difference between the medical and the lay, but also implying a cultural unity for medicine itself. (The latter is more often assumed than demonstrated in practice.) The asymmetry of the encounter thus provides occasion for the sociological exploration (or at least *invocation*) of authority, control and power. (They are not always distinguished adequately or explored with sufficient sensitivity, however.) None the less, the medical encounter is seen as the occasion for the professional manipulation of talk and appearances. Often in ironic contrast with the claimed or imported ideals of medical practice, the consultation may be portrayed as controlled rather than collaborative, repressive rather than receptive, inhibiting rather than facilitating. The smooth accomplishment of medical consultations thus appears to be the outcome of the medical practitioner's coercive control over the form and content of talk. The lay client – powerless and dominated – is therefore excluded from the discourse. The medical problem ceases to be his or hers and is transformed into the object of the medical practitioner's own gaze. This asymmetric encounter may become the vehicle whereby existing inequalities are reproduced or amplified. The injuries of class, race and gender may be recapitulated in the consultation. The medical encounter thus becomes more a microcosm for the mechanisms of exclusion that characterize the wider cleavages of modern society.

The clinical consultation has exerted a special fascination not least because of this convergence of formal and political concerns. The analysis of interpersonal communication and negotiation has repeatedly been used to demonstrate mechanisms of domination and control in operation. The social distance between the doctor and his or her patient, and the asymmetrical distribution of expert knowledge and interactional resources, provide grist for the sociological mill. Sociologists and discourse analysts have therefore produced a substantial literature on the consultation. It includes analyses of encounters wherein social class and gender are shown to amplify social difference and in turn give rise to interactional processes of manipulation and exclusion. (This voluminous literature includes: M. Bloor, 1976a; Davis, 1988; Fisher, 1984; Fisher and Todd, 1983; Frankel, 1984; Hak, 1994; Mishler, 1984; Silverman, 1987; Waitzkin, 1989, 1991; Waitzkin and Stoeckle, 1978; West, 1984; Woolhandler and Himmelstein, 1989.)

In the course of these encounters the lay person is widely represented as losing his or her problem. It is appropriated by the practitioner and incorporated into his or her discourse of expert knowledge. This alienation of the client's own medical or health experience is mirrored in the micro-sociological literature by the medical transformation of his or her *identity*. The confrontation between the medical and the lay is reflected in the objectification of the person of the client. Just as the problem is appropriated, so too is the client.

The sociology of medical encounters is therefore replete with accounts of how the personhood of the patient is transformed into the case of the practitioner. This is the professional equivalent of the impersonal bureaucratic processing of cases. The organized routines of everyday practice transmute the unique, biographically constituted troubles of the person into the appropriate classes of diagnosis and management. The individual thus becomes fixed in a domain of typified actors, actions and outcomes. The consultation becomes one of a series of functionally equivalent encounters, and the patient one of a series of typified clients. That process of typification serves and legitimates the recipes of knowledge and action that are the stock-in-trade of the experienced practitioner. Medical sociology adopts an ambivalent perspective. It recognizes on the one hand the pervasive – even necessary – presence of practical reasoning in the most specialized and arcane of fields. It acknowledges that the practitioner must draw upon such devices as typification and recipe-knowledge in order to render his or her work manageable. The practicability and stability of the social world are ordered by such cognitive and interactional devices. There is no escape from them if the world is not to be recreated afresh at each and every social encounter. On the other hand, the sociological imagination recoils from the deperson-alizing consequences of these *im*personal routines and recipes. Once more, the world of medicine is ironically contrasted with a (largely mythical) alternative in which patient and practitioner encounter one another as fully realized persons. The patient retains control not only of his or her 'problem' but also of his or her biography.

The consequences of typification are typically held to be especially shocking when they deprive the patient not only of the problem, not only of his or her identity, but even of dignity. The production and use of disparaging or stigmatizing typifications is an especial offence for micro-sociology. It seems to represent the utmost abuse of the professional's discursive power. The asymmetry of the relationship is exaggerated to the point that the lay client becomes not the beneficiary but the *victim* of the consultation. In so far as the sociological perspective readily aligns itself with that of the lay person (and of the underdog) then the analysis of the consultation affirms the otherness of the medicine.

This bias in the coverage of medical encounters has one immediate consequence. The sociological treatment of doctor–patient interaction, and the almost exclusive attention devoted to that dyadic relationship, has meant that other types of encounter, and other types of participant, are all but invisible. The implicit assumption of what counts as social has meant that sociologists have collectively misrepresented the variety of medical encounters and medical settings. There is a rich diversity of social action and interaction that escapes the obsessive focus on doctor–patient dyads. In contrast with the doctor–patient consultation, there is precious little analysis of how medical practitioners deal with one another. In other words, doctor–doctor interaction is poorly researched. Indeed, the entire range of possibilities is under-researched. With some notable exceptions we know little of how interaction is managed within clinical teams or firms – how superiors and inferiors in the medical profession engage with one another. Apart from some studies that focus primarily on educational work in such contexts, there is little specific attention to the discourse of medical teams. Likewise, there is little to guide the sociological understanding of how clinicians interact with non-clinical specialists – medically qualified and others. Within the complex division of labour of modern medicine, the clinician or clinical team may draw on the expertise and advice of many others – pathologists, geneticists, radiologists, haematologists and so on. Those consulting services themselves include medical practitioners, laboratory scientists and technicians. There are many occasions when consultation between practitioners takes place: sometimes in face-to-face interaction and sometimes by less direct means.

The net effect, however, is that too much sociological work treats virtually all medical settings and all medical work as synonymous with the consultation. The entire organization of medical institutions and the complex division of labour is imploded into this one microcosm. The naive observer, who had access only to mainstream sociological research, could all too readily assume that medical work was a predominantly solitary affair that occurred within the consulting rooms of family practitioners and their hospital counterparts.

By contrast, great tracts of work remain all but invisible. There is little or no sociological illumination of most of the back regions of medical institutions. We know next to nothing about the laboratories of modern hospitals; of the regular encounters between practitioners at case conferences, grand rounds, mortality and morbidity reviews. We know as little about the myriad interactions – some fleeting and informal, others more formally contrived – through which medical practitioners consult one another. We know depressingly little about how the work of the laboratory relates to the work of the clinic. There is far too little research on how medical practitioners from different specialties cooperate or compete in the management of particular conditions. The implicit assumption that the social is to be found with the patient, and his or her consultation, is therefore a limiting one. In consequence, much of contemporary medicine is left under-explored. Again, the danger is in assuming that the interesting sociological issues – of cultural variation, of belief, practical reasoning – are to be found only in the interaction of the patient's biography and the practitioner's expert knowledge. This bias therefore parallels the classic sociological preoccupation with illness behaviour. The 'purely' medical and technical knowledge of medical science goes by default. The sociological and anthropological literature tell us far too little about how medical science is produced and reproduced, how it is shared and transmitted, how it is legitimated in practice. The contemporary sociological literature all too often portrays a solitary craft worker, who makes no use of other experts, of scientific evidence or of published research.

The emphasis on the consultation has over-simplified the representation of medicine as a social domain. The dyadic doctor–patient interaction offers an elementary exemplar. Each individual may be held to stand for two respective cultures, or two elements in a social system. They furnish a simple model for culture-clash, for the play of power, for gender inequalities, for professional dominance (or whatever analytic axe the sociologist grinds). Moreover, this microcosm is readily grasped and documented because it is *bounded*. The doctor–patient consultation can be encapsulated within Aristotelian dramatic unities. (I return to this issues in the next chapter when I discuss representations of decision-making.) It is a commonplace of the sociological and psychological analyses of consultations that they are characteristically short. Though the length is demonstrably affected by the patient's social position and personal characteristics, the modal length of medical encounter is relatively brief. The consultation routinely occupies no more than a few minutes. It characteristically takes place in one physical location. Within the privacy of the consulting room, then, the interaction is bounded in time and space. This relatively brief, focused, dyadic interaction thus provides manageable strips of spoken and unspoken activity that are amenable to recording and analysis. The structure of the consultation provides the analyst with manageable episodes. A substantial corpus of such episodes can be assimilated fairly straightforwardly, and the results aggregated quite readily. Medical work is thus isolated in time and place, apprehended in convenient chunks. The dyad presents little complexity in analysing patterns of interaction. Again, therefore, we can see how the opportunity offered by the consultation is ultimately a limitation. The tendency is for medical work and medical interaction to be seen as bounded spatially and temporally. The analysis of doctor–patient interaction, conventionally conducted, cannot capture the more protracted and dispersed processes of work that are pervasive of modern medical organizations. The division of labour is lost: the lone practitioner stands for the whole occupation. The diverse settings for medical work are represented only by the consulting room. Protracted investigations and deliberations are reduced to a single episode. Multiple meetings and conferences are condensed into one fleeting interaction. As we shall see, this means that the one-to-one medical consultation is a kind of *synecdoche*: that is, it stands in a part-for-whole relationship with the whole field of medical work, interaction and discourse (Kuipers, 1989). This means, in turn, that the very character of medical work is condensed within this one episodic encounter. The process(es) of trouble formulation, history-taking, investigation, discussion, debate, judgement, management and so on become represented as single *acts*. Rather than diffuse and protracted, the cognitive and linguistic tasks of medicine are all too easily summarized as if they were virtually instantaneous events....

REFERENCES

Atkinson, J. M. and Drew, P. (1979) *Order in Court: The Organisation of Verbal Interaction in Judicial Settings*. London: Macmillan.

Bloor, D. (1976) *Knowledge and Social Imagery*. London: Routledge and Kegan Paul.

Davis, K. (1988) *Power Under the Microscope*. Dordrecht: Floris Publications.

Fisher, S. (1984) 'Doctor–patient communication: a social and micro-political performance', *Sociology of Health and Illness*, 6: 1–29.

Fisher, S. and Todd, A. D. (eds) (1983) *The Social Organization of Doctor–Patient Communication*. Washington, DC: Center for Applied Linguistics.

Frankel, R. (1984) 'From sentence to sequence: understanding the medical encounter through micro-interactional analysis', *Discourse Processes*, 7: 135–70.

Hak, T. (1994) 'The interactional form of professional dominance', *Sociology of Health and Illness*, 16: 469–88.

Kuipers, J. C. (1989) ' "Medical discourse" in anthropological context: views of language and power', *Medical Anthropology Quarterly*, 3: 99–123.

Mehan, H. (1979) *Learning Lessons: Social Organization in the Classroom*. Cambridge, Mass.: Harvard University Press.

Mishler, E. (1984) *The Discourse of Medicine: Dialectics of Medical Interviews*. Norwood, NJ: Ablex.

Silverman, D. (1987) *Communication and Medical Practice: Social Relations in the Clinic*. London: Sage.

ten Have, P. (1989) 'The consultation as a genre' in B. Torode (ed.), *Text and Talk as Social Practice*. Dordrecht: Floris Publications. pp. 115–35.

Waitzkin, H. (1989) 'A critical theory of medical discourse: ideology, social control, and the processing of social context in medical encounters', *Journal of Health and Social Behaviour*, 30: 220–39.

Waitzkin, H. (1991) *The Politics of Medical Encounters: How Patients and Doctors Deal with Social Problems*. New Haven, Conn.: Yale University Press.

Waitzkin, H. and Stoeckle, J. (1978) 'Information control and the micropolitics of health care: summary of an ongoing research project', *Social Science and Medicine*, 10: 263–76.

West, C. (1984) *Routine Complications*. Bloomington: Indiana University Press.

Woolhandler, S. and Himmelstein, D. V. (1989) 'Ideology in medical science: class in the clinic', *Social Science and Medicine*, 28: 1205–9.

Source: P. Atkinson, *Medical Talk and Medical Work: The Liturgy of the Clinic*
(London: Sage, 1995).

Study Questions and Activities

1. Outline the reasons why you think sociologists and others have found the doctor–patient relationship attractive as a focus of research.
2. Atkinson argues that too much sociological work treats almost all medical settings and all medical work as synonymous with the doctor–patient consultation. Make a note of the medical relationships and settings that he thinks need to receive further attention. Can you think of any others?
3. Look for some examples, in this Reader and in the library and/or on the internet, of books and articles that focus on healthcare relationships other than the doctor–patient one. Are the arguments similar or different to the ones that Atkinson suggests characterise the literature surrounding doctor–patient consultations?

--------------------------- **Further Reading** ---------------------------

In addition to this reading, Reading 3 (and associated further reading) turn to Part V of the book for further examples of power and control within healthcare encounters. Reflecting specifically on issues of language and communication within such encounters, look for any of the following: Deborah Lupton's 'Consumerism, reflexivity and the medical encounter', *Social Science and Medicine*, 45:3 (1995) 373–81; Elliot G. Mishler's *The Discourse of Medicine: Dialectics of Medical Interviews* (Norwood, NJ: Ablex, 1984); David Silverman's *Communication and Medical Practice: Social Relations in the Clinic* (London: Sage, 1987); and Howard Waitzkin's 'A critical theory of medical discourse: ideology, social control, and the processing of social context in medical encounters', *Journal of Health and Social Behaviour*, 30 (1989) 220–39. For a consideration of the place of emotion within medical encounters, look at Readings 19, 21 and 22 in this book.

The Sociological Imagination

C. Wright Mills

The Sociological Imagination, the book from which this reading is taken, was first written in 1959 but remains extremely influential today. Neither the reading nor the book is specifically related to health and illness or healthcare experiences. However, we have included it here in the hope that as you progress through, or dip in and out of this Reader, you will be developing your own 'sociological imagination' in relation to your own development and practice. For C. [Charles] Wright Mills, the sociological imagination involves an awareness of three things – history, structure and biography – and an understanding of the relationship between them. Thus, as Mills puts it, 'The sociological imagination enables us to grasp history and biography and the relations between the two within society. That is its task and its promise' (p. 12). So the sociological imagination is a tool that enables us to understand individual experience with reference to time and place. It also enables us to understand and explain the relationship between 'the personal troubles of milieu' and 'the public issues of social structure'. In other words, it enables us to question whether those problems and experience that are sometimes defined as private and thus the responsibility of the individual are really the result of wider issues relating to society and societal norms and values. Hopefully, you now see the relevance of this argument to the other readings in this first part of this reader, and more generally to a sociological understanding of health, illness and healthcare. The examples Mills uses in the reading relate to the time (1950s) and place (America) within which he was writing, yet by focusing on different and contemporary examples we can see that his analysis is as useful today as it was when his book was first published.

Nowadays men often feel that their private lives are a series of traps. They sense that within their everyday worlds, they cannot overcome their troubles, and in this feeling, they are often quite correct: what ordinary men are directly aware of and what they try to do are bounded by the private orbits in which they live; their visions and their powers are limited to the closeup scenes of job, family, neighbourhood; in other milieux, they move vicariously and remain spectators. And the more aware they become, however vaguely, of ambitions and of threats which transcend their immediate locales, the more trapped they seem to feel.

Underlying this sense of being trapped are seemingly impersonal changes in the very structure of continent-wide societies. The facts of contemporary history are also facts about the success and the failure of individual men and women. When a society is industrialized, a peasant becomes a worker; a feudal lord is liquidated or becomes a businessman. When classes rise or fall, a man is employed or unemployed; when the rate of investment goes up or down, a man takes new heart or goes broke. When wars happen, an insurance salesman becomes a rocket launcher; a store clerk, a radar man; a wife lives alone; a child grows up without a father. Neither the life of an individual nor the history of a society can be understood without understanding both.

Yet men do not usually define the troubles they endure in terms of historical change and institutional contradiction. The well-being they enjoy, they do not usually impute to the big ups and downs of the societies in which they live. Seldom aware of the intricate connexion between the patterns of their own lives and the course of world history, ordinary men do not usually know what this connexion means for the kinds of men they are becoming and for the kinds of history-making in which they might take part. They do not possess the quality of mind essential to grasp the interplay of man and society, of biography and history, of self and world. They cannot cope with their personal troubles in such ways as to control the structural transformations that usually lie behind them.

Surely it is no wonder. In what period have so many men been so totally exposed at so fast a pace to such earthquakes of change? That Americans have not known such catastrophic changes as have the men and women of other societies is due to historical facts that are now quickly becoming 'merely history'. The history that now effects every man is world history. Within this scene and this period, in the course of a single generation, one sixth of mankind is transformed from all that is feudal and backward into all that is modern, advanced, and fearful. Political colonies are freed; new and less visible forms of imperialism installed. Revolutions occur; men feel the intimate grip of new kinds of authority. Totalitarian societies rise, and are smashed to bits – or succeed fabulously. After two centuries of ascendancy, capitalism is shown up as only one way to make society into an industrial apparatus. After two centuries of hope, even formal democracy is restricted to a quite small portion of mankind. Everywhere in the underdeveloped world, ancient ways of life are broken up and vague expectations become urgent demands. Everywhere in the overdeveloped world, the means of authority and of violence become total in scope and bureaucratic in form. Humanity itself now lies before us, the super-nation at either pole concentrating its most coordinated and massive efforts upon the preparation of the Third World War.

The very shaping of history now outpaces the ability of men to orient themselves in accordance with cherished values. And which values? Even when they do not panic, men often sense that older ways of feeling and thinking have collapsed and that newer beginnings are ambiguous to the point of moral stasis. Is it any wonder that ordinary men feel they cannot cope with the larger worlds with which they are so suddenly confronted? That they cannot understand the meaning of their epoch for their own lives? That – in defence of selfhood – they become morally insensible, trying to remain altogether private men? Is it any wonder that they come to be possessed by a sense of the trap?

It is not only information that they need – in this Age of Fact, information often dominates their attention and overwhelms their capacities to assimilate it. It is not only the skills of reason that they need – although their struggles to acquire these often exhaust their limited moral energy.

What they need, and what they feel they need, is a quality of mind that will help them to use information and to develop reason in order to achieve lucid summations of what is going on in the world and of what may be happening within themselves. It is this quality, I am going to contend, that journalists and scholars, artists and publics, scientists and editors are coming to expect of what may be called the sociological imagination.

1

The sociological imagination enables its possessor to understand the larger historical scene in terms of its meaning for the inner life and the external career of a variety of individuals. It enables him to take into account how individuals, in the welter of their daily experience, often become falsely conscious of their social positions. Within that welter the framework of modern society is sought, and within that framework the psychologies of a variety of men and women are formulated. By such means the personal uneasiness of individuals is focused upon explicit troubles and the indifference of publics is transformed into involvement with public issues.

The first fruit of this imagination – and the first lessons of the social science that embodies it – is the idea that the individual can understand his own experience and gauge his own fate only by locating himself within his period, that he can know his own chances in life only by becoming aware of those of all individuals in his circumstances. In many ways it is a terrible lesson; in many ways a magnificent one. We do not know the limits of man's capacities for supreme effort or willing degradation, for agony or glee, for pleasurable brutality or the sweetness of reason. But in our time we have come to know that the limits of 'human nature' are frighteningly broad. We have come to know that every individual lives, from one generation to the next, in some society; that he lives out a biography, and that he lives it out within some historical sequence. By the fact of his living he contributes, however minutely, to the shaping of this society and to the course of its history, even as he is made by society and by its historical push and shove.

The sociological imagination enables us to grasp history and biography and the relations between the two within society. That is its task and its promise....

No social study that does not come back to the problems of biography, of history, and of their intersections within a society, has completed its intellectual journey. Whatever the specific problems of the classic social analysts, however limited or however broad the features of social reality they have examined, those who have been imaginatively aware of the promise of their work have consistently asked three sorts of questions:

(1) What is the structure of this particular society as a whole? What are its essential components, and how are they related to one another? How does it differ from other varieties of social order? Within it, what is the meaning of any particular feature for its continuance and for its change?

(2) Where does this society stand in human history? What are the mechanics by which it is changing? What is its place within and its meaning for the development of humanity as a whole? How does any particular feature we are examining affect, and how is it affected by, the historical period in which it moves? And this period – what are its essential features? How does it differ from other periods? What are its characteristic ways of history-making?

(3) What varieties of men and women now prevail in this society and in this period? And what varieties are coming to prevail? In what ways are they selected and formed, liberated and repressed, made sensitive and blunted? What kinds of 'human nature' are revealed in the conduct and character we observe in this society in this period? And what is the meaning for 'human nature' of each and every feature of the society we are examining?

Whether the point of interest is a great power state or a minor literary mood, a family, a prison, a creed – these are the kinds of questions the best social analysts have asked. They are the intellectual pivots of classic studies of man in society – and they are the questions inevitably raised by any mind possessing the sociological imagination. For that imagination is the capacity to shift from one perspective to another – from the political to the psychological; from examination of a single family to comparative assessment of the national budgets of the world; from the theological school to the military establishment; from considerations of an oil industry to studies of contemporary poetry. It is the capacity to range from the most impersonal and remote transformations to the most intimate features of the human self – and to see the relations between the two. Back of its use there is always the urge to know the social and historical meaning of the individual in the society and in the period in which he has his quality and his being.

That, in brief, is why it is by means of the sociological imagination that men now hope to grasp what is going on in the world, and to understand what is happening in themselves as minute points of the intersections of biography and history within society. In large part, contemporary man's self-conscious view of himself as at least an outsider, if not a permanent stranger, rests upon an absorbed realization of social relativity and of the transformative power of history. The sociological imagination is the most fruitful of this self-consciousness. By its use men whose mentalities have swept only a series of limited orbits often come to feel as if suddenly awakened in a house with which they had only supposed themselves to be familiar. Correctly or incorrectly, they often come to feel that they can now provide themselves with adequate summations, cohesive assessments, comprehensive orientations. Older decisions that once appeared sound, now seem to them products of a mind unaccountably dense. Their capacity for astonishment is made lively again. They acquire a new way of thinking, they experience a transvaluation of values: in a word, by their reflection and by their sensibility, they realize the cultural meaning of the social sciences.

2

Perhaps the most fruitful distinction with which the sociological imagination works is between 'the personal troubles of milieu' and 'the public issues of social structure'. This distinction is an essential tool of the sociological imagination and a feature of all classic work in social science.

Troubles occur within the character of the individual and within the range of his immediate relations with others; they have to do with his self and with those limited areas of social life of which he is directly and personally aware. Accordingly, the statement and the resolution of troubles properly lie within the individual as a biographical entity and within the scope of his immediate milieu – the social setting that is directly open to his personal experience and to some extent his wilful activity. A trouble is a private matter: values cherished by an individual are felt by him to be threatened.

Issues have to do with matters that transcend these local environments of the individual and the range of his inner life. They have to do with the organization of many such milieux into the institutions of a historical society as a whole, with the ways in which various milieux overlap and interpenetrate to form the larger structure of social and historical life. An issue is a public matter: some value cherished by publics is felt to be threatened. Often there is a debate about what the value really is and about what it is that really threatens it. This debate is often without focus if only because it is the very nature of an issue, unlike even widespread trouble, that it cannot very well be defined in terms of the immediate and everyday environments of ordinary men. An issue, in fact, often involves a crisis in institutional arrangements, and often too it involves what Marxists call 'contradictions' or 'antagonisms'.

In these terms, consider unemployment. When, in a city of 100,000, only one man is unemployed, that is his personal trouble, and for its relief we properly look to the character of the man, his skills, and his immediate opportunities. But when in a nation of 50 million employees, 15 million men are unemployed, that is an issue, and we may not hope to find its solution within the range of opportunities open to any one individual. The very structure of opportunities has collapsed. Both the correct statement of the problem and the range of possible solutions require us to consider the economic and political institutions of the society, and not merely the personal situation and character of a scatter of individuals. . . .

What we experience in various and specific milieux, I have noted, is often caused by structural changes. Accordingly, to understand the changes of many personal milieux we are required to look beyond them. And the number and variety of such structural changes increase as the institutions within which we live become more embracing and more intricately connected with one another. To be aware of the idea of social structure and to use it with sensibility is to be capable of tracing such linkages among a great variety of milieux. To be able to do that is to possess the sociological imagination.

3

What are the major issues for publics and the key troubles of private individuals in our time? To formulate issues and troubles, we must ask what values are cherished yet threatened, and what values are cherished and supported, by the characterizing trends of our period. In the case both of threat and of support we must ask what salient contradictions of structure may be involved.

When people cherish some set of values and do not feel any threat to them, they experience *well-being*. When they cherish values but *do* feel them to be threatened, they experience a crisis – either as a personal trouble or as a public issue. And if all their values seem involved, they feel the total threat of panic.

But suppose people are neither aware of any cherished values nor experience any threat? That is the experience of *indifference*, which, if it seems to involve all their values, becomes apathy. Suppose, finally, they are unaware of any cherished values, but still are very much aware of a threat? That is the experience of *uneasiness*, of anxiety, which, if it is total enough, becomes a deadly unspecified malaise.

Ours is a time of uneasiness and indifference – not yet formulated in such ways as to permit the work of reason and the play of sensibility. Instead of troubles – defined in terms of values and threats – there is often the misery of vague uneasiness; instead of explicit issues there is often merely the beat feeling that all is somehow not right. Neither the values threatened nor whatever threatens them has been stated; in short, they have not been carried to the point of decision. Much less have they been formulated as problems of social science.

In the thirties there was little doubt – except among certain deluded business circles – that there was an economic issue which was also a pack of personal troubles. In these arguments about 'the crisis of capitalism', the formulations of Marx and the many unacknowledged reformulations of his work probably set the leading terms of the issue, and some men came to understand their personal troubles in these terms. The values threatened were plain to see and cherished by all; the structural contradictions that threatened them also seemed plain. Both were widely and deeply experienced. It was a political age.

But the values threatened in the era after the Second World War are often neither widely acknowledged as values nor widely felt to be threatened. Much private uneasiness goes unformulated; much public malaise and many decisions of enormous structural relevance never become public issues. For those who accept such inherited values as reason and freedom, it is the uneasiness itself that is the trouble; it is the indifference itself that is the issue. And it is this condition, of uneasiness and indifference, that is the signal feature of our period.

All this is so striking that it is often interpreted by observers as a shift in the very kinds of problems that need now to be formulated. We are frequently told that the problems of our decade, or even the crises of our period, have shifted from the eternal realm of economics and now have to do with the quality of individual life – in fact with the question of whether there is soon going to be anything that can properly be called individual life. Not child labour but comic books, not poverty but mass leisure, are at the centre of concern. Many great public issues as well as many private troubles are described in terms of 'the psychiatric' – often, it seems, in a pathetic attempt to avoid the large issues and problems of modern society. Often this statement seems to rest upon a provincial narrowing of interest to the Western societies, or even to the United States – thus ignoring two thirds of mankind; often, too, it arbitrarily divorces the individual life from the larger institutions within which that life is enacted, and which on occasion bear upon it more grievously than do the intimate environments of childhood.

Problems of leisure, for example, cannot even be stated without considering problems of work. Family troubles over comic books cannot be formulated as problems without considering the plight of the contemporary family in its new relations with the newer institutions of the social structure. Neither leisure nor its debilitating uses can be understood as problems without recognition of the extent to which malaise and indifference now form the social and personal climate of contemporary American society. In this climate, no problems of 'the private life' can be stated and solved without recognition of the crisis of ambition that is part of the very career of men at work in the incorporated economy....

Source: C. Wright Mills, *The Sociological Imagination* (Harmondsworth: Penguin, 1970 [1959]).

Study Questions and Activities

1. According to C. Wright Mills what is the task and promise of the sociological imagination?
2. Using the example of unemployment, Mills demonstrates the relationship between the 'personal troubles of milieu' and the 'public issues of social structure'. Using heart disease, breast cancer, infertility, arthritis (or another medical condition of your choice) as an example, do the same.
3. Re-read any one of the earlier readings in this part of the book. If you re-read Reading 1 or 2 consider how the sociological imagination can help us to explain why a twenty-first century woman might 'choose' to have a breast implant, or a baby with the help of medical assistance such as in vitro. If you re-read Reading 3 or 4 consider how the sociological imagination can help to understand the contemporary doctor/patient relationship and/or other healthcare encounters.
4. Reflect on your own career choices with reference to the issues of history, structure and biography.
5. You will be aware that, at times, Mills (and other authors in this section) uses the generic he to refer to both men and women. However, for the last 30 years or so, sociologists have been more aware of the negative consequences of excluding women and other groups through language. Look at the website of the British Sociological Association (http://www.britsoc.co.uk/) for guidelines on a more inclusive approach to language.

Further Reading

As noted in the introductory comments to this reading, Mills' work is as relevant today as it was in the 1950s. Over the years since *The Sociological Imagination* was published, sociologists have returned to a consideration of Mills' work and, recently, scholars in Britain and the United States have argued, like Mills, that sociology and sociologists have a political responsibility. Michael Burawoy, the then president of the American Sociological Association, began the debate in the United States with 'For public sociology' in *American Sociological Review*, 70 (2005) 4–28 and John Scott's 'Sociology and its others: reflections on disciplinary specialisation and fragmentation', *Sociological Research Online*, 7:2 (2005) was followed by a series of articles on the subject (see http://www.socresonline.org.uk/home.html). Of course, feminists, too, promote the political significance and the responsibility of social science, and for a piece that considers the specific influence of feminism on sociology, see Liz Stanley's 'A child of its time: hybrid perspectives on othering in sociology', *Sociological Research Online*, 10:3 (2005), http://www.socresonline.org.uk/10/3/stanley.html.

For another piece on sociological thinking, see: Z. Bauman (with T. May), *Thinking Sociologically* (Oxford: Blackwell, 2001); for an accessible introduction to the life and works of several influential sociologists – including C. Wright Mills – see: G. Crow, *The Art of Sociological Argument* (Houndmills: Palgrave, 2005); and for a general introduction to sociological theory see: T. May, *Situating Social Theory* (Buckingham: Open University Press, 1996).

Part II

Making Sense of Health and Healthcare

Introduction

Following on from a consideration of some of the concepts, concerns and theories that are of interest when studying the sociological perspectives of health and healthcare, in Part II of the book the focus is on research methods and processes. In other words, the concern is with how sociologists measure and understand the social experience of health and illness and medical treatment and care. In this part of the book, there are readings focusing on issues of *method* (the tools for data gathering, e.g. questionnaires, interviews, conversational analysis), of *methodology* (the analysis of the methods used) and of *epistemology* (the theory of knowledge). Sociologists, like other social scientists (and physical scientists), need to be clear about their motivations for research, their methods of data collection and how the research process affects the research product (the findings and the theoretical pronouncements). Thus, any account of sociological research that you read – in this reader or elsewhere – should include some reference to the research process. In addition, there is a large amount of sociological writing focusing on the research process itself, a very small selection of which is represented here.

All of the six readings in this part of the book are concerned with research issues of general concern to social scientists, some of which do this through a consideration of health-related research. In Reading 6, Keith F. Punch provides an overview of data collection methods that involve the collection and/or the analysis of numbers (quantitative) and of those that involve the collection and or the analysis of words and observations (qualitative). Punch's approach moves beyond the merely descriptive. He offers a critique of each of these approaches and highlights the importance of choosing the research method that best suits the research question. Whereas Keith Punch's concern is largely with primary data collection – data collected specifically for the research – Sarah Mallinson and colleagues (Reading 7) detail their experience of working on a research project that involved the combination of secondary data (documents or statistics that are already available) and primary data. Mallinson et al.'s overall focus is historical in that they use local historical archives and oral histories to map historical factors that may be important in understanding contemporary variations in health, and, as such, their research questions, as well as their consideration of research methods, are relevant for this reader. Shifting from a focus on methods to a consideration of epistemology, Nick Fox (Reading 8) reflects on the relationship between politics and research, both in relation to the research process and the research product. As such, Fox's concern is with both the practice of research and research-informed practice. The politics of research is also of interest to Beth Humphries in Reading 9. Humphries' piece brings to our attention the similarities between traditional and emancipatory research approaches. She does this, rather than focus on the differences between them, as some of the other readings in this part do. In Reading 10, Helen Roberts' concern is, again, with research politics. Here though the focus is on the relationship with respondents, the methodological experience of the researcher and the researched, and the ethical responsibility of researchers within this relationship. Finally, in Reading 11, Carole Truman draws on her own experiences of obtaining external ethical approval for a health-based research project. This reading is interesting in that attention is given to issues of method, methodology and epistemology and the sometimes taken-for-granted power of the researcher is called into question.

Quantitative and Qualitative Approaches

Keith F. Punch

The readings in this section of the book are all concerned with different aspects of the 'doing' of social research. This first reading, which is from a chapter in a book by Keith F. Punch, is a useful piece to start with as it provides an introductory overview of quantitative (those which involve the collection and/or analysis of numbers) and qualitative (those which involve observation and/or words) methods. But Punch does more than merely outline the benefits and limitations of these approaches as some introductory textbooks do. Instead, he provides a detailed discussion of the relationship between research questions, value judgements, causation and quantitative and qualitative research approaches. Punch begins by identifying good and bad research questions, which leads him to consider two of the types of problems that can lead to inappropriate or unsatisfactory research questions: value judgements (moral judgements or statements) and causation (cause–effect relationships). Punch briefly considers some of the arguments against the view that researchers who adopt 'scientific' approaches (historically and to date still associated with the privileging of quantitative methods) to studying the social world are value-free. He also challenges the view that, when using qualitative methods, a researcher is not involved in thinking causally. Following this, Punch outlines some of the particular methods (tools of data collection) used by quantitative and qualitative researchers. He reminds us that the type of data used and the use of quantitative methods alone, qualitative methods alone, or a combination of both quantitative and qualitative methods should always be determined by the research question, that is, by what the researcher(s) is trying to find out.

This [reading focuses on] research questions, but concentrates ... on linking the questions to the data. Data link content to method through the empirical criterion for research questions (or hypotheses).

THE EMPIRICAL CRITERION

According to this criterion, a well stated research question indicates what data will be necessary to answer it. It is useful to apply it to all research questions, as they are developed; where hypotheses are appropriate, it can also be applied, in the same way. Another way of saying this is that 'a question well asked is a question half answered': the way the question (or hypothesis) is stated shows what data will be necessary to answer (or test) it, and probably suggests also how and from where or from whom the data will be obtained. Since empirical research means using data, we will not know how to proceed if the research questions do not give clear indications of the data needed to answer them.

This criterion applies most clearly to prespecified research questions. What about when there are no clearly prespecified research questions – where, instead, the research strategy is for the questions to emerge? There still has to be the fit between questions and data, but now, rather than questions leading to data, we may have data leading to questions. In fact it is more likely that there will be a 'reciprocal interaction' between the questions and the data. In this sort of unfolding situation, the question identification and question development processes are delayed. Instead of before the research, they come in later, with the data influencing the way the questions are identified and developed. But it is still important that the questions and the data fit with each other, so the criterion is applicable whether the research questions are prespecified or whether they unfold.

LINKING CONCEPTS AND DATA

Empirical research requires the linking of data to concepts, the connecting of a concept to its empirical indicators.[1] In quantitative research, this idea is described as operationalism. Variables have conceptual definitions, where they are defined using abstract concepts, and operational definitions, where they are connected by means of empirical operations to data indicators. The same idea applies in qualitative research, but comes up in the analysis of data.

The empirical criterion stresses the link between research questions and data, or between concepts and their empirical indicators. This link is an important part of the fit between the different parts of a research project.... It is also part of the overall logical chain within a piece of research. Tight logical connections are needed between all levels of abstraction in that chain.... First-order facts are very concrete, empirical generalizations use abstract concepts, and theories use even more abstract concepts. There must be firm connections between concepts at each level of abstraction in this hierarchical structure.

We can illustrate these points using Charters's example in his discussion of the hypothesis, remembering that a hypothesis is a predicted answer to a research question. Charters (1967) shows propositions at different levels of generality, and demonstrates the need for logical links between those levels:[2]

Theoretical proposition	Aggression occurs when a person is frustrated in getting to his goals. That is, whenever a person is prevented from getting something he wants, an aggressive urge arises within him that induces him to behave aggressively toward the party responsible for his frustration.
Conceptual hypothesis	Elementary school children who are prevented by their teacher from going to recess on a sunny day will express greater hostility in their remarks to the teacher during the remainder of the school day than elementary school children who are not prevented by the teacher from going to recess, other things being equal.
Operational hypothesis	The ratio of 'hostile' to 'non-hostile' remarks made by pupils and classified as 'directed towards teacher', based upon the observation of classroom interaction by a trained observer between 2.00 and 3.30 in the afternoon of sunny days, will be significantly lower under condition A (27 second-grade pupils in Hawthorne School whose teacher said, 'You may go to recess now') than under condition B (36 second-grade pupils in Hawthorne School whose teacher said, 'Instead of going to recess today, I think we had better work some more on spelling').

In a tightly prefigured quantitative study such as is used in this example, the linking of concepts and data is done ahead of the empirical work of data collection and analysis. The link is made *from concepts to data*. In the language of quantitative research, the variables are operationally defined. In a more 'open-ended' qualitative study, say a grounded theory study, that linking is done during the empirical work. In fact, one purpose of such a study is to develop concepts linked to, or grounded in, the data. In that sort of study, the link is made *from data to concepts*. Earlier, in the comparison between theory verification and theory generation research, I used Wolcott's theory-first or theory-after description. Here, it is concepts-first or concepts-after. Whenever it is done, before or during the empirical part of the research, the careful linking is necessary, and the principles are the same....

As stated, it is useful to apply the empirical criterion to all research questions. When all questions satisfy this criterion, we are ready to move from content to method. When research questions fail the test of this criterion, one of two situations will usually apply. Either we have more conceptual-analytic question development work to do, which means that the questions are most likely still not specific enough. This is typical of questions which are being developed deductively, from the general to the specific. Or we have research questions which are faulty in some way. This leads to the topic of good and bad research questions.

GOOD AND BAD RESEARCH QUESTIONS

... good research questions are:

▨ *Clear* They can be easily understood, and are unambiguous.

▨ *Specific* Their concepts are at a specific enough level to connect to data indicators.

▨ *Answerable* We can see what data are required to answer them, and how the data will be obtained.

▨ *Interconnected* They are related to each other in some meaningful way, rather than being unconnected.[3]

▨ *Substantively relevant* They are interesting and worthwhile questions for the investment of research effort.

Bad research questions do not satisfy one or more of these criteria. Mostly, this is because either they are unclear and not specific enough, or they fail on the test of the empirical criterion, which is expressed in the second and third points above. If we cannot say how we would answer each research question, and what evidence would be required to answer it, we cannot proceed.

While there are many different ways in which research questions can be inappropriate or unsatisfactory, there are two types of problems which often occur. The first concerns value judgements, the second concerns causation. They are not directly related, but both are important philosophical issues, and both have been prominent in the paradigm discussions referred to earlier.

VALUE JUDGEMENTS

Value judgements are moral judgements or statements. They are statements about what is good or bad, right or wrong (or any synonyms of these words), not in the sense of instrumental values (means) but in the sense of terminal values (ends). They are often described as statements of 'ought' (or 'should'), and are contrasted with statements of 'is'.[4] The problem is that it is not clear how (or whether) we can use empirical evidence to support or refute such value judgements. There are two main positions on this important issue.

One position (the conventional positivist position) is that we cannot use empirical evidence in the making of value judgements, because of the so-called 'fact-to-value gap'. The fact-to-value gap maintains that there is a fundamental difference between facts and values, and that, because of that difference, there is no logical way to get from statements of fact to statements of value. If this is true, it means that evidence is irrelevant to the making of value judgements, and that value judgements cannot be justified by evidence. Some other basis will be required for their justification. For proponents of this view, science must remain silent on value judgement questions, since scientific research, being based on empirical data, can deal only with the facts. This is no small problem, since value judgements, on an individual, collective and societal level, are among the most important judgements people must make. In this view, science has no role in making those value judgements. Nor do value judgements have any place in scientific inquiry. As noted, this is the conventional, positivist, 'science-as-value-free' view, and it has a long history.[5]

The other main view is that this gap is based on a mistaken dualism which sees facts and values as quite different things. In this view, that distinction is invalid, and the fact-to-value gap is therefore a misleading fallacy. [Lincoln and Guba (1985)] indicate the many possible meanings of values, they show why the fact–value dualism is discredited, they stress the value-ladenness of all facts, and they show the four main ways in which values have a direct impact on the research. They [make the] plea that we discontinue the fallacious dichotomy between facts and values, and stop trying to exclude values from research:

> At this point, *at a minimum*, we should be prepared to admit that values do play a significant part in inquiry, to do our best in each case to expose and explicate them ... and, finally, to take them into account to whatever extent we can. Such a course is infinitely to be preferred to continuing in the self-delusion that methodology can and does protect one from their unwelcome incursions. (1985: 186)

This rejection of the positivist view comes from several quarters. Feminist scholars, for example, have repeatedly challenged the 'persistent positivist myth' (Haig, 1997) that science is value free, and critical theorists and feminists alike regard the distinction between facts and values as simply a device which disguises the role of conservative values in much social research. Instead of value-free research, critical theorists especially argue that research should be used in the service of the emancipation of oppressed groups – in other words, that it should be openly ideological (Hammersley, 1995)....

While the positivist value-free position has a long history, its rejection has grown strongly in importance in the last 20 years. Ironically, the positivist position is itself a statement of values, and many see it as discredited in maintaining that inquiry can be value free. The problem with the rejection of the value-free position, however, is that it is not clear where it leads.[6] This can complicate the development of research questions, since the area of value judgements is controversial. In the face of that, I suggest three points to keep in mind. First, we should be aware that there are different positions on this issue, and therefore not be surprised if we encounter different reactions to it. Second, we should recognize when value statements are being made, and be careful about phrasing research questions in value judgement terms.[7] We should be aware of synonyms for 'good–bad' and 'right–wrong', which may camouflage the value judgements, but do not remove the issue.[8] Third, if value judgement terms are used in questions, we can first determine whether they are being used in the instrumental or terminal sense. If instrumental, we can rephrase the question to get rid of the value judgement term(s). If the terms are being used in the terminal value sense, we should indicate how the evidence will be used in conjunction with the value judgements.

There is another point worth noting about the positivist belief in value-free inquiry. The choice of a research area, and of problems and questions within that area, clearly involves value judgements. This is because, in some sense, the proposed area or question is judged to be more worthwhile, or better, or more valuable, than others that could be studied. As Addelson (1991) points out, whether something is a social problem or not depends on one's social position and perspective, and it is often also a political question.[9] Having made that value judgement, the positivist researcher then aims to carry out the research in a value-free way. A similar situation arises after the research, when the findings are discussed and interpreted, and their implications for action and practice are drawn out. In doing this, value judgements will be involved, since any recommendation for action based on research findings contains value judgements. Thus the positivist has a value judgement at the start of the research (when the selection of the research area and research questions is made) and value judgements at the end of the research, if recommendations for practice are involved. In between, the idea is to do value-free empirical work. The empirical research is sandwiched between value judgements.[10]

CAUSATION

Scientific research has traditionally sought the causes of effects, events or phenomena. Indeed, a useful definition of scientific research in any area is that it seeks to trace out cause–effect relationships. In this sense, science reflects everyday life. The concept of causation is deeply ingrained in our culture, and saturates our attempts to understand and explain the world. On the everyday level, we find it a very useful way to organize our thinking about the world: the word 'because', for example, is one of the most central in our language, and in our world view. As Lincoln and Guba (1985) point out, our preoccupation with causation may be related to our needs for prediction, control and power. Whether that is true or not, the concept of causation is deep seated, and perhaps built into the way we think about the world.

But causation is also a difficult philosophical concept. What does causation mean, and how do we know when we have a cause (or the cause, or the causes) of something? The definitional question about causation has no easy answer. [For example] Brewer and Hunter (1989) discuss different types of causes. Without going into the definitional details, one way to simplify this complicated issue is to see the difference between the constant conjunction view of causation and the necessary connection view.

In the *constant conjunction* view, to say that X (for example, watching violence on television) causes Y (for example, the development of antisocial attitudes) is to say that every time X occurs, Y occurs. This means simply that Y always follows X, that there is a constant conjunction between them. This view is clear enough, but it also has problems. For example, night always follows day, yet we don't want to say that day causes night. Therefore constant conjunction alone does not seem to be enough to define causation.

On the other hand, in the *necessary connection* view, to say that X causes Y is to say not only that X is followed by Y, but that X must be followed by Y. In this view causation means that the variables are necessarily connected. The problem with this view is that we cannot observe that X must be followed by Y. We can only observe whether or not X is followed by Y. We cannot observe the necessity part. Since we cannot observe it, we are forced to infer it. Thus causation, in this view, is not observable, it can only be inferred. It is not, in other words, an empirical concept.

The necessary connection view of causation therefore leads to this question: under what conditions is it plausible to infer that an observed relationship is a causal one? This is a difficult question, precisely because the world is full of relationships we can observe, but most of them are not causal. It is a question to which many answers have been proposed (see, for example, Lincoln and Guba, 1985; Rosenberg, 1968; Brewer and Hunter, 1989). Without attempting here a full treatment of this question, the main conditions for inferring that X (watching violence on television) causes Y (the development of anti-social attitudes) are:

- The variables X and Y must be related.[11]

- A time order between the variables must be demonstrated, with the cause X preceding the effect Y.[12]

- There must be a plausible theory showing the links by which the variables are causally related: that is, the missing links which bring about the causal connection must be specified.

- Plausible rival hypotheses to the preferred causal one must be eliminated.

Perhaps no topic has received more attention in quantitative research design than this. For a long time, and in some quarters still, the experiment has been the preferred empirical research design, because, by imposing a time order and by systematically eliminating rival hypotheses, it is the safest basis we have for inferring causal relationships between variables.... More recently, there have been advances in designs for inferring causation, both in quantitative research through the development of quasi-experimental and non-experimental designs, and also in qualitative research (see, for example, Miles and Huberman, 1994: 143–71).

Different researchers have different views of causation (Huberman and Miles, 1994: 434), and the credibility of causal claims depends on the view one holds. Despite the resistance to the concept and terminology of causation among some qualitative researchers, and despite the view of Lincoln and Guba (1985) that the concept may have outlived its usefulness, it seems a safe assumption that many researchers will continue to want to think causally about the world. But it is important to be careful about the way we use the word 'cause(s)'. In particular, we need to remember that causation can only be inferred, according to the necessary connection view described above. This is one reason that the word 'cause(s)' itself is not often used among experienced researchers. Other words are substituted. We therefore need to be careful about such statements in a proposal as 'In this research we will find the cause(s) of ...'. Still more must we be careful of statements in a finished report that 'In this research we have found the cause(s) of ...'.[13]

On the assumption that we retain the idea of causation, I suggest that we proceed as follows. First, when we are thinking causally, we replace the words 'cause' and 'effect' by other terms, choosing from those shown in Table 1, especially in quantitative studies. Second, we proceed to study the extent to which and the ways in which things are interconnected and variables are interrelated, according to whatever design we have chosen. Third, we reserve any causal description of observed relationships until it is time to interpret the results. It is one thing to observe, describe and report the relationship. It is another to interpret it, to say how it came about. If the interpretation we prefer is a causal one, we are on safe ground if we point out that this interpretation is an inference, and then argue for it on the basis of the sorts of conditions mentioned earlier....

Multiple Causation

The discussion in this section has been simplified, by talking basically about one cause and one effect, and by talking about only one direction for causation (from X to Y). In social research today, especially quantitative research, single cause and effect thinking is uncommon, and multiple causation is seen as much more realistic. Multiple causation means that there will likely be more than one cause, and probably several causes, for any particular effect. Effects are thought to have several causes, and these causes can act together in various ways, and can fluctuate in importance in how they bring about the effect. The terms 'multiple causes', 'conjunctional causes'

Table 1 Substitute terms for cause and effect

Cause	Effect
Independent variable	Dependent variable
Treatment variable	Outcome variable
Predictor variable	Criterion variable
Antecedents	Consequences
Determinants	

1 'Correlates' is sometimes used for both causes and effects.
2 Sometimes 'cause–effect relationship' is replaced by 'functional relationship'.

and 'conjectural causes' express these ideas. While the discussion in this section has been simplified, and put in terms of one cause and one effect, everything we have said about the nature of causes and the logic of causation holds for the more complicated case of multiple causation....

Causation in Qualitative Research

... The term 'causation' has positivist connotations (Hammersley and Atkinson, 1995: 233), and this, combined with the difficulty of assessing causal claims, makes some qualitative researchers reluctant to use the concept. Some postmodernists, for example, as pointed out by Neuman (1994), reject the search for causation because they see life as too complex and rapidly changing. For such reasons, causation has been more a preoccupation of quantitative research.

However, as Hammersley and Atkinson (1995) point out, causal theories and models are common in ethnographic work, even if they are used implicitly. Similarly, Miles and Huberman (1994) make clear the importance of causation in qualitative research. Indeed, they claim that qualitative studies are especially well suited to finding causal relationships. Qualitative studies can

> look directly and longitudinally at the local processes underlying a temporal series of events and states, showing how these led to specific outcomes and ruling out rival hypotheses. In effect, we get inside the black box; we can understand not just that a particular thing happened, but how and why it happened. (Huberman and Miles, 1994: 434)

Again:

> We consider qualitative analysis to be a very powerful method for assessing causality ... Qualitative analysis, with its close-up look, can identify *mechanisms*, going beyond sheer association. It is unrelentingly *local*, and deals well with the complex network of events and processes in a situation. It can sort out the *temporal* dimension, showing clearly what preceded what, either through direct observation or *retrospection*. It is well equipped to cycle back and forth between *variables* and *processes* – showing that 'stories' are not capricious, but include underlying variables, and that variables are not disembodied, but have connections over time. (Miles and Huberman, 1994: 147)

In *Qualitative Data Analysis*, Miles and Huberman show how causal networks can be developed to model qualitative data, just as causal path diagrams model quantitative data.

FROM RESEARCH QUESTIONS TO DATA

At this point in the process, let us assume that we have stabilized our research questions.... The substantive or content side of the research is now under control. We know what we are trying to find out, and we can now move from content to method. The connection from content to method is through data: what data will be needed, and how will they be collected and analysed? Before we get down to details of method, therefore, we need to consider the nature of data.

What are data? As noted earlier, synonyms for data are evidence, information, or empirical materials. The essential idea is first-hand observation and information about (or experience of) the world. Obviously, that could include all sorts of things, so 'data' is a very broad term, and is subdivided into quantitative and qualitative.

Quantitative Data

The key concept here is quantity, and numbers are used to express quantity. Therefore quantitative data are numerical; they are information about the world, in the form of numbers.

Information about the world does not occur naturally in the form of numbers. It is we, as researchers, who turn the data into numbers. We impose the structure of the number system on the data, bringing the structure to the data. The fact that we bring the structure to the data means there is nothing 'God-given' about the numerical structure we impose; on the contrary, that structure is 'man made'. It is therefore not inevitable, or essential, that we organize our empirical data as numbers. The question is whether we find it useful to impose this structure on the data. If we find it useful (and if it is feasible), we can do it. If not, we are not at all bound to do it. Measurement is the process by which we turn data into numbers. Measurement involves assigning numbers to things, people, events or whatever, according to particular sets of rules.... Therefore to collect quantitative data is to collect measurements. By definition, quantitative data collected with measuring instruments are prestructured.... The numerical structure is imposed on the data, ahead of the research.

Two types of operations produce numbers – counting and scaling. Counting is such a common everyday occurrence that we don't think about it. We do it automatically, it is straightforward and not problematic, and we find it extremely useful in dealing with the world. When we count, we are counting with respect to something. There is a dimension of interest, some scale or quantity we have in mind, which gives meaning to the counting.

Scaling[14] is rather different, though again we do it all the time. The basic idea here is that we have in mind some characteristic, or property, or trait – we will use trait – and we envisage a continuum, or scale, ranging from a great deal (or perhaps 100%) of that trait, to very little (or perhaps 0%) of that trait. Further, we envisage different locations along that continuum, corresponding to different amounts of that trait. We use this sort of thinking and describing very frequently in everyday language, and it is not difficult to find many examples. Nor do we normally consider it a problem to do that. In other words, the idea of scaling (though we do not normally call it that) is deeply ingrained into our world view and into our language. This needs stressing because of the controversies which can arise with this same operation in a research situation. As a final step, in actual measurement, we assign numbers to represent those different locations along the scaled continuum. We do not normally make this last step in everyday life, and it seems to be here that the controversies arise. The idea of a scale is useful to us in everyday life because it helps us to be systematic in our thinking, and because it helps us to compare things (or events, or people) in a standardized way. Making standardized comparisons is something we often want to do, and measurement formalizes those comparisons, enabling us to make them more precise and systematic. It is interesting to note the similarities on this point between quantitative and qualitative research: making comparisons is also central in the analysis of qualitative data....

Qualitative Data

We have defined quantitative data as empirical information in the form of numbers. Qualitative data can therefore be defined as empirical information about the world, not in the form of numbers. Most of the time but not always ... this means words.

This definition covers a very wide range, and qualitative data do indeed include many different types of things. Denzin and Lincoln (1994) use the term 'qualitative empirical materials', and point out that it includes interview transcripts, recordings and notes, observational records and notes, documents and the products and records of material culture, audio-visual materials, and personal experience materials (such as artefacts, journal and diary information, and narratives). The qualitative researcher thus has a much wider range of possible empirical materials than the quantitative researcher, and will typically also use multiple data sources in a project. For some qualitative researchers, literally everything is data. [Here], we concentrate on qualitative data from observation (and participant observation), interviews or documents – or, as Wolcott (1992) puts it, on data from 'watching, asking or examining'.

We saw that quantitative data have a predetermined structure, being at the left hand end of the structure continuum. What about qualitative data? As with research questions and research designs, qualitative data can fall anywhere along this continuum. Thus, they can be towards the left hand end, and well structured, as in the case of standardized interview questions with response categories, or observations based on a predetermined observation schedule.[15] On the other hand, qualitative data can be totally unstructured at the point of collection, as in the transcript of an open-ended interview, or field notes from participant observation. In this case, there would be no predetermined categories or codes. Rather, the structure in the data will emerge during the analysis. The basis of this structure is codes and categories, and they are typically derived from the data in the initial stages of analysis....

... Here it is a case of structure-before or structure-after in the data.... 'Structure-before' means that the researcher imposes codes and/or categories and/or concepts on the data; these are researcher-imposed concepts. Measurement in quantitative research is a clear example of concepts and structure imposed on the data by the researcher. By contrast, 'structure-after' allows respondents in research to 'tell it in their own terms' to a much greater extent.[16] This is often a big issue in a research project. A common criticism of prestructured data is on this very point: that pre-structuring the data does not permit people to provide information using their own terms, meanings and understandings. On the other hand, when we collect data using people's own terms and meanings, it is difficult to make standardized comparisons. This is an example of the sort of choice often facing the researcher. Like all other such choices, it needs to be analysed, and there are advantages and disadvantages in each way of doing it. Thus, it will often seem good to begin with the data in respondents' own terms and concepts. But the systematic comparisons which structure and measurements permit are also valuable, and they require that the same terms and concepts be used across different respondents – that they be standardized. That suggests combining the two approaches in such a way as to retain the advantages of each....

Open-ended qualitative data are often appealing to researchers who are keen to capture directly the lived experience of people. But unstructured qualitative data require some processing to prepare them for analysis (for example, recordings need to be transcribed and edited, and field notes need to be corrected). Therefore the data themselves represent a text constructed by the researcher. It is one thing to experience (some aspect of) the world. It is another thing to represent that experience in words. Once data are put into words, it is the researcher-constructed text which is used in the analysis. It is inevitable that the words we use to record data from the field will reflect, to some extent, our own concepts. Thus, as Miles and Huberman (1994: 10) write, behind the apparent simplicity of qualitative data there is a good deal of complexity,[17] requiring care and self-awareness from the researcher. In this sense, too, qualitative research is similar to quantitative: in both, the researcher brings something to the data.

The surge of interest in qualitative methods which has occurred in the last 20 years has meant the opening up of many different forms of data in social science research. It has also brought with it specialized techniques in the collection and, particularly, in the analysis of those data, along with recognition of the central role of language....

COMBINING QUANTITATIVE AND QUALITATIVE DATA

We can now summarize these sections on the nature of data. Quantitative data are information about the world in numerical form, whereas qualitative data are (essentially) information about the world in the form of words. Quantitative data are necessarily structured in terms of the number system, and reflect researcher-imposed constructs. Qualitative data may range from structured to unstructured, and may or may not involve researcher-imposed constructs. The basic difference between the two types of data lies in the process of measurement, which has often engendered rigid positions about research, and which has been at the centre of debates between proponents of the two approaches.

To move past these rigid positions does not of course mean that we must combine the two types of data – only that we can do so when appropriate. Thus there are three possibilities for any study. It can have all quantitative data, it can have all qualitative data, or it can combine both types in any proportions. Which of these three should apply is not a matter for rules. The type of data we finish up with should be determined primarily by what we are trying to find out, considered against the background of the context, circumstances and practical aspects of the particular research project. Concentrating first on what we are trying to find out means that substantive issues dictate methodological choices. The 'substantive dog' wags the 'methodological tail', not vice versa....

NOTES

1. In quantitative research, the key concepts are variables, so there the link is between variables and data, as in the operational definition of variables.
2. This paper by Charters is a valuable discussion of the 'functions, anatomy and pathology' of the hypothesis. However, to my knowledge it has not been published.
3. They should form a coherent whole, rather than being a 'random collection of queries about the topic' (Maxwell, 1996: 107).
4. Terminal values are ends in themselves. Instrumental values are means towards achieving these ends. A discussion of value judgements in science is given in Broudy et al. (1973: 502–48) and in Brodbeck (1968: 79–138).
5. See, for example, O'Connor (1957) especially Chapter 3.
6. Thus different writers reach different conclusions about how values are to be involved in empirical inquiry.
7. To admit the value-ladenness of facts does not justify the making of sweeping value judgements.
8. Examples are 'worthwhile–worthless', 'effective–ineffective' and 'efficient–inefficient'.
9. Thus, for example, bank robbing, pot smoking and homosexuality are social problems in the eyes of certain segments of the population, but not others.
10. Naturally, this whole paragraph makes no sense to the anti-positivist, since it is based on the 'mistaken distinction' between facts and values.
11. For convenience, the ideas are expressed here quantitatively, in terms of variables. The ideas generalize to the qualitative situation.
12. If the time order cannot be established, the 'relative fixity and alterability' of the variables must support the proposed causal inference: see Rosenberg (1968).
13. Sometimes, words other than 'cause' are used, but the causal connotations remain. Some examples are 'due to', 'affects', 'contributes to', 'has an impact on', 'is a function of', and 'determines'.
14. Scaling is used here to mean placing on a scale, or continuum. In Chapter 6, the more general term 'measurement' is used. Here scaling, along with counting, is seen as one type

of measurement. In general, the term 'scaling' is used more often in psychology, the term 'measurement' more often in educational research.

15. Highly structured interview responses or observational data are often described as quantitative.... they would not be described as quantitative here unless they are actually turned into numbers, but they are clearly highly structured.

16. But not necessarily totally, since questioning already introduces some structure. However, some questions are more structured than others.

17. This complexity has another aspect too, centring on the use of language and the analytic status of qualitative data.

REFERENCES

Addeslon, K.P. (1991) 'The man of professional wisdom', in M.M. Fonow and J.A. Cook (eds), *Beyond Methodology: Feminist Scholarship as Lived Research*. Bloomington and Indianapolis, IN: Indiana University Press. pp. 16–34.

Brewer, J. and Hunter, A. (1989) *Multimethod Research: A Synthesis of Styles*. Newbury Park, CA: Sage.

Brodbeck, M. (ed.) (1968) *Readings in the Philosophy of the Social Sciences*. London: Macmillan.

Broudy, H.S., Ennis, R.H. and Krimerman, L.I. (1973) *Philosophy of Educational Research*. New York: Wiley.

Charters, W.W. Jr (1967) 'The hypothesis in scientific research'. Unpublished paper, University of Oregon, Eugene.

Denzin, N.K. and Lincoln, Y.S. (eds) (1994) *Handbook of Qualitative Research*. Thousand Oaks, CA: Sage.

Haig, B.D. (1997) 'Feminist research methodology', in J.P. Keeves (ed.), *Educational Research, Methodology, and Measurement: An International Handbook*. 2nd edn. Oxford: Elsevier. pp. 180–5.

Hammersley, M. (1995) *The Politics of Social Research*. London: Sage.

Hammersley, M. and Atkinson, P. (1995) *Ethnography: Principles in Practice*. 2nd ed n. London: Routledge.

Huberman, A.M. and Miles, M.B. (1994) 'Data management and analysis methods', in N.K. Denzin and Y.S. Lincoln (eds), *Handbook of Qualitative Research*. Thousand Oaks, CA: Sage. pp. 428–44.

Lincoln, Y.S. and Guba, E.G. (1985) *Naturalistic Inquiry*. Beverley Hills, CA: Sage.

Maxwell, J.A. (1996) *Qualitative Research Design: An Interactive Approach*. Thousand Oaks, CA: Sage.

Miles, M.B. and Huberman, A.M. (1994) *Qualitative Data Analysis*. 2nd edn. Thousand Oaks, CA: Sage.

Neuman, W.L. (1994) *Social Research Methods: Qualitative and Quantitative Approaches*. 2nd edn. Boston: Allyn and Bacon.

Rosenberg, M. (1968) *The Logic of Survey Analysis*. New York: Basic Books.

Wolcott, H.F. (1992) 'Posturing in qualitative inquiry', in M.D. LeCompte, W.L. Millroy and J. Preissle (eds), *Handbook of Qualitative Research in Education*. San Diego, CA: Academic Press. pp. 3–52.

Source: K. F. Punch, *Introduction to Social Research: Quantitative and Qualitative Approaches* (London: Sage, 1998).

Study Questions and Activities

1. What do you understand by the term value judgement? According to Keith Punch, why is the positivist position that argues for 'value-freedom' a contradiction?
2. Punch argues that researchers should avoid the use of the phrase 'In this research we will find the cause(s) ...' Why?
3. Is causation relevant to qualitative research?
4. As Punch argues, it is always important to use the appropriate method, i.e. the method should be determined by what you are trying to find out. Pick an area relevant to your practice and imagine you are conducting a study concerned with the *prevalence* and the *experience* of a condition. Formulate some research questions. What methods would you use and why?

Further Reading

There are a large number of books written by sociologists and other social scientists that provide an overview of the methods, methodology and epistemology of the social sciences. Tim May's *Social Research: Issues, Methods and Experiences*, 2nd edn (Buckingham: Open University Press, 1997) and Malcolm Williams' *Making Sense of Social Research* (London: Sage, 2002) provide accessible and detailed overviews. In addition, you may want to read the rest of Keith Punch's book *Introduction to Social Research: Quantitative and Qualitative Approaches* (London: Sage, 1998). There are also books written specifically about the social aspects of health, illness and medical treatment and/or aimed at healthcare professionals who wish to undertake social research, one example being C. Taylor and S. White, *Practicing Reflexivity in Health and Welfare: Making Knowledge* (Buckingham: Open University Press, 2000). There is much, often heated, debate about the advantages and disadvantages, and values and problems of quantitative and qualitative methods and data. One aspect of this is the suggestion by some that historically quantitative methods are linked to male researchers and qualitative methods to female researchers. If you are interested in this, look at the debate in the journal *Sociology* between Ann Oakley and Gayle Letherby – A. Oakley, 'Gender, methodology and people's ways of knowing: some problems with feminism and the paradigm debate in social science', *Sociology*, 32:4 (1998) 707–31; G. Letherby, 'Quoting and counting: an autobiographical response to Oakley', *Sociology*, 38:1 (2004) 175–89; A. Oakley, 'Response to quoting and counting: an autobiographical response to Oakley', *Sociology*, 32:1 (2004) 191–2; and G. Letherby, 'Reply to Oakley', *Sociology*, 38:1 (2004) 193–4.

Reading 7

Historical Data for Health Inequalities

Sara Mallinson, Jennie Popay, Eva Elliott, Sharon Bennett, Lisa Bostock, Anthony Gatrell, Carol Thomas and Gareth Williams

In this reading, the authors focus on their experience of a pilot study conducted to assess the feasibility of using local historical archives and oral histories to map historical factors that may be important in understanding contemporary variations in health. Focusing on housing clearances in the 1950s, 1960s and 1970s, the pilot study drew on a wide range of primary and secondary data to explore how changes to local housing impacted upon the local social and psychological landscape. As such this reading is interesting substantively as well as methodologically and you may like to compare it to Reading 13 in Part III that is also concerned with geographical health inequalities. For our purposes here though Mallinson et al.'s paper is interesting and useful in terms of the authors' use of documentary evidence (secondary data) – including newspaper archives, local authority archives and autobiographical literatures – and oral history interviews (primary data) with 12 people who had had various roles and responsibilities within the study locality during the last 50 years. The pilot study, therefore, made use of a variety of historical research methods and the researchers were able to convincingly argue that taking an historical focus within sociological research on health inequalities adds to an understanding of contemporary patterns of morbidity and mortality in particular areas. However, as the authors note, the inclusion of historical evidence in research is not completely unproblematic and concerns include the status of historical evidence and the integration of historical analyses into contemporary social research data sets.

INTRODUCTION – CONCEPTUALIZING AND MEASURING THE HEALTH IMPACT OF 'PLACE'

There is now a considerable body of evidence pointing to the direct and indirect links between unequal social and material circumstances and health inequalities (see for example, Marmot and Wilkinson, 1999; Graham, 2000). However, there is also evidence of differences in the health outcomes of people who, on the face of it, have similar levels of material deprivation but live in different places (Graham, 2000). It appears that some 'places' have an impact on people's health experiences above and beyond the impact of those factors traditionally used to measure material deprivation. Within research on inequalities in health, there is considerable interest in methods that allow for the separate measurement of possible causal factors associated with people living in particular places (such as social class, ethnicity and gender – known as 'compositional effects') from factors associated with places themselves (known as 'contextual or area effects'). However, there is a need for greater sophistication in the way that these 'area' effects are conceptualized and measured in order to identify what it is that makes the health impact of places unique.

Until relatively recently, 'place' has rarely featured in health inequalities research, except as 'the canvas on which events happen' (Jones and Moon, 1993: 515). In the early 1990s a literature review by MacIntyre and colleagues (1993) identified two ways in which place was being used in health inequalities research. First, there were studies that focused on the physical environment and the genesis of diseases. Second, there were studies that used area population data to explore the impact of deprivation on health. Since MacIntyre and colleagues conducted their literature review, place has been a more regular feature on inequalities research agendas. However, a large proportion of the research has focused on area population data and the development of ever more complex modelling techniques to separate out contextual from compositional factors. While advancing statistical techniques, these models have been a source of some debate (see for example, Gatrell et al., 2000). Researchers are now attempting to incorporate better and more diverse measures of contextual factors, such as the degree of rurality, and measures of social relationships within places. Some research has also begun to explore the links between levels of vandalism and crime, access to recreational facilities, transport and other 'opportunity structures' and differential health outcomes between places (MacIntyre et al., 1993; MacIntyre, 1997).

In attempting to unravel the complex relationship between people, places and health outcomes, and in particular the mechanisms through which people negotiate and mediate the health-damaging effects of their neighbourhoods, a considerable proportion of recent work, including some of the research described earlier, has focused on the concept of social capital (Cooper et al., 1999; Putnam, 1993). Although this term is plagued by definitional vagaries, for the purpose of this article, we are referring to the 'resources' that flow from the networks, formal and informal, in which people are engaged. One reason why the amount and nature of social capital present in localities has become the focus of research interest in relation to health inequalities is its emphasis on the imbalances in power that ensue from the erosion of social capital. It is argued that high levels of social capital enable people to establish links to social systems and institutions, thereby facilitating access to health and welfare resources. Conversely, it is suggested, low levels of social capital can lead to disengagement and a lack of social cohesion (which is linked to reduced trust), factors that have been shown to be linked to poor health outcomes (Baum, 1999; Baum, 2000; Popay, 2000).

Research around the issue of social capital has helped to focus attention on the relationship between place and health and particularly the role of the 'social' in the genesis of geographical inequalities in health experiences, but significant challenges remain. In particular, as Popay et al. (1998) have argued, research seeking to understand the contribution of particular places to health inequalities must both conceptualize places as social phenomena with histories, and consider the ways in which the meanings people give to places and the social relationships that develop within them have emerged over time.

Research on health inequalities that has incorporated an historical focus has been limited but important. This research has highlighted, for example, how differences in the industrial/economic and cultural histories (including for example, differences in public housing initiatives in the past) can help to explain contemporary patterns of morbidity and mortality in particular areas (Barker and Osmond, 1987; Phillimore, 1993; Phillimore and Morris, 1991). However, such isolated examples of research taking an historical perspective are not adequate. Rather, we would argue that sociological accounts of the development and reproduction of health inequalities in places should, as a matter of course, incorporate an historical context. In seeking to understand the complexities, uncertainties and apparent contradictions of local people's accounts of 'place' in relation to other 'measures' of area characteristics, we need to look beyond the moment of the research and focus 'upstream' on the historical roots of contemporary relationships. As a modest contribution to this project we have recently begun to explore how future research might begin to gain, in the words of C. Wright Mills (1959: 145), 'an historical scope of conception and a full use of historical materials' and regard the historical as intrinsic to understanding and 'not merely general background' (1959: 150).

We now outline exploratory research conducted in a locality of Salford in the northwest of England that used historical resources to explore how social relationships between populations and local institutions were shaped by key events in one aspect of the area's recent past, namely its housing history. [We] discuss the nature and status of the different types of data we used, issues around memory and bias in historical evidence and illustrate the challenges (and benefits) of drawing together diverse accounts and perspectives on historical events.

THE STUDY RATIONALE

...

The fieldwork was conducted in 1992–2000 and had two strands. First, we identified potentially relevant local archives with material on people's experiences of living in particular places, or their experiences of health, and documents relating to socio-economic changes. Second, we used archives and newly collected oral histories to explore a bounded topic in order to assess the contribution that this approach could make to the larger study of health inequalities we were engaged in. This discussion relates to the second of these two strands of work.

Housing was selected as the topic for exploration for a number of reasons. First, the inner-city area being studied had undergone a series of major physical changes within living memory ('slum' clearances in the post-war period followed by demolition of high-rises during the 1980s and 1990s). It was now in the throes of a third wave of regeneration. We were interested in exploring whether local housing history had had a long-term impact on the social and psychological landscape and we wanted to understand how 'popular memories' (Johnson and Dawson, 1998) of events in the relatively recent past might inform the perspectives of people living there today....

METHODOLOGICAL ISSUES IN HISTORICAL RESEARCH

Historians have numerous sources of data available to them but, as in most academic disciplines, there exists a hierarchy of evidence that is a source of contention and debate (Lummis, 1998). Traditionally great store has been set by 'authenticated' documentary evidence in the form of official records, reports, newspapers and so forth. Much lower down the hierarchy of evidence are autobiographical accounts and oral histories (Thompson, 1988). The strengths and weaknesses of forms of evidence were not the particular concern of the research. Suffice to say that our perspective is that particular forms of evidence are of different value depending on the question one is asking. In our case, we were interested in establishing an outline chronology of events as part of the preparation for oral history work (Grele, 1998). For this reason, various forms of documentary evidence have been used, as outlined later. However, as our primary purpose was not simply to describe events but to gain some insight into the meaning people attached to those events, we also conducted a series of oral history interviews. Oral history offers the potential to look behind the 'public representations'[1] of a particular time and seek out 'private memories', which include everyday talk, comparisons and narratives (Johnson and Dawson, 1998).

While an oral history interview is acknowledged to be partial, variable and in some ways artificial (Thompson, 1988), it nevertheless offers a unique opportunity to hear people's memories about their past and its impact on their present. In other words, it offers an opportunity to explore what people *did*, what they *thought* at the time, what they *wanted* to do and what they *think* about it now. This approach acknowledges the dynamic nature of people's memories and experiences as they weave together past and present....

TYPES OF HISTORICAL DATA RELEVANT TO RESEARCH ON HEALTH INEQUALITIES

Documentary Evidence

The research began with a review of materials held in the local library archives, other historical collections and by local community projects. The key documentary materials identified in this work were: newspaper archives; local authority archives; contemporaneous literatures (e.g. academic texts and 'grey literature' from local organizations); autobiographical literatures; and research literatures (more recent analyses).

Local archives revealed a wealth of resources that the research team used to build a chronology of events and a sense of local and national context for the work. For example, we were able to explore the national state of public housing and compare this with local conditions. The strength of the documentary resources was in generating a 'factual' framework but there were also some clues as to the 'mood' of the era, the saliency of housing to local people and the various perspectives that needed to be explored during the oral history phase of the study. For example, housing issues are front-page, headline news almost every week in 1967 in the local newspaper. Some specific topics we identified as important for additional exploration were rents, property quality, pace of new build and problems of deferred demolition property.

While we found that autobiographical accounts added some depth to the reports in papers and other materials, in this instance people in relative positions of power and influence wrote these texts. Given our interest in exploring the potential mechanisms through which social capital is eroded or maintained, we needed to ensure a more balanced set of perspectives. The main avenue for this was the oral history interviews.

Oral History Interviews

While we were conscious of the need to explore the 'lay' perspective by speaking to people who had been rehoused during the period of our historical investigation, we also wanted to engage with other people involved in the housing process. In doing so, we hoped to gain some insight into the 'private memories' of people who were part of the 'bureaucracy' and those who were not.

We interviewed 12 people who had had various roles and responsibilities within the study locality during the last 50 years. People were identified and asked to take part in the research using a snowballing technique. The interviews were unstructured and lasted between 45 minutes and 1.5 hours. They were tape-recorded, partially transcribed and analysed using an indexing technique (Spencer and Ritchie, 1994). The 12 interviewees can be broadly categorized as follows: six local residents (five female and one male); one local councillor (male); one former housing officer (male); two former senior council officers (male); and two former members of parliament (male).[2]

While an unstructured approach was used in the interviews, people were guided with prompts. The prompts related to particular events or issues that we had identified in the documentary review. While this will have imposed some boundaries on people's accounts, the historical methods literature (and other psychological literatures) on recall point to the considerable utility of adding particular memory anchors in order to get beneath 'public representations' of an era (Bornat, 1998; Johnson and Dawson, 1998; Pearson et al., 1992). There is evidence to show that without specific anchors (e.g. times or places) people tend to forget important details about their personal experiences and their memories are then more likely to be influenced by other 'public' accounts such as those in newspaper articles.

The accounts given by the interviewees reflected their different backgrounds as a housing officer, or an MP, or a resident,[3] as well as their different expectations and interpretations of the purpose of the research. As one might expect, the interviews with 'local residents' were largely about memories of being rehoused and of living in the housing that replaced the terraces. Key themes were perceptions of choice and involvement in local housing plans, the intelligibility of council policy on rehousing, and 'theories' about why the new housing was (and continues to be) plagued with problems. Interviews with people who had had a role in local bureaucracy tended to focus on procedures and policies for rehousing and the outcomes of decisions. Key issues were perceptions of local people, sources of conflict between planners and housing officers, mistakes in housing strategy and 'theories' about the long-term consequences of poor management of rehousing processes and housing stock.

Our interviewees brought diverse knowledge and experience to the research because of their different roles in the local community. This diversity made the analysis and synthesis of the data challenging but there are two key benefits to this approach. First, given the different standpoints of the interviewees, areas of convergence suggest a strong theme for future in-depth historical research. For example, in talking about the process of notifying people of slum clearance orders, there was a consensus across all the interviewees that information and consultation processes were poor. Housing officers and local residents gave insightful accounts of the reasons for the lack of consultation and its impact, not only on local housing plans but on future relationships between various local agencies and people. The long-term consequences of the atmosphere of mistrust and uncertainty that the interviewees linked to inadequate consultation is a topic for more detailed scrutiny....

The second advantage of a diverse sample is that it allows 'special' knowledge and experience to be drawn into the data set to illuminate issues raised but not described in detail in other historical records. For example, 'bad management decisions' was a prominent theme developed by the interviewees who we had contacted because of their work-role in the locality. In particular there was an indepth discussion of the policy of deferred demolition (a process whereby an area was designated for demolition but was not cleared for anything up to ten years because of funding shortages). In our analysis of documentary evidence the problems arising from deferred demolition were frequently mentioned and were therefore noted as a topic for exploration. The advantage of having 'specialist' knowledge in the oral history accounts was that the factual reports of events and policies could be explored in more depth and supplemented with a personal narrative in which the interviewees reflected upon their perspective during the time period in question and their perspective now. The time and relative distance of the events were key to the type of account that the interviewees with 'special knowledge' gave, even though the confidentiality of the accounts was guaranteed. All the interviewees suggested that 'mistakes' they now see in the management of housing in the past have had long reaching effects.

In summary, the examples above demonstrate the value of the oral history accounts in three ways. First, they give some depth to the factual policy details on housing during the era that were garnered from documentary sources. Second, they introduce some personal meanings to the data set. Third, our data reinforce the claim of some historians that oral history allows one to see the dynamic nature of history and memories of the past. People are able to reflect upon the changes in their own perspective over time. This capability is important to the project of historically rooting contemporary meanings attached to places. There are some challenges involved in unravelling the influence of the present from people's memories of the past and a thoughtful interviewing and analysis strategy is important. Nevertheless, with the help of local people, or people 'who know', we can begin to explore how and why things are as they are.

CONCLUSIONS

. . .

The pilot research mapped a wealth of historical resources that are largely untapped in contemporary social research. In other places, historical data archives may not be as accessible or as plentiful, but in explorations of people's experiences of events in the relatively recent past (which is potentially a fruitful area of investigation to inform policy development) oral history interviews can be used to generate new resources. The methodological challenge is to find ways of addressing the limitations of the different forms of historical evidence which have been outlined here, such as the power/status issues around perspectives likely to be found in documentary evidence or the interweaving of past and present perspectives in oral history interviews. There is then the issue of integrating historical analyses into contemporary social research data sets.

Despite these challenges, we suggest that future research on health inequalities needs to draw on existing archives and on people's memories in order to build in an historical context for local people's experiences. Without this context an understanding of the dynamic nature of the places in which we live will remain out of reach both for researchers and policy makers.

NOTES

1. The memories recorded in documents, newspapers and other accounts are acknowledged to be shot through with the power and pervasiveness of dominant institutions (Johnson and Dawson, 1998).
2. It is interesting to note the gender divisions in the study sample. Female interviewees are represented only in the 'residents' category. All the other categories (MP, council officer, etc.) are exclusively male.
3. Some interviewees had multiple roles and perspectives to bring.

REFERENCES

Barker, D.J.P. and C. Osmond (1987) 'Inequalities in Health in Britain: Specific Explanations in Three Lancashire Towns', *British Medical Journal* 294: 749–52.

Baum, F. (1999) 'Social Capital: Is it Good for Your Health? Issues for a Public Health Agenda', *Journal of Epidemiology and Community Health* 53: 409–10.

Baum, F. (2000) 'Social Capital, Economic Capital and Power: Further Issues for a Public Health Agenda', *Journal of Epidemiology and Community Health* 54: 195–6.

Bornat, J. (1998) 'Oral History as a Social Movement', *Oral History* 17: 16–20.

Cooper, H., S. Arber, L. Fee and J. Ginn (1999) *The Influence of Social Support and Social Capital on Health*. London: HEA.

Gatrell, A., C. Thomas, S. Bennett, L. Bostock, J. Popay, G. Williams and S. Shahtahmasebi (2000) 'Understanding Health Inequalities: Locating People in Geographical and Social Spaces', in H. Graham (ed.) *Understanding Health Inequalities*. Buckingham: Open University Press.

Graham, H. (2000) *Understanding Health Inequalities*. Buckingham: Open University Press.

Grele, R.J. (1998) 'Movement Without Aim: Methodological and Theoretical Problems in Oral History', in R. Perks and A. Thomson (eds) *The Oral History Reader*, pp. 38–52. London: Routledge.

Johnson, R. and G. Dawson (1998) 'Popular Memory: Theory, Politics, Method', in R. Perks and A. Thomson (eds) *The Oral History Reader*, pp. 75–86. London: Routledge.

Jones, K. and G. Moon (1993) 'Medical Geography: Taking Space Seriously', *Progress in Human Geography* 17: 515–24.

Lummis, T. (1998) 'Structure and Validity in Oral Evidence', in R. Perks and A. Thomson (eds) *The Oral History Reader*, pp. 273–83. London: Routledge.

MacIntyre, S. (1997) 'The Black Report and Beyond: What Are the Issues?', *Social Science and Medicine* 44(6): 723–45.

MacIntyre, S., S. McIver and A. Sooman (1993) 'Area Class and Health: Should We be Focusing on Places or People?', *Journal of Social Policy* 22: 213–34.

Marmot, M. and R.G. Wilkinson (1999) *Social Determinants of Health*. Oxford: Oxford University Press.

Mills, C.W. (1959) *The Sociological Imagination*. Oxford: Oxford University Press.

Pearson, R.W., M. Ross and R.M. Dawes (1992) 'Personal Recall and the Limits of Retrospective Questions', in J. Tanur (ed.) *Questions About Questions: Enquiries into the Cognitive Bases of Surveys*. New York: Russell Sage Foundation.

Phillimore, P. (1993) 'How do Places Shape Health? Rethinking Locality and Lifestyle in North East England', in S. Platt, H. Thomas, S. Scott and G. Williams (eds) *Locating Health: Sociological And Historical Explorations*. Aldershot: Avebury.

Phillimore, P. and D. Morris (1991) 'Discrepant Legacies: Premature Mortality in Two Industrial Towns', *Social Science and Medicine* 33(2): 139–52.

Popay, J. (2000) 'Social Capital: The Role of Narrative and Historical Research', *Journal of Epidemiology and Community Health* 54: 401.

Popay, J., G. Williams, C. Thomas and A. Gatrell (1998) 'Theorising Inequalities in Health: The Place of Lay Knowledge', in M. Bartley, D. Blane and G. Davey-Smith (eds) *The Sociology of Health Inequalities*. London; Blackwell.

Putnam, R.D. (1993) *Making Democracy Work. Civic Traditions in Modern Italy*. Princeton, NJ: Princeton University Press.

Spencer, J. and L. Ritchie (1994) 'Qualitative Data Analysis for Applied Policy Research', in A. Bryman and R.G. Burgess *Analysing Qualitative Data*, pp. 173–94. London: Routledge.

Thompson, P. (1988) *The Voice of the Past: Oral History*. Oxford: Oxford University Press.

Source: S. Mallinson, J. Popay, E. Elliott, S. Bennett, L. Bostock, A. Gatrell, C. Thomas and G. Williams, 'Historical data for health inequalities: a research note', *Sociology*, 37:4 (2003) 771–80.

Study Questions and Activities

1. Re-read Reading 5. How successful or not are Sara Mallinson and her colleagues in utilising Mills' concept of the sociological imagination?
2. Detail the secondary and primary data collected in the pilot study described. How do these types of data complement each other?
3. How do you think Mallinson and her colleagues can address the limitations of historical data collection that they identify in their conclusion?
4. With reference to the research questions you established for study question 4 in Reading 6, consider how taking a historical perspective would benefit (or not) your own practice.

Further Reading

As this reading highlights, researchers who want to study the past often need to use secondary as well as primary data. Examples of books and articles that detail the use of primary data for historical research include: R. Perks and A. Thomson (eds), *The Oral History Reader* (London: Routledge, 1998); J. Popay, 'Social capital: the role of narrative and historical research', *Journal of Epidemiology and Community Health*, 54 (2000) 401; and P. Thompson, *The Voice of the Past: Oral History*

(Oxford: Oxford University Press, 1988). Almost any already published material can be useful secondary data for researchers and, in addition to the secondary data referred to in Reading 7 Shulamit Reinharz in her chapter on 'Experiential research: a contribution to feminist theory', in G. Bowles and R. D. Klein (eds) *Theories of Women's Studies* (Oxford: Oxford University Press, 1992) cites (amongst other things) children's books, billboards, non-fiction and fiction postcards, medical texts and works of art as potential sources of secondary data.

Reading 8

Practice-Based Evidence

Nick J. Fox

The central concern of this reading is the relationship between social science research and 'practice'. As Nick J. Fox argues practitioners are sometimes criticised for failing to base actions on research evidence, while academic research is, on occasion, condemned as irrelevant to practice. In this reading, Fox argues that this conflict derives in part from an academic model of research constructed in opposition to practice. He offers an alternative to 'evidence-based' practice and attempts to re-privilege the role of the practitioner whilst not rejecting the skills of the academic researcher. His 'practice-based evidence' model necessitates the acknowledgement of research 'findings' as local and contingent; a sensitivity to and respect for difference; and the acceptance that theory building should be an adjunct to practical activity. Having stated his case, Fox goes on to outline the development of an 'practice-based evidence' approach though a consideration of different aspects of the research process including setting a research question; research design; data collection and reliability and data analysis. In this reading, Fox is arguing for a praxis (theory and action) model of social research – an explicitly political approach to studying the social world – and it is interesting to compare this with the 'scientific' model identified by Punch and other authors referred to in the Further Reading section of Reading 6. Yet, Fox is not only concerned with the political significance of the research product but also with the political aspects of the research process (just as Mallinson et al. (Reading 7) are with reference to historical research methods). Fox insists that adopting a 'practice-based evidence' approach leads to the breakdown of the unequal researcher/researched and research/practice positions found in traditional research approaches and, as such, is an ethically, as well as politically engaged, research approach.

INTRODUCTION

Social scientific research into 'practice' (for example, education, social services, health-care, policing) has contributed a mass of data on how services are delivered and offered important recommendations for improvements to services. Yet in academic circles there is a culture which implies that research ends when the paper has been published, a seminar or two has been given and the subjects have all – metaphorically and literally – gone home. This view is mediated in research methods texts, in institutional processes for funding research and in most research contracts (Elton, 2000; Print and Hattie, 1997).[1] Traditionally, the application of a piece of research in practical settings is seen as non-problematic, something which naturally flows from the conclusions of the research and is best left to the 'practitioners', be they citizens, education or care professionals or other social scientists (see, for example, Dawson, 1995, Lomas et al., 1993).

In reality, the uptake of service-oriented research findings in professional practice is extremely patchy; an issue which has begun to exercise those who have promulgated the 'evidence-based' approach (Dawson, 1995; NHS Executive, 1998). A consequent authoritarianism towards practitioners is reflected in developments such as the Cochrane Collaboration, which has promulgated a view that the randomized controlled trial is unequivocally the 'gold standard' of research evidence (often to the exclusion of social science research) (Sackett et al., 1996). Health practitioners have been recently presented with distillations of evidence in the form of National Service Frameworks for various disease categories and in future these will be benchmarks against which actual practice will be measured and judged (NHS Executive, 1999).

Critical responses to this 'academic encirclement' (Strong, 1984) of service-based practice have come from a number of different perspectives, ranging from critical theory (Carr and Kemmis, 1986), Foucauldian critiques of ever-burgeoning 'technologies of the self' (Gastaldo, 1997: 126–9; Lupton, 1998: 206; Rose, 1989) to attacks on the 'irrelevance' and over-theorized nature of educational research conducted by academics in university departments, rather than by teachers and educational policymakers addressing issues of effectiveness (Hargreaves, 1996). [Here] I want to unpack the 'problem of implementation' from a different perspective; to re-evaluate the hierarchy of knowledge which situates research evidence in a position superior to other forms of knowing. The objective is to re-privilege the role of the 'practitioner' in generating useful knowledge, without rejecting the skills and perspectives of the 'academic' researcher.

WHY IS RESEARCH NOT IMPLEMENTED?

Some studies of the failure to adopt research findings into practice have not started from the assumption that research findings are top of a 'hierarchy of evidence'....

A study by Wood et al. (1998) looked at evidence-based guidelines on the use of oral anticoagulants for stroke prophylaxis, laparoscopic surgery for inguinal hernia repair and the proposals for obstetric care set out in a government circular known as 'Changing Childbirth'. While there appeared to be general acceptance of the latter, other initiatives were often adopted patchily and, in the case of anticoagulant prophylaxis, very slowly – despite the evidence of reduced morbidity and mortality. Wood et al. suggested that practitioners were not convinced by disembodied research findings, but wanted to see these findings contextualized within their own practical experience. They found it essential that practitioners 'bought in' to the proposed changes and that research had to take account of locally-situated practices which engage with the research. 'Research findings' represent not so much truth about reality, as one 'reified moment' in the ongoing saga of 'practice' (Wood et al., 1998: 1735).

Research and practice need to be seen as differing world-views on the same subject matter: researchers see data while practitioners see people (Haines and Jones, 1994) and research data must be translated from the former to the latter world-view before it is recognized as relevant by practitioners. Shaugnessy et al. (1994) suggest that practitioners' perceptions of the utility of evidence will depend on its relevance to a particular setting and its validity for that setting. Practitioners need to recognize a problem for which the evidence is relevant before research will be seen as applicable in a practice setting (Williamson, 1992) and research evidence is most likely to be adopted by practitioners if it is first 'digested', replacing specific findings (the usual outcome of a particular study), with a 'big picture' (Brown and Duguid, 1991; Haynes, 1993). Dawson (1995: 202) concludes that practitioners and researchers must work together as part of a 'bottom-up' approach to implementation (Grimshaw and Russell, 1993; Haines and Jones, 1994).

From these various studies and different theoretical perspectives, three readings are possible.

1. Practitioners know best and should be left to get on with it, free of interference from the professional researcher (the conservative view).
2. Practitioners are lacking in key knowledge and ways must be found to re-educate them into effective service delivery (the evidence-based practice approach).
3. Rather than blaming practitioners for disregarding research evidence, the fault lies with the model of research which has been developed in academia. This research model does not readily articulate with the practical imperatives of service professionals. Research does contribute knowledge, but it is up to the researcher to change her mode of working so it contributes to practice.

This paper explores the third of these perspectives and argues that because 'evidence' is contingent and needs to be contextualized, 'evidence-based practice' should be supplemented by 'practice-based evidence' and a model of 'practice-based research' (PBR).

POST-STRUCTURALISM AND POSTMODERNISM: THE TRUTH IS NOT OUT THERE

Post-structuralist contributions to social theory over the past decade have led to various models of postmodern social theory and research.... Postmodernism is suspicious of and rejects 'grand narratives' that offer a unified or monolithic perspective on the world, human-ness, or knowledge in general (Lyotard, 1984)....

... Despite this, the desire for the *logos*: truth about the object of study, remains a core value for many social scientists and is most clearly exemplified in the language of research-funding applications and the assertions of methods texts (Feinstein, 1992). In the latter, this orientation towards truth-seeking (perhaps dressed-up as 'authenticity', 'credibility' and so on) is mediated in discourses on the concepts of internal and external validity in research.

First, 'internal validity' (the extent to which a study measures what it claims to be measuring) articulates a scientific *logocentrism* based on the premises of the particular discipline in question. Scientific methodology, according to this line of thinking, makes reality accessible, removing or minimizing distortions that methods of observation or analysis may introduce. Thus, research methodology is not just a matter of technique, but stems from pronouncements on epistemology: of how we may legitimately 'get to truth' (Denzin and Lincoln, 1998; Lakatos, 1978; Popper, 1982)....

If only – the argument goes – our methodology is adequate and appropriate, then we will be able to achieve an understanding based upon the observations that we make and the theory we develop to explain those observations. Scientific logo-centrism – while on the one hand privileging research data gathered through specified methods – downgrades the 'mere experience' which is developed in practical settings (Lomas et al., 1993: 405; Wood et al., 1998: 1730). Methods texts are science's equivalent of a religion's holy book: setting out the right way to do things and the 'threats to validity' which come from not following the prescriptions and precedents. This has also led proponents of 'evidence-based practice' to assert a hierarchy of research designs, with meta-analysis of randomized controlled trials at the top and qualitative studies somewhere close to divination (Denzin and Lincoln, 1998: 7; Greenhalgh, 1997).

Secondly, the 'external validity' of research is concerned with the generalizability of research findings to practical settings. This is of importance, both in terms of inferences that can be made from the study group to the whole population and for the application of findings in practice. The basis for 'evidence-based practice' is the external validity of research. Thus, for example, health professionals, teachers or social workers should manage their patients, students or clients according to guidelines based on research evidence, rather than drawing upon their own experiences or harking back to their original training. If a study possesses external validity, the failure of research findings to be translated into practice can be blamed on the practitioners, who are assumed to be either recalcitrant or incapable of grasping the relevance of the research for their practice setting.

These two elements of research 'validity' do more than just set up rules for generating trustworthy evidence. Together, they differentiate between the claimed rationality and enlightenment of research evidence and the messy, 'irrational' uncertainty of practice (see, for example, Hammersley, 1997: 147; Silverman, 1999: 2). Form such a perspective, 'research' constructs 'practice' as an irrational *other*, the other pole of a binary opposition. As such, the 'truth' of research – paradoxically – must sustain itself unsullied by the threatening irrationality of the practical world, while at the same time claiming to be supremely relevant and valid for these practical settings....

Exposing this constructed binary opposition between research and practice is the starting point for re-thinking their relationship. We must immediately overturn the imputed hierarchy of evidence that claims privilege for a certain kind of practice called 'research'.... It follows that research must be seen as an *extension* – as one form – of practice: research and practice are intertwined rather than opposite poles....

If researchers can no longer stand apart from their research setting, it follows that their relationship with subjects should be wider than simply that of researcher/researched. Consequently, researchers must adopt an ethical and political position that structures the engagement which they have with the subjects of research. The politics of such a model of research are radical and are concerned with resistance and change (Fox, 1995; Game, 1991; MacLure, 1996).

Reporting research changes from efforts to represent or to persuade, to a reflection upon the relationship between the research text and other texts (Richardson, 1993; Sanger, 1995; Tyler, 1986), including those texts which comprise practice. Rather than excluding these, researchers may draw upon them to provide the context for their research in a way which is more substantive than simply 'locating the study' within the 'literature'. Indeed the form of the research output may be radicalized: offering polyvocality (for example, Curt, 1994; Mulkay, 1985), or in the form of a direct engagement (teaching, therapy, protest, worship). Whatever form is chosen, the research becomes part of the setting it is exploring and research becomes a facet of practice, inextricably tied up with the wider issues of political engagement, power and justice.

This analysis of research leads to a number of propositions concerning how we may seek knowledge of the world. Firstly, the pursuit of knowledge must be recognized as a *local and contingent* process. While understanding of the environment may be achieved through observation and inductive reasoning, it cannot be assumed that these observations or this reasoning can be translated to other settings, or even from the research setting to 'real life'....

Secondly, research as a political activity should be *constitutive of difference*, rather than demonstrative of similarity (for example, generalizability)... research which is constitutive of difference acknowledges different qualities, yet accepts them as of equal value rather than privileged in hierarchical or oppositional relationships to each other....

Thirdly, *theory building* – while necessarily part of any activity of 'understanding' – should be seen not as an end in itself but as an *adjunct to practical activity* within the setting in question.… Understanding makes sense only if data are placed in context (Mauthner et al., 1998). Given the commitments of those engaged in practice, in this formulation 'research' and 'theory' will be similarly committed to an ethical and political engagement with 'practice'. It is to this issue that I now turn by way of an exploration of action research.

ACTION RESEARCH: ENGAGING ETHICALLY AND POLITICALLY WITH PRACTICE

Action and practitioner research implicitly link to practice. Despite a long history within the social sciences, these models have been marginalized and are often ignored in methodology texts. Action research grew up in the 1940s and 1950s, underpinned by the principle that theory would be developed and tested by practical interventions or actions; that there would be consistency between project means and desired ends; and that ends and means were grounded in guidelines established by the host community (Stull and Schensul, 1987).

Such an advocacy model for research sustained a distinction between researcher and researched, while acknowledging the importance of the perspectives of the researched subjects. Nixon (1981) described a model of 'practitioner research' which embodied professional ideals, focused on changing practice, identified and explained inconsistencies between aspiration and practice and involved professional practitioners in testing new forms of practice and related theories. Practitioner research is a developmental process in which practice is a form of research and vice versa (Elliott, 1995).

Schensul (1987) suggests that collaborative action research can:

- bring together people with diverse skills and knowledge;
- de-mystify the research process, allowing practitioners to shape the data collection process;
- build a research capacity into a community which can operate independently;
- increase the likelihood that practitioners will use the research findings; and
- improve the quality of research by enabling access to key bodies of knowledge in a community.

The varieties of action research have been categorized by Carr and Kemmis (1986) as:

- technical (in which an outside expert undertakes the research within a practice setting);

- practical (in which the researched are encouraged to participate in the research process); and

- emancipatory (in which the researcher takes on the role of a 'process moderator' assisting participants to undertake the research themselves).

The third of these models is of most interest here, because of its challenge to a researcher/researched opposition. Zuber-Skerritt (1991) suggests that, within this paradigm, action research is participative and collaborative, emancipatory, interpretive and critical, so that 'action and practical experience may be the foundations of ...research and research may inform practice and lead to action' (Zuber-Skerritt, 1991: 11)....

TRANSGRESSING THE RESEARCH/PRACTICE DIVIDE

I now want to set out some further thoughts on what is entailed in doing practically engaged research. While not intending to be prescriptive, this will assist in both deconstructing traditional research and re-constructing something very different.... At the heart of what follows will be the three propositions of practice-based research (PBR) identified earlier (contingency, constitution of difference and relation to practice) and the rejection of three dualisms: researcher versus researched, research versus experience and theory versus practice.

To assist in developing this PBR perspective, I will look at four 'moments' in the research process....

Setting a Research Question

Over a number of years spent teaching (modernist) research methods I emphasized to students that, without a clear research question, it is impossible to undertake research and that all subsequent stages in the research process are bedevilled by an absence of clarity which undermines the efforts of the researcher. However, this argument is based on the assumption that research is a linear process and the end result of research must be some kind of answer to a question....

From a PBR perspective things are rather different. Taking the first proposition established earlier, if *knowledge is local and contingent*, then it may be impossible to establish what are the correct questions to ask until one has a fairly clear understanding of the characteristics of the setting. A research question would only emerge after a considerable period spent familiarizing oneself with the local issues. This kind of approach to setting a research question is not wholly dissimilar to that of ethnographers and other qualitative researchers who work in a field for an extended period, creating research questions which link to the specificities of the setting.

Taking the second proposition, if the *research should be constitutive of difference*, then it is important that the research question should not have the effect of closing down or limiting the ways in which the subjects of the research will be understood or will conceive of themselves. The ethics and politics of the research thus begin with the question which is asked – indeed, the concept of a 'subject' of research must be challenged and deconstructed in the research process. Within research conducted from this kind of perspective, 'subjects' become 'participants' and are not 'subjected' to research or to the will of the researcher. Thus it will be important to involve participants in the process of setting a research question which is relevant to their own concerns and which will open up rather than close down the possibilities of action open to the participants....

The final proposition, that *theory should be related to practice*, means that research questions should be developed in such a way that the theoretical consequences will be of direct practical relevance. This does not rule out 'blue sky' or pure research, but does mean that researchers involved in these areas need to think carefully about the application of their research findings over a longer time period than the single investigation they are undertaking....

Research Design, Study and Instrument Validity

In traditional research, the issue of research design and the validity of the study and the instruments used are tied up with questions of whether they are appropriate and may adequately answer the research question (Cain and Finch, 1981; Denzin and Lincoln, 1998). Thus a randomized controlled trial would not be considered appropriate to answer an exploratory question of a 'how' type. Similarly, a survey would not be appropriate or adequate to compare two alternative forms of treatment. In the PBR approach, these 'technical' questions are subsumed within epistemological, political and ethical propositions developed previously.

First, if knowledge is local and contingent, we can make no assumptions about the methodological approach or the tools or instruments which should be used to uncover this 'knowledge'. Similarly, we cannot assume that one research design or instrument will be sufficient to answer a question – methodological pluralism or eclecticism may well be the key here....

This relates to the second proposition of PBR, in that this period of exploration should be conducted with the full involvement of all those concerned with the research, specifically the 'subjects' or participants, as in action research designs. Conversely, the politics and ethics of difference militate against such designs as randomized and blind studies or surveys, which sustain differences between 'researcher' and the 'researched'. Methodologies which fit into this principle include qualitative approaches which enable participation, such as interviews, focus groups, Delphi groups and other discursive contexts, as well as case studies which are concerned with specific settings and small- rather than large-scale approaches.

The use of such methods would also support the final proposition, inasmuch as the theory that is developed from the research would be closely linked to the practical concerns of the participants, as opposed to the concerns of a 'disinterested' researcher or scientific community. As was noted earlier in this paper, the difference between traditional and PBR research can be seen clearly in relation to issues of internal and external validity of a study. If a study concerns itself with the development of contingent and local knowledge through methods that ensure participation and the involvement of all those in a setting, then the internal validity (the extent to which a study measures what it sets out to measure) will be high. On the other hand, the external validity or generalizability to other settings will be low or non-existent. Measurements of internal and external validity would be more valuable as indicators that one's approach fits within the PBR propositions rather than as ends in themselves....

Data Collection and Reliability

In the traditional paradigm of research, validity and reliability are closely related, with both contributing to the accuracy of the data. While validity is affected by systematic error and is a consequence of the instrumentation or procedures developed for data collection, reliability is concerned with random error. Thus reliability is affected not so much by the adequacy of the instruments used to collect the data, but by the processes of data collection themselves....

If the propositions of PBR were applied to the process of data collection, from a traditional standpoint the reliability of the data would be seriously compromised, as should be obvious bearing in mind the previous discussion of design and validity. There is a requirement for a degree of reflexivity within PBR which would make the process of data collection prone to both inter- and intra-observer biases. For example, it is probable that an instrument such as a questionnaire or interview schedule would be developed in close consultation with the people who would eventually be the respondents. Indeed, the conflation of the identities of 'researcher' and 'researched' would make the concept of 'observer bias' deeply problematic.

However, rather than confounding the research process, within the PBR paradigm, the 'bias' would be seen as a virtue, guaranteeing that the research was relevant and adequate to answer the research question. While this way of thinking about data collection is highly appropriate for social science, it might also be considered appropriate in biomedical research. For example, a research study could be devised to explore the effects of a particular drug upon patients suffering from some condition. The design of the study would involve the patients, so they would identify the parameters which were relevant for them in assessing the utility of the drug for them. These would vary from 'hard' measures of efficacy, through to the acceptability of the drug for individual patients. As a result, the assessment of the drug might be highly transgressive of medical and health economic commitments! ... Within the PBR perspective, given the reservations commented upon earlier concerning internal and external validity, subjectivity and bias would be seen as advantages, ensuring that the research findings were relevant to the study population....

Data Analysis and Hypothesis Testing

In traditional research paradigms, the phase of data analysis completes the cycle of the research process and should enable the research question to be answered. Where there is a hypothesis, this can be tested using inferential statistics or methods such as analytic induction (Mitchell, 1983). The PBR perspective is more open-ended than this linear or cyclical model of research. Just as the research question emerged during a preliminary exploration of the research setting, the analysis of the research data is likely to be part of an ongoing process of evaluation and reflection.

In terms of the proposition that knowledge is local, the analysis of the data will be intimately linked with the reflections on the research process by the participants and researchers. Indeed, the data would include these processes of reflection and it would be impossible to understand fully the data if the context were to be lost or ignored (Mauthner et al., 1998). The second proposition, that all action should be constitutive of difference, requires that the analysis of the data is constituted within the ethical and political commitments of the participants. Finally, the proposition that theory should be related to practice requires that data analysis would inform the practical concerns of participants and researchers, for example, through recommendations for changes in practice.

The data analysis phase is also implicated in the more general issue of the translation of research findings into practice and, for these reasons, it is hard to see a clear end point to the research process within this paradigm. There is a blurring of the phase of 'research' with that of 'normal practice', so that it is impossible to discern where one begins and the other finishes. It should be obvious from the assessment of this phase of the research process that, within the PBR model, research cannot be seen as an independent activity, but must be seen within the ongoing ethical and political engagements of all the participants: both researchers and researched....

These four moments in the research process address many of the important issues in designing a research programme which meets the expectations established in the propositions for practice-based research. However it is worth reflecting briefly on a further aspect: the ethics of the research process. In many traditional research studies, ethical issues are often tagged on to a discussion of methods: the discussions of design, data collection and analysis are strangely stripped of ethical or political contexts and these have to be grafted on at a later stage. Bauman (1989) suggests that modernist organizations lack an intrinsic morality, making activities like the Nazi genocide simply another organizational problem to be solved by instrumental means. Similar criticism may be raised against many research practices which have flourished in the 20th century, including many studies in psychology and the use of animals in experimentation. Research ethics weigh the benefits of research against the ethical principles on which they impinge and make judgements based on privileging ends against means. By contrast, PBR – as it has been set out here – has no requirement for an additional section on the ethics of research, because the ethics and politics are integral to the propositions and practices of research in this paradigm. A commitment to difference (as operationalized in the emphases on reflexivity, collaboration and transgression) is in itself ethical and political. The research process flows from these propositions, rather than remaining separate and unengaged.

DISCUSSION: OVERCOMING THE RESEARCH/PRACTICE DIVIDE

...

... while this paper sets out some practical suggestions for a PBR, the intention is not to create yet another model of the 'best' way to research. If PBR is intrinsically transgressive, this rules out a single truth about how things should be done. Indeed, reflexivity about practice requires that one is always critical and open to new ways of thinking. The ideas developed here have much to say to the academic and the contract researcher, to those who fund research and to those engaged in practice. Research which is integral to practice, which is 'everybody's business', can lead to 'practice-based evidence', but also challenges many deeply-held commitments and will inevitably transgress norms, values and interests in the research community.

NOTE

1. Research councils and other funding bodies request information from grant applicants about how users will be involved in research. Acceptable responses tend to focus on evidence of prior consultation with stakeholders and strategies for the dissemination of research findings.

REFERENCES

Bauman, Z. (1989) *Modernity and the Holocaust*. Cambridge: Polity.
Brown, J.S. and P. Duguid (1991) 'Organizational Learning and Communities of Practice: Towards a Unified View of Working, Learning and Innovation', *Organization Science* 2: 40–57.
Cain, M. and J. Finch (1981) 'Towards a Rehabilitation of Data', in P. Abrams, R. Deem, J. Finch and P. Rock (eds) *Practice and Progress: British Sociology* 1950–80. London: Macmillan.
Carr, W. and S. Kemmis (1986) *Becoming Critical: Knowing through Action Research*. Victoria: Deakin University Press.
Curt, B. (1994) *Textuality and Tectonics: Troubling Social and Psychological Science*. Buckingham: Open University Press.
Dawson, S. (1995) 'Never Mind Solutions: What are the Issues? Lessons of Industrial Technology Transfer for Quality in Health Care', *Quality in Health Care* 4: 197–203.
Denzin, N. and Y.S. Lincoln (1998) 'Introduction', pp. 1–29 in N. Denzin and Y.S. Lincoln (eds) *Collecting and Interpreting Qualitative Materials*. Newbury Park: Sage.
Elliott, J. (1995) 'What is Good Action Research?', *Action Researcher* 2: 10–11.

Elton, L. (2000) 'The UK Research Assessment Exercise: Unintended Consequences', *Higher Education Quarterly* 54: 274–83.

Feinstein, A.R. (1992) 'Invidious Comparisons and Unmet Clinical Challenges', *American Journal of Medicine* 92: 117–20.

Fox, N.J. (1995) 'Intertextuality and the Writing of Social Research', *Electronic Journal of Sociology* 1 (3).

Game, A. (1991) *Undoing the Social*. Buckingham: Open University Press.

Gastaldo, D. (1997) 'Is Health Education Good for You? Re-thinking Health Education through the Concept of Bio-power', pp. 113–33 in A. Petersen and R. Bunton (eds) *Foucault, Health and Medicine*. London: Routledge.

Greenhalgh, T. (1997) 'How to Read a Paper: Papers that Report Diagnostic or Screening Tests', *British Medical Journal* 315: 540–3.

Grimshaw, J.M. and I.T. Russell (1993) 'Effects of Clinical Guidelines on Medical Practice: A Systematic Review of Rigorous Evaluations', *Lancet* 342: 1317–22.

Haines, A. and R. Jones (1994) 'Implementing Findings of Research', *British Medical Journal* 308: 1488–92.

Hammersley, M. (1997) 'Educational Research and Teaching: A Response to David Hargreaves' TTA lecture', *British Educational Research Journal*, 23: 141–61.

Hargreaves, D. (1996) 'Educational Research and Evidence-based Educational Practice – a Response to Critics', *Research Intelligence* 58: 12–16.

Haynes, R.B. (1993) 'Some Problems in Applying Evidence in Clinical Practice', *Annals of the New York Academy of Science*, 73: 21–4.

Lakatos, I. (1978) 'Introduction', in *The Methodology of Scientific Research Programmes Volume 1*. Cambridge: Cambridge University Press.

Lomas, J., J.E. Sisk and B. Stocking (1993) 'From Evidence to Practice in the United States, the United Kingdom and Canada', *Milbank Quarterly*, 71: 405–10.

Lupton, D. (1998) 'Medicine and Health Care in Popular Media', in A. Petersen and C. Waddell (eds) *Health Matters*. St Leonards, Australia: Allen and Unwin.

Lyotard, J. (1984) *The Postmodern Condition, A Report on Knowledge*. Minneapolis: University of Minnesota Press.

MacLure, M. (1996) 'Telling Transition Boundary Work in Narratives on Becoming an Action Researcher', *British Educational Research Journal* 22: 273–6.

Mauthner, N.S., O. Parry and K. Backett-Milburn (1998) 'The Data are Out There, or Are They? Implications for Archiving and Revisiting Qualitative Data', *Sociology* 32: 733–45.

Mortimore, P. (2000) 'Does Educational Research Matter?', *British Journal of Educational Research* 26: 5–24.

Mitchell, J.C. (1983) 'Case and Situation Analysis', *Sociological Review* 31: 187–211.

Mulkay, M.J. (1985) *The Word and the World*. London: George Allen and Unwin.

NHS Executive (1998) *A First Class Service*. Quality in the NHS. London: Department of Health.

NHS Executive (1999) *Clinical Governance. Quality in the New NHS*. London: Department of Health.

Nixon, J. (1981) *A Teacher's Guide to Action Research*. London: Grant McIntyre.

Popper, K. (1982) 'Science: Conjectures and Refutations', pp. 87–93 in P. Grim (ed.) *The Philosophy of Science and the Occult*. Albany: New York State University Press.

Print, M. and J. Hattie (1997) 'Measuring Quality in Universities: An Approach to Weighting Research Productivity', *Higher Education* 33: 453–69.

Rose, N. (1989) *Governing the Soul*. London: Routledge.

Sackett, D.L., M.C. Rosenberg, J.A. Muir Gray, R.B. Haynes and W. Scott Richardson (1996) 'Evidence-based Medicine: What It Is and What It Isn't', *British Medical Journal* 12: 71–2.

Sanger, J. (1995) 'Five Easy Pieces: The Deconstruction of Illuminatory Data in Research Writing', *British Educational Research Journal* 21: 89–97.

Schensul, J.J. (1987) 'Perspectives on Collaborative Research', in D.D. Stull and J.J. Schensul (eds) *Collaborative Research and Social Change*. Boulder, Colorado: Westview Press.

Shaugnessy, A.F., D.C. Slanson and J.H. Bennett (1994) 'Becoming an Information Master: A Guidebook to the Medical Information Jungle', *Journal of Family Practice* 39: 89–99.

Silverman, M. (1999) *Facing Postmodernity*. London: Routledge.

Strong, P. (1984) 'Viewpoint: The Academic Encirclement of Medicine', *Sociology of Health & Illness* 6: 339–58.

Stull, D.D. and J.J. Schensul (1987) (eds) *Collaborative Research and Social Change*. Boulder, CO: Westview Press.

Tyler, S.A. (1986) 'Postmodern Ethnography', pp. 122–40 in J. Clifford and G.E. Marcus (eds) *Writing Culture: The Poetics and Politics of Ethnography*. Berkeley: University of California Press.

Williamson, P. (1992) 'From Dissemination to Use: Management and Organisational Barriers to the Application of Health Services Research Findings', *Health Bulletin* 50: 8–86.

Wood, M., E. Ferlie and L. Fitzgerald (1998) 'Achieving Clinical Behaviour Change: A Case of Becoming Indeterminate', *Social Science and Medicine* 47: 1729–38.

Zuber-Skerritt, O. (1991) *Action Research in Higher Education*. Brisbane: Centre for Advancement of Learning and Teaching.

Source: N. J. Fox, 'Practice based evidence: towards collaborative and transgressive research', *Sociology*, 37:1 (2003) 81–102.

Study Questions and Activities

1. What leads Nick Fox to argue that 'practice-based experience' and a model of 'practice-based research' should replace 'evidence-based practice'? Thinking about the research evidence that you use in your own practice do you agree with him?
2. What are the differences between internal and external validation?
3. In what ways is the approach Fox advocates 'transgressive'?
4. Fox argues that ethics and politics are integral to 'practice-based research'. Do you agree? Why?

Further Reading

For further reading on the possibilities, and critique, of evidence-based research see, for example, T. Greenhalgh, 'Narrative based medicine in an evidence based world', in T. Greenhalgh and B. Hurwitz (eds) *Narrative Based Medicine: Dialogue and Discourse in Clinical Practice* (London: BMJ, 1998); L. Locock and A. Boaz, 'Research, policy and practice – worlds apart?', *Social Policy and Society*, 3:4 (2004) 375–84; C. Sharp, *The Improvement of Public Sector Delivery: Supporting Evidence Based Practice Through Action Research* (Edinburgh: The Scottish Executive Knowledge Transfer Research Findings 2, 2005). In addition to this particular genre of research writing, there is a plethora of work focusing on the political potential of social research. You might find it interesting to compare one of the first pieces written by an academic – for example, Howard Becker's 'Whose side are we on?', *Social Problems*, 14 (1967) 239–47 – to a piece written by a recent UK Secretary of State of Education and Employment – David Blunkett's *Influence or Irrelevance: Can Social Science Improve Government? Secretary of State's ESRC Lecture Speech 2nd February* (London: Department for Education and Employment, 2000). See also: M. Bloor, 'Addressing social problems through qualitative research', in D. Silverman (ed.) *Qualitative Research: Theory, Method and Practice* (London: Sage, 1998); P. Beresford, 'Service users' knowledges and social work theory: conflict or collaboration?', *British Journal of Social Work*, 30 (2000) 489–503; S. Hood, B. Mayall and S. Oliver (eds) *Critical Issues in Social Research* (Buckingham: Open University Press, 1999); and J. Radford, M. Friedberg and L. Harne (eds) *Women, Violence and Strategies for Action: Feminist Research, Policy and Practice* (Buckingham: Open University Press, 2000) for a small selection of the contributions to this debate by sociologists and other social scientists.

Reading 9

'Traditional' and 'Emancipatory' Research

Beth Humphries

In this reading, Beth Humphries, like Keith F. Punch in Reading 6, challenges some simplistic stereotypical understandings within the philosophy of research. Also, and like Nick J. Fox in Reading 8, she provides a critique of 'traditional' and 'scientific' approaches arguing for praxis-orientated research. In the article from which this reading is taken, Humphries draws on two books: Patti Lather's *Getting Smart* (London: Routledge, 1991) – who writes from a feminist perspective – and Martyn Hammersley's *The Politics of Social Research* (London: Sage, 1995) – which is critical of this and other explicitly political research. In the early part of the article, Humphries briefly outlines the debate between these two positions, which are both in their own ways value-laden (for example, see Punch in Reading 6). We pick up her argument halfway through the article at the point where she notes the similarities, rather than the differences, in traditional and emancipatory approaches. The reading concludes with a consideration of the possibilities for a praxis-orientated research that may lead to possibilities for emancipatory action.

Humphries' article stimulated a debate in the journal *Sociological Research Online* (see M. Hammersley, 'A reply to Humphries', 2:4 (1997), http://www.socresonline.org.uk/2/4/6.html and B. Humphries, 'The baby and the bath water: Hammersley, Cealey Harrison and Hood-Williams and the emancipatory research debate', 3:1 (1998), http://www.socresonline.org.uk/ 3/1/9.html). This is just an example of a debate between sociologists about research practice and process (also see Further Reading section of Reading 8, as well as Further Reading below).

APPEALS TO A METANARRATIVE OF EMANCIPATION

… The production and dissemination of scientific knowledge is legitimated on the grounds that it represents the disinterested pursuit of truth, the pursuit of which will contribute to progress and to the ultimate general good of humanity. As Lyotard notes, although there have been wars and disputes over the name of the subject we are to help to become emancipated, 'all the parties concurred that enterprises, discoveries and institutions are legitimate only insofar as they contribute to the emancipation of mankind' (Lyotard, 1993: p. 172). Alternative approaches on the other hand, embrace more particular emancipatory goals and claim empowerment for specific oppressed groups. And although we need to acknowledge a range of critical positions and feminisms, the knowledge assumptions which underpin them are similar to those of scientific knowledge, rooted in the ideals of the Enlightenment – that is a view of the subject as powerful and self-consciously political: a belief in reason and rationality; and a belief in social and economic progress through grand schemes of change (Barrett and Phillips, 1992: p. 5). Where they have diverged is in the exposure by feminists, critical theorists and anti-racists of capitalist and male-centred interest at the root of claims to 'neutrality' in the construction of scientific knowledge. Further, feminism developed a critique of critical and participatory perspectives (Maguire, 1996) for their failure to take account of gender in any serious way. In its turn white feminist theory and research has had its universalist and imperialist assumptions challenged by black and third world feminists, by lesbian feminists and by disabled feminists. In these ways, although the *nature* of knowledge is hotly contested (who can be a knower and what kinds of knowledge are legitimate as 'truth'), the debate is premised on a tacitly agreed set of rules within a metanarrative of the liberation of humankind.

The shift to post-structuralist thinking has had an influence on the development of feminist thinking in particular. Post-structuralism has displaced the subject as conscious, rational and coherent, pointing to a variety of different subjectivities and realities. It has challenged the materialist, determinist and structuralist mode of explanation for social phenomena and emphasized representation, symbols and language. In place of the development of societies as an onward movement of progress, post-structuralism focuses on the specifics of time and space and localized struggle. In the consideration of post-structuralism's contribution to feminism, there has been recognition of its conflict with emancipatory ideals in its concern to emphasize *difference* and the *particular*.

So to summarize, scientific research and alternative research approaches both appeal to a metanarrative of emancipation and have their roots in Enlightenment ideals. Post-structuralism challenges these roots and dismisses a metanarrative of justice as an organising concept. I shall return to this presently.

The Will to Power

Emancipatory research approaches identify traditional research as deeply implicated in power, and set as their goals the equalizing of power between researcher and research subjects and the changing of oppressive relations of power. However both approaches are implicated in power. The very act of engaging in an activity implicates us in power, so that our efforts to liberate perpetuate the relations of dominance. The concept to 'empower' is a metaphor similar to Derrida's definition of 'to enlighten', which he describes as a light-based metaphor which positions the emancipators as senders of light and receivers as passive. Foucault (1993) argues that there may be projects whose aim is to modify some constraints, 'to loosen, or even to break them, but none of these projects can simply, by its nature, assure that people will have liberty ... Liberty is a *practice*' (p. 162). Emancipation cannot be conferred on one group by another. Martin's (1994, 1996) descriptions of experiences of feminist participatory research return again and again to this contradiction. In her attempts to share power as a researcher, she is inevitably implicated in power in the process.

The issue of the will to power has been less overt in traditional approaches to research, largely because where power issues are acknowledged, they are seen as a problem to be solved through greater reliability of the research instruments or through the application of ethical standards. It is in critiques of traditional methods that the relations of power are foregrounded (in for example Oakley, 1981, Reinharz, 1992), and in the debates which are central to alternative discourses. For example Williams (1993) points out the differences amongst feminists in the debate on power. Oakley (1974, 1981) and McRobbie, 1982) for example, both recognize the complex dynamics of researcher-researched relationships but:

> ... while the former sees close kinship between women researchers and women subjects of research, the latter is concerned that women's willingness to talk to researchers is an index of their powerlessness. Finch (1984) taking yet another view, writes that women as a group are powerless, whether they are researchers or subjects of research, and it is precisely this which underlines kinship. (Williams, 1993, p. 581)

Other research in the emancipatory tradition such as Critical approaches (Harvey, 1990) and participatory approaches (Tandon, 1996) are pre-occupied with issues of power in traditional research, and in the implications of power in the research process in which they are engaged.

The uncovering of power as intrinsic to all social research demonstrates that instead of a scientific community which is autonomous and free from political interest, we now know that an intimate relationship exists between the projects of science and other intellectual and political interests in the cultures where science is practised.

GOING BEYOND OURSELVES

The identification of these commonalities between scientific and emancipatory research – appeals to a metanarrative of emancipation and the will to power – leads me to ask a number of questions:

If both appeal to a metanarrative of emancipation are we then simply talking about different approaches of equal status which have the same ends in their sights?

What are we to make of the post-structuralist challenge to emancipatory ideals, and its concern to emphasize *difference* and the *particular*?

What does emancipatory research mean if researchers are inevitably implicated in power, so that our efforts to liberate perpetuate the very relations of dominance?

In the light of my arguments here, it would not be appropriate to offer a recipe for resolving these tensions. Instead I shall point up a number of areas which emancipatory researchers will need to confront, if their efforts are not to perpetuate relations of dominance. First, we need to remind ourselves that the status of scientific knowledge has been privileged over other forms of knowledge. It has been sanctioned by the state, which spends a lot of money in the production of knowledge to obtain public consent to its decisions. Further the dominance of such a discourse is predicated upon the authority of a research community concerned about the truth of claims to knowledge. Hammersley [1995] depends on such a community and appeals to a set of rules and ideas about the construction of knowledge which have been the orthodoxy in social research. Such authority is invested with the force of exclusion and enforcement. Edwards and Usher say:

> ... the logic of modern scientific knowledge and its assumptions of its own legitimacy as a discourse of truth about the world results in the exclusion of other ... forms of knowledge and a denial of their legitimacy. (Edwards and Usher, 1994: p. 158)

Such 'Other' knowledge belongs to a different mentality – 'savage, primitive, underdeveloped, backward ...' (Lyotard, 1984: p. 27). Writers such as Hammersley (1995) exercise that exclusion by declaring feminist, anti-racist, critical and emancipatory 'truths' outside the norms of legitimate research. By a discourse of derision they are dismissed as prejudiced, ignorant and ideological. In doing so the threat to notions of knowledge and to sources of income, is diverted. We are not talking about different kinds of knowledge of equal status. Stanley (1990: p. 5) describes how, within the 'academic mode of production' official and unofficial gatekeepers use myriad ways of controlling academic inputs and outputs. At the centre of these is a notion of scientism, grounded in Cartesian dualisms as to who can be a knower and what can be known, and concerned with producing knowledge through the observation of the real – those objects which exist independently of our beliefs about them. It explicitly excludes knowledge produced through alternative research approaches. It is therefore of crucial importance to claim the legitimacy of low status knowledge, of subjugated knowledge, of the knowledge of the Other which has been silenced and excluded, and to continue the deconstructive process of thinking about 'the danger of what is powerful and useful' (Spivak, 1989: p. 135). Although scientific knowledge appeals to a metanarrative of the liberation of all, the general thrust of the knowledge produced is *ownership by a privileged research community in the interests of dominant groups*. The claim to a metanarrative of emancipation in both scientific and alternative research should not be a source of discomfort to emancipatory researchers. *Both* have to be interrogated as to the basis for such claims, and *both* may be found wanting.

The challenges of post-structuralism lead us to ask: Can we appeal to a metanarrative of emancipation whilst retaining a concern with the particular and the local? McNay, from a feminist perspective, has grappled with this, and she concludes:

> ... feminists cannot afford to relinquish either a general theoretical perspective, or an appeal to a metanarrative to justice. I contend that gender issues cannot be fully comprehended without an understanding of general social dynamics, nor can gender oppression be overcome without some appeal to a metanarrative of justice. (McNay, 1992: p. 7)

Surely it is possible to recognize the particularities of struggle without abandoning metanarratives of emancipation and justice. There can be no universalizing in the sense that struggles have to be open and contingent on changing conditions. Both Lather and Harding [1991], from different starting points, argue that the greatest resource for would-be knowers is our 'non-essential, nonnaturalizable, fragmented identities and the refusal of the delusion of a return to "original unity"' (Harding, 1986: p. 193). Here is a basis for continuing the struggle to throw off the regulating 'regimes of truth', whatever form they take – an acceptance of the permanent partiality of the point of view of those of us seeking to construct emancipatory research.

The issue of power has been treated (by feminists as well as others) in terms of a commodity which can be handed over from one person to another, or wrested from one group by another – possessed rather than exercised. Equally empowerment has been used in simplistic and reductionist ways which treat it as just a matter of will, either on the part of those who are disempowered, or on the part of those in a position to empower. People who do emancipatory research are as much at risk of depoliticizing their activities as others who use the concept of empowerment. Elsewhere I have written about the culture of empowerment (Humphries, 1996) identifying themes in the discourse. These include *containment* – where the demands of oppressed groups are incorporated or accommodated without a radical reordering of social structures. Related to this is a theme of *collusion* – where subordinate groups accept unequal terms and in turn obtain resources in competition with other oppressed groups. Moreover, a discourse of empowerment is located largely *within existing socially powerful groups* – it is not the oppositional agency of the poor and disenfranchised, but the enforcement of the concerns of hegemonic groups. Finally, a theme of *empowering nihilism* (Grossberg, 1988) leads to the identity of the Other being appropriated by marginalized groups to form a clear, strong identity and sense of power. At the same time this identity is disrupted by a confirmation of the characteristics displayed by them as of the essence of their alien nature, therefore requiring containment. Is this what is meant by emancipatory action?

Any notion of emancipatory research needs to recognize these contradictions, and must refuse a naive and self-deluding approach. It will acknowledge the *practice of liberty* – it is not something which can be conferred; it is not something gained once and for all, but has a view of power as fluid, a back and forward movement rather than binary; which is available to dominated groups; which is multifaceted and contradictory; which recognizes both discursive and material realities; which is historically and culturally specific; and which is grounded in the struggle for survival of the most disadvantaged and the poorest, not in the privileging of the researcher or other groups as the norm or referent (Humphries, 1994). As researchers, commitment to self-reflexivity is fundamental, although this can deteriorate into a self-indulgence which places the researcher as the norm. An emancipatory intent is no guarantee of an emancipatory outcome (Acker et al, 1983: p. 431). A self-critical account that situates the researcher at the centre of the text can perpetuate the dominance our emancipatory intentions hope to fight. Our own frameworks need to be interrogated as we look for the tensions and contradictions in our research practice, paradoxically aware of our own complicity in what we critique. Said talks about 'writing turning back on itself to consider, questioningly, its beginning validity and principles' (Said, 1975: p. 335). This I think, lays the groundwork for praxis-oriented research which can open up new possibilities for emancipatory action.

REFERENCES

BARRETT, M. & PHILLIPS, A. (editors) (1992) *Destabilising Theory: Contemporary Feminist Debates*. Cambridge: Polity Press.
EDWARDS, R. & USHER, R. (1994) *Postmodernism and Education*. London: Routledge.
FOUCAULT, M. (1993) 'Space, Power and Knowledge', in S. During (editor) *The Cultural Studies Reader*. London: Routledge.
GROSSBERG, L. (1998) 'Putting the Pop Back in Postmodernism' in A. Ross (editor) *Universal Abandon*. University of Minnesota Press.
HAMMERSLEY, M. (1995) *The Politics of Social Research*. London: Sage.
HARDING, S. (1986) *The Science Question in Feminism*. Milton Keynes: Open University.
HARVEY, L. (1990) *Critical Social Research*. London: Unwin Hyman.
HUMPHRIES, B. (1996) 'Contradictions in the Culture of Empowerment' in B. Humphries (editor) *Critical Perspectives on Empowerment*. Birmingham: Venture Press.
LATHER, P. (1991) *Getting Smart: Feminist Research and Pedagogy with/in the Postmodern*. London: Routledge.
LYOTARD, J. F. (1993) 'Defining the Postmodern' in S. During (editor) *The Cultural Studies Reader*. London: Routledge.
MAGUIRE, P. (1996) 'Proposing a More Feminist Participatory Research: Knowing and Being Embraced Openly' in K. de Koning & M. Martin (editors) *Participatory Research in Health*. London: Zed Books.

MARTIN, M. (1994) 'Developing a Feminist Participative Research Framework: Evaluating the Process' in B. Humphries and C. Truman (editors) *Rethinking Social Research*. Aldershot: Avebury.

MARTIN, M. (1996) 'Issues of Power in the Participatory Research Process' in K. de Koning & M. Martin (editors) *Participatory Research in Health*. London: Zed Books.

McNAY, L. (1992) *Foucault and Feminism*. Cambridge: Blackwell.

McROBBIE, A. (1982) 'The Politics of Feminist Research: Between Talk, Text and Action', *Feminist Review*, vol. 12, pp. 46–57.

OAKLEY, A. (1974) *The Sociology of Housework*. London: Martin Robinson.

OAKLEY, A. (1981) 'Interviewing Women: A Contradiction in Terms?' in H. Roberts (editor) *Doing Feminist Research*. London: Routledge and Kegan Paul.

REINHARZ, S. (1992) *Social Research Methods: Feminist Perspectives*. Oxford: Oxford University Press.

SPIVAK, G. (1989) 'In a Word: Interview by Ellen Rooney', *Differences*, vol. 1, no. 2, pp. 124–56.

STANLEY, L. (editor) (1990) *Feminist Praxis*. London: Routledge.

TANDON, R. (1996) 'The Historical Roots and Contemporary Tendencies in Participatory Research: Implications for Health Care' in K. de Koning & M. Martin (editors) *Participatory Research in Health*. London: Zed Books.

WILLIAMS, A. (1993) 'Diversity and Agreement in Feminist Ethnography', *Sociology*, vol. 27, no. 4, pp. 575–89.

Source: B. Humphries, 'From critical thought to emancipatory action: contradictory research goals', *Sociological Research Online*, 2:1 (1997), http://www.socresonline.org.uk/2/1/3.html.

Study Questions and Activities

1. Beth Humphries includes reference to some debates and concepts that you may be unfamiliar with. Spend some time finding the definitions of words and phrases that you do not recognise – these may include: enlightenment, post-structuralism, academic mode of production, and so on.
2. In what ways does research that aims to be emancipatory differ from that which aims to be scientific?
3. What does this reading and the others in this section tell us about the issue of power within the research process?
4. Download the full article from which this reading is taken. Also download the reply by Hammersley, and Humphries' response to this reply. Summarise the argument in 500 words.
5. Make a list of the positive and negative aspects of taking an overtly 'political' stance when undertaking health-related research.

Further Reading

Another example of a debate involving Martyn Hammersley can be found in the journal *Sociology*: Martyn Hammersley, 'On feminist methodology', *Sociology*, 26:2

(1992) 187–206, and Caroline Ramazanoglu's 'On feminist methodology: male reason versus female empowerment', *Sociology*, 26:2 (1992) 207–12.

For a consideration of the relationship between research and social change, and an acknowledgement that the research process is also a social and political endeavour, see: G. Letherby, *Feminist Research in Theory and Practice* (Buckingham: Open University Press, 2003). You might also like to look at G. Letherby and P. Bywaters, *Extending Social Research: Application, Implementation and Publication* (Buckingham: Open University Press, 2007) for a critique of the traditional research timeline as design, funding, access, fieldwork, analysis and output. Letherby and Bywaters argue for research training and texts to also include reference to how researchers can be involved in working with and for research stakeholders beyond the traditional research boundaries.

Women Respondents in Health Research

Helen Roberts

The relationship between researchers and respondents is of concern to any researcher interested in the politics of the research process. Helen Roberts begins this reading by noting that research on women's health cannot be carried out without women participating, whether they know it or not, within research. Roberts gives several examples of the lack of attention and, arguably, the lack of respect given to women respondents in clinically based research. She argues that in health-related research, those who are researched are more likely to be the powerless – rather than the powerful – and she considers the implications of this when the agenda of respondents is different to the agenda of researchers. Towards the end of the reading, Roberts outlines some of the positive ways in which respondents' views can be used within research reports and, as such, highlights the position of respondents as thinking, feeling, theorising individuals rather than being mere data vessels.

I would just like to thank everyone involved in this questionnaire because it has made me realise a lot of my feelings and help do something about them.

(Questionnaire 2: 0610, Pritchard and Teo, forthcoming)

From randomized clinical trials to the 'softest' of social research on women's health, the respondent, participant, or 'subject' of the research is crucial to the enterprise. Research on women's health cannot be carried out without women participating, knowingly or not, in the research process. They may be relatively passive participants, taking a particular drug, or having a particular procedure carried out, with the results simply being observed; there may be no real part played by the main players, the patients, other than taking the drugs and recovering or not. Or they may have their opinions actively sought about the desirability of a particular service such as family planning or well women's clinics; they may be questioned on their willingness or otherwise to participate in breast or cervical screening or they may be asked to describe their experience of maternity care. In the finished research 'product', however, the respondents are normally curiously absent. The absence of the respondents from many finished research projects is indicative of their objectification throughout the research. They are there right up until the last moment, and then they are excluded. They are made mere objects from the beginning, and the human material for the research is frequently relegated to the position of inhabitants of a different world from that of the observer.

In reports of clinical trials or case reports in the medical literature for instance, doctors referring patients to a particular trial, or drawing a colleague's attention to an 'interesting case', are frequently acknowledged while the patients themselves may go entirely unacknowledged. An issue of the *British Journal of Obstetrics and Gynaecology* (1990), chosen at random, contained a mix of case-studies, trials and other studies, as well as commentaries and research reports. Some of the articles described studies which required no active co-operation from women. Their tissue was examined, or they were entered into a study, and the outcome reported required no conscious input from the women. Other studies required varying degrees of time, effort or discomfort. (One, which required thirty-six women to agree to an extra venesection at delivery, is confusingly entitled 'Determinants of fetal and maternal atrial natiuretic peptide concentrations at delivery *in man*' (my emphasis) (Voto *et al.* 1990: 1123). As well as blood tests, women who provided the raw data for the articles in this journal also provided urine, tissue, diary cards and symptom questionnaires (in one case completed on 7 occasions by a set of respondents). Table 1 shows the pattern of acknowledgements in the fourteen articles which comprised this issue of the journal.

While no paper acknowledged the patients, one acknowledged the assistance of a nurse in 'the management of patients' and others acknowledged colleagues for

Table 1 Acknowledgements appearing
in obstetrics and gynaecology journal

Acknowledgements to:	
No one	3
Funders	8
Colleagues	5
Clinic staff	1
Computing help	1
Preparation of the manuscript	4
Total no. of articles:	14

'access to the clinical records of patients under their care'. That it is possible to extend the courtesy of acknowledgement to the women who participate in research in a scientific article may be seen in the acknowledgements to the scholarly report on the Canadian multi-centre trial of chorion villus sampling and amniocentesis; in it the participants are thanked before the funders: 'We thank the women who; generously and altruistically, took part in this study ...' (Canadian collaborative CVS-amniocentesis clinical trial group 1989: 6)....

In some large-scale studies, research respondents may be at several removes from a piece of research, particularly where secondary analyses are concerned. The General Household Survey (GHS) for instance, ... collects data from a very large number of households, and respondents are, of course, aware that this is part of a research enterprise. The detailed analyses of GHS data to look at, for instance, sex differences in sickness absence and care of the elderly (Arber 1990) or differences in health and health status between men and women may not have been foreseen by the original research respondents, but it is difficult to foresee any undesirable consequences for those who participated in the survey. This is not always the case. In some clinical research, women may not always be aware that as well as receiving treatment, they are also the subjects of research. A patient who found herself in two randomized clinical trials without her knowledge or consent subsequently wrote, 'Withholding information about the trials may have invalidated them. It was forgotten that patients, unlike laboratory animals, can move around and communicate with each other. Treatments are discussed and unexplained differences discovered ... the stress produced may be the very factors which affect health and well being' (Thomas 1988). Meanwhile, some doctors argue that it is wrong to inform patients with life-threatening illnesses that one treatment or another means that they are entered into one arm or another of a clinical trial, since this may be an added source of stress: 'If protection of the subject is the reason for obtaining informed consent, the possibility of iatrogenic harm to the subject as a direct result of the consent ritual must be considered' (Loftus and Fries 1979: 11). As Ann Oakley points out, the term 'ritual', used in a derogatory sense, gives a view of how these investigators regard the task of informing people what is being done to them (Oakley 1990)....

Research published in 1990 in *The Lancet* compared the survival of a group of women with breast cancer undergoing only conventional treatment with a group who supplemented conventional treatment with the more holistic therapies of the Bristol Cancer Help Centre (Bagenal *et al.* 1990). Early results, which were the subject of a press conference and therefore attracted wide publicity outside the medical press, indicated a reduced survival period in the group who had attended the Bristol Cancer Help Centre. Within a few weeks, attention had been drawn to a number of serious methodological flaws in the study (Hayes *et al.* 1990; Heyse-Moor 1990; Munro and Payne 1990). The director of research of one the funding organizations involved wrote, 'Our own evaluation is that the study's results can be explained by the fact that women going to Bristol had more severe disease than control women' (Bodmer 1990: 1188).

Less prominence was given in the national press to criticisms of the study. While many research subjects are not in a position to be aware of, let alone comment on, research to which they have contributed, the wide publicity given to this study meant that few of the women who had participated could have been unaware of the initial findings. Thus, late entries to the public debate over this study were some of the research subjects themselves. In a letter to a national newspaper, one wrote, 'As one of the women surveyed in the ill-fated *Lancet* study, I ... am at a turning point. Serious issues arise for patients who are used in such surveys. A support group is being formed to share experiences and to consider what action should be taken' (Goodare 1990: 16).

THE ROLE OF RESEARCH RESPONDENTS IN WOMEN'S HEALTH RESEARCH

Those who are researched, as others have noted, are more likely to be the powerless than the powerful: patients are more likely to come under scrutiny than hospital consultants or general managers in the National Health Service and are less likely to have the opportunity to comment on such scrutiny.

A great deal of research on health depends on the good will, participation and time of women, although the choice of women as respondents is not always dictated by an overwhelming desire to explore women's needs and experiences as such. Women may become research respondents because they are less willing to slam the door on the researcher, more likely than are men to be socialized to want to be helpful, and because they are perceived as being more flexible in relation to demands on their time....

George Brown and Tirril Harris, whose work on depression among women is a classic, frankly admitted,

> We needed as many people as possible to agree to co-operate in what we knew would be a lengthy interview. Such an interviewing programme is expensive and one way to reduce its cost was to study women only, as they probably suffer from depression more than men. It also seemed likely that women, who are more often at home during the day, would be more willing to agree to see us for several hours.
>
> (Brown and Harris 1978: 22)

Women's willingness to act as respondents is a compelling reason to use them as such. The time after the birth of a child is unlikely to be the most leisured period in a woman's life, yet surveys conducted to explore women's experiences of childbirth can expect responses of at least 75 per cent (Mason 1989: 1) which compares very favourably with responses to research enquiries from medical practitioners.

Given the importance of human subjects to research on health, it is perhaps surprising that the role of women as participants in research has received little more attention than the role of the rats in the physiology department animal house (and perhaps rather less, since the interest taken in the latter by the Animal Liberation Front). With the exception of Hilary Graham's (1983, 1984) work, such literature as there is tends to concentrate on ethical matters. The questions of whether researchers are doing right by their respondents; whether they are benefiting or harming them; whether respondents are active participants in research or unwitting 'subjects', are important and deserve the serious attention they have received.... From a feminist perspective, Ann Oakley's article on interviewing women (Oakley 1981) and Janet Finch's discussion of the ethics and politics of interviewing women (Finch 1984) are classics.

Other aspects of the role of respondents have been less thoroughly explored. In an early research project in which I was involved, looking at variations in consultation rates in middle-aged women at the general practitioner's surgery (Roberts 1981), I became uncomfortably aware that research respondents may have an agenda of their own, quite at variance with that which interests the researcher. Just as a doctor taking a history may discard those symptoms which seem important to the patient, but which don't fit a particular 'story' or disease pattern, so researchers may prefer to frame their questions so as to induce the minimum of 'interference' from respondents. It is clearly simpler, more convenient, and will lead to less equivocal research results to ask a woman to rate the discomfort from her episiotomy on a scale of 1 to 5 than to ask her a more general question about her experience of childbirth. General or so-called 'open' questions may be difficult for respondents to answer, are untidy and time-consuming at the analysis stage, and at the end of the day may be difficult to use. There is an understandable tendency in research reports where responses to open questions are used, to concentrate examples on those women providing witty, unusual or otherwise colourful responses. Val Mason, whose survey manual provides an excellent guide to those wishing to carry out a survey into women's experiences of maternity care, suggests:

> [Open questions] are less likely to be answered fully, for example by groups such as those with no educational qualifications and those for whom English is not their first language .... [Responses] can provide useful illustrative material in a survey report. Indeed they can bring to life for the reader the experiences behind the necessarily more standardised answers printed in the questionnaire.
>
> (Mason 1989: 17)

...

It seems to me that there are a number of positive ways in which respondents' views could be used over and above the cosmetic use of apt quotations to enliven research reports. As well as using open comments in the analysis and discussion of a study where appropriate as a matter of course, funding for the following needs to be built into projects:

1. Respondents should receive reports on the findings of the research to which they have contributed, with an invitation to comment.

2. Where hospitals or clinics are used to recruit respondents, they should be sent not only the formal research report, but also any comments made, positive or otherwise, on service provision.
3. Where respondents make recommendations for future research, these should be brought to the attention of funders by way of an appendix.
4. There should be effective dissemination of project findings not simply to academic but also to service providers and wider audiences.

As researchers, we do have particular skills in the collection, analysis and dissemination of research findings (see, for example, Roberts 1984) but ordinary people use the skills of observation and experience in their everyday lives to make sense of the world in a way which may not be dignified by the lofty term research, but could have similar results. Oakley points out that

> Experience does alter the way people (experts and others) behave: this is part of the scientific method that theories should be tested empirically, not just once under artificial conditions, but constantly in the real world.... It is *from* their own experience in this world that most people (who are not scientists) develop their theories, build up their generalisations, become confident about asserting things generally to be true.
>
> (Oakley 1979: 308)

The *intention* of the current imperative to conduct research into 'consumer satisfaction' is unlikely to be targeted towards the use of these kind of data, however freely given they may be, and however cost effective. But in developing health services truly responsive to patients, clients, customers or consumers, we need to take their views seriously, use them effectively, and draw from and build on their knowledge.

The typical concern of social scientists has been with the unique character of research into human subjects which arises from the humanity of the scholar, from the fact that she is both an observer and a part of the thing being observed. But there is another side. For whilst the scholar is also potentially a subject, the subject is potentially as much a source of interpretation, understanding and criticism as is the observer. In their concern to understand the place of their own feelings and suppositions in the interpretation of the human subjects from which they are only artificially, by the process of scholarship, separated, social scientists have been led to neglect the isolation of the thinking object of their research. If the common humanity of object and subject make it impossible for the social scientist to be treated as simply objective, it makes it to the same extent impossible for respondents in a survey to be treated simply as data or the source of data....

A further reason for looking afresh at the active role of the human participants in research arises from the aspiration on the part of many social scientists and those who fund them, to make research 'useful', or helpful in the making or refinement of government, health authority or other policies. If research is to be policy relevant, then the conventional separation of observer and subjects is even more inappropriate.

For until an objective criterion of needs is established, what other source of policy objectives can there be than the aspirations of policy users?

The objection to the exclusion of human participants from the business of research is therefore both epistemological and has a market and a democratic dimension. For if the human object of research and policy is a customer, then the customer is always right. And if she is a citizen, then the people are sovereign. There is a further reason why the thinking subjects of research ought wherever possible to be employed. A social or governmental policy is not applied to inert matter, but to active human beings. Its success will depend in considerable measure on its relation to their aspirations and aversions. Drawing on the active contribution of citizens to research is a necessary way of ensuring that policies which arise from that research can in a meaningful and effective way be connected with the lives of those towards whom they are directed.

REFERENCES

Arber, S. (1990) 'Revealing women's health: Re-analysing the General Household Survey', in H. Roberts (ed.) *Women's Health Counts*, London: Routledge.

Bagenal, F. S., Easton, D. F., Harris, E., Chilvers, C. E. D., McElwain, T. J. (1990) 'Survival of patients with breast cancer attending Bristol Cancer Help Centre', *The Lancet* 336(8715): 606–10.

Bodmer, W. (1990) 'Bristol Cancer Help Centre' (letter), *The Lancet* 336(8724): 1188.

British Journal of Obstetrics and Gynaecology (1990) 87(12).

Brown, G. H. and Harris, T. (1978) *The Social Origins of Depression: A Study of Psychiatric Disorder in Women*, London: Tavistock.

Canadian Collaborative CVS-Amniocentesis Clinical Trial Group (1989) 'Multi-centre randomised clinical trial of chorion villus sampling and amniocentesis', *The Lancet* 1(8628): 1–6.

Finch, J. (1984) ' "It's great to have someone to talk to": The ethics and politics of interviewing women', in C. Bell and H. Roberts (eds) *Social Researching: Politics, Problems and Practice*, London: Routledge & Kegan Paul.

Goodare, H. (1990) 'Bristol survey support group' (letter), *Independent on Sunday* 30 December: 16.

Graham, H. (1983) 'Do her answers fit his questions? Women and the survey method', in E. Gamarnikov, D. Morgan, J. Purvis, D. Taylorson (eds) *The Public and the Private*, London: Heinemann.

Graham, H. (1984) 'Surveying through stories', in C. Bell and H. Roberts (eds) *Social Researching: Politics, Problems, Practice*, London: Routledge & Kegan Paul.

Hayes, R. J., Smith, P. G., Carpenter, L. (1990) 'Bristol Cancer Help Centre' (letter), *The Lancet* 336(8724): 1185.

Heyse-Moore, L. (1990) 'Bristol Cancer Help Centre' (letter), *The Lancet* 336(8717): 734.

Loftus, E. F. and Fries, J. F. (1979) 'Informed consent may be hazardous to health', *Science* 204: 11.

Mason, V. (1989) *Women's Experience of Maternity Care: A Survey Manual*, London: HMSO.

Munro, J. and Payne, M. (1990) 'Bristol Cancer Help Centre' (letter), *The Lancet* 336(8717): 734.

Oakley, A. (1981) 'Interviewing women: A contradiction in terms', in H. Roberts (ed.) *Doing Feminist Research*, London: Routledge & Kegan Paul.

Oakley, A. (1990) 'Who's afraid of the randomised controlled trial? Some dilemmas of the scientific method and "good" research practice', in H. Roberts (ed.) *Women's Health Counts*, London: Routledge.

Pritchard, C. and Teo, P. (forthcoming) 'Women's experiences during pregnancy', Glasgow: Public Health Research Unit.

Roberts, H. (1981) 'Power and powerlessness in the research process', in H. Roberts (ed.) *Doing Feminist Research*, London: Routledge & Kegan Paul.

Roberts, H. (1984) 'Putting the show on the road: The dissemination of research findings', in C. Bell and H. Roberts (eds) *Social Researching: Politics, Problems, Practice*, London: Routledge & Kegan Paul.

Thomas, E. (1988) 'How doctors' secret trials abused me', *The Observer*, 9 October: 12.

Voto, L. S., Hetmanski, D. J., Broughton-Pipkin, F. (1990) 'Determinants of fetal and maternal atrial natiuretic peptide concentrations at delivery in man', *British Journal of Obstetrics and Gynaecology* 97(12): 1123–9.

Source: H. Roberts, 'Answering back: the role of respondents in women's health research', in H. Roberts (ed.) *Women's Health Matters* (London: Routledge, 1992).

Study Questions and Activities

1. How many of the issues raised by Helen Roberts do you think are also relevant to research on men and male experience?
2. Do you think that social scientists are more or less likely than physical scientists to acknowledge the part played in research by respondents? Why?
3. Towards the end of the reading, Roberts identifies several ways in which respondents' views could be used in research. Spend an hour looking through some journals. In the years since Robert's chapter was written, have her recommendations been heeded? Do you think her suggestions improve research both academically and in terms of implications for practice?

Further Reading

Helen Roberts is concerned, amongst other things, with the privileging of 'respondents' voices' and with the researcher–respondent power relationship. With these concerns in mind, it is important to note that Roberts' piece is part of a long debate – started in the 1980s by feminist researchers – and is continued today by feminists and others concerned with the politics of the research process (see also Letherby (2003) referred to in Further Reading section of Reading 9). Early examples that focus on researching women and men include Janet Finch's '"It's great to have someone to talk to": the ethics and politics of interviewing women', in C. Bell and H. Roberts (eds) *Social Researching: Politics, Problems, Practice* (London: Routledge and Kegan Paul, 1984) and David Morgan's 'Men, masculinity and the process of sociological inquiry', in H. Roberts (ed.) *Doing Feminist Research* (London: Routledge and Kegan Paul, 1981). If you look, you will find many recent articles and books that add to this debate. A small selection includes: K. Ramsay,

'Emotional labour and organisational research: how I learned not to laugh or cry in the field', in S. E. Lyon and J. Busfield (eds) *Methodological Imaginations* (London: Macmillan, 1996); M. Padfield and L. Proctor, 'The effect of interviewer's gender on the interviewing process: a comparative enquiry', *Sociology*, 30:2 (1996) 355–66; and J. Ribbens and R. Edwards (eds) *Feminist Dilemmas in Qualitative Research* (London: Sage, 1998). You might also like to look at S. Wilkinson and C. Kitzinger (eds) *Representing the Other: A Feminism and Psychology Reader* (London: Sage, 1996) that focuses on the significance of other aspects of difference and diversity between respondents and researchers including age, sexuality, ethnicity and class. *Women's Health Matters* – focusing on qualitative, heath-related research – was published as a companion to *Women's Health Counts* (also edited by H. Roberts, London: Routledge, 1990) – which focused on quantitative health-related research. Look at both of them for further practical examples of research methods in action and for interesting articles on women and health.

Ethics and Ethics Committees

Carole Truman

Carole Truman, the author of this reading, draws on her own experiences of gaining ethical approval for a research study that focused on user participation within a community mental health service to consider specific and more general ethical issues. As such, the focus in this reading, as in others in this part of the book, is with the politics of research. Truman is concerned specifically with the expansion of external (to the academy) research ethics committees in the United Kingdom. She argues that ethics committees hold a powerful role as gatekeepers within the research process and that underpinning the provision of ethical guidelines and the call for research governance are a range of measures that protect institutional interests, without necessarily providing an effective means to address the moral obligations and the responsibilities of researchers to those that they research. On one level, this reading provides us with a practical account focusing on strategies used to gain ethical approval for a particular project and on another provides a critique of the need to gain ethical approval of this kind. Through a discussion of the ethical issues that emerged from the perspective of one respondent during the actual research process, Truman highlights contradictions between the formal ethical regulation of research and the experiences of research respondents.

INTRODUCTION

Debates relating to ethics and research governance have gathered new momentum in recent years with social research coming under increased scrutiny and social researchers being held more accountable for what research they undertake and how they undertake it. Within the UK, professional associations across different branches of social research have begun to reformulate guidelines on ethical practice. The process of ethical review has become reinstitutionalised as role of research ethics committees (RECs) has expanded across the UK and North America. RECs have gained a powerful role as gatekeepers within the research process. Approaches to ethics within traditional (scientific/positivist) approaches to research frequently assume a role to 'protect' dependent and 'vulnerable' research subjects within the research process. The usefulness and appropriateness of such an approach is questionable in relation to qualitative and/or participatory approaches to research design. Researchers working within qualitative and/or participatory research paradigms are often acutely aware of ethical dilemmas contained within the process of conducting research with vulnerable groups, but try to address such dilemmas within an emergent process consistent with conducting democratic research. Too often, such research proposals are treated in a hostile way when scrutinised under traditional regimes of ethical scrutiny. There is little debate relating to the types of ethical dilemmas faced by researchers working within a participatory research paradigm and yet a consequence of re-institutionalising ethical review may be detrimental to some of the most user-friendly approaches to social research. At the same time, underpinning the re-constitution of ethical guidelines and research governance are a range of measures which clearly protect institutional interests. Such measures operate within a legal framework of liability and as a consequence deflect attention away from open debate about the moral obligations and responsibilities of researchers in relation to the production of social research (Homan 1991,1992).

In this paper I draw upon experiences of gaining ethical approval for a research study about user participation within a community mental health service[1]. I discuss the strategies used to gain ethical approval and the 'formal concerns' raised by the ethics committee. I then describe and discuss ethical issues which emerged from a participants' perspective during the actual research as it was carried out....

ETHICAL CONCERNS FROM THE STANDPOINT OF RESEARCH PARTICIPANTS

The research study which I draw upon is an evaluation of community mental health project. The project was an exercise facility in the form of a community gym for people with, or at risk of developing mental health problems. The gym was funded by the health authority, but operated within a framework of strong inter-sectoral collaborations between health and social care. Users of the Gym came from a wide range of medical and non-medical referral routes. By using exercise as a basis for promoting health and well-being, the gym drew upon a social model of mental health and well-being, more than the medical model of treatment for mental health problems. The Gym placed considerable emphasis on user involvement in the management, development and running of the service. Users were represented on the management committee; they produce their own newsletter; and a formal volunteer scheme exists which has enabled some users to become trained as fitness instructors (Truman and Raine 2002).

As an innovatory project, and in climate of evidence-based health and social welfare, senior management in the Region wanted to attach a research study to the project. The gym was located in a geographically isolated part of the region with an array of economic problems, and the Region was keen to develop a research culture in that area, on the grounds that if a service could be successful in that location, it could succeed anywhere. I was commissioned to write a research proposal to evaluate the gym. This proposal outlined a qualitative study to explore users' experiences of the gym. It was refereed by peers within health research and subsequently approved. I was notified that funding for the research would be released once LREC approval had been secured. The research protocol followed a funding trajectory that is familiar to most researchers in health and social care: although the methodology and context for the research, were approved as suitable for funding through a process of peer-review, the funders themselves insisted that the research protocol receive 'independent' ethical review....

Control over the Material Production of Research

The funding process I have briefly described is one which will be familiar to those who have applied for research funding. It is a process which is subject to rigorous scrutiny and control. The process requires lengthy applications, peer review, and budgets subject to justification to the minutest detail. This extensive review process determines what are worthy research topics, and who the worthy researchers are....

Ethics as Aligned with Methodology

It is often the methodology of a research study which provides the focus for ethical committees (Ramcharan and Cutliffe 2001). LRECs thus use judgements about whether or not a study is well-designed as the basis for granting or refusing ethical approval. Current debate around research governance has pressed questions about whether or not it is within the competence of ethical committees to judge the methodological merits of the full spectrum of research methods (Gauld and MacMillan 1999, Gelling 1999). Guidelines issued by my LREC states that it

> 'receives many applications and has developed a form of application which enables it to deal expeditiously with new applications. It is not, therefore, prepared to receive applications on any other form than that which is made available to potential applicants' (South Cumbria Research Ethics Committee 1997: 1).

The application form I was required to use to describe my research had clearly been designed around assumptions which favour deductive research using quantitative methodologies (van den Hoonaard 2001). Ethical issues in qualitative methodologies often emerge as research studies unfold, but current systems of ethical review are unable to address the nature of this process (Ramcharan and Cutliffe 2001). In practice, many qualitative researchers struggle to describe their research within the required format. This means that research proposals may go backwards and forwards whilst questions are asked and responded to whilst underlying ethical issues within the research remain unaddressed (Popay *et al.* 1998). Consequently, researchers often view the process of ethical approval more as a bureaucratic hurdle to be negotiated, rather than as a constructive part of the research process.

The DoH guidelines (DoH 2001:12) reiterate the view of Lynoe *et al.* (1999: 52) that 'a poorly designed study is by definition unethical'. Underpinning this perspective is a question about who is best placed to judge the value of whether or not a study is well-designed. However, research design, on paper at least, is one area of research that can be left in the capable hands of trained, professional researchers – especially if, as in the case of this research, the proposal has had to undergo extensive peer review in order to get funding. But even the most robust research design requires the co-operation of research participants, as the following example illustrates:

> *In our research study, an array of outside experts had approved a research protocol which outlined that eight focus groups would take place over a twelve-month period; each group would involve between eight and ten users. The project's full-time research assistant spent considerable time at the gym, making links with service users with a view to recruiting participants to the first focus group. Although payment of expenses was offered to participants, recruitment proved difficult. Many users were unwilling to take part in a focus group, and half of those who agreed to take part failed to attend on the day. The research assistant for the project felt that she had developed a good relationship with users, so in the end, we began to ask direct questions about what prevented them from joining focus groups. Various factors emerged, including: variation in mental health symptoms which could preclude attendance; users felt they had little to contribute; and anxiety concerning group situations. In some cases, no specific reasons were given by individuals who simply did not want to join a focus group. For example, a number of users, whilst happy to talk to the research assistant, clearly had no interest in the research study and simply 'drifted off' at the point that focus groups were mentioned.*

This example illustrates that what appeared to be a sound research design on paper failed to stand up to the test of what service users might consider to be an appropriate design to ensure their participation. However, the concerns, or barriers identified by users were not the ones raised in processes of ethical approval or peer review.

In line with guidance given by the LREC, our research proposal stated that users would be paid appropriate expenses for their involvement. 'Appropriate' expenses are deemed as sufficient recompense for taking part in the study, but not so much that they could 'be seen as an undue inducement' (SCREC 1997:1). Six users who did participate in Focus Group One took part in ice-breaking exercises and contributed to discussions. Feedback at the end of the session suggested that those who took part were reasonably comfortable with the process. Recruitment improved for Focus Group Two. Although the drop-out rate (50%) was consistent with that of Focus Group One, two users who were present in the facility at the time of the group agreed to take part, thus boosting the numbers participating. This may have been because for the second focus group, we provided participants with lunch as well as travelling expenses. As researchers, we believe that provision of lunch provided an inducement for users of the gym to take part in the research. Provision of lunch made the experience of a focus group more of a social event, and less the experience of groupwork within a clinical setting. Most members of the focus groups participated in discussions and exercises, and thus contributed to the research. But what of those whose main motivation for attending the focus group was to receive a free lunch? Could this be considered undue inducement? My own perceptions of a providing lunch which was shared by researchers and research participants, was it transformed the research process from being a scientific event into more of a social event. By doing this, the ambience of the research process became more closely aligned with the ambience of the gym which draws upon a social model of mental health.

Inside 'Informed' Consent

The principle of informed consent is also something that appears within almost all statements of ethical guidelines that professional bodies have developed (Bulmer 1982). Superficially at least, the principle of informed consent, is designed to ensure that research participants are made fully aware of the nature of the research in which they are taking part, and the consequences of their participation. The issue of 'informed consent' came under scrutiny by the Alder Hey Inquiry, where it was revealed that the public are often quite ignorant of what they are consenting to in the context of medical research. Informed consent also raises questions about the competency of some groups and individuals to agree on their own behalf to take part in research. Consequently, the topic of whom, and under what circumstances, consent may be given has received extensive discussion, particularly in research with vulnerable groups such as in the field of learning disability (Brown and Thompson 1997, Stalker 1998), mental health (Usher and Arthur 1998) and in research relating to women and children (Ribbens and Edwards 1998).

In the case of our research, the LREC required that research participants are given an information sheet about the research. Guidance also suggested that consent forms should be used, and these should provide reference to a written information sheet and space for signatures of the participant and witness. Informed consent has taken on greater importance within UK research following the Alder Hey inquiry where it was revealed that the safeguards which are supposed to follow informed consent may be ambiguous. Informed consent is often seen as a means to 'protect research participants' and to ensure that they are informed about research processes. However, it is clear that the principle of informed consent also operates within a legal framework which safeguards research organisations if adverse events occur within research. In this respect, informed consent becomes aligned with processes of indemnity and thus operationalised within a legal framework. In practice, this means that from a participant's perspective, signing forms to agree to take part in research may appear to take on similar legal significance to writing a Will or getting married. Whilst this process may satisfy the legal obligations of research organisations, it does not address some core issues about consent to take part in research.

Within social research, informed consent goes beyond an understanding of the nature of the research in question and extends into the terrain of the social consequences or repercussions of taking part in research. For example Coomber (2002) describes how the process of obtaining informed consent from participants to take part in a research study of criminal populations may contravene anonymity and thus expose research participants to risk. Alderson (1999: 60) notes how, in the case of children, formal ethics requirements, which have the intention of protecting vulnerable people, can lead to them being excluded from research studies. She argues that the requirement to opt into a study will silence those who would participate more easily in research based upon informal personal contact, rather than those which deploy consent forms and formal protocols. Alderson also identified issues relating to confidentiality and risk, where parents are required to give parental consent on behalf of children as this may be seen as a threat to confidentiality between the child and the researcher.

Consent as Contingent

As an alternative to insisting that formal consent is obtained, Alderson (1999) suggests that ethics committees could have a more productive role by ensuring that research studies are respectful to their participants, and not against their interests. For this to happen, ethical research would be highly contingent upon the relationship of research participants to the research process in terms of its approach and the methods used.

Within our research study, we drew up an information sheet and pre-designed a form that followed a standardised format since we felt that this approach was most likely to get the approval of the LREC. All research participants who took part in the first two focus groups had a copy of the information sheet and signed our consent form. Under ethical guidelines, informed consent is often constructed as a binary division between research participants and non-participants; between those who provide consent against those who do not. Many ethical guidelines stress that the granting of consent is something that has to be reviewed throughout the research process and as such protect participants' right to withdraw from research. In practice, we found that consent from the perspective of research participants was far more contingent than is allowed for within the narrow definition used in most ethical guidelines. Some service users said they would like to take part in the research, but only if they could be interviewed on their own, rather than within a focus group.

Within the gym, there is a high level of user involvement and positive environment for service users (Raine *et al.* 2002). Many of the users viewed being involved in the research as a way of giving something back to the service. Consent was thus contingent upon the methods we used to enable users to take part in the research along the lines in which they participated within the gym. In order to meet the aims and objectives for the research, we made on-going changes and constant adjustments to the study. Eventually, we fully embraced a participatory research approach developed which centralised experience of users within the research process. Our exit strategy for the research, was to leave the gym with a fully operational user-led evaluation process (see Truman and Raine 2001a). By this point, some users had become researchers, and were undertaking research with others. The boundaries of who was party to informed consent had thus become quite blurred.

Replacing 'Risk' with 'Well-Being' in Research

A shift in the social relations towards a more participatory research process provided some interesting insights into how being involved in research can be a positive experience for research participants. The new guidelines on research governance identify that 'research can involve an element of risk, both in terms of return on investment and sometimes for the safety and well-being of research participants' (Department of Health 2001:1). Within our research, notions of risk and well-being varied with the construction of social relations within the research process. As our research became more participatory in nature, users identified a range of positive reasons for being involved in the research. For example, a member of the evaluation group wrote about her experiences of being involved in the research:

> My name is Rebecca and I have been nominated by the evaluation group to tell you what we are about. The evaluation group consists of a staff member, two researchers and four gym users. As part of Lancaster University's research, the evaluation group was set up to compile information on the gym by way of a questionnaire. For the evaluation group this posed quite a challenge. We had to organise a set of questions that would:
>
> ▓ Give answers that could be put in a database.
>
> ▓ Ask questions that would highlight both positive and negative aspects of the Gym.
>
> ▓ Show areas in which the gym could make improvements.
>
> ▓ Give gym users a voice.
>
> ▓ But most importantly, be COMPLETELY ANONYMOUS
>
> **Personally, I found the process of setting up the questionnaire a challenge with many rewards. What originally seemed a very daunting task soon became interesting, fun and it gave me the chance of doing something worthwhile. Another reward was the chance to work with a fantastic group of people! Cheers Everyone!**

We have now finished the questionnaire and are hoping to send it out to users. We would appreciate your help and co-operation in completing these questionnaires. Don't worry these are not going to be personal questionnaires and they are anonymous. But, when the answers are compiled on database, it should highlight areas in which the gym is working, areas that need improvements, and also find out what YOU the users want from YOUR gym. Please don't think, oh no, not another form, as it is the results from these questionnaires that will give you the user what you want. So be warned a questionnaire will be circulating in your area soon. I wish to thank you all in advance for filling out the questionnaires and also everyone that helped make this happen.

Thanks, Rebecca.

(Extract reproduced from a booklet which provides a short summary of the research)

In the above extract I have highlighted Rebecca's description of the benefits she describes of being involved in the research. The extract as a whole also raises issues relating to anonymity and confidentiality which are almost always a feature within ethical guidelines. However, anonymity and confidentiality are contingent, rather than absolute (Robinson 1991). In describing the research to other users, Rebecca addresses their concerns about anonymity which were present throughout the research process. Anonymity was an area where users expressed most concern and suspicion since they needed to know how the data were to be treated. They were conscious that protocols of anonymity would not prevent them from being identified on the basis of what they said. Similarly, users also talked about the importance of being able to trust researchers, and this trust developed over time. Trust enabled users to feel confident about telling researchers about their experiences in ways that was different from what they would have said to professionals who might exercise control over their lives. Rebecca's reference to the questionnaire as a form provides an illustration of this point. Service users in the NHS are familiar with having information about them recorded on forms. Participants in our research talked about how they often had a general mistrust of forms because the information gets used by professionals who make judgements about their mental health status and thus use the information to control their lives. For users involved in the process of developing a questionnaire, it was important to build trust in the questionnaire as being different from the forms which are routinely used in systems of mental healthcare.

Feminists have highlighted ways that trust is an integral but complex part of the research process (Stacey 1988, Finch 1984, Oakley 1981, Song and Parker 1995). It is often articulated as something which occurs between researchers and research participants on a personal basis, as individuals. However, within our research, trust was an on-going process which was transferred between service users, as one user identified:

'well I didn't want to do it [interview] at first, and then I saw [another service user] giving you information, and I thought "oh well, go on, do it yourself." '

In this example, trust was fundamental to being able to carry out the research. The nature of trust is such that it is given a social meaning within the research process, in terms of how it is experienced by users, rather than as something which can be conferred either by researchers or through processes of ethical review.

'Adverse' Incidents in Research

The new DoH guidelines for research governance reflect concerns about the occurrence of 'adverse events' within research. The LREC which gave ethical approval to our research asked to be informed of such events. When such events occur, there are questions about who defines them as being adverse. For example, it is clear from the findings of the Alder Hey Inquiry that established medical practice was not considered 'adverse' until it came to the attention of the public. How such events are dealt with, depends upon what is at stake for the parties involved with the event. Having research users directly involved in producing the research presented different types of ethical dilemma, as illustrated by the following example:

> *The user evaluation group (referred to in the extract from Rebecca) undertook to do an on-going user-led evaluation of the gym. This involved users designing, administering and analysing an evaluation tool which took the form of a short questionnaire. The evaluation group usually worked in pairs to administer the questionnaire. On one occasion, they approached another user of the gym and asked him if he would be willing to complete a questionnaire. The user said that he was experiencing a psychotic episode at that moment (he said he was hearing voices). The researchers said they could easily ask the questions at some other time and thought it best to leave him alone. However, the user said that he was trying to manage this psychotic episode by being active and that he would like them to help him complete the questionnaire. The researchers sat with him and helped him to do this.*

When the researchers reported this incident to me, my first reaction was one of anxiety about the intrusion and possible harm that may have occurred to the user as a consequence of taking part in the research whilst experiencing a psychotic episode. This incident represents a real ethical dilemma in research, and was identified as such by the user-researchers. It is likely that the LREC would have viewed the incident differently to me, and that had I administered the questionnaire, my response would have been different to that of the users. I believe that had the LREC known about this event, it might have been labelled as an 'adverse incident' and outlawed as legitimate research practice. As a researcher, I would have been reluctant to continue the research process with someone experiencing psychological distress. However, in this case, the user wanted to manage his distress by being engaged with other users. Upon reflection, I believe that it would have been harmful to ignore the user's wishes that he wanted to take part in the research at that time, within the context through which the research was taking place.

Hidden within this scenario are various investments and risks in pursuing different courses of action. Such courses of action are underpinned by the social relations of research production and the power relations that underpin those actions. Within this scenario, the judgement of the LREC would always carry more weight and authority than the judgements of the user-researchers. Yet, from the perspective of the research participant, the decision to proceed with the research, seems to be less harmful than the alternative which was to exclude him from the process. LRECs make their judgements based upon the norms of the medical profession, which is translated into written guidance for those who apply for research funding. In contrast, the user-researchers decided upon their course of action as a result of engaging in dialogue within the context of the situation itself. This is an approach advocated by Rossiter *et al.* who state that:

> 'Professional codes of ethics are the justified norms of the profession. However, the application of those norms is interpretive, and depends on the local and particular features of each situation.... the interpretive aspect of application is best carried out in a dialogical process ... a partner in dialogue helps us to recognise our unconscious investments, our blind spots, unrecognised feelings, or unchallenged attitudes ... the centrality of ethics ... depends upon the possibility of unconstrained dialogue' (Rossiter *et al.* 2000: 95).

The Ethics of 'Ethics Avoidance'?

My discussion of ethics within research has a range of implications for the conduct of researchers and the way that we articulate and address the ethical dimensions of research. Furthermore, my analysis also provides insights into how professional researchers relate to those who seek to govern ethical conduct in research.

A condition of ethical approval being granted, is that LRECs ask to be informed of any changes to the research protocol. Many professional researchers share anecdotes of research designs on paper which do not translate into practice when fieldwork actually begins. As I have already illustrated, ethical issues are intricately woven into the social relations of research processes. Research methodology is often required to change once research participants become part of the research process, yet the relationship of LRECs to research processes means that some researchers may be reluctant to re-enter the ethical approval process once initial approval has been given. There are two reasons for this - first, re-submission could risk ethical approval being withdrawn; secondly, the bureaucratic nature of LRECs means that they are not able to respond in a timely or constructive way to genuine ethical concerns which unfold during the course of a study. For this to happen, there needs to be 'a shift in our common-sense understanding of ethics as a property of individuals who monadically reflect on dilemmas, to a notion of ethics as social relations that produce individuals and organisations in ways that limit or potentiate ethical decision making.... it requires attention to issues of communicative process, and ... it requires a much broader set of activities than is associated with conventional professional ethics.' (Rossiter *et al.* 2000: 97).

In the research that I have described, a communicative process, albeit limited, was established by the LREC which prescribed the format in which they were prepared to review ethical issues within research. The research study in question has subsequently been highly regarded at a Regional and national level. For example, it has been used as a case-study in a national review of participatory research (Baxter *et al.* 2001). Even so, we felt reluctant to take our design modifications back to the LREC as the research evolved. Firstly, the research process became one which went through a series of changes, so at what point should we report those changes to the LREC? Secondly, we were not convinced that the views of the LREC could add anything constructive to the ethical aspects of the research process. In contrast, the views of research participants added considerably to the efficacy of the research and also provided a means for addressing ethical issues from the perspective of those who are participants within the research process.

My experiences are not dissimilar from those of others who operate under professional codes of ethics. Research undertaken with professionals in human services settings found that most participants treated ethics codes as irrelevant and they tended not to employ internal cognitive schemes to resolve ethical dilemmas. Within each setting, there were multiple interacting forces which create participants' ethical subjectivities. 'These subjectivities, forged as they are within power relations, condition what is perceived as ethics, and how ethical dilemmas can be resolved.' (Rossiter *et al.* 2000: 95).

NOTE

1. The research was funded by the Research and Development Programme of the North-west NHS Executive grant number RDO/11/11/5.

REFERENCES

ALDERSON, P. (1999) 'Disturbed young people, research for what, research for whom?' in S. Hood, B. Mayall and S. Oliver (eds.) *Critical Issues in Social Research: Power and Prejudice* Buckingham: Open University Press.

BAXTER, L., THORNE, L. and MITCHELL, A. (2001) *Lay Involvement in Health Research* Exeter: Washington Singer Press.

BROWN, H. and THOMPSON, D (1997) The ethics of research with men who have learning disabilities and abusive sexual behaviour: a minefield in a vacuum. *Disability and Society* 12 (5), 695–707.

BULMER, M. (1982) *Social Research Ethics* London: Macmillan.

CAMPBELL, M. and MANICOM, A. (1995) *Knowledge, Experience and RulingRelations: Studies in the Social Organization of Knowledge* Toronto: University of Toronto Press.

COOMBER, R. (2002) Signing your life away?: Why Research Ethics Committees (REC) shouldn't always require written confirmation that participants in research have been informed of the aims of a study and their rights – the case of criminal populations. (Commentary). *Sociological Research Online* Vol. 7 no. 1. <http://www.socresonlin e.org.uk/7/1/coomber.html>.

DEPARTMENT OF HEALTH (2001) *Research Governance Framework for Health and Social Care* London: HMSO.

FINCH, J. (1984) ' "It's Great to Have Someone to Talk to": The Ethics and Politics of Interviewing Women.' In C. Bell and H. Roberts (eds.) *Social Researching: Politics, Problems, Practice.* London: Routledge and Kegan Paul.

GAULD, R. and MACMILLAN, J. (1999) Ethics Committees and Qualitative health research in New Zealand *New Zealand Medical Journal* 112 (1089) 195–197.

GELLING, L. (1999) 'Role of the Research Ethics Committee' *Nurse Education Today* 19, 564–569.

HOMAN, R. (1991) *The Ethics of Social Research* London: Longman.

HOMAN, R. (1992) The Ethics of Open Methods *British Journal of Sociology* 43 (3) 321–332.

LYNOE, N., SANDLUND, M., JACOBSSON, L. (1999) Research Ethics Committees: a comparative study of assessment of ethical dilemmas. *Scandanavian Journal of Psychiatry* 2, 152–159.

OAKLEY, A. (1981) "Interviewing Women: A Contradiction in Terms" in H. Roberts (ed.) *Doing Feminist Research* London: Routledge and Kegan Paul.

POPAY, J. ROGERS, A. WILLIAMS, G. (1998) Rationale and standards for the systematic review of qualitative literature in health services research. *Qualitative Health Research* 8, 341–351.

RAINE, P. TRUMAN, C and SOUTHERST, A. (2002) 'The Development of A Community Gym for People with Mental Health Problems: Influences on Accessibility' *Journal of Mental Health* 11, 143–53.

RAMCHARAN, P. and CUTLIFFE, J. (2001) Judging the Ethics of Qualitative Research: considering the 'ethics as process' model *Health and Social Care in the Community* 9 (6), 358–366.

RIBBENS, J. and EDWARDS, R. (eds.) (1998) *Feminist Dilemmas in Qualitative Research: Public Knowledge and Private Lives* London: Sage.

ROBINSON, I. (1991) 'Confidentiality for Whom?' *Social Science and Medicine* 32 (3) 279–286.

ROSSITER, A., PRILLELTENSKY, I., and WALSH-BOWERS, R. (2000) 'A postmodern perspective on professional ethics' in B. Fawcett, B. Featherstone, J. Fook and A. Rossiter (eds.) *Practice and Research in Social Work: postmodern feminist perspectives* London and New York: Routledge.

SONG, M. and PARKER, D. (1995) Commonality, difference and the dynamics of disclosure in in-depth interviewing *Sociology* 29 (2) 241–256.

SOUTH CUMBRIA RESEARCH ETHICS COMMITTEE (1997) Information/Guidelines for Application Kendal: Morecambe Bay Health Authority.

STACEY, J. (1988) Can there be a feminist ethnography? *Women's Studies International Forum* 11 (1), 21–27.

STALKER, K. (1998) Some ethical and methodological issues in research with people with learning disabilities *Disability and Society* 13 (1), 5–19.

TRUMAN, C. and RAINE P. (2001a) 'Involving Users in Evaluation: the social relations of user involvement in health research' (with P. Raine) *Critical Public Health*, Vol. 11 No 3: September pp. 215–232.

TRUMAN, C and RAINE, P. (2002) 'Experience and Meaning of User Involvement - Some Explorations From A Community Mental Health Project' Health and Social Care in the Community 10 (3), 136–143.

USHER, K. and ARTHUR, D. (1998) Process and Consent; a model for enhancing informed consent in mental health research. *Journal of Advanced Nursing* 27, 692–697.

VAN DEN HOONAARD, W. (2001) 'Is Ethics Review a Moral Panic?' *Canadian Review of Sociology and Anthropology* 38, 1. 19–35.

Source: C. Truman, 'Ethics and the ruling relations of research',
Sociological Research Online, 8:1 (2003),
http://www.socresonline.org.uk/8/1/truman.html.

Study Questions and Activities

1. Carole Truman argues that the external research ethics committee model 'reserves or at best distances research participants from processes of research, and hence knowledge production'. Drawing on ALL of the articles in this section of the book, what consequences does this have in terms of power within the research process? In answering this question consider the power (or not) of the researched; of the researcher(s), of commissioners, of ethics committee members and of others affected by the research process and the product.
2. What do you understand by the term 'informed consent' within research? How does it compare to the need for informed consent in a practice context? Can researchers ever be sure that respondents are truly fully 'informed'?
3. Look at the latest British Sociological Association ethical guidelines on http://www.britsoc.co.uk. Which of these would you need to consider in the research product you designed for study question 4 in Reading 6?
4. Having read all of the readings in this part of the book, make a list of the things you have learnt and reflect on how your view of social science research has changed.

Further Reading

For additional research method texts aimed specifically at healthcare research and researchers see: A. Edwards and R. Talbot, *The Hard Pressed Researcher: A Research Handbook for the Caring Professions* (London: Pearson, 1999) and T. E. Dinero (ed.) *Selected Practical Problems in Health and Social Research* (Binghamton, NY: Haworth, 1996). For a good 'how to' book, see L. Blaxter, C. Hughes and M. Tight, *How to Research*, 2nd edn (Buckingham: Open University Press, 2001). For useful social research dictionaries, look at one or both of the following: V. Jupp (ed.) *The Sage Dictionary of Social Research* (London: Sage, 2006) and R. L. Miller and J. D. Brewer (eds) *The A-Z of Social Research: A Dictionary of Key Social Science Research* (London: Sage, 2003). *Social Research Update* (www.soc.surrey.ac.uk/sru/) is also a useful online resource; updated by Nigel Gilbert – a sociologist – from the University of Surrey, it contains a number of papers on research methods and methodological problems – examples include using diaries in social research; correspondence analysis; telephone focus groups; paying respondents; safety in social research; and using e-mail as a research tool.

Health and Healthcare: Inequalities and Diversity

Introduction

Part III of this book is set out to explore the challenges of diversity in health and healthcare and, continuing with some of the themes set out in Part II, considers the ways in which such diversity can be measured and understood. Here, you will be focusing specifically on spatial difference, gender, ethnicity, and socio-economic diversity. We could, of course, have focused on other examples, so the selections given here are not the only important areas to consider, but they do provide a range of examples that highlight the significance of inequalities and diversity in health and healthcare. Part III also explores the issues of inequalities in health and healthcare by considering the health status of women, children, Black and minority ethnic groups, and people living in disadvantaged communities and by highlighting some differences in healthcare provision.

As you have already seen in previous parts of this book, sociologists are concerned with the relationship between the individual and society. Sociologists are also concerned with understanding why some people are more likely to get sick and die than others. Whilst there is no clear sociological explanation for inequalities in health and associated differences in healthcare, sociologists are keen to examine how social and physical environments influence the health of individuals and social groups.

There are five readings in this part of the book and the first, by Robert Crawford (Reading 12), offers a critique of the ideology of individual responsibility for health, an ideology that still persists amongst health professionals and policy makers and that can be clearly identified within government rhetoric and policy across the United Kingdom, and elsewhere. The concepts of 'self-surveillance', 'self-care' and the 'expert patient', amongst others, provide a framework for contemporary definitions and practices in health and healthcare. Crawford argues that whilst public health should not abandon strategies that attempt to change individual lifestyle and behaviour, area-based initiatives – which recognise the structural barriers to change – are most likely to be effective. Continuing with this theme, the next reading by Heather Joshi *et al.* (Reading 13) focuses on geographical inequalities in health, asking the questions: does where you live matter, and why? This reading – which draws on analyses of data from the Office for National Statistics Longitudinal Study and the Health & Lifestyle Survey – is interesting because it highlights how individual differences in socio-economic status, employment and patterns of migration cannot, in themselves, account for spatial differences in health status between social groups. In Reading 14, Kathryn Backett-Milburn and her colleagues consider the important issue of children's health inequalities. They do this by exploring the contrasting lives and views of children and parents living in differing social circumstances. Unlike other studies of children's health inequalities, however, Reading 14 draws on the perspectives of children themselves. In the next reading, Lesley Doyal (Reading 15) considers the gendered experiences of sickness and health by focusing on women's health. Here, Doyal considers the differences in mortality between men and women, and also health differences between women. In doing so, she argues that whilst crude universalism should be rejected, so, too, should theories of crude difference. That is, this reading suggests that whilst it is important to identify commonalities between women, it is also important to acknowledge the diversity that exists within this social group. In the final reading in this part of the book, you will consider the work of Mel Bartley (Reading 16), who examines ethnic inequalities in health. Bartley reflects on the factors that influence ethnic definitions and how these are different in different places and at different times. She also considers the complex relationship between ethnicity and health inequalities.

The Politics of Victim Blaming

Robert Crawford

All of the readings within this part of the book are concerned with the relation-ship between the health of individuals and the society in which they live. In this piece, Robert Crawford writes about the ideology and politics of victim blaming, exploring the way in which policy and rhetoric lay the blame for health very firmly at the feet of the poor. This piece was written at a time of increasing recognition that proliferation in health service provision would not lead to further improve-ments in public health, and in reply to the way that governments responded to this. For example, in *A New Perspective on the Health of Canadians*, Lalonde (1974) argued that attention should be paid to biological, environmental and behavioural factors in health, as well as to the role of the health service. The British government consultation paper *Prevention & Health: Everybody's Busi-ness* (DHSS, 1976) also highlighted the individual's responsibility for health. Some would say that with the British government's White paper *Choosing Health: Making Healthier Choices Easier* (DoH, 2004) and similar documents across the United Kingdom, we have now come full circle and that Crawford's critique is more powerful than ever. However, Crawford argues that the ideology of victim blaming serves to inhibit an understanding of what really influences health – the environment. Whilst he recognises that individual actions play a part in determining health and that health education has a role to play, Crawford stresses the need to focus on the social causation of illness and disease, and on the structural barriers that prevent individuals from achieving health.

References

DHSS, *Prevention and Health – Everybody's Business* (HMSO: London, 1976).
DoH, *Choosing Health: Making Healthier Choices Easier* (TSO: London, 2004).
M. Lalonde, *A New Perspective on the Health of Canadians* (Ministry of Supply and Services: Ottawa, 1974).

THE CHALLENGE TO MEDICINE

During the last twenty years and especially the last decade we have witnessed a remarkable expansion in the health sector. Health expenditures in the United States were 4.1 percent of the gross national product in 1950, 5.2 percent in 1960, 7.1 percent in 1970, and 8.1 percent in 1976. Estimates are that they will exceed 10 percent of the GNP by the early 1980s. Other growth indicators, including employment, the extent of corporate investment, physical infrastructure, and numbers of people obtaining services, have been steadily climbing. Health sector expansion has been powered by a growth coalition able to win the extension of employee health benefits, the socialization of costs for the aged and many of the poor, and the direct subsidization of medical research and provider and training institutions. Medicine has come to capture the imagination and hope of the American public, some observers claiming that the hospital has become the archetype institution of American life.

In the last few years, however, the hegemony of medicine has been challenged. First, the women's and self-help movements have undercut professional authority and raised the issue of overmedicalization. Of more immediate interest for this discussion has been the profusion of monographs, conferences, and policy statements shifting debate from a concern with issues of equality of access to the irrelevancy or limits of medicine for maintaining health. Impressive evidence on the relative ineffectiveness of medicine in reducing mortality and morbidity is being added to the academic literature by McKeown (2, 3), Cochrane (4), Powles (5), and others, and is being popularized in the United States by Illich (6), Fuchs (7), and Carlson (8). Illich has had a particularly profound effect in writing *Medical Nemesis* and lecturing widely on his views.

More concrete recommendations for a reorientation from medical care to health promotion by the Canadian Minister of National Health and Welfare, Marc Lalonde (9), have generated considerable interest. In the U.S., Anne Somers (10) seems to have sparked a new interest in health education as an alternative to continued expansion of the medical system. Medicine, in short, confronts a number of critiques ranging from what has been called "therapeutic nihilism" (11) to more modest proposals for therapeutic constraint ....

The victim blaming ideology as applied to health is emerging alongside the limits of medicine argument. Indeed, that argument is its first premise. Basing itself on the irrefutable and increasingly obvious fact that medicine has been oversold, the new ideology argues that individuals, if they take appropriate actions, if they, in other words, adopt life-styles which avoid unhealthy behavior, may prevent most diseases. "Living a long life is essentially a do-it-yourself proposition," as it was put by one pundit. Policy, it is argued, must be redirected away from the extension of social programs which characterized the 1960s toward a health promotion strategy which calls upon the individual to become more responsible for his or her own health rather than to rely on ineffective medical services.

While the emergence of the new victim blaming ideology seems to have been facilitated by the attack on medicine, it is the conjuncture and contradictions contained in three political phenomena which best explain its emergence and the political functions it has acquired ....

THE NATURE OF THE CRISIS

The Crisis of Costs

Foremost is the current crisis of costs, a crisis which is transforming the entire political landscape in the health sector. The cost crisis has several dimensions, most of which have been repeated so often that they are all too familiar. High medical costs have always been a problem. What makes health sector inflation so critical in the 1970s is not only its spectacular rate but its concurrence with wider economic and fiscal crises. High medical costs have become a direct threat to the corporate sector, adding significantly to the costs of production through increases in health benefit settlements with labor, aggravating inflation, and diverting private and governmental resources ...

The costs of production for corporations in unionized sectors have been rapidly escalating, in large part due to increasing costs of benefit settlements. The Council on Wage and Price Stability reports that in the auto, rubber, and steel industries, gross average hourly earnings between 1965 and 1974 increased 83, 59, and 85 percent, respectively, but that in the same industries, negotiated employee benefits jumped 240, 150, and 160 percent for the same period. Overall, between 1966 and 1972, total employer payments for insurance and health benefits increased 100 percent while wages increased only 47 percent (12, p. 94).

General Motors claims it spent more money with Blue Cross and Blue Shield in 1975 than it did with U.S. Steel, its principal supplier of metal. Standard Oil of Indiana announced in 1976 that employee health costs for the corporation had tripled over the past seven years (13). In 1976, Chrysler estimates it paid $1500 per employee for medical benefits or a total of $205 million in the U.S. (14, p. 656). "Unlike most other labor costs that can and do vary with the level of production," the corporation complains, "medical costs continue to rise in good times as well as in bad" (14, p. 660).

The implications for consumer costs are obvious. GM added $175 to the price of every car and truck in passing on its employee medical benefit costs. In a period in which consumption and investment are stalled, and foreign competition adds an additional barrier to raising prices, figures such as those given above are startling. Corporate and union leaders are expressing in every possible forum their concern over the impact of rising medical costs upon prices, wages, and profits.

Mounting fiscal pressures on both federal and local governments are also worrying political and economic leaders. As the Council on Wage and Price Stability reports (12, p. 94),

The portion of the Federal budget expended for health has increased from 8.9 percent in 1969 to 11.3 percent in 1975 and is projected to be 11.7 percent in 1977. Only national defense, interest on the national debt, and income security programs now consume a larger share.

The fiscal crisis at the local level is dramatically forcing the issue. Steps are being taken daily to cut back public programs and otherwise to attempt to control the escalating costs. The cost problem has hurt almost every major economic interest group in the country, resulting in a fundamental coalitional shift from support for expansion to "get tough" cost control measures. Large corporate interests and government officials are at the center of the coalition. Substantial political pressures are being mobilized to cut the direct costs to corporations and to cut the indirect costs of social programs generally (15). Just as the politics of expansion dominated the last period in health politics, the politics of cost control will dominate the next (16, 17). The terms of agreement in the new coalition as well as its fragility are still to be tested, but it is clear that expansionary forces are facing their most serious challenge to date.

Politicization of the Social Production of Disease

The second phenomenon underlying the emergence of the ideology of individual responsibility, occurring simultaneously with the cost crisis, is a rapid politicization of the social production of disease. Widely reported scientific and popular critiques of environmental health dangers and occupational health and safety hazards have resulted in a growing awareness, concern, and polarization over these issues. First, there is now almost universal agreement in the scientific community that most cancers are environmentally caused, anywhere from 70–90 percent by most estimates. ...

The American people have been inundated in just the last few years with a constant flow of environmental warnings and disasters: air pollution, contamination of drinking supplies, ozone watches in which "vulnerable" people are advised to sharply reduce their activities and to stay indoors, food additive carcinogens, the PCB disaster in Michigan, the asbestos disaster in Minnesota, and the kepone disaster in Virginia, vinyl chlorides, pesticides, the controversy over nuclear power plants, and more. The Environmental Protection Agency, the Occupational Safety and Health Administration, and the Food and Drug Administration have been among the most embattled government agencies in recent years. While there is considerable debate over threshold limit values, the validity of animal research applications to humans, and specific policy decisions by the above agencies, awareness is growing that the public is being exposed to a multitude of environmental and workplace carcinogens. Although many people still cling to the "it won't happen to me" response, the fear of cancer is becoming more widespread. ...

From within industry, an occupational health and safety movement is gaining momentum. The UMW, OCAW, USW, and UAW are among the most active unions in developing programs and confronting corporate management on health and safety issues. Occupational health and safety has also sparked some radical challenges to established union leadership (18). Industry has reacted to these events by warning of unemployment, inflation, and economic stagnation if government regulations are expanded, and by presenting industry-sponsored research to alleviate fears. In addition, massive advertising campaigns herald the environmental efforts of public-spirited corporations. The "manufacturers of illness" confront what they fear will be a serious threat to corporate autonomy: the forging of labor, environmental, consumer, and populist groups into a new public health movement. The example of political constraints on the growth of the nuclear power industry is not lost on other industries.

Medical Care as a Right

Third, in the present period people's expectations of medicine have been lifted to their highest point, and the idea that medical care is a right is widely accepted. Belief in medicine is the result of many factors: years of conditioning by the medical profession; a research and philanthropy establishment deeply committed to the medical model; a few spectacular medical successes; a general, society-wide glorification of science and technology; and the medicalization of society, the cultural roots of which extend far beyond professional imperialism (6, 19, 20). Further, in a period in which people feel vulnerable to epidemic-proportion diseases, and powerless to do much about it, the tendency is to rely on medicine all the more. Dependency grows, even as anxiety increases over the inability of medicine to find a cure for the new diseases. The great promise of the twentieth century will not easily be dispelled. The hope of deliverance is perhaps more pervasive than ever. Finally, the idea that access to medical services is an essential component of personal and family security has long been a politicized matter. It has emerged from a long history of union and popular struggles negotiated in labor contracts and promoted through legislation. The campaign for national health insurance goes back several decades, was a primary political force in the adoption of Medicare and Medicaid, and in the last six or seven years has gained a new vitality.

In summary, on the one hand, America is a society ridden with anxiety about disease and yet infatuated with the claims of scientific medicine, in which access to medical care is believed to be a basic right. On the other hand, the cost of medical services and the fiscal crisis are making services more difficult to obtain and are forcing a retreat from public programs. At a time when people seem to want medicine most, its continuing availability and expansion threaten powerful economic and political interests. Further, much to the concern of industry, medicine is clearly inadequate in dealing with the contemporary social production of disease, and is therefore increasingly unable to perform its traditional role of resolving societal tensions which emerge when people identify the social causes of their individual pathologies. In the face of these trends, it is fascinating and revealing that we are witnessing the proliferation of messages about our own personal responsibility for health and an attack on individual life-styles and at-risk behaviors....

THE POLITICS OF DIVERSION

Social causation of disease has several dimensions. The complexities are only beginning to be explored. The victim blaming ideology, however, inhibits that understanding and substitutes instead an unrealistic behavioral model. It both ignores what is known about human behavior and minimizes the importance of evidence about the environmental assault on health. It instructs people to be individually responsible at a time when they are becoming less capable as individuals of controlling their health environment (21, 22). Although environmental dangers are often recognized, the implication is that little can be done about an ineluctable, modern, technological, and industrial society. Life-style and environmental factors are thrown together to communicate that individuals are the primary agents in shaping or modifying the effects of their environment....

Thus, the practical focus of health should not be on the massive and expensive task of overhauling the environment, which, it is argued, would threaten jobs and economic growth. Instead, the important, i.e. amenable, determinants of health are behavioral, cultural, and psychological.

The diffusion of a psychological world view often reinforces the masking of social causation. Even though the psychiatric model substitutes social for natural explanations, problems still tend to be seen as amenable to change through personal transformation – with or without therapy. And with or without therapy, individuals are ultimately held responsible for their own psychological well-being. Usually, no one has to blame us for some psychological failure; we blame ourselves. Thus, psychological impairment can be just as effective as moral failing or genetic inferiority in blaming the victim and reinforcing dominant social relations (23). People are alienated, unhappy, dropouts, criminals, angry, and activists, after all, because of maladjustment to one or another psychological norm.

The ideology of individual responsibility for health lends itself to this form of psychological social control. Susceptibility to at-risk behaviors, if not a moral failing, is at least a psychological failing. New evidence relating psychological state to resistance or susceptibility to disease and accidents can and will be used to shift more responsibility to the individual. Industrial psychologists have long been employed with the intention that the best way to reduce plant accidents in lieu of costly production changes is to intervene at the individual level (24). The implication is that people make themselves sick, not only mentally but physically. If job satisfaction is important to health, people should seek more rewarding employment. Cancer is a state of mind.

In another vein, many accounts of the current disease structure in the United States link disease with affluence. The affluent society and the life-styles it has wrought, it is suggested, are the sources of the individual's degeneration and adoption of at-risk behaviors. Halberstam, for example, writes that "most Americans die of excess rather than neglect or poverty" (quoted in 10, p. 22). Knowles' warning about "sloth, gluttony, alcoholic intemperance, reckless driving, sexual frenzy and smoking" and later about "social failure" (1, pp. 2, 3) are reminiscent of a popularized conception of a decaying Rome. Thus, even though some may complain about environmental hazards, people are really suffering from over-indulgence of the good society. It is that over-indulgence which must be checked. Further, by pointing to life-styles, which are usually presented as if they reflect the problems of a homogenized, affluent society, this aspect of the ideology tends to obscure the reality of class and the impact of social inequality on health. It is compatible with the conception that people are free agents. Social structure and constraints recede amidst the abundance.

Of course, several diseases do stem from the life-styles of the more affluent. Discretionary income usually allows for excessive consumption of unhealthy products; and as Eyer (25) argues, everyone suffers in variable and specific ways from the nature of work and the conditioning of life-styles in advanced capitalist society. But are the well-established relationships between low income and high infant mortality, diseases related to poor diet and malnutrition, stress, cancer, mental illness, traumas of various kinds, and other pathologies (26–30) now to be ignored or relegated to a residual factor? While long-term inequality in morbidity and mortality is declining (31), for almost every disease and for every indicator of morbidity incidence increases as income falls (32, pp. 620–621). In some specific cases, the health gap appears to be widening (33, 34)....

Finally, by focusing on the individual instead of the economic system, the ideology performs its classical role of obscuring the class structure of work. The failure to maintain health in the workplace is attributed to some personal flaw. The more than 2.5 million people disabled by occupational accidents and diseases each year and the additional 114,000 killed (35, 36) are not explained by the hazards or pace of work as much as by the lack of sufficient caution by workers, laziness about wearing respirators or the like, psychological maladjustment, and even by the worker's genetic susceptibility....

Corporate management appears to be increasingly integrating victim blaming themes into personnel policies. Physical and especially psychological health have acquired more importance for management faced with declining productivity and expanding absenteeism. The problem for management becomes more serious with its growing dependence on high-skilled and more expensive labor, and on a more complex, integrated, and predictable production process.... Holding individual workers responsible for their susceptibility to illness, or for an "unproductive" psychological state, reinforces management attempts to control absenteeism and enhance productivity. Job dissatisfaction and job-induced stress (in both their psychological and physical manifestations), principal sources of absenteeism and low productivity, will become identified as life-style problems of the worker....

Workers who are found to be "irresponsible" in maintaining their health or psychological stability, as manifest in attendance records, will face sanctions, dismissals or early retirement, rationalized as stemming from employee health problems....

If such practices do become widespread, the facilitating device will likely be health screening. Screening potential and current employees for behavioral, attitudinal, and health purposes has already gained considerable popularity among large corporations. Among the specific advantages cited for health screening are selection "of those judged to present the least risk of unstable attendance, costly illness, poor productivity, or short tenure"; development of a "medical placement code" to match employees to jobs by health specifications; and "protection of the company against future compensation claims" (37, p. 31). In addition, screening holds out the possibility of cost savings from reduced group insurance rates. In a 1974 survey of over 800 corporations with more than 500 employees each, 71 percent of the companies gave preemployment health screening examinations to some or all new employees, compared with 63 percent ten years ago. General periodic examinations jumped from 39 to 57 percent over the same period (37). New businesses are now selling employee risk evaluations, called by one firm "health hazard appraisals." The American Hospital Association is also developing health appraisal programs for use by employers. Of course, many screening practices, such as psychological testing for appropriate work attitudes, alcoholism, or screening for mental illness records, have long been in use. The availability to employers of computerized information from health insurance companies for purposes of screening has drawn criticism from groups concerned about invasion of privacy. Women have often been asked questions during job interviews about their use of birth control, and women planning to have children continue to face barriers, especially to those jobs requiring employer investment in training.

Programs are now being expanded to screen workers for susceptibility to job hazards. Not only genetic susceptibility but also other at-risk health behaviors, such as smoking, use of alcohol, or improper diet, help legitimize screening programs. But while alerting individual workers to their susceptibility, these programs do not address the hazardous conditions which to some degree affect all workers. Thus, all workers may be penalized *to the extent* that such programs function to divert attention from causative conditions. To the degree that the causative agent remains, the more susceptible workers are also penalized in that they must shoulder the burden of the hazardous conditions either by looking for another, perhaps nonexistent job, or, if it is permitted, by taking a risk in remaining. It is worth noting in this regard that some women of childbearing age barred from working in plants using lead are reported to be obtaining sterilizations in order to regain their jobs....

Thus, whether or not the individual is personally blamed for some at-risk behavior, excluding the "susceptible" worker from the workplace is like asking "vulnerable" people to reduce activity during an ozone watch: it may be helpful for particular individuals, but under the guise of health promotion, it may also act as a colossal masquerade.

SOME RELATED ISSUES

It is important to recognize and address the issue that a significant portion of socially caused illness is, at some level, associated with individual, at-risk behavior which can be changed to improve health. A deterministic view which argues that individuals have no choice should be avoided. What must be questioned is both the effectiveness and the political uses (as well as the scientific narrowness) of a focus on life-styles and on changing individual behavior without changing the social and economic environment.... McKinlay has convincingly argued that the frequent failure of health education programs designed to change individual behavior is attributable to the failure to address the social context. In reviewing some of the strategies adopted by the "manufacturers of illness" to encourage profitable at-risk behaviors and to shape conducive self-images in American consumers, McKinlay observes that (47, pp. 9–10):

> ... certain at-risk behaviors have become so inextricably intertwined with our dominant cultural system (perhaps even symbolic of it) that the routine display of such behavior almost signifies membership in this society .... To request people to change or alter these behaviors is more or less to request the abandonment of dominant culture.

Certainly, the development of health education programs should be encouraged. Concurrent with expansion of access to primary medical services, health personnel should be trained to work with patients in developing practices which reduce risk factors. Lack of information about the dangers of smoking, high cholesterol intake, or obesity, for example, could be considerably reduced by such efforts.... Health educators, however, would be engaging in victim blaming if such efforts were allowed to suffice; and only marginal results would be achieved as well.

Unfortunately, at a time when the health education profession needs to develop a new strategy which, as Podell argues, enlarges the focus "to include the political and social context in which the individual's health-related choices are being made" (32, pp. 171–172), the individual-behavior orientation of the field has become more pronounced in response to the developments described in this article.... (32, p. 88).

CONCLUSION

The ideology of individual responsibility promotes a concept of wise living which views the individual as essentially independent of his or her surroundings, unconstrained by social events and processes. When such pressures are recognized, it is still the individual who is called upon to resist them. Nevertheless, an alternate political understanding, directed not toward individuals, but toward relations among individuals, will profoundly influence the politics of health in the coming period. The commercial and industrial assault on health is becoming too grave to be ignored. A crisis characterized by an increasing involvement of unions, consumer groups, and environmental activists in confrontation with the "manufacturers of illness" threatens to extend far beyond the normal boundaries of health politics.

This politicization of environmental and occupational health issues suggests an erosion of the power of medicine to function as a diversion from social causation. This may be occurring even though overall utilization of medical services continues to rise and the hope for medical deliverance remains intense. The failure of medicine to contain the new epidemics is a partial explanation for that erosion. The cost crisis also leads to an ideological shift away from medicine. Given people's expectations and political pressures for protection and extension of entitlements, a justification for retrenchment must be offered. Thus, people are told that they rely too much on ineffective medical services, and they must think instead about prevention. However, to the extent that medicine is delegitimized, its traditional social control function of individualizing disease through the biological model, and of providing a "technological fix" as a substitute for social change, is also weakened. As people come to understand the limitations of medicine and technology as a means to better health, there is increasing potential for the development of a movement willing to confront dominant interests over the systematic denial of health.

The ideology of individual responsibility poses an alternate social control formulation. It replaces reliance on therapeutic intervention with a behavioral model which only requires good living. Like medicine, the new ideology continues to "atomize both causation and solution to illness" (39), although now that ideological function is performed outside the therapeutic structure.

The success of such an approach, however, is problematic. A deinstitutionalized individualism cannot perform as an effective social control device in a technological age. For this reason it is important not to overemphasize the abandonment of medicine. If cost control and other organizational reforms can be successfully imposed, and the provision of services divorced from popular demands for rights and entitlements, medicine may again become more amenable to dominant interests. The continuing utility of medicine will come not so much from a newly found effectiveness, but from its potent redemptive and other social control qualities. Although medicine is not the only institution capable of performing such critical functions, the therapeutic ideology will remain the "paradigm for modernized domination" (40, p. 8). Through masking political relations by calling them medical (23), and through the technical definition of social problems, medicine provides an institutionalized form of control that the concept of individual responsibility cannot.

Finally, although the victim blaming ideology is linked with the attack on medicine, there is no inherent reason why the celebration of a "reformed" medicine and notions of individual responsibility cannot coexist. Each counterbalances the weakness of the other. Even as the attack on medicine gains popularity, a reintegration may be under way. After all, victim blaming may let medicine off the hook as well.

REFERENCES

1. *Conference on Future Directions in Health Care: The Dimensions of Medicine.* Sponsored by Blue Cross Association, The Rockefeller Foundation, and Health Policy Program, University of California, New York, December 1975.
2. McKeown, T. *Medicine in Modern Society.* G. Allen and Unwin, London, 1965.

3. McKeown, T. An historical appraisal of the medical task. In *Medical History and Medical Care: A Symposium of Perspectives*, edited by T. McKeown and G. McLachlan, pp. 29–55. Oxford University Press, London, 1971.

4. Cochrane, A. L. *Effectiveness and Efficiency: Random Reflections on Health Services*. Nuffield Provincial Hospitals Trust, London, 1972.

5. Powles, J. On the limitations of modern medicine. *Sci. Med. Man* 1(1): 1–30, 1973.

6. Illich, I. *Medical Nemesis: The Expropriation of Health*. Pantheon Books, New York, 1975.

7. Fuchs, V. *Who Shall Live? Health, Economics, and Social Choice*. Basic Books, New York, 1974.

8. Carlson, R. *The End of Medicine*. John Wiley & Sons, New York, 1975.

9. Lalonde, M. *A New Perspective on the Health of Canadians: A Working Document*. Information Canada, Ottawa, 1975.

10. Somers, A. *Health Care in Transition: Directions for the Future*. Hospital Research and Educational Trust, Chicago, 1971.

11. Starr, P. The politics of therapeutic nihilism. *Working Papers for a New Society* 4(2): 48–55, 1976.

12. *The Complex Puzzle of Rising Health Costs: Can the Private Sector Fit It Together?* Council on Wage and Price Stability, Washington, D.C., December 1976.

13. *Chicago Sun-Times*, March 16, 1976.

14. Inflation of Health Care Costs, 1976. Hearings before the Subcommittee on Health of the Committee on Labor and Public Welfare, United States Senate, 94th Congress. U.S. Government Printing Office, Washington, D.C., 1976.

15. O'Connor, J. *The Fiscal Crisis of the State*. St. Martin's Press, New York, 1973.

16. Fox, D., and Crawford, R. Health politics in the United States. In *Handbook of Medical Sociology*, edited by H. E. Freeman, S. Levine, and L. Reeder, Ed. 3. Prentice-Hall, Englewood Cliffs, N.J., forthcoming.

17. Kotelchuck, R. Government cost control strategies. *Health/PAC Bulletin* No. 75, 1–6, March/April 1977.

18. Berman, D. Why work kills: A brief history of occupational safety and health. *Int. J. Health Serv.* 7(1): 63–87, 1977.

19. Zola, I. Medicine as an institution of social control. *Sociological Review* 20(4): 487–504, 1972.

20. Ehrenreich, B., and Ehrenreich, J. Medicine and social control. In *Welfare in America: Controlling the "Dangerous Classes,"* edited by B. R. Mandell, pp. 138–167. Prentice-Hall, Inc., Englewood Cliffs, N.J., 1975.

21. Special Issue on the Economy, Medicine, and Health, edited by Joseph Eyer. *Int. J. Health Serv.* 7(1): 1–150, 1977.

22. The Social Etiology of Disease (Part I). *HMO-A Network for Marxist Studies in Health* No. 2, January 1977.

23. Edelman, M. The political language of the helping professions. *Politics and Society* 4(3): 295–310, 1974.

24. *New York Times*, April 3, 1977.

25. Eyer, J. Prosperity as a cause of disease. *Int. J. Health Serv.* 7(1): 125–150, 1977.

26. Hurley, R. The health crisis of the poor. In *The Social Organization of Health*, edited by H. P. Dreitzel, pp. 83–122. Macmillan Company, New York, 1971.

27. *Infant Mortality Rates: Socioeconomic Factors*, Series 22, No. 14. U.S. Public Health Service, Washington, D.C., 1972.

28. *Selected Vital and Health Statistics in Poverty and Nonpoverty Areas of 19 Large Cities, United States, 1969–71*, Series 21, No. 26. U.S. Public Health Service, Washington, D.C., 1975.

29. Kitagawa, E., and Hauser, P. *Differential Mortality in the United States: A Study in Socioeconomic Epidemiology*. Harvard University Press, Cambridge, 1973.
30. Sherer, H. Hypertension. *HMO-A Network for Marxist Studies in Health* No. 2, January 1977.
31. Antonovsky, A. Social class, life expectancy, and overall mortality. *Milbank Mem. Fund Q.* 45(2, part I): 31–73, 1967.
32. *Preventive Medicine USA*. Prodist, New York, 1976.
33. Jenkins, C. D. Recent evidence supporting psychologic and social risk factors for coronary heart diseases. *N. Engl. J. Med.* 294(18): 987–994, 1976, and 294(19): 1033–1038, 1976.
34. Eyer, J., and Sterling, P. Stress related mortality and social organization. *Review of Radical Political Economy*, forthcoming.
35. Page, J. A., and O'Brien, M. *Bitter Wages*. Grossman Publishers, New York, 1973.
36. Brodeur, P. *Expendable Americans*. Viking Press, New York, 1974.
37. Lusterman, S. *Industry Roles in Health Care*. The Conference Board, Inc., New York, 1974.
38. McKinlay, J. A Case for Refocussing Upstream–The Political Economy of Illness. Unpublished paper, Boston University, 1974.
39. Ziem, G. Ideology, the State, and Victim Blaming: A Discussion Paper for the East Coast Health Discussion Group. Unpublished paper, Johns Hopkins University, 1977.
40. McKnight, J. The Medicalization of Politics. Unpublished paper, Northwestern University, undated.

Source: R. Crawford, 'You are dangerous to your health: the ideology and politics of victim blaming', *International Journal of Health Services*, 7:4 (1977) 663–80.

Study Questions and Activities

1. Think about what Robert Crawford has written about the ideology and politics of victim blaming. Now think about your own practice and reflect on whether you ever engage in victim blaming.
2. Contemporary western societies (and parts of some developing societies) have experienced an epidemiological transition with an increase in the numbers of people living with long-term conditions such as chronic obstructive pulmonary disease and diabetes. Can health education tackle this disease burden? What structural issues should be addressed?
3. How might lifestyle advice contribute to the experience of health, illness and healthcare?

Further Reading

The ideology of victim blaming has been widely discussed. For example, the following article discusses the negative health effects of lifestyle advice within general practice and argues that patients often feel blamed for their health problems and health behaviour by doctors: H. Richards, M. Reid and G. Watt, 'Victim-blaming revisited: a qualitative study of beliefs about illness causation and responses to chest pain', *Family Practice*, 20:6 (2003) 711–16. In a review of lay understandings, J. Popay, S. Bennett, C. Thomas, G. Williams, A. Gatrell and L. Bostock in their 2003 article 'Beyond 'beer, fags, egg and chips'? Exploring lay understandings of social inequalities in health', *Sociology of Health and Illness*, 25:1, 1–23 show how lay people do not just locate the blame for health inequalities not only in lifestyle and behaviour, but also on social and structural issues. If you are interested in complementary and alternative medicines (CAMs), the following two readings will be of interest in that they focus on how CAMs also promote a victim-blaming ideology: S. Mclean, "The illness is part of the person': discourses of blame, individual responsibility and individuation at a centre for spiritual healing in the North of England', *Sociology of Health & Illness*, 27:5 (2005) 628–48 and S. Wilkinson and C. Kitzinger, 'Towards a feminist approach to breast cancer', in S. Wilkinson and C. Kitzinger, (eds) *Women and Health: Feminist Perspectives* (Taylor and Francis: London, 1994), pp. 124–40. Ideologies of individual responsibility are widespread but no more so than in relation to discourses of disease and excess. For example, you will find the following two readings on obesity really interesting in that they show how individuals are assumed to have a moral and medical responsibility to manage their weight: A. C. Saguy and R. W. Riley, 'Weighing both sides: morality, mortality, and framing contests over obesity', *Journal of Health Politics, Policy and Law*, 30:5 (2005) 869–923 and M. Gard and J. Wright, *The Obesity Epidemic: Science, Morality and Ideology* (Routledge: London, 2005).

Reading 13

The Determinants of Geographical Inequalities in Health

Heather Joshi, Richard D. Wiggins, Mel Bartley, Richard Mitchell, Simon Gleave and Kevin Lynch

In this reading, the authors point out how the geography of disease has remained constant over the past 150 years in that inequalities in health persist across the North/South divide, with the best health still distributed amongst the South and East of England. Geographical inequalities in health have frequently been explained by examining the particular socio-economic or cultural differences between people living in different areas. So, just as Robert Crawford has drawn attention to an ideology that locates responsibility for health with the individual, according to this approach, the families living in the most economically derived areas are the least likely to adopt health education messages and, thus, are the most likely to get sick and die young. However, Heather Joshi and her colleagues argue that composition (the characteristics of individuals living in an area) and context (the characteristics of the area in which people live) must, both, be considered. Drawing on census data from England and Wales, this reading considers the evidence base for area-based inequalities in health. It concludes by pointing out that both individual and area characteristics matter. So if you take individuals with similar socio-economic characteristics and place them in different contexts, the individuals located in the poorest neighbourhoods will be at a higher risk of illness. The policy and practice implications of this are that individual inequality and area inequalities in health each should be tackled.

INTRODUCTION

The analysis of geographical differentials in health in Great Britain has a long tradition. In the mid-nineteenth century, William Farr established the practice of taking 'healthy districts' as a baseline from which to compare the state of industrial cities. In those times, most of the healthy districts were in more rural areas and in the South and East of England. The spatial distribution of health and illness has changed remarkably little in the past century and a half, despite the passage of the UK through the 'epidemiologic transition'. This transition, from a situation in which infectious diseases of childhood and young adulthood were the most common causes of mortality, to one in which the chronic diseases of older age predominate, might have been expected to bring about a shift in the geography of disease. But this has not proved to be the case.

The dominant paradigm, within which these persistent spatial inequalities have been understood, has been one based on individual characteristics and behaviour. One generally accepted reason for spatial health inequality derives from a spatial variation in employment structure. There is still a preponderance of manual work in the old northern industrial areas. Manual workers and their families are more likely to experience economic deprivation and are less likely to adopt the health education messages aimed at countering the new major diseases such as heart disease and cancer. For example, manual workers are still smoking when other groups are giving up; neither have they adopted whole heartedly the recommended changes in diet and exercise....

Research on the reasons for observed area differences now distinguishes between the effects of social composition and of social context (Macintyre *et al.* 1993). Composition refers to the aggregated characteristics of individuals living in an area, while context refers to characteristics of the area which are independent of its individual inhabitants. Context could include features of the physical environment, such as climate or pollution, and features of the local economy, such as the housing stock or the structure of employment. It could also include the provision of services such as shops, transport and schools, as well as the quality of healthcare available. Finally, there are features of the social fabric which may make a place less or more 'healthy', such as the level of crime or community cohesion.

Sooman *et al.* (1993) have studied the types of shops and transport available in different areas of Glasgow, an example of clearly contextual features. However, at a certain level of density, composition may become a form of context: as one example, when in deprived areas with high rates of smoking, an individual is more likely to smoke than a similar individual in an area with lower smoking rates (Duncan *et al.* 1996).

In order to disentangle these complex influences, evidence is required both about individuals and the places they live in. We also need a statistical framework capable of analysing the relationships between them. An appropriate statistical framework is provided by a multi-level model, which allows for separate relationships between individual and area characteristics (Goldstein 1997).

A multi-level model explicitly recognizes that individuals behave in context. They act out their lives in households and within neighbourhoods, and in larger areas and broad regions. Areas provide natural groupings, or clusters of units, for our analysis, reflecting features of context or population composition. In contrast to conventional regression analysis, the multi-level framework provides an appropriate way of being able to take account explicitly of any clustering (Cheung *et al.* 1990). We are also able to examine the interplay of individual and area-level characteristics in determining individual health. By separating out the between-area and within-area contribution of area effect, it is possible to see the extent to which they actually explain any differences between areas, once the characteristics of the individuals who reside there have been taken into account. The failure of many studies to take account of the multi-level nature of the data obtained has been a prominent theme in methodological criticisms of epidemiological (Langford and Bentham 1996), educational (Goldstein 1997) and sociological (Willms and Patterson 1995) research over the last 20 years. We were able to avoid the 'ecological fallacy' by making a pioneering application of multi-level modelling to the Office for National Statistics Longitudinal Study (ONS-LS), not previously possible with individual data.

Earlier analysis of individual and ward-level data in this study (but which did not use the multi-level technique) suggested that individual characteristics are the most important source of geographical variations in mortality (Sloggett and Joshi 1994, 1998a). However, some ward and regional 'effects' remained in models of limiting long-term illness (LLTI), even after allowance for effects at both personal and community levels (Sloggett and Joshi 1998a, 1998b). In these models, the risk of LLTI was raised by about 17 per cent, moving across areas towards those with worse composite indices of deprivation in steps of one standard deviation. Shouls *et al.* (1996) also analysed limiting long-term illness in the 1991 census, using multi-level modelling on larger areas (local authorities or groups thereof). With more information at the area-level included (for example, affluence as well as deprivation), a greater geographical element was detected alongside the effects of individual inequality on health.

This chapter explores some of the evidence on area-based inequalities in health. It begins by describing the evidence before asking what role may be played in these area effects by two specific factors among the many: economic change and social cohesion. It concludes with a discussion of the relevance of the spatial aspect of health inequality for policy.

INDIVIDUAL DISADVANTAGE OR AREA TYPE?

The ONS-LS allows us to look at the health of individuals within areas with the additional dimension of time by examining social and spatial mobility. This is because the ONS-LS links information from the 1991 census of England and Wales, to information from 1971 and 1981 for up to 800,000 individuals (Hattersley and Creeser 1995). The 1991 census asked a question on limiting long-term illness. We used this information to examine whether a certain type of work life-history between 1971 and 1991 was more likely to result in LLTI in men of working age. We also examined how far geographical differences in typical work life-histories could go towards explaining the marked regional inequalities in health.

The first step was to look at differences in LLTI between all 403 of the county districts of England and Wales. County districts are administrative units averaging 120,000 population. Previous analysis of the 1991 census data had shown large differences in the prevalence of LLTI, ranging between 48 per cent of all households having at least one person with a long-term illness, in the Rhondda (Wales), to 15 per cent in Surrey Heath (southern England) (Charlton and Wallace 1994). Were these area differences any more than a matter of the collection of individuals with higher susceptibility to ill-health? This question was approached by using multi-level models, a technique not previously available on ONS-LS microdata. These showed that individual characteristics were indeed important, the more so as we looked at movement between social classes, and into and out of unemployment over successive census reports. Having been out of work in either 1971 or 1981, having been in a manual job in 1971, having moved from a higher to a lower social class, not having a degree and being a member of an ethnic minority were all risk factors for LLTI. These variables explained around half of the area differences. However, after taking account of the fact that some areas contain far more disadvantaged men than others, it still seemed to matter where a man lived.

In order to begin the task of discovering what it might be about areas which makes a difference to health risks, each of the 403 county districts was classified according to the ONS grouping of local authorities (Wallace and Denham 1996). The classification is based on a range of social and economic data collected at the time of the 1991 census, concerning what kinds of industries predominate in different areas, car and home ownership, unemployment, the type of housing and the area's demographic structure....

Including this information on area type in the multi-level model explained another quarter of the differences in illness between areas. Fewer inhabitants of areas described as 'growth areas' or among the most economically prosperous areas had LLTI, having already taken account of their individual characteristics and the occupational histories. Conversely, the health of men in coalfield areas, and areas dominated by ports and heavy industries, was poorer than would have been expected on the basis of their own social and occupational histories alone. This leaves about one quarter of the health variations (age-standardized) between districts unaccounted for, either by measured characteristics of individuals or by their local economy: a variation possibly explained by climate, culture or other particular local conditions (Wiggins *et al.* 1998).

This type of analysis of the ONS-LS was extended to consider health variations among women as well as men, taking car ownership and housing tenure as indicators of individual circumstances (Wiggins *et al.* 1999). These analyses looked at the influence of a third, intermediate level – that of the electoral ward, of which there are 9369 in England and Wales.

For women and men, the chance of reporting LLTI was affected by the persistence over time of disadvantaged individual circumstances. Each observed occurrence of a disadvantageous state added to the chances of an adverse outcome: those who were, say, unemployed or council tenants at both previous censuses reported worse health than those who reported such states only once. There was a milder effect of repetition of residence in a deprived area, but otherwise little difference in LLTI for those who were geographically mobile or not. Migration into the South-East region did, however, appear to be beneficial. In line with findings by Macintyre and Ellaway (1998), cars and tenure appear to be useful markers of social and material advantage. For individuals, owning a car and a home in 1971 and 1981 both protected against the risk of reporting LLTI; not having either at either date raised the odds of LLTI by a factor of 1.7.

After adjusting for individual circumstances and histories, area differences persisted. A deterioration in ward poverty by one standard deviation of an index (based on census small area statistics) raised the chances of LLTI by a factor of about 1.18: much the same as in the analysis of Sloggett and Joshi (1998a), but less than the impact of individual circumstances. For men, the majority of local authority districts with a worryingly high level of unexplained rates of LLTI are largely accounted for by virtue of their classification as a former coalfield. For women, almost all of the remaining variation between county districts is explained by taking account of the composition of the wards in these areas. Multi-level analysis also revealed the existence of variation between wards in otherwise unspecified effects of place – however, investigation of these variations would require more information than is available in the census.

How far did this combination of individual and area variables explain the 'North–South divide' in illness? Once the geographical distribution of people with different kinds of employment histories, and the characteristics of areas in terms of industry, housing and degree of urbanization, are taken into account, little difference in health remained between northern and southern areas of England and Wales. This does not mean there is no role for health-related behaviour, as it still may be that individuals with certain types of work histories, living in certain types of area, smoke more, take less exercise and eat a poorer diet. This analysis tells us that area does matter, as well as individual factors, but it does not tell us all the reasons why this might be....

HOW MIGHT AREA MAKE A DIFFERENCE TO HEALTH?

What specific characteristics of an area might affect the health of its inhabitants? Of the various ways in which an area itself might generate poor or good health, we focus here on one aspect of the economic environment (de-industrialization) and one of the social environment (social capital). In these analyses, the source of data was the

Health and Lifestyle Survey (HALS), a representative sample of the British population in 1984–5 spatially clustered in electoral wards (Cox *et al.* 1987). Poor health was defined as having more than the average number of symptoms in the past two weeks.

De-industrialization

One area characteristic with a potential health effect is de-industrialization: economic decline with associated socio-demographic change. Champion and Townsend (1990) report a net loss of 2.8 million manufacturing jobs in Britain between 1971 and 1989. Since the manufacturing and mining industries were spatially concentrated, the effects of their loss were also spatially (and therefore socially) concentrated. There are likely to be changes in the nature of everyday life for the entire population of a de-industrialized community, even for those not directly involved in the declining industries. Areas experiencing de-industrialization during the 1980s have shown a relative deterioration in health (Phillimore *et al.* 1994). We therefore investigated the relationship between local de-industrialization and levels of health reported by all residents, men and women, employed and unemployed.

The source of data on de-industrialization was the Small Area Statistics for 1981 and 1991. We categorized wards into those with high and low levels of heavy industrial employment in 1981, which experienced high or low decreases in this type of employment up to 1991. To see whether differences in the degree of community cohesion made any difference to the health impact of economic recession, we also included in the analysis people's answers to a question on how far they felt they were part of the local community.

Residents in areas that had once had a high level of heavy industry, and then lost a large number of such jobs between 1981 and 1991, were indeed more likely to report poor current health. Of residents in such areas, 14.2 per cent reported a high number of symptoms, compared with 10.5 per cent in areas with low levels of industrial employment in 1981 and with low loss of industrial employment over the next ten years. These two types of area accounted for 38 per cent and 40 per cent of the sample respectively. The remaining 22 per cent lived in areas with other combinations of the level and change of industrial employment and had intermediate levels of health. Multi-level analysis expressed the higher risk of poor health among individuals in the de-industrializing areas as an odds ratio of 1.35 relative to the areas of low industrialization and low industrial decline. This took account of whether they themselves were unemployed or employed in manual work, and applied regardless of the extent to which they felt integrated into their community. The odds of poor health for those in unskilled social class V were 1.78 (relative to social class I); while the odds for those who did not feel part of the community (relative to those who did) were 1.33.

Thus, while there was a specific effect on health of adverse change in the local economic structure, regardless of the situation of individual people, there were still bigger health differentials for individual disadvantageous situations like being in social class V. Socially integrated people who felt part of their communities were healthier, too, but this was so whatever the economic state of the area they lived in. Feeling part of their community might help protect people against the effects of de-industrialization, but de-industrialization does not explain the whole of the area differences in health (Mitchell *et al.* 2000).

Social Capital

The concept of social capital has been described as 'the resources that emerge from one's social ties' (Portes and Landolt 1996: 26). Putnam, in his highly influential analysis, suggests that social capital is a community-based resource which includes 'civic engagement'. This he defines as 'people's connections with the life of their communities' (1995: 1).

We examined whether a higher level of civic engagement was positively associated with health, independently of other socio-economic characteristics of individuals and the areas in which they live. HALS records the frequency and nature of contact with family and friends, attendance at a place of worship and any voluntary or community work, in the two weeks prior to interview. Responses revealed three distinct tendencies characterized by high levels of contact with family, with friends and with fellow citizens. A civic orientation was characterized by attendance at church and by involvement in voluntary work. We tested directly the nature of the relationship between health and these orientations to family, friends and fellow citizens.

Logistic regression analysis of poor health (again measured as having above average numbers of symptoms) controlled for the individual's age and fitness and then successively introduced controls for the individual's socioeconomic circumstances and those of the local population. Individual fitness (as measured by sports participation and limiting long-standing illness) was included in the model to allow for the effects of chronic ill-health, as well as the effect of current symptoms, on social contacts. Area deprivation was measured by the Breadline Britain Index (Gordon and Pantazis 1997). This estimates the number of households likely to be in poverty in an area, using the local rates at the 1991 census of non-home ownership, non-access to a car, low social class, unemployment, lone parents and LLTI, weighted in accordance with responses to the Breadline Britain survey. It is positively, but not perfectly, correlated with the de-industrialization score (0.25) and more closely related to the ward scores used in the ONS-LS, though these use different weights and do not include LLTI.

The analysis is shown in Table 1. The effects of any explanatory variable are shown as odds ratios: any ratio under 1 suggests that the attribute will improve the chances of good health, whereas a ratio greater than 1 suggests the opposite.

Table 1 Results of logistic regression models, predicting ill-health.[1] Odds ratios (and confidence intervals)

Model	Social orientation, individual fitness	Social orientation, individual fitness individual socio-economics	Social orientation, individual fitness individual socio-economics, area characteristics
Predictor variable			
More civic oriented[2]	0.65 (0.57, 0.74)	0.72 (0.63, 0.83)	0.72 (0.63, 0.83)
More family oriented[2]	0.86 (0.77, 0.96)	0.81 (0.72, 0.91)	0.80 (0.72, 0.90)
More friend oriented[2]	0.88 (0.79, 0.99)	0.93 (0.82, 1.04)	0.93 (0.82, 1.04)
Age[3]	0.95 (0.92, 0.98)	0.90 (0.86, 0.93)	0.91 (0.87, 0.94)
Does sport/physical activity[4]	0.59 (0.52, 0.67)	0.64 (0.56, 0.72)	0.65 (0.57, 0.73)
Has LLTI[5]	5.78 (5.03, 6.64)	5.60 (4.86, 6.45)	5.59 (4.85, 6.44)
Manual class[6]		1.48 (1.30, 1.67)	1.41 (1.25, 1.60)
Low income[7]		1.45 (1.67, 1.26)	1.39 (1.58, 1.20)
High income[8]		0.68 (0.65, 0.69)	0.71 (0.68, 0.73)
Area poverty[9]			1.21 (1.13, 1.30)
−2 Log likelihood	7525	7360	7341
N with full data for this analysis = 7020			

Notes:
1. Reporting more than the mean number of symptoms in the past two weeks.
2. Odds relative to those who had a negative score.
3. Age in 10 years, modelled as a continuous variable.
4. Those who reported doing some kind of sport/physical activity in the two weeks prior to interview. Odds relative to those who did not report any such activity.
5. Those reporting limiting long-term illness. Odds relative to those who did not.
6. Those in social classes IIIM, IV or V. Odds relative to classes I, II or IIIN.
7. Those in the lowest income bracket (under £79 per week, net, per week in 1984) relative to those in the middle income bracket (£79–£173). There are 28 per cent of cases in the low income bracket, just under half all cases in the middle bracket and another 28 per cent in the top.
8. Those in the top income bracket (£174 or more per week in 1984). Odds relative to the middle bracket.
9. The Breadline Britain Index. Unit equivalent to a 10 per cent difference in the fitted proportion of households in poverty in the respondent's ward of residence in 1991.

The first model (column labelled social orientation, individual fitness) showed those with a greater degree of civic engagement or family contact gave a significantly better report on their state of health than those with less, whether or not they had a chronic disease. Civic engagement was the form of social activity most strongly related to current health (odds of reporting above average symptoms of 0.65, in comparison with 0.86 and 0.88, for family and friend orientations respectively).

The second model (column labelled social orientation, individual fitness, individual socio-economics) adds a simple indicator of low or high social class, and a three-category measure of income. The effect of being in a low social class is to raise the chances of experiencing more than average symptoms (odds ratio 1.48). Those in the highest income band are only about half as likely to report poor health as those in the lowest band. The effects of class and income are independent of the other characteristics already in the model. Although the association between civic orientation and health was weakened after adjusting for socio-economic circumstances, it remains significant.

The final model (column labelled social orientation, individual fitness, individual socio-economics, area characteristics) introduces a measure of area deprivation. An increase of 10 per cent in the proportion of households estimated to be living in poverty in the area is associated with an increase of 21 per cent in the chances of a person reporting poor health. It is a significant, independent, predictor of poor health at the individual level despite the inclusion of individual socio-economic characteristics. Its inclusion slightly reduces the impact of these individual terms, but makes no difference to the association between civic orientation and health. Indirectly, this tells us that the poor areas do not have systematically less civic engagement. Civic engagement has about the same protective effect in the full model (0.72) as does 'feeling part of the community' in the de-industrialization model (0.75). The reason that civic engagement appears to protect health is not that it is more common in rich areas poor areas seem to have health disadvantage beyond those associated with the individual and with the community as we have measured them.

The socio-economic health divide therefore has individual, social and local components. Although a low level of civic engagement is associated with poorer health, socio-economic status is no less important at both the individual and area levels. In the presence of wealth, weaker friendship networks and lower levels of civic orientation have relatively small health penalties attached to them. Personal circumstances seem at least as strong an influence as area. The odds of poor health increase by 1.39 between the median to the poorest income group, and by 1.21 if the deprivation score is increased by ten points (which it does between the middle of the most deprived quarter of the sample and its mid-point). Combining the impact of individual and local deprivation, the model predicts that a gap in income of this magnitude accompanied by an equivalent contrast in area deprivation and a shift from non-manual to manual occupation, would more than double the odds (2.37) of poor health.

The size of the Breadline Britain area effect on current illness is very similar to the corresponding analyses of LLTI in the ONS-LS, despite the difference in outcome measures. When adjusted by the standard deviation of the Breadline Britain Index, the odds ratio is 1.16. For the ONS-LS, we have around 1.18....

CONCLUSION

Do individual or area characteristics matter? Both do. Our analyses of the ONS-LS and HALS produced a remarkably consistent set of findings about the contribution of context and composition to area differences in health. Area differences in self-reported ill-health, long-term or current, are mainly, but not simply, attributable to the socio-economic characteristics, occupational and migration histories of individual residents. But where people live also matters. Both men and women living in deprived wards have higher risks than those with similar characteristics in more affluent wards of reporting LLTI in the census and of reporting high numbers of symptoms in HALS. Men are especially at risk of ill health if they live in former coalfields or other areas of industrial decline. The magnitude of ward effects is strikingly similar in the present and previous analysis of census data, and in the survey data on current illness in the working-age population. In all cases, too, the estimates of the impact of individual disadvantage were more important, even if they did not account for all the area variation.

As well as looking at individuals' socio-economic circumstances, we attempted to look at social relations. We have not been able to identify areas which are rich in the kinds of collective activity and public provision which adds value to the quality of life of poorer residents. But we have found evidence, in two separate exercises, for individual social inclusion having an independent impact on health. But lack of participation in the community and lack of civic engagement are not the only reasons that poor people in poor places are at a health disadvantage.

What are the implications for public health policy? Should policies be targeted at particular areas (Smith 1999)? The geographical clustering of people at high health risk makes area-based initiatives look attractively cost effective. This would apply even if local health variations were all due to local concentrations of individual disadvantage, assuming some economies of scale in delivering services at these points. This would be all the more effective if the place itself gives rise to poor health. However, if only individuals living in particular areas are to benefit, then individuals at risk who happen to live outside targeted areas will obviously miss out. In the 1981 census of England, the majority (55 per cent) of the most 'deprived' individuals (those owning neither a home nor a car at both 1971 and 1981) lived outside the most deprived wards (Sloggett and Joshi 1994). Similarly, for England and Wales in 1991, 51 per cent of 'deprived' individuals did not live in the wards containing the most deprived fifth of the population. A similar picture emerges from our analysis of HALS. The bottom income group in our HALS sample, though over-represented in the bottom fifth Breadline Britain wards, or those with high de-industrialization, were not confined to these areas. Of the low-income group, 71 per cent lived in the better-off four fifths of wards, and 53 per cent lived outside the areas of greatest industrial decline.

Equally, if individuals rather than areas are targeted, the nature of area differences will continue to deflate potential benefits to those individuals. This suggests that policymakers need targeting strategies which combine redistributive initiatives at an individual and area level. Policies could be crafted which start with individuals and provide enhancements/premiums, depending on the deprivation profiles persisting at ward and broader levels of aggregation. Such resource allocation mechanisms cannot be foolproof, particularly as much variation in health remains unaccounted for by our models. To improve allocation, we need to continue to deepen our understanding of why area differences persist.

Our finding that individual dimensions are important sources of health disadvantage implies that public health needs to be concerned with economic inequalities. Our finding that there are spatial dimensions to these disadvantages further suggests that area-based initiatives need not be futile. But they will not be a panacea, if individual inequality is neglected.

REFERENCES

Social Exclusion Unit (1998) *Bringing Britain Together: A National Strategy for Neighbourhood Renewal*. London: The Stationery Office.

Sundquist, J. and Johansson, S.E. (1997) Self reported poor health and low educational level predictors for mortality: a population based follow up study of 39, 156 people in Sweden, *Journal of Epidemiology and Community Health*, 51: 35–40.

Townsend, P., Phillimore, P. and Beattie, A. (1988) *Health and Deprivation: Inequality and the North*. London: Routledge.

Wallace, M. and Denham, C. (1996) *The ONS Classification of Local and Health Authorities of Great Britain*. London: The Stationery Office.

Watson, D. and Pennebaker, J. (1989) Health complaints, stress and distress: exploring the central role of negative affectivity, *Psychological Review*, 96: 234–54.

Zigmond, A. and Snaith, R. (1976) The Hospital Anxiety and Depression Scale, *Acta Psychiatrica Scaninavica*, 67: 361–87.

Blane, D., Mitchell, R. and Bartley, M. (in press) The 'Inverse Housing Law' and respiratory health, *Journal of Epidemiology and Community Health*.

Champion, A. and Townsend, A. (1990) *Contemporary Britain: A Geographical Perspective*. London: Edward Arnold.

Charlton, J. and Wallace, M. (1994) Long-term illness: results from the 1991 Census, *Population Trends*, Spring: 18–25.

Cheung, K.C., Keeves, J.P., Sellin, N. and Tsoi, S.C. (eds) (1990) The analysis of multilevel data in educational research: studies of problems and their solutions, *International Journal of Educational Research*, 14: 215–319.

Cox, B.D., Blaxter, M. and Buckle, A.L.J. *et al.* (1987) *The Health and Lifestyle Survey*. London: Health Promotion Trust.

Duncan, D., Jones, K. and Moon, G. (1996) Health related behaviour in context: a multilevel approach, *Social Science and Medicine*, 42(6): 817–30.

Goldstein, H. (1997) *Multilevel Models in Educational and Social Research*. London: Charles Griffin & Co. Ltd.

Gordon, D. and Pantazis, C. (1997) *Breadline Britain in the 1990s*. Aldershot: Ashgate.

Hattersley, L. and Creeser, R. (1995) *Longitudinal Study 1971–1991: History, Organisation and Quality of Data*. London: HMSO.

Langford, I.H. and Bentham, G. (1996) Regional variations in mortality rates in England and Wales: an analysis using multilevel modelling, *Social Science and Medicine*, 42: 897–908.

Macintyre, S. and Ellaway, A. (1998) Ecological approaches: rediscovering the role of the physical and social environment, in L. Berkman and I. Kawachi (eds) *Social Epidemiology*. Oxford: Oxford University Press.

Macintyre, S., MacIvers, S. and Sooman, A. (1993) Area, class and health: should we be focusing on places or people? *Journal of Social Policy*, 22: 213–34.

Mitchell, R., Gleave, S., Bartley, M., Wiggins, R.D. and Joshi, H. (2000) Do attitude and area influence health? *Health and Place*, 6: 67–79.

Phillimore, P., Beattie, A. and Townsend, P. (1994) Widening inequality of health in Northern England, 1981–91, *British Medical Journal*, 308(6937): 1125–8.

Portes, A. and Landolt, P. (1996) The downside of social capital, *The American Prospect*, 26: 18–21.

Putnam, R. (1995) The strange disappearance of civic America, *The American Prospect*, 24(Winter).

Shouls, A., Congdon, P. and Curtis, S. (1996) Modelling inequality in reported long term illness: combining individual and area characteristics, *Journal of Epidemiology and Community Health*, 50(3): 366–76.

Sloggett, A. and Joshi, H. (1994) Higher mortality in deprived areas: community or personal disadvantage? *British Medical Journal*, 309(6967): 1470–4.

Sloggett, A. and Joshi, H. (1998a) Deprivation indicators as predictors of life events, 1981–1992, *Journal of Epidemiology and Community Health*, 52(4): 228–33.

Sloggett, A. and Joshi, H. (1998b) Indicators of deprivation in people and places: longitudinal perspectives, *Environment and Planning A*, 30(6): 1055–76.

Smith G.R. (1999) *Area Based Initiatives: The Rationale for and Options for Area Targeting*, CASEpaper 25. London: London School of Economics.

Sooman, A., Macintyre, S. and Anderson, A. (1993) Scotland's health – a more difficult challenge for some? The price and availability of healthy foods in socially contrasting localities in the West of Scotland, *Health Bulletin*, 51(5): 276–84.

Wallace, M. and Denham, C. (1996) *The ONS Classification of Local and Health Authorities of Great Britain*. London: HMSO.

Wiggins, R.D., Bartley, M. and Gleave, S. *et al.* (1998) Limiting long-term illness: a question of where you live or who you are? A multilevel analysis of the 1971–1991 ONS Longitudinal Study, *Risk, Decision and Policy*, 3(3): 181–98.

Wiggins, R.D., Gleave, S. and Bartley, M. *et al.* (1999) Health, area and the individual: a multilevel analysis of reporting a limiting long-term illness for men and women in the ONS Longitudinal Study of England and Wales. Paper presented at Royal Statistical Society Conference on Risk, University of Warwick, July.

Willms, J.D. and Patterson, L. (1995). A multilevel model for community aggregation, *Journal of Mathematical Sociology*, 20(1): 23–40.

Source: H. Joshi, R. D. Wiggins, M. Bartley, R. Mitchell, S. Gleave and K. Lynch, 'Putting health inequalities on the map: does where you live matter, and why?', in H. Graham (ed.) *Understanding Health Inequalities* (Buckingham: Open University Press, 2000), pp. 143–55.

Study Questions and Activities

1. With reference to the community in which you live, make some notes on key environmental features such as housing, leisure facilities, transport and schooling. How far does this environment facilitate, or impede, the achievement of good health?
2. The authors of this reading make a distinction between 'composition' and 'context'; how can an understanding of these influence health practice?
3. In what ways can individual social exclusion directly influence health?
4. How would you set about improving the health of an economically disadvantaged patient or client living in a poor neighbourhood?

Further Reading

The piece you have read here can be found in Hilary Graham's *Understanding Health Inequalities* (Buckingham: Open University Press, 2000). You may find some of the other chapters within this book useful, in particular: S. Macintyre, R. Hiscock, A. Kearns and A. Ellaway, 'Housing tenure and health inequalities: a three dimensional perspective on people, homes and neighbourhoods' and A. Gatrell, C. Thomas, S. Bennett, L. Bostock, J. Popay, G. Williams and S. Shahtahmasebi, 'Understanding health inequalities locating people in geographical and social spaces'. Further discussions of compositional and contextual effects on health can be found in S. Curtis and I. R. Jones, 'Is there a place for geography in the analysis of health inequality?', *Sociology of Health & Illness*, 20:5 (1998) 645–72. The relationship between geography, social capital and health inequalities can be explored in J. Mohan, L. Twigga, S. Barnard, and K. Jones, 'Social capital, geography and health: a small-area analysis for England', *Social Science and Medicine*, 60:6 (2005) 267–1283. In this, the authors argue that whilst much has been made of the relationship between geography and social capital as a determinant of health inequalities, little evidence can be found to support this assertion. Another interesting article is that written by Morrow in 2000 that examines young people's views on community and neighbourhood: V. M. Morrow, "Dirty looks' and 'trampy places' in young people's accounts of community and neighbourhood: implications for health inequalities', *Critical Public Health*, 10:2 (2000) 141–53. Here, Morrow argues that environments can both support and exclude young people and that age must be considered in any analysis of environment and health inequality.

Children Reflecting on Health

Kathryn Backett-Milburn, Sarah Cunningham-Burley and John Davis

Epidemiological studies have highlighted the importance of poverty and social exclusion in determining patterns of health and illness in children and families. For example, low birth weight – which is associated with higher levels of morbidity and mortality – is more prevalent in babies born to fathers in manual, rather than non-manual, occupations. Children's health is important, not just for its own sake but because health and health behaviours in childhood are thought to continue into adult life. However, attention is seldom given to children's own voices and experiences, with most knowledge about children's health being derived from parents and other adults. In this reading, Kathryn Backett-Milburn, Sarah Cunningham-Burley and John Davis report on the findings from a qualitative study examining the social and cultural context of children's lifestyles and inequalities in health. This study was based on semi-structured interviews with 35 boys and girls, aged 9–12 years, living in two contrasting areas in a Scottish city – one relatively advantaged, the other relatively disadvantaged. Thirty of their parents were also interviewed and community profiling and observations were undertaken. Many children rejected straightforward explanations for illness, demonstrating considerable understanding of the interplay between the factors that influence health. They also showed how familial and personal challenges – such as experiences of bullying and divorce – cut across material and structural difference.

BACKGROUND

It is increasingly recognised that children's socioeconomic, cultural and familial circumstances and experiences are part of the pathways implicated in health and illness in adulthood (Graham, 1997; Wadsworth, 1997). Quantitative analyses in the UK suggest many linkages between social class in childhood and subsequent patterns of adult mortality (Davey Smith, Hart, Blane, & Hole, 1998; Brunner, Shipley, Blane, Davey Smith, & Marmot, 1999; Blane & Montgomery, 2000), though such findings are inevitably bounded by the health concerns and theories of causation at the time of data collection (Razzell, Barker, & Braham, 2000). However, in all of this work, children's own voices are absent and adult-defined data about health and illness continue to be collected. Consequently, little is known about the social and cultural processes, in children's very different childhoods, which underpin and ultimately constitute these epidemiological findings.

Over the past decade there has been renewed emphasis on poverty as a relative concept and further evidence has accumulated regarding the adverse effects of child poverty on future health and well-being (Shaw, Dorling, Gordon, & Davey Smith, 1999; Gordon et al., 2000). This, alongside findings on the relationship between adolescent health and lifestyles and their perceptions of their futures (West & Sweeting, 1996), supports the importance of exploring younger children's theorising of their structural position and its implications for health (Backett-Milburn & Cunningham-Burley, 2001). The mechanisms involved in the reproduction of health inequalities are complex and continue to be debated (Graham, 2001). However, if childhood experience is indeed creating and recreating inequalities which affect health in adult life, clearly, understanding children's own perspectives and how they exercise agency in making sense of and recreating the health cultures in which they grow up are missing links.

Although the importance of lay theorising for understanding health relevant behaviour is now acknowledged (Backett & Davision, 1995; Milburn, 1996; Popay & Williams, 1996), the ways in which adults (let alone children) recognise and interpret health inequalities, and how these may impact on behaviour, has yet to be documented in any detail (Mielck, Backett-Milburn, & Pavis, 1998; Blaxter, 1997). Moreover, there are few studies which examine the extent to which children exercise agency over health-relevant issues and how their choices in these respects are influenced by parents and other adults (Kalnins, McQueen, Backett, Curtice, & Currie, 1992; Mayall, 1998). Research using the 'Draw and Write' technique has provided insights into children's perspectives on health and illness (Williams, Wetton, & Moon, 1989; Oakley, Bendelow, Barnes, Buchanan, & Hussain, 1995; Pridmore & Bendelow, 1995). However, such work has been conducted mostly in the school setting (Backett-Milburn & McKie, 1999); studies have only recently focussed on how children perceive, manage and negotiate everyday health relevant behaviours in other contexts such as their homes or neighbourhoods (Backett & Alexander, 1991; Mayall, 1994, 1998; Hood, Kelley, Mayall, & Oakley, 1996; Valentine, 1997; Dixey, 1998, 1999; Harden, 2000). Although medical sociologists and anthropologists have conducted insightful research with children on health-relevant issues (James, 1993; Mayall, 1998; Christensen, 1999; Morrow, 2000; Prout, 2000), many of these studies have taken health inequalities as the background to rather than the focus of understanding children's perspectives. In order to understand the origins of survival, resistance and salutogenesis, as well as the reproduction of health inequalities, it is important to explore children's own perceptions of differentiated experience.

This limited research base exists despite the considerable growth in the social study of childhood during the 1990s. Here there has been a focus on children as active agents which acknowledges that both childhood and health are social constructions and, as such, are dynamic, contested and negotiated realities (Mayall, 1994). This has resulted in studies developing child-appropriate research techniques which try to move away from what may be termed more 'adultist' approaches. In essence this means acknowledging that children are social actors in their own right and not simply the passive recipients of adult socialisation; and understanding how they make sense of their lives with and alongside adults and in their own social worlds of childhood (Mayall, 1998; Christensen & James, 2000). Moreover, in addressing health inequalities, such an approach emphasises the importance of paying attention to children's *present time* quality of life and of not simply being driven by perspectives which prioritise them as future citizens (Qvortrup, 1994).

These issues, alongside an increasing policy and public health interest in children's rights and perspectives (Morrow & Richards, 1996), shaped the development of a recently completed qualitative study carried out in Scotland (Backett-Milburn & Cunningham-Burley, 2001). This study aimed to illuminate children's everyday experience of inequalities and the production of health inequalities through qualitative research with boys and girls in the latter years of primary school and their parents....

CHILDREN, HEALTH AND INEQUALITIES

...

As with adults, children drew on both abstract and experientially based knowledge, but often faltered in linking the two. Their abstract knowledge about inequalities and health often related to experience very distant from their own, such as talking about the effects of poverty in Africa; or, occasionally, to observation or guesses about homeless people or those living in one of the stereotypically poor areas of their city. However, it was evident that, with few exceptions, the children in the more affluent area could *only* relate to health, health relevant behaviours, inequalities and poor areas in such abstract terms. For instance, 'sometimes if they don't have much money, sometimes maybe parents feel better smoking or drugs and alcohol' (Eleanor); and, thinking about an area she had driven through which she described as 'tatty' and 'none of my friends live there', Kirsten explained that, 'you think that people might be like drinking or taking drugs—cos it gives them a kind of boost'. In contrast, children living in the less affluent area described encounters with a nearby 'unsafe' area and its residents and spoke of parts of their area which they were not allowed to go to. Laura said she would like to make her area better 'cos people get spray paint an they draw over the walls and em, there's loads y like teenagers up here and some a them take drugs an that'.

When asked hypothetical questions about health and illness, all of the children tended to rehearse individually based health promotion messages, such as smoking is bad for you; exercise is good for you; eating the wrong foods makes you fat; or sweets damage your teeth. However, the ways in which they made sense of such knowledge might be contradictory. Some children from both areas, for example, expressed a fairly sympathetic appraisal of why people in poverty might indulge in potentially health damaging behaviour; others said that parents should look after their children, making sure they did not allow these things to happen; and yet others put forward both of these structural and individually based interpretations. So, children, like adults, struggled with linking causes and effects of health inequalities. In addition, children often indicated that it was not appropriate to make generalised statements. For example, many challenged the notion that children today were unfit, a proposition given to them by the interviewer as a popular media message. Most children reported being physically active, whether or not they were involved in organised sport and exercise, and, as Deirdra from the less affluent area said:

> When I go out to play we get a game eh like stuff outside. And that's like running and stuff, you know like. You would, you'd get more chance because you can, there's loads of space and you can run about. (less affluent area)

A much more nuanced understanding of the children's perspectives and experiences of health and illness came from embedding questions within their own everyday lives. As indicated earlier, the children were uncomfortable with abstract questions and more expansive when talking about their own concerns. Again, the ways in which they talked about health and illness tended to be grounded in social and family relationships, and emotional upsets. Many children speculated that bad experiences in childhood, involving illness or social or physical issues, could, mainly through psychological effects, result in future ill health. Often such future scenarios were described in quite dramatic terms, for example Jocelin said:

> I think that you could be ill like with upset and you can be because like if you were really upset about something you can just like sulk for ages and it can make you quite ill. And if you don't eat anything and drink then you can die from that. (more affluent area).

Similarly, following the interviewer's probe after Eve had mentioned that adults get depression, she said, '*Well they get upset and don't communicate. Just run away, explode. Not explode, but sort of don't know how to explain it*' (less affluent area). Another girl, Keri, said she thought that from her own observations of a friend, too much parental control (such as being over-protective or making a child go to church) could have long-term effects on children's well being in that, '*they might be scared all their lives*' or that '*it could affect anybody, you could get broken hearted and you could go mad*'. But when the interviewer probed for any future effects as an adult she replied, '*Nah, because you'll be grown up and you'll know not do it to your child*' (less affluent area).

Experientially based knowledge was, of course, easier for the children to talk about but here their knowledge appeared to be limited by that experience or their willingness to talk about it. Only a few mentioned any illness or accidents that they had themselves experienced. Moreover, whilst parents told us about a child having witnessed say an illness episode with an elderly relative, having to visit a grandparent with dementia, or the parent him/herself having to go into hospital, their children tended not to mention these experiences. Thus, with a few exceptions, even when questioned more directly about such issues, it was hard to know if many of these children had direct knowledge of ill health in their friends or their families, far less what sense they made of this for themselves or to use as information to make a wider point about health, illness and inequality. For several children, when specifically asked to explain death or illness in adults, the response was in terms of 'old age'.

However, although the children rarely discussed physical health or ill-health, they did talk about adult stress. Several, from both areas, described stress symptoms which they had observed in their parents; sometimes indicating how they tried to help them in various ways; sometimes simply expressing worries about what they had witnessed. Such accounts and the ways children spoke about other health relevant issues suggested that most of these children embraced a sense that parents and children had some responsibility for their own and each other's health. Most of the children's interviews also showed considerable awareness of the multi-factoral nature of illness as well as the diversity of its experience. Their accounts and understandings were nuanced and qualified. So, although most tended to claim that individuals had responsibility for their own good health and, moreover, that parents should look after their children in these respects, this was matched with an unwillingness to blame, especially when discussing people they knew. For example, one boy discussed, as follows, eating the wrong foods as causing fatness but said that this was not the case for the fat boy in his class:

JD: But this issue about children not being fit. Do you have any views?

Adrian: Well there's certainly quite a lot of people look like flab in my class.

JD: And why are they like that do you think?

Adrian: I don't know like. But there's one boy in my class who's really just sort of taken it on from like his parents. He's sort of just inherited like a gene or something, not cause he eats, it's just

JD: The way they look.

Adrian: Yeah it's just the way he is basically.

JD: And then are there some children who it's to do with what they eat and?

Adrian: I don't really think it is to do with what they eat. I think they just sort of are like that. (more affluent area)

Just as the children talked about inequalities in terms of relationships, so they also made links between relationships and health or well-being both in the present and future. For instance, when asked about the short and long-term effects of bullying most described the immediate emotional and physical consequences, such as not wanting to go out to play. Many children further stressed that access to emotional resources and support was as important as access to material resources. In these respects parents' care was viewed as important and protective (though occasionally overprotective!), and the lack of good care detrimental to health. To explain these views children frequently cited example of the difference between good parents and bad parents; in this there was no great difference between the children from the two social groupings. They all said that having a good parent involved: being cared for and looked after; being given the opportunity to make choices and enter in to dialogue; and being listened to. For them, a bad parent was one who smacked, shouted, and ignored or neglected children.

These accounts of their everyday experiences and observations involved many children speaking about how they came to terms with or developed resilience to unfairness and inequalities in relationships and the impact these might have on their health and well-being. For example, they suggested that with the support of friends or by developing their own resilience they could prevent life events and experiences from adversely affecting their sense of self and future health. This did not mean that children were unaware of social and material inequalities and unfairnesses, rather that they appeared to cushion the blow by thinking to themselves, 'it doesn't really affect me that much'. For instance, David, whose parents were unemployed and had moved around a lot, suggested that structural pressures, like changing towns and schools frequently, were not always negative and that you got used to it, explaining that:

Well in a way I've found it quite annoying because we've never been secure and had loads of friends in the one place. But in a way I found it quite reassuring that I've found out about all these places and I know about them a little bit and I know what kind of people are there. (less affluent area)

Parents from both areas who had experienced or had direct contact with poverty had no doubts about its effects on health. A mother from the less affluent area said about being on Family Credit (UK government support for families on low incomes), '*I think it affects your health, definitely mental health, good grief yeah*' (Natasha's mum). Another from the more affluent area spoke graphically of her own experiences of going to school in one of the poorer areas of the city explaining that, '*two of my classmates died while I was at school. Partly, you know, just simply because of where they were living and the social conditions*' (George's mum). Similarly, although many more affluent parents expressed concerns that their children would not become snobbish and should appreciate their privilege, some describing themselves as having had working class backgrounds, they acknowledged that their childrens' present lives and future health and prospects were protected by material and social advantage. For example, one respondent pointed out that her son would never feel he had to face adversity and '*fight for things*' (Adrian's mum) and another commented that:

> I don't think Robin or I would recognise poverty if it hit us in the face. We sometimes overspend on our disposable income, but that's not the same as being skint. That's poverty. (Robin's mum, residence less affluent area, child at private school in affluent area)

Like their children, parents' views of the causes of health and illness were multi-faceted. Many spoke of health, health behaviours and illness as being mediated through social attitudes and psychological well-being. Parents from both areas often stated that it was not money per se that made a difference to health and well-being but how people chose to spend it, which was a matter of values and attitudes. For some wealth was not seen as necessarily health protective and they justified this with personal examples of poor health and well-being amongst the better-off.

Finally, it was evident from both parents' and children's interviews that only a minority of children actively experienced both wealthier and poorer areas and a wide range of poverty and wealth. For instance, although one of the schools in the less affluent area had pupils from very poor areas and greater school-based opportunities for social contact occurred, most children and parents described putting boundaries against going to those areas, which were not considered safe. Only one boy in the more affluent area described direct knowledge of a poor area in another city where his father now lived. The state schools previously attended by some of the private school children were in predominantly middle class catchment areas. Furthermore, when parents spoke about people living in contrasting areas some of their broader views about the promotion of good health and protections of priviledge became more evident. For instance, many parents in the affluent area considered that their better material circumstances promoted quality of life, well-being and a better environment for their children, such as pleasant spacious homes and extensive play facilities. Thus, the parents' interviews echoed those of their children in indicating that, with a few exceptions, the out of school experience of the majority of the children in the sample as a whole of health, wealth, poverty and inequalities was spatially and socially relative, bounded by area or parental control/facilitation of friendships.

REFERENCES

Backett, K., & Alexander, H. (1991). Talking to young children about health: Methods and findings. *Health Education Journal, 11*, 2–24.

Backett, K., & Davison, C. (1995). Lifestyle and lifecourse: The social and cultural location of health behaviours. *Social Science & Medicine, 40*, 629–638.

Backett-Milburn, K., & Cunningham-Burley, S. (2001). *The socio-economic and cultural contexts of children's lifestyles and the everyday production of health variations*. ESRC Health Variations Programme Phase 2, Final Report. Swindon: ESRC.

Backett-Milburn, K., & McKie, L. (1999). A critical appraisal of the Draw and Write technique. *Health Education Research: Theory and Practice, 14,* 387–398.

Blane, D., & Montgomery, S. (2000). Workplace factors within a lifecourse perspective and their influence on health in early old age. *Paper presented to the Eighth ESRC Health Variations Programme Meeting.* Lancaster House Hotel, Lancaster: ESRC, September 25/26.

Blaxter, M. (1997). Whose fault is it? People's own conceptions of the reasons for health inequalities. *Social Science & Medicine, 44,* 747–756.

Brunner, E., Shipley, M. J., Blane, D., Davey Smith, G., & Marmot, M. G. (1999). When does cardiovascular risk start? Past and present socio-economic circumstances and risk factors in adulthood. *Journal of Epidemiology and Community Health, 53,* 757–764.

Christensen, P. H. (1999). 'It Hurts': Children's cultural learning about everyday illness. *Etnofoor, 12,* 39–52.

Christensen, P., & James, A. (Eds). (2000). *Research with children: Perspectives and practices.* London, New York: Falmer Press.

Davey Smith, G., Hart, C., Blane, D., & Hole, D. (1998). Adverse socioeconomic conditions in childhood and cause specific adult mortality: Prospective observational study. *British Medical Journal, 316,* 1631–1635.

Dixey, R. (1998). Improvements in child pedestrian safety: Have they been gained at the expense of other health goals? *Health Education Journal, 57,* 60–69.

Dixey, R. (1999). Keeping children safe: The effect on parents' daily lives and psychological well-being. *Journal of Health Psychology, 4*(1), 45–57.

Gordon, D., et al. (2000). *Poverty and social exclusion in Britain.* York: Joseph Rowntree Foundation.

Graham, H. (1997). *Risking and protecting health in poverty.* Paper presented to Edinburgh Health Research Group, University of Edinburgh, May 12. Edinburgh: Research Unit in Health and Behavioral Change.

Graham, H. (Ed.). (2001). *Understanding health inequalities.* Buckingham: Open University Press.

Hood, S., Kelley, P., Mayall, B., & Oakley, A. (1996). *Children parents and risk.* London: Social Science Research Unit, Institute of Education.

James, A. (1993). *Childhood identities: self and social relationships in the experience of the child.* Edinburgh: Edinburgh University Press.

Kalnins, I., McQueen, D. V., Backett, K. C., Curtice, L., & Currie, C. E. (1992). Children, empowerment and health promotion: Some new directions in research and practice. *Health Promotion International, 7,* 53–59.

Mayall, B. (1994). *Negotiating health: primary school children at home and school.* London: Cassell.

Mayall, B. (1998). Towards a sociology of child health. *Sociology of Health and Illness, 20,* 269–288.

Mielck, A, Backett-Milburn, K., & Pavis, S. (1998). *Perception of health inequalities in different social classes, by experts and laypersons, health professionals and health policy makers in Germany and the United Kingdom.* Review Report commissioned by Wissenschaftszentrum Berlin fur Socialforschuing, Reichpretschufer 50, Berlin.

Milburn, K. (1996). The importance of lay theorising for health promotion research and practice. *Health Promotion International, 11,* 41–46.

Morrow, V. (2000). 'Dirty looks' and 'trampy places' in young people's accounts of community and neighbourhood: Implications for health inequalities. *Critical Public Health, 10,* 141–152.

Morrow, V., & Richards, M. (1996). The ethics of social research with children: An overview. *Children and Society, 10,* 28–40.

Oakley, A., Bendelow, G., Barnes, J., Buchanan, M., & Hussain, O. A. (1995). Health and cancer prevention: Knowledge and beliefs of children and young people. *British Medical Journal, 310,* 1029–1033.

Popay, J., & Williams, G. (1996). Public health research and lay knowledge. *Social Science and Medicine, 42,* 759–768.

Pridmore, P., & Bendelow, G. (1995). Images of health: Exploring beliefs of children using the 'draw and write' technique. *Health Education Journal, 54,* 473–488.

Prout, A.(Ed). (2000). *The body, childhood and society.* Houndmills and London: Macmillan Press Ltd.

Qvortrup, J. (1994). Preface. In J. Qvortrup, M. Bardy, G. Sgritta, & H. Wintersberger (Eds.), *Childhood matters: Social theory, practice and politics.* Vienna: Avebury/European Centre.

Razzell, P.E., Barker, D., & Braham, P. (2000). *Unravelling the childhood determinants of adult health: A methodological pilot study.* Final report to ESRC. Swindon: ESRC.

Shaw, M., Dorling, D., Gordon, D., & Davey Smith, G. (1999). *The widening gap: health inequalities and policy in Britain.* Bristol: The Policy Press.

Valentine, G. (1997). 'Oh yes I can.' 'Oh no you can't': Children and parents' understandings of kids' competence to negotiate public space safely. *Antipode, 29,* 165–189.

Wadsworth, M E. J. (1997). Health inequalities in the life course perspective. *Social Science & Medicine, 44,* 850–869.

West, P., & Sweeting, H. (1996). Nae joy, nae future: Young people and health in the context of unemployment. *Health and Social Care in the Community, 4,* 50–62.

Williams, T., Wetton, N., Moon, A. (1989). *A picture of health: What do you do that makes you healthy and keeps you healthy?* Health Education Authority. London: HEA.

Source: K. Backett-Milburn, S. Cunningham-Burley and J. Davis, 'Contrasting lives, contrasting views? Understandings of health inequalities from children in differing social circumstances', *Social Science and Medicine,* 57 (2003) 613–23.

Study Questions and Activities

1. Reading 14 builds on a growing tradition of sociological (and other) research that seeks to give children a voice. In what ways can this principle be applied to your own professional practice? Has reading this piece encouraged you to relate differently to children and their parents/guardians?

2. Do you think that the similarities amongst children are more important than the differences between them?

3. Who is responsible for children's health? Make a list of these people and place them in order of those with the greatest, to the least, responsibility for children's health.

4. How would you define childhood? What is the difference between a child and a young person? At the other end of the age spectrum, what are the similarities and differences between an adult, an old person and an elderly person? How does age influence access to, and experiences of, healthcare?

––––––––––––––––––––––– **Further Reading** –––––––––––––––––––––––

For general sociological texts on children and childhood, consider reading one of the following: A. James and A. Prout (eds) *Constructing and Reconstructing Childhood: Contemporary Issues in the Sociological Study of Childhood*, (Falmer Press: London, 1997) or A. James and A. L. James, *Constructing Childhood: Theory, Policy and Social Practice* (Houndmills: Palgrave, 2004). Some sociologists have argued that the subject of children's health has been relatively neglected within the sociology of health and illness. However, if you are specifically interested in children's health, then the journals *Children's Health Care* and *Children and Society* may be of interest to you as they both carry relevant articles on the subject. Alternatively, this book has a more explicit focus on health: B. Mayall, *Children, Health and the Social Order* (Buckingham: Open University Press, 1966). Backett-Milburn et al. draw on children's own views – if you are especially interested in children's perspectives of health and illness, then either of the following would provide useful further reading: M. Hill, A. Laybourn, M. Borland and J. Secker, 'Promoting mental and emotional well-being: the perspectives of younger children', in D. R. Trent and C. A. Reed (eds) *Promotion of Mental Health, Vol. 5* (Aldershot: Avebury, 1997); J. Shucksmith and L. B. Hendry, *Growing Up and Speaking Out: Young People's Perceptions of Their Own Health Needs* (London: Routledge, 1998). In the Further Reading section of Reading 13, we suggested an article focusing on social capital, geography and health. With reference to the issues of children and social capital, you might like to look for: K. M. Ferguson, 'Social capital and children's wellbeing: a critical synthesis of the international social capital literature', *International Journal of Social Welfare*, 15:1 (2006) 2–18. In preparation for the remaining readings in this part of the book, find: J. L. Locher, C. S. Ritchie, D. L. Roth, P. S. Baker, E. V. Bodner and R. M. Allman, 'Social isolation, support, and capital and nutritional risk in an older sample: ethnic and gender differences', *Social Science & Medicine*, 60:4 (2005) 747–61.

Reading 15

Gender and Women's Health

Lesley Doyal

Many people would argue that one of the most fundamental inequalities in health is that which exists between women and men. However, whilst sex differences may account for some of these inequalities, feminist scholars would argue that gender – the socially constructed differences between women and men – is to blame for this. In this reading, Lesley Doyal provides an introduction to women's health and argues that gender has a profound effect on the health of both sexes. She discusses gendered differences in mortality and morbidity, showing that whilst women generally live longer than men, they experience much higher levels of illness, particularly in later life. In this reading, Doyal also calls for a rejection of crude universalism, that is, the idea that all women experience health similarly, pointing out how differences in class, ethnicity, sexuality and so on influence health. That said this reading also rejects theories of crude difference, suggesting that whilst there might be differences between women, there are also important commonalities in values, beliefs, interests and experience.

INTRODUCTION

There are obvious differences between male and female patterns of sickness and health. Not surprisingly, these stem in part from biological differences between the sexes. But as we shall see, the situation is more complex than might at first appear. All societies continue to be divided along the 'fault line' of gender and this too has a profound effect on the well-being of both men and women (Moore, 1988; Papanek, 1990).

Gender differences are especially significant for women, since they usually mean inequality and discrimination. Though female subordination can take many forms it is an extremely pervasive phenomenon, demonstrating 'both endless variety and monotonous similarity' (Rubin, 1975). This does not, of course, mean that all women are worse off in every way than all men. But it remains true that in most societies the male is valued more highly than the female. Men are usually dominant in the allocation of scarce resources and this structured inequality has a major impact on women's health.

Material discrimination against women has been extensively documented. World-wide, they do more work than men, yet their labour is seen to be of less value. Typically they receive about 30–40 per cent less pay than men if employed and no pay at all for most domestic work. They hold only 10–20 per cent of managerial and administrative jobs and are very poorly represented in the ranks of power, policy and decision making (United Nations, 1991, p. 6). As a result, many face major challenges in acquiring the material resources needed for a healthy life.

Cultural devaluation is also important, though more difficult to map. All social groups operate through a variety of discourses that naturalise gender differences and inequalities. Women have to create their identity – their sense of themselves – within the framework of these culturally constructed and sometimes conflicting definitions of womanhood (Martin, 1987; Ussher, 1989). They may be revered as mothers for instance, or as the guardians of morality, while also being regarded as 'sickly', neurotic, polluted or just fundamentally less valuable than men. The dominant message is that women are not just different, but physically, psychologically and socially inferior. In a world defined by and for men, women are 'the other' (de Beauvoir, 1972). Under these circumstances it is hardly surprising that many find it difficult to develop the feelings of competence and self-worth associated with positive mental health.

However these similarities do not mean that women constitute a unified and homogeneous group. Though they share a gender identity and a common biology, women are differentiated by factors such as age, sexual preference, race, class and, very importantly, geopolitical status – the wealth or poverty of the country in which they live....

Rejecting Crude Universalism

During the last decade, women from many different constituencies – working-class women, lesbians, black women, women with disabilities and women from third world countries – have challenged the white, western, middle-class domination of feminist theory and practice (Humm, 1992, Ch. 5; Lovell, 1990; Segal, 1987; McDowell and Pringle, 1992). In particular they have been critical of those feminists who prioritise gender over other social divisions, representing all women as members of the same oppressed group, unified by their experience of male domination and their uniquely female emotionality. This political critique has been reinforced by a shift towards post-modernism in much feminist thinking. Women working in this tradition have emphasised the dangers of inaccurate and inappropriate generalisations, stressing instead, the importance of 'hearing many voices' (Barrett and Phillips, 1992; Braidotti *et al.*, 1994; Mohanty *et al.*, 1991; Nicholson, 1991).

In response to these arguments, many feminist writers are now placing much greater emphasis on the differences between women. Rejecting the ideas of 'universal sisterhood' that characterised much feminist thinking in the 1980s, they have begun to develop a more sophisticated understanding of the relationships between race, class and gender. The analysis contained in this book should be seen as a contribution to that process, with the social construction of health and sickness offering important examples of how such links are forged in concrete historical circumstances.

As we shall see, there are very marked inequalities in the health status of women from different classes and racial backgrounds and these will be explored in detail as the book progresses. However the greatest disparities are those that divide the majority of women in the developed countries from the majority of those living in what is often called the 'third world'. Though the diversity of social forms in 'third world' countries is immense, they are similar enough to generate comparable patterns of disease and death for the mass of their female populations. It is important therefore that we specify these common features, as well as defining the term 'third world' more precisely.

About two thirds of the world's women live in countries where per capita income is low and life expectancy relatively short, where the fertility rate continues to be high and a comparatively small percentage of the paid labour force is female, where class and gender inequalities in income and wealth continue to be very great and the state provides few health and welfare services. Though they are both culturally and materially heterogeneous most of these countries do share common experiences of colonialism and imperialism, which have resulted in varying degrees of subordination within the world economic system. Geographically they are located in the southern part of the globe in the Latin American, Caribbean, African, Asian and Pacific regions.

All the terms currently used to summarise the complex reality of these economic and social divisions are problematic. They tend inevitably towards over simplification – there are huge differences for instance, between the newly industrialising nations of Asia and Latin America and the majority of African countries. Such terms also have the potential to reinforce economic, cultural and ideological hierarchies (Mohanty, 1991). Yet it is difficult to avoid their use altogether. 'Third world' is probably the most frequently used and widely understood of currently available options (Mohanty, 1991, p. 75, note 1; Sen and Grown, 1988, p. 9, note 3). It also continues to be employed as an affirmative identification by many political activists around the world, and will therefore be used here (with care) to locate women's lives within a broader geopolitical context.

However we need to acknowledge that this categorisation of global reality into first and third worlds excludes those countries that used to be called 'second world' but are now 'post-communist' or 'desocialising'. A number of recent texts have made the lives of women in Central and Eastern Europe much more visible outside their own countries (Buckley, 1989; Corrin, 1992; Funk and Mueller, 1993). Though health has not been their major focus, most of these accounts imply that the rapid social changes now taking place in this part of the world have been detrimental to women's well-being....

Rejecting Crude Difference Theories

It is clear that women's lives vary enormously and recognition of this reality must remain at the heart of any analysis of their health and welfare. However this rejection of crude universalism does not mean that we should embrace crude difference instead – that we should deny any possibility of women having beliefs, values or interests in common.

A number of strands in contemporary women's studies contain within them the implication of radical difference, the belief that we cannot make meaningful judgements about the relative situations of women in different cultures. For some, this relativism reflects a political commitment to the acceptance of all 'other' cultural beliefs and practices. To do otherwise is said to denigrate those who live their lives in accordance with values that are different from our own. In the context of women's health, this can mean a refusal to engage with the hazards of procedures such as genital mutilation because they are defined as 'traditional' practices. It has also led in some instances to a reluctance to condemn male violence in cultures where it is widely condoned.

Similar tendencies are evident in the work of some post-modernist writers (Maynard and Purvis, 1994; Nicholson, 1991). Their rejection of any universal criteria for determing what is right or wrong, good or bad, real or unreal, implies that the situations of women in different cultures cannot be compared in any meaningful way. Thus even 'worse' or 'better' health cannot be measured, except perhaps by the crudest measure of all – survival. According to some writers even the category 'woman' is itself so culturally variable – so discourse – specific – that it is not a useful category for social analysis. Thus the very project of feminism is called into question as women are seen to have radically different interests.

This has led in some parts of the world to a political paralysis that is becoming increasingly intolerable (Maynard and Purvis, 1994; Ramazanoglou, 1993). Despite their undoubted heterogeneity, women do have important things in common. All share broadly similar bodily experiences, even though the meanings they attach to them may vary dramatically (Martin, 1987). Their bodies are not merely social constructs as some post-modernist writers seem to imply (Haraway, 1991). Nor are they infinitely malleable. Bodies do impose very real (though varying) constraints on women's lives as well as offering enormous potential, and this is evidenced by the fact that the fight for bodily self-determination has been a central feature of feminist politics across very different cultures (Jacobus *et al.*, 1990; Lupton, 1994, Ch. 2; Morgan and Scott, 1993; Pringle, 1992).

Women also share the reality of occupying (more or less) subordinate positions in most social and cultural contexts. Though this subordination is linked in complex ways with divisions of race, class and nationality, women do have common experiences as the objects of sexist practices. Some of these are psychological, as women struggle to construct their sense of themselves in the face of cultural messages about their intrinsic 'otherness' and inferiority. However they also have a material dimension as women deal with the consequences of poverty and economic inequality between the sexes. Again, women in very different cultures have identified similar processes of gender discrimination as powerful obstacles to their achievement of both mental and physical well-being.

As we shall see, it is a common recognition both of their need for control over their own bodies, and of the social origins of many of their health problems, that has led many women into political action. Physical and mental health are universal and basic human needs and all women have an equal right to their satisfaction....

A PICTURE OF HEALTH?

All women whose physical or mental health is damaged will therefore be harmed in broadly similar ways, and morbidity and mortality rates can give us a preliminary indication of the global distribution of this harm. Of course such statistics can provide only a partial picture since they are not measuring the subjective or experiential aspects of illness. Moreover they offer a negative view of sickness and death rather than a positive picture of well-being. However they do represent important points of reference between societies and social groups as well as offering clues to structural factors underlying any perceived inequalities.

Inequalities in Mortality

In most of the developed countries women can now expect to survive for about 75 years (United Nations, 1991, p. 55). However this average conceals significant variations in life expectancy between women in different social groups. In Britain women married to men in semiskilled or unskilled jobs are about 70 per cent more likely to die prematurely than those whose husbands are professionals (OPCS, 1986). Similar social divisions are apparent in the United States, where black women now have a life expectancy of 73.5 years compared with 79.2 for white women while their risk of dying in pregnancy or childbirth is three and a half times greater (US National Institutes of Health, 1992, pp. 8, 13). In most underdeveloped countries the social inequalities in health are even more dramatic.

There are also major differences in mortality rates between rich and poor nations. In Latin America and the Caribbean average life expectancy is lower than in developed countries but still relatively high at around 70. In Asia and the Pacific it is 64 and in Africa as low as 54 (UN, 1991, p. 55). The lowest rates recorded for individual countries are in Afghanistan, East Timor, Ethiopia and Sierra Leone, where women can expect to live for only about 43 years (ibid.) These inequalities are at their most extreme in deaths related to childbearing. In developed countries mortality of this kind is rare, with less than five deaths for every 100 000 live births. In South Asian countries, on the other hand, the rate is more than 650 deaths per 100 000 with the African average a close second at around 600 deaths (UN, 1991, p. 56).

Though these figures are extremely dramatic they do not show the true extent of the inequalities in reproductive hazards facing women in different parts of the world. The maternal mortality rate reflects the risk a woman runs in each pregnancy. However we also need to examine fertility rates to assess the lifetime risk to an individual woman of dying of pregnancy-related causes. Recent estimates suggest that for a woman in Africa this risk is 1 in 23 compared with only 1 in 10 000 in developed countries (Rooney, 1992). Pregnancy causes almost no deaths among women of reproductive age in developed countries but between a quarter and a third of deaths elsewhere (Fortney *et al.*, 1986). Reproductive deaths are therefore an important indicator both of the different health hazards facing men and women and also of the heterogeneity of women's own experiences.

Turning from mortality to morbidity statistics – from death to disease – we are immediately faced with what appears to be a paradox. Around the world, women usually live longer than men in the same socio-economic circumstances. In most of the developed countries the gap between male and female life expectancy is about 6.5 years (UN, 1991, p. 55). In Latin America and the Caribbean it is 5.0 years, in Africa 3.5 years and in Asia and the Pacific, 3.0 years (ibid.) Only in a few countries in Asia do women have a lower life expectancy than men. Yet despite their generally greater longevity, women in most communities report more illness and distress. This pattern of excess female morbidity is reasonably well documented in the developed countries and we examine that evidence first. The more limited information on women in third world countries will be considered later.

Sickness and Affluence

A number of studies in the United Kingdom have found that women's own assessment of their health is consistently worse than that of men (Blaxter, 1990; Whitehead, 1988). Similar findings have emerged from studies in the United States (Rodin and Ickovics, 1990; Verbrugge, 1986). US women are 25 per cent more likely than men to report that their activities are restricted by health problems and they are bedridden for 35 per cent more days than men because of acute conditions (US National Institutes of Health, 1992, p. 9). In community surveys throughout the developed world, women report about twice as much anxiety and depression as men (Paykel, 1991; Weissman and Klerman, 1977).

Women also use most medical services more often. This fact cannot be taken as a straightforward indicator of the relative well-being of the two sexes since admitting illness may well be more acceptable for women than for men. However it does highlight certain important features of women's health status. The most immediate reason for their greater use of medical care is longevity. Deteriorating health and increasing disability are a frequent, though not inevitable accompaniment of the ageing process and women make up a large proportion of the elderly in the population – especially the 'old old' (Doty, 1987). In the United States 72 per cent of those over 85 are female (US National Institutes of Health, 1992, p. 8). Older women appear to receive less assistance from relatives and friends than older men of the same age, despite the fact that they suffer higher rates of certain disabling diseases, including arthritis, Alzheimer's Disease, osteoporosis and diabetes (Heikkinen *et al.*, 1983; Verbrugge, 1985).

Because of the incorporation of birth control and birthing itself into the orbit of doctors, younger women too make more use of medical services. This is not usually associated with organic pathology but reflects the growing role of medicine in the management of the 'normal' process of pregnancy and childbirth (or its prevention). Women also appear to experience more problems with their reproductive systems than men, and again this is likely to bring them into more frequent contact with the formal healthcare system.

Finally, evidence from across the developed world suggests that more women than men consult doctors about psychological and emotional distress. In the United Kingdom, female consultation rates with general practitioners for depression and anxiety are three times and nearly two and a half times, respectively, those of males (Office of Health Economics, 1987; UK Royal College of Practitioners, 1986). Over the course of a year one British woman in every twenty aged between 25 and 74 seeks help for emotional problems from her GP, compared with one in fifty men. There is also evidence from a range of countries that women are at least twice as likely as men to be prescribed mild tranquillisers (Ashton, 1991; Balter *et al.*, 1984).

Broadly speaking then, the picture in the developed countries is one where women live longer than men but appear 'sicker' and suffer more disability. They are ill more often than men and use more medical services. Men do not suffer such frequent illness though their health problems are more often life-threatening. But sex and gender are not the only factors influencing women's health status, as we can see if we look again at the differences between women themselves.

Even within developed countries there are major variations in the health of women in different social groups. In the United States, strokes occur twice as often in black women as in white women, and they have the highest incidence of gonorrhoea and syphilis (US National Institutes of Health, 1992, p. 13). Though black women have a lower incidence of breast cancer than white women it is significant that they are more likely to die from it (ibid.) In the United Kingdom women in the lowest social class are much more likely to experience chronic illness than their more affluent counterparts. In a national survey 46 per cent of unskilled and semi-skilled women aged between 45 and 64 reported a long-standing illness compared with 34 per cent of professional and managerial women (Bridgewood and Savage, 1993). Women in the lowest social groups were also more likely than those in the professional and managerial groups to report that illness limited their daily activities (30 per cent in comparison with 20 per cent) (ibid.)

Sickness and Poverty

However it is in the poorest countries that the state of women's health is at its worst. Though some affluent women are as healthy as those in the developed countries, it is clear that millions of others live in a state of chronic debility, afflicted by the diseases of poverty and the hazards of childbearing (Jacobson, 1992; Smyke, 1991). Estimates suggest that for every one of the half million women who die of pregnancy-related causes each year, at least 16 suffer long-term damage to their health – an annual total of about eight million (Royston and Armstrong, 1989, p. 187). Reproductive tract infections are also extremely common (International Women's Health Coalition, 1991). In some African countries gonorrhoea is estimated to affect as many as 40 per cent of women (WHO, 1992). These diseases are not just distressing and disabling in themselves, but often result in chronic infection with serious effects on women's overall well-being.

Millions of women in third world countries also have to cope with the broader health consequences of poverty – communicable diseases and undernutrition. While they risk contracting the same endemic diseases as men, both biological and social factors may increase their exposure or worsen the effects. Malaria, hepatitis and leprosy, for instance, can be especially dangerous during pregnancy, while women's responsibility for domestic tasks increases their chance of contracting water-borne diseases.

The extent of undernutrition in girls and women is dramatically documented in the incidence of anaemia. Estimates suggest that at least 44 per cent of all women in third world countries are anaemic compared with about 12 per cent in developed countries (WHO, 1992, p. 62). In India the figure is as high as 88 per cent (World Bank, 1993, p. 75). This is an important indicator of general health status, suggesting that many women are chronically debilitated, never reaching the levels of good health that most women in the first world take for granted.

In these conditions of poverty, deprivation and disruption, mental distress is clearly a major risk. Though there is little statistical evidence of its prevalence, most community surveys show a pattern similar to that of developed countries, with more women than men reporting feelings of anxiety and depression. However the pattern of treatment is very different, with many more men than women receiving psychiatric help (Paltiel, 1987). Indeed evidence from many third world countries suggests that women receive less medical treatment of all kinds than men, despite their greater need. Rural women in particular are often unable to gain access to modern services, even for obstetric care. Around 75 per cent of all births in South Asia and 62 per cent in Africa still take place without a trained health worker, compared with about 1 per cent in the developed countries (UN, 1991, p. 58). While this reflects very low levels of health spending overall, it also suggests a particular reluctance to invest in the health of women and girls.

Though female life expectancy continues to rise in most third world countries, the 'harsh decade' of the 1980s and the economic rigours of structural adjustment policies have meant deteriorating health for many women (Smyke, 1991; Vickers, 1991). The number of those who are malnourished has risen, resulting in an increased incidence of high-risk pregnancies and low birth-weight babies. Diseases of poverty such as tuberculosis are re-emerging while the so-called 'diseases of affluence' are beginning to proliferate, with cancer already one of the leading causes of death for women between the ages of 25 and 35. Environmental degradation has made many women's lives harder and millions are without access to clean water or sanitation. Yet fewer resources are available to care for them. In recent years a real decline in per capita health spending has been documented in three quarters of the nations in Africa and Latin America and women appear to have been the major losers (UNICEF, 1990)....

BIBLIOGRAPHY

Ashton, H. (1991) 'Psychotropic drug prescribing for women', *British Journal of Psychiatry*, vol. 158, supplement 10, pp. 30–5.

Balter, M., Manheimer, D., Mellinger, G. *et al.* (1984) 'A cross-national comparison of anti-anxiety/sedative drug use', *Current Medical Research and Opinion*, vol. 8 (supplement 4), pp. 5–18.

Barrett, M. and Phillips, A. (1992) *Destabilising Theory: contemporary feminist debates* (Cambridge: Polity Press).

Blaxter, M. (1990) *Health and Lifestyles* (London: Routledge).

Braidotti, R., Charkiewicz, E., Häusler, S. and Wieringa, S. (1994) *Women, the Environment and Sustainable Development: towards a theoretical synthesis* (London: Zed Press).

Bridgewood, A. and Savage, D. (1993) *General Household Survey 1991* (UK Office of Population Censuses and Surveys).

Buckley, M. (1989) *Women and Ideology in the Soviet Union* (Brighton: Harvester).

Corrin, C. (1992) *Superwomen and the Double Burden: women's experience of change in central and eastern Europe and the former Soviet Union* (London: Scarlet Press).

de Beauvoir, S. (1972) *The Second Sex* (ed.) H. M. Parshlay (Harmondsworth: Penguin) (first published 1949).

Doty, P. (1987) 'Health status and health services among older women: an international perspective', *World Health Statistics Quarterly*, vol. 40, pp. 279–90.

Fortney, J., Susanti, I., Gadalla, S., Saleh, S., Rogers, S. and Potts, M. (1986) 'Reproductive mortality in two developing countries', *American Journal of Public Health*, vol. 76, no. 2, pp. 134–8.

Funk, N. and Mueller, M. (eds) (1993) *Gender, Politics and Post Communism: reflections from Eastern Europe and the former Soviet Union* (London: Routledge).

Haraway, D. (1991) 'A manifesto for Cyborgs: science, technology and socialist feminism', in L. Nicholson (ed.) *Feminism/Post-Modernism* (London: Routledge).

Heikkinen, E., Waters, W. and Brzezinski, Z. (eds) (1983) *The Elderly in Eleven Countries – a socio medical survey* (Public Health in Europe no. 21) (Copenhagen: WHO Regional Office for Europe).

Humm, M. (ed.) (1992) *Feminisms: a reader* (Brighton: Harvester Wheatsheaf).

International Women's Health Coalition (1991) *Reproductive tract infections in women in the Third World: national and international policy implications* (New York: IWHC).

Jacobson, J. (1992) 'Women's health, the price of poverty', in M. Koblinsky, J. Timyan and J. Gay (eds) *The Health of Women: a global perspective* (Boulder, Co: Westview Press).

Jacobus, H., Keller, E. and Shuttleworth, S. (1990) *Body/Politics: women and the discourses of science* (London: Routledge).

Lovell, T. (1990) *British Feminist Thought: a reader* (Oxford: Basil Blackwell).

Lupton, D. (1994) *Medicine as Culture: illness, disease and the body in western societies* (Newbury Park, Ca: Sage).

Martin, E. (1987) *The Woman in the Body: a cultural analysis of reproduction* (Milton Keynes: Open University Press).

Maynard, M. and Purvis, J. (eds) (1994) *Redefining Women's Lives from a Feminist Perspective* (London: Taylor and Francis).

McDowell, L. and Pringle, R. (1992) *Defining Women* (Oxford: Polity Press).

Mohanty, C., Russo, A., and Torres, L. (1991) *Third World Women and the Politics of Feminism* (Bloomington and Indianapolis: Indiana University Press).

Moore, H. (1988) *Feminism and Anthropology* (Oxford: Polity Press).

Morgan, D. and Scott, S. (1993) 'Bodies in a social landscape', in S. Scott and D. Morgan (eds) *Body Matters, essays on the sociology of the body* (Brighton: Falmer Press).

Nicholson, L. (1991) 'Introduction', in L. Nicholson (ed.) *Feminism/Post Modernism* (London: Routledge).

Office of Health Economics (1987) *Women's Health Today* (London: OHE).

Office of Population Censuses and Surveys (OPCS) (1986) *Occupational Mortality: Decennial Supplement, England and Wales 1979–80* (London: HMSO).

Paltiel, F. (1987) 'Women and mental health: a post Nairobi perspective', *World Health Statistics Quarterly*, vol. 40, pp. 233–66.

Papanek, H. (1990) 'To each less than she needs, from each more than she can do: allocations, entitlements and value', in I. Tinker (ed.) *Persistent Inequalities: women and world development* (Oxford: Oxford University Press).

Paykel, E. (1991) 'Depression in women', *British Journal of Psychiatry*, vol. 158 (suppl. 10), pp. 22–9.

Pringle, R. (1992) 'Absolute sex? Unpacking the sexuality/gender relationship', in R. Connell and G. Dowsett (eds) *Rethinking Sex: social theory and sexuality research* (Melbourne: Melbourne University Press).

Ramazanoglou, C. (1993) *Up Against Foucault: explorations of some tensions between Foucault and feminism* (London: Routledge).

Rodin, J. and Ickovics, J. (1990) 'Women's health: review and research agenda as we approach the 21st century', *American Psychologist*, vol. 45, no. 9, pp. 1018–34.

Rooney, C. (1992) *Antenatal Care and Maternal Health: how effective is it?, A review of the evidence* (Geneva: WHO).

Royston, E. and Armstrong, S. (1989) *Preventing Maternal Deaths* (Geneva: World Health Organisation).

Rubin, G. (1975) 'The traffic in women: notes on the "political economy" of sex', in R. Reiter (ed.) *Toward an Anthropology of Women* (Boston: Monthly Review Press).

Segal, L. (1987) *Is the Future Female: troubled thoughts on contemporary feminism* (London: Virago).

Sen, G. and Grown, C. (1988) *Development, Crises and Alternative Visions* (London: Earthscan).

Smyke, P. (1991) *Women and Health* (London: Zed Press).

UK Royal College of General Practitioners (1986) *Morbidity Statistics from General Practice 1981–2 Third National Survey* (London: HMSO).

UNICEF (1990) *The State of the World's Children 1989* (Oxford: Oxford University Press).

United Nations (1991) 'The world's women 1970–1990: trends and statistics', *Social Statistics and Indicators*, Series, K, no. 8. (New York: UN).

United Nations Institute for the Advancement of Women (INSTRAW) (1991) 'Women, water and sanitation', in S. Sontheimer (ed.) *Women and the Environment, a Reader: crisis and development in the third world* (London: Earthscan).

United States National Institutes of Health (1992) *Opportunities for Research on Women's Health* (NIH Publication no. 92–3457) (Washington, DC: US Department of Health and Human Services).

Ussher, J. (1989) *The Psychology of the Female Body* (London: Routledge).

Verbrugge, L. (1985) 'An epidemiological profile of older women' in: M. Haug, A. Ford and M. Sheafor (eds) *The Physical and Mental Health of Older Women* (New York: Springer).

Verbrugge, L. (1986) 'From sneezes to adieux: stages of health for American men and women', *Social Science and Medicine* vol. 22, no. 11, pp. 1195–212.

Vickers, J. (1991) *Women and the World Economic Crisis* (London: Zed Press).

Weissman, M. and Klerman, G. (1977) 'Sex differences and the epidemiology of depression', *Archives of General Psychiatry*, vol. 24, pp. 98–111.

Whitehead, M. (1988) *The Health Divide: inequalities in health in the 1980s* (Harmonds-worth: Penguin).

World Bank (1993) *World Development Report 1993: investing in health* (Oxford: Oxford University Press).

World Health Organisation (1992) *Women's Health: across age and frontier* (Geneva: WHO).

Source: L. Doyal, *What Makes Women Sick: Gender and the Political Economy of Health* (Basingstoke: Basingstoke, 1995), pp. 1–26.

Study Questions and Activities

1. To what extent do you think that biology plays a role in gendered inequalities in health?
2. Lesley Doyal argues that 'gender differences are especially significant for women, since they usually mean inequality and discrimination'. Reflect on your own experiences of practice: in the light of this, do you agree with this statement?
3. In the context of healthcare provision, how useful is it to think of either women or men as homogenous groups?
4. If you would like to consider gender issues further now, turn to and read Reading 19 and attempt study question 2.

──────────────── **Further Reading** ────────────────

In the above reading, Lesley Doyal warns against crude universalism, emphasising the importance of differences between women. To explore the relationships between gender and ageing, read the following: S. Arber and J. Ginn, *Connecting Gender and Ageing: A Sociological Approach* (Buckingham: Open University Press, 1995). To explore sexuality and women's health, consider: P. Stern, *Lesbian Health: What are the Issues?* (Washington: Taylor & Francis, 1992) and to read about reproductive health, consider: S. Earle and G. Letherby (eds) *Gender, Identity and Reproduction: Social Perspectives* (Houndmills: Palgrave, 2003). If you are interested in gender and ethnicity, try: S. Loue, *Gender, Ethnicity, and Health Research* (Guildford: Kluwer Academic/Plenum Publishers, 1999). For more general literature on women's health, Jocelyn Cornwell's *Hard Earned Lives: Accounts of Health and Illness from East London* (London: Tavistock, 1984) is a fascinating read (also referred to in the Further Reading section of Reading 3) and E. Annandale and K. Hunt, *Gender, Inequality and Health* (Buckingham: Open University Press, 2000) is also useful. To consider men's health, the following texts are worth reading: M. Luck, M. Bamford and P. Williamson, *Men's Health: Perspectives, Diversity and Paradox* (Oxford: Blackwell Science, 2000) and J. Watson, *Male Bodies: Health, Culture and Identity*, (Buckingham: Open University Press, 2000). For a wider discussion of gender issues, see also: J. Marchbank and G. Letherby, *Introduction to Gender: Social Science Perspectives* (Harlow, Pearson, 2007).

Reading 16

Understanding Ethnic Inequalities in Health

Mel Bartley

This reading focuses on the problems of defining ethnicity and subsequent difficulties with measuring ethnic inequalities in health. Mel Bartley argues that ethnicity is defined in relation to differences in geographical origin, language and religion but that the definition and measurement of ethnicity varies across countries and over time (thus making comparisons quite difficult). In this reading, Bartley considers the merit of biological explanations for health, concluding that the notion of 'genetic homogeneity' is unlikely to account for ethnic inequalities. She also considers whether cultural diversity – differences in lifestyle, such as diet – can account for the disproportionate levels of mortality and morbidity experienced by people from minority ethnic groups. However, similar to other readings in this part of the book, the crux of Bartley's argument is that ethnic inequalities in health cannot be explained in relation to either biological or cultural differences, but are best understood in terms of the social structures in which different groups are situated.

Definitions of what is a 'race' or what constitutes 'ethnicity' vary over time and between countries (Jones, 2001; Aspinall, 2002). The term 'race' has been used to refer to groups of people who are thought to differ from each other in some biological way, whereas 'ethnicity' refers to cultural differences, such as language or religion. During the 1970s and 1980s, the term 'race' became discredited as a useful concept for scientific research on human health (Cooper, 1984; Rathwell and Phillips, 1986), as it was realized that there was no scientific basis for the idea that groups of people defined as 'races' shared biological features that had significance for health. 'Race' is now regarded as a socially and politically constructed concept that is used to justify the inferior treatment and greater exploitation of certain groups within a given society

(Cooper, 1986). 'Ethnicity' is usually defined in terms of the combination of common geographical origin and linguistic and/or religious differences from the 'majority' or dominant population. So we may think of the Polish communities in England and Scotland as an ethnic group, for example, because they have ancestors from Poland, many still speak Polish and almost all are Catholic.

In many nations, the official statistical organizations have definitions of race and/or ethnicity which are used in censuses and official surveys. These definitions change rapidly and are the subject of so much debate that one could devote an entire book to this topic alone. The US government defines four 'races': White, Black, American Indian/Alaskan Native and Asian or Pacific Islander. Hispanic people are described not as a race but as an ethnic group. Ethnic identification in Great Britain has been classified in many different ways, which differ over time, and between England and Wales, Scotland and Northern Ireland (Aspinall, 2002)....

The problem with the concept of ethnicity is that the notion of 'ethnic differences in health' was at one time used to imply that health problems in groups of people subjected to discrimination and racial harassment were due to their 'culture' (dietary customs, for example). In many ways this was considered to be just as bad as attributing health differences to biology. It was still an excuse, in the eyes of many, for giving insufficient attention to the position of ethnic or racial minority groups in the social structure, and to the ways in which they have been exploited, often over a long period of history, to the benefit of the majority and more powerful groups. For this reason, most groups who are in any context defined as a racial or ethnic minority support the recording by official surveys of race or ethnicity in one form or another: in order to monitor discrimination and its consequences....

The largest-scale historical phenomena giving rise to the existence of racial or ethnic minority groups in industrial nations at the present time have been slavery and colonialism. Slavery brought many thousands of people forcibly from Africa to the Americas in the eighteenth and nineteenth centuries. Slavery was enormously important in the development of the economic system we would now call industrial capitalism, the exploitation of African people allowing massive accumulations of wealth that later led to the rise of whole industries in the UK and the USA. British colonialism moved many groups of people round the world in various ways. Three of these streams of migration are most relevant to the present discussion. The first of these was the mass recruitment of Irish workers to build canals and railways in Great Britain in the eighteenth and early nineteenth centuries (Abbotts et al., 1997). Then there was the post-war migration of people from the Caribbean Islands and South Asia (India, Pakistan and Bangladesh), recruited to make up for severe shortages of workers in the UK. In the late 1960s and 1970s, there was also movement of people who had originally migrated from India to Kenya and Uganda when these were all part of the British Empire, who were expelled from the African nations. In 1974, people migrated from Cyprus at the time of the Turkish invasion of the island. However, the Immigration Act of 1962 brought an end to large-scale migration from the 'New Commonwealth' nations to Britain (the 'Old Commonwealth' nations being Australia, Canada and New Zealand) (Smaje, 1995).

What are defined as the characteristic differences in appearance between races or ethnic groups are indefinite and bound to their social and historical context (Williams, 1997; Dyson, 1998; Jones, 2001). Both the definition of a group as ethnically or racially distinct and the expression of discriminatory attitudes and practices are outcomes of economic and social forces. In the 1930s, there were 'race riots' in West London (UK) against Welsh people. They were regarded as unwanted aliens at that time, because people from Wales were brought in to work at lower wages in the new industries that were springing up, displacing the Londoners. In Switzerland in the 1960s and 1970s, myths abounded about the strange cooking and sexual behaviour of Italians. The status of an 'ethnic minority' was in this case due to the position of Italian guest workers, brought in to do unskilled and hazardous jobs at lower wages than Swiss citizens would have accepted. Korean workers in Japan occupy a somewhat similar position. These are examples of the ways in which economic forces produce 'ethnic minority' status. An example of the ways in which political forces do the same thing could be taken from the position of people from Eastern European nations in Western Europe at the present time. These people are at high risk of becoming the target of negative stereotyping, harassment and discrimination. If an outsider were to see an Italian and a Swiss person sitting side by side in a café, it would be impossible to tell which was which. Nor would it be possible for the average British, American or Swiss to tell the difference between a Welsh person and an English person. In the USA, England, Wales and Scotland, studies of health inequality pay no attention to religion itself. But in the Netherlands, it is customary automatically to 'adjust' statistically for Catholic and Protestant religion, because the health differences between these groups are so consistent, in the same way that one takes account of gender. So we can see that the components of 'race/ethnicity' that are seen as important in terms of defining a group that might be at risk of some kind of health disadvantage depend on time and place.

ETHNICITY, BIOLOGY AND HEALTH

In this light, it is no surprise that most researchers now consider it a mistake to explain health differences between races or ethnic groups in terms of biology. Many studies in the past were based on the assumption that there are biological similarities among members of the same racial groups (genetic homogeneity) and differences between groups that might give rise to differences in disease risk. This is very rarely true. Certain genes do influence some of the characteristics that are used in some situations to distinguish racial or ethnic groups, such as hair or skin colour. But these genes do not seem to be very important for the ways in which the body works or responds to disease hazards (Cruickshank and Beevers, 1989; Cavalli-Sforza, Menozzi and

Piazza, 1994; Senior and Bhopal, 1994). In most respects, the genetic differences between groups of people defined in terms of their ethnicity are less than the genetic differences between individuals within any of those groups (Cruickshank and Beevers, 1989). Knowing an individual's racial or ethnic group, for example, is little help in predicting what their blood group will be (Jones, 1981).

It is not particularly surprising that the 'genes' that determine hair, eye or skin colour, for example, do not predict ethnic or racial differences in disease vulnerability. After all, it is not hair, eye or skin colour that create an 'ethnic minority' category. 'Genes' may determine who has auburn hair, green eyes and freckly skin, not the countries in which people with this appearance might or might not be regarded as 'similar' in the sense of constituting a racial or ethnic minority. People of this appearance might be viewed as an ethnic minority in the Spanish Basque country, but not in Italy, for example. However, in David Williams's words, race or ethnicity can, in many places, act as a 'master status': as sex and age do (Williams, 1997). They are one of the first things that people register when they first meet each other. A stream of assumptions follow about what a person is like in many ways (Jones, 2001). Because of this, when discovering pockets of illness in social groups who are regarded as racially or ethnically 'different', doctors have tended to think first of biological or cultural causes. Nazroo (1997) has described this as the 'traditional epidemiological approach'. It focuses on particular diseases and how biological or cultural variations across ethnic groups may be used to provide clues to aetiology. This can lead to 'blaming' members of minority groups for their greater vulnerability to certain diseases. He contrasts to this the 'race relations approach' which 'raises questions about the motives for, and the methods used in, work on ethnicity and health and the implications that this has for the potentially discriminatory conclusions drawn. It focuses on the health disadvantages faced by ethnic minority groups and how the health services ... may be failing to find appropriate ways to meet needs' (Nazroo, 1997: 2–3).

Understanding of disease causation that is sufficient to help in prevention and treatment is more likely to be gained by paying attention to differences in material and psycho-social hazards across the life course (Onwuachi Saunders and Hawkins, 1993; Lillieblanton and Laveist, 1996; Lillieblanton et al., 1996). Dressler (1993) tested three conventional models of health inequalities affecting African-American people in a US study. He terms these the 'racial-genetic model', the 'health behaviour or lifestyle model' and the 'socio-economic status model'. No one model was found to explain the health differences in the study, so he arrived at a fourth, 'social structural model'. Like Williams, Dressler concludes that skin colour is a kind of 'master status', which serves as a criterion of social class in colour-conscious societies such as that of the United States and most European nations. The reason for differences in health between, in particular, White and Black Americans is the effect that their racial master status has on access to better education, jobs and careers.

There is, however, a considerable debate on the meaning of this kind of exercise. Many studies take two different ethnic or racial groups and adjust for various measures that are plausible explanations for higher ill health or mortality in one of them. If all these adjustments still leave an excess of ill health, how is this to be viewed?

In the past, studies concluded that this remaining difference was due to 'racial' genetic differences. This kind of explanation, as we have seen, is now largely discredited.

HOW GREAT ARE ETHNIC OR RACIAL DIFFERENCES IN HEALTH?

...

Official statistics on the risk of death (mortality statistics) therefore may not give us a very good picture of health differences between races or ethnic groups. Official government mortality statistics depend on having a good system for recording deaths, recording the ethnic group to which a deceased person belonged, and recording the numbers of persons in the ethnic group in the country as a whole. Only in this way is it possible to get an accurate 'rate' (the number of deaths divided by the population and then multiplied by 100 for a percentage, or by whatever other number is required to get rates per 1,000, 100,000 and so on). There are various ways in which inaccuracies can creep into this kind of procedure, most of which can be envisaged by common sense. If members of some ethnic groups are less likely than others to be accurately classified in a national census, but their origins are accurately recorded when they die, then their apparent death rate will be too high. To calculate the rate, the 'correct' number of deaths in this group will have been divided by a population number that is lower than it should be. If, for some reason, ethnicity or race is not correctly classified when a person's death is officially registered, then the death rate will be too low. The same will happen if a large number of people from a certain group return to the country from which they, or their forbears, originated when they become old or ill. So perhaps we should look outside official records at studies specifically designed to investigate health in different races.

Harding and Rosato have looked more closely at cancer incidence (how many people are newly diagnosed each year) among persons born in Scotland, Northern Ireland, the Irish Republic, Caribbean Common-wealth and Indian subcontinent and living in England and Wales. They also found that the incidence of all cancers, including breast cancer, was low among West Indians and South Asians. Looking more carefully at differences between religious groups, they found that, among South Asians, this pattern was consistent for Hindus, Sikhs and Muslims. In contrast, Irish and Scottish women suffered more cancers of the lung, mouth and liver, and men suffered more leukaemia and cancer of the lung, mouth and liver, and men suffered more leukaemia and cancer of the mouth and stomach (Harding and Rosato, 1999). Krieger and colleagues similarly examined ethnic differences in cancer incidence of several common forms of cancer in the San Francisco Bay Area. They found that incidence rates varied as much, if not more, by socio-economic position than by ethnicity. For example, lung cancer incidence was higher in people with less socio-economic advantage, except in Hispanic people: in this group the more affluent had higher incidence. They argue for the use of a social class measure in routine official statistics for cancer in the USA, such as exists in the UK (Krieger et al., 1999).

ETHNICITY AND SOCIO-ECONOMIC CONDITIONS

Nazroo has reported on a variety of health problems in various groups in the UK, using the first large study designed for this purpose. He is sharply critical of 'lumping' groups together in an unconsidered manner, and of ignoring the importance of socio-economic position and circumstances. For example, within the category of people with Indian family origins, he distinguishes Hindus, Sikhs, Muslims and Christians, and shows that the difference in general health between these groups, as well as between each of these and White people, was considerable. While the general health of Hindu and Christian people from ethnic minorities differed little from Whites, that of Muslims was considerably worse (Nazroo, 1998). Furthermore, within groups classified broadly according to ethnic origins, there were large health differences according to socio-economic circumstances. When he looked at individual diseases, the importance of socio-economic circumstances was equally striking. In this study, as in others, diabetes was higher in people of Caribbean origins, Indian people who had migrated from both India and Africa, Pakistani and Bangladeshi people than it was in Whites. However, within each of these ethnic groupings, the disease was more prevalent among those in workless households and those engaged in manual occupations (Nazroo, 1997: 103–6). When the excess risk of a number of diseases in ethnic minority groups was adjusted for the average standard of living in each group, this excess was greatly reduced and in many cases disappeared altogether (Nazroo, 1997: 103–7).

The attention paid in this report to the more precise definition of ethnicity enabled it to show that high rates of ill health relative to the White population were a far greater problem for Pakistani and Bangladeshi people than for other groups, such as Indian and Chinese. A more careful definition of socio-economic position and circumstances was the other important innovation. Rather than using social class alone, Nazroo devised an index of social conditions that included household overcrowding, quality of household amenities and ownership of consumer durables. It was this careful attention to defining both the groups involved and the nature of the disadvantages experienced that allowed many of the 'ethnic' differences to be explained (Nazroo, 2001).

SOCIAL ECOLOGY OF ETHNICITY AND HEALTH

Residential area is another important variable. People defined as belonging to ethnic or racial minorities do not only tend to find themselves in less advantaged occupations with lower incomes but also in areas that suffer from environmental disadvantage (Acevedo-Garcia et al., 2003; Northridge et al., 2003). In some studies, once account has been taken of income, social class and area of residence, there are no visible 'ethnic effects' at all. In other words, the ethnic 'minority' groups studied were in no poorer health than members of the ethnic 'majority' living in the same conditions in similar areas (Sundquist et al., 1996; Deaton and Lubotsky, 2003; Chandola, 2001).

The economic system that created migration patterns of African people to and within the USA, and of Irish, Indian, Pakistani and Bangladeshi people to and within England and Wales, has not disappeared. In particular, the need for labour power to carry out large-scale agricultural and industrial projects, combined with the problem of what happens to these workers after economic recessions and changes in patterns of employment, still remains. The areas in towns and cities where immigrants have congregated while they worked in these industries often remain polluted, run down and under-developed. When the work is finished, as with the railways, or the industry becomes obsolete, as with the textile and pottery industries, those who worked in them are often forgotten. Hard and hazardous labour is replaced by unemployment. But there is often no good infrastructure of schooling and further education to equip the children of those whose labour has built the old industries to move on and benefit from change.

It is not possible to compare the mortality of first-generation African-American people to that of their descendants born in the USA, as these events took place long before the existence of censuses and health surveys. But we can relate the health disadvantage of African-Americans today to the alarming deterioration in the health experience of the children and grandchildren of Irish people who migrated to England and Wales at the end of the nineteenth century. Whereas first-generation people from the Irish Republic had around 35 per cent higher risk of death between 1971 and 1985, second-generation Irish people had a 54 per cent higher risk (Harding and Balarajan, 1996). The reasons for this persistent and worsening health disadvantage among people of Irish descent is not understood, any more than we clearly understand the reasons for the health disadvantage suffered by African-American people. These questions need to be addressed by consideration of political as well as economic factors. Groups that are discriminated against often find it impossible to break into local power structures that determine which areas will have new schools, better transport and improved health services. The social geography of racism and its implications for health are only just beginning to be understood. For example, Chandola has reported that a combination of social class, a measure of material standard of living and an area-based measure of local deprivation explains away all of the health differences between British South Asians and the White population (Chandola, 2001). Increasing use is now being made of new research methods combined with measures that take account of social and economic conditions, both contemporary and (where relevant) over historical time. These methods may eventually come to be extended beyond the investigation of ethnic or racial differences in health and improve our understanding of differences between social classes and status groups as well.

EXPLANATIONS FOR RACIAL AND ETHNIC DIFFERENCES IN HEALTH

Overall, these studies from both the UK and the USA seem to support the idea that socio-economic position and circumstances are an important reason for such ethnic or racial differences as we do see in the statistics. Health differences between racial or ethnic groups are nothing like as clear or consistent as socio-economic differences. In many groups defined as racial or ethnic minorities, smoking, alcohol consumption and diet are more favourable to health than those of the 'majority' population, despite the fact that most of the groups studied are subject to various forms of discrimination. When studies attempt to explain the ethnic health inequalities that do exist, however, social class, education and income do not seem to be the whole answer. It seems that we should also take account of the environment in which people live. Areas with very high concentrations of certain ethnic and racial groups seem to experience lower levels of services and worse environmental conditions that add to the disadvantages measured in individual socio-economic terms. This brings us back to the questions concerned with the historical forces that result in any group migrating from their region of origin to a different region. One interesting aspect of the new approach is that it widens out a 'life-course political economy' perspective from concentration on individual nations towards consideration of global forces over long periods of time. This new way of looking at ethnic differences in health is at an early stage of development. It is likely to have important implications for the ways in which we analyse all forms of health inequality.

REFERENCES

Abbotts, J., Williams, R., Ford, G., Hunt, K., and West, P. (1997), Morbidity and Irish Catholic descent in Britain: an ethnic and religious minority 150 years on. *Soc Sci Med* 45, 3–14.

Acevedo-Garcia, D., Lochner, K. A., Osypuk, T. L., and Subramanian, S. V. (2003), Future directions on residential segregation and health research: a multilevel approach. *Am J Public Health* 93, 215–21.

Aspinall, P. J. (2002), Collective terminology to describe the minority ethnic population. *Sociology* 36, 803–16.

Cavalli-Sforza, L. L., Menozzi, P., and Piazza, A. (1994), *The History and Geography of Human Genes*. Princeton: Princeton University Press.

Chandola, T. (2001), Ethnic and class differences in health in relation to British South Asians: using the new National Statistics Socio-Economic Classification. *Soc Sci Med* 52, 1285–96.

Cooper, R. (1984), A note on the biological concept of race and its application in epidemiological research. *Am Heart J* 108, 715–23.

Cooper, R. (1986), Race, disease and health. In T. Rathwell and D. Phillips (eds), *Health, Race and Ethnicity*, 21–79. London: Croom Helm.

Cruickshank, J., and Beevers, D. (1989), *Ethnic Factors in Health and Disease*. Sevenoaks: Wright.

Deaton, A., and Lubotsky, D. (2003), Mortality, inequality and race in American cities. *Soc Sci Med* 56, 1139–53.

Dressler, W. W. (1993), Health in the African-American community: accounting for health inequalities. *Med Anthropol Q* 7, 325–45.

Dyson, S. M. (1998), 'Race', ethnicity and haemoglobin disorders. *Soc Sci Med* 47, 121–31.

Harding, S., and Balarajan, R. (1996), Patterns of mortality in second generation Irish living in England and Wales: longitudinal study. *BMJ* 312, 1389–92.

Harding, S., and Rosato, M. (1999), Cancer incidence among first generation Scottish, Irish, West Indian and South Asian migrants living in England and Wales. *Ethnicity and Health* 4, 83–92.

Jones, C. P. (2001), Invited commentary: 'Race', racism and the practice of epidemiology. *Am J Epidemiol* 154, 299–304.

Jones, J. (1981), How different are human races? *Nature* 293, 188–90.

Krieger, N., Quesenberry, C., Peng, T., Horn Ross, P., Stewart, S., and Brown, S. (1999), Social class, race/ethnicity, and incidence of breast, cervix, colon, lung, and prostate cancer among Asian, black, Hispanic, and white residents of the San Francisco Bay Area, 1988–92 (United States). *Cancer Causes Control* 10, 525–37.

Lillieblanton, M., and Laveist, T. (1996), Race/ethnicity, the social-environment, and health. *Soc Sci Med* 43, 83–91.

Lillieblanton, M., Parsons, P. E., Gayle, H., and Dievler, A. (1996), Racial-differences in health – not just black and white, but shades of gray. *Annu Rev Public Health* 17, 411–48.

Nazroo, J. Y. (1997), *The Health of Britain's Ethnic Minorities*. London: PSI.

Nazroo, J. (1998), Genetic, cultural or socio-economic vulnerability? Explaining ethnic inequalities in health. *Sociol Health Illn* 20, 710–30.

Nazroo, J. Y. (2001), South Asian people and heart disease: an assessment of the importance of socioeconomic position. *Ethn Dis* 11, 401–11.

Northridge, M. E., Stover, G. N., Rosenthal, J. E., and Sgerard, D. (2003), Environmental equity and health: understanding complexity and moving forward. *Am J Public Health* 93, 209–14.

Rathwell, T., and Phillips, D. (1986), *Health, Race and Ethnicity*. London: Croom Helm.

Senior, P. A., and Bhopal, R. (1994), Ethnicity as a variable in epidemiological research. *BMJ* 309, 327–30.

Smaje, C. (1995), *Health, 'Race' and Ethnicity*. London: Kings Fund Institute.

Sundquist, J., Bajekal, M., Jarman, B., and Johansson, S. E. (1996), Underprivileged area score, ethnicity, social-factors and general mortality in district health authorities in England and Wales. *Scand J Prim Health Care* 14, 79–85.

Williams, D. R. (1997), Race and health: basic questions, emerging directions. *Ann Epidemiol* 7, 322–33.

Source: M. Bartley, *Health Inequality: An Introduction to Theories, Concepts and Methods* (Cambridge: Polity Press, 2004).

Study Questions

1. How would you describe your own ethnic identity?
2. In what ways might the ethnicity of your patient or client influence the care that you provide? How relevant is your own ethnicity to the care you provide for individuals from the same or from different ethnic groups than yourself?
3. In Reading 12, Robert Crawford examined the politics of victim blaming. How far do Crawford's ideas help you to make sense of ethnicity and health?
4. Think back to the readings in Part II of this book. Make some notes on any particular issues that you might need to consider when carrying out research with people from minority ethnic groups.

─────────────────────── **Further Reading** ───────────────────────

For a general introduction and discussion of 'race' and ethnicity, you might try reading the book by K. Woodward and D. Goldblatt, *Race and Ethnicity* (Buckingham: Open University Press, 2001). To further explore the relationship between health and ethnicity, either of the following would be worth looking at: H. Macbeth and P. Shetty (eds) *Health and Ethnicity* (London: Routledge, 2000) or L. Culley and S. Dyson, 'Ethnicity and health', in E. Denny and S. Earle (eds) *Sociology for Nurses* (Oxford: Polity Press, 2005). The journal *Ethnicity & Health* would also be a useful resource. In the next two suggestions, the focus is on ethnicity within nursing. The first piece outlines the general paucity of research on ethnicity within nursing and the second, which draws on an ethnographic study of nurses, illustrates how nurses can engage in victim blaming and have limited cultural knowledge of minority ethnic groups: L. Serrant-Green, 'Breaking traditions: sexual health and ethnicity in nursing research: a literature review', *Journal of Advanced Nursing*, 51:5 (2005) 511–19 and V. Vydelingum, 'Nurses' experiences of caring for South Asian minority ethnic patients in a general hospital in England', *Nursing Inquiry*, 13:1 (2006) 23–32.

Part IV

Health and Healthcare: Bodies, Minds and Emotions

Introduction

Sociology began at a time of considerable political, social and technological change. Concerned to explain and account for these changes, sociologists concentrated on the public sphere: the world of work, the marketplace and political arenas. To a large extent then, until quite recently, sociologists paid little attention to the personal and private and to minds, bodies and emotions. It was the influence of feminist work and the claim that the 'personal is political' that encouraged sociologists and other social and cultural theorists to consider these issues. On the other hand, health professionals, by virtue of their occupations, have always been interested in issues pertinent to minds, bodies and emotions. So, how can a sociological perspective of bodies, minds and emotions help you in your study and in your practice? Thinking sociologically about these issues will encourage you to challenge your taken-for-granted assumptions and stereotypes about the status and the experience of the body and bodies, and of the mind and emotions. Sociology also provides a challenge to medical practice, which sometimes separates the body from the mind and the bodily experience from the emotional experience, both in terms of patient experience and healthcare work.

The first of the six readings in this section is by Deborah Lupton (Reading 17). In it she provides an overview of the reasons for an increased sociological interest in the body. In the second half of the reading, Lupton focuses on the dead body and considers, amongst other things, the rituals surrounding dead bodies, including the meanings and the use of body parts after death. In Reading 18, Peter Conrad and Heather T. Jacobson are concerned with body 'enhancement', specifically in relation to breast augmentation. This reading provides further evidence of how medicine and values within medical practice reflect the social norms of time and place (see also Part I) in that both small and large breasts have, on occasion, been defined as medically problematic. Although this reading focuses on an issue relating to the body, it also demonstrates the close relationship among bodies, minds and emotions in that individuals who opt for medical assistance speak of unhappiness and inadequacy prior to surgery. Alison Chapple and Sue Ziebland's reading (Reading 19) also encourages us to reflect on the holistic nature of self. This time the emphasis is on how men use humour as a tool to manage their bodily experience of testicular cancer and how, sometimes, they feel that humour is used against them. Chapple and Ziebland's reading draws on data from qualitative research, as does the reading by Stephanie Tierney (Reading 20). The respondents in Tierney's research also struggle to maintain a positive sense of self in managing their experience of anorexia. Tierney outlines the positive and negative consequences of defining anorexia as a disability and considers the support for, and challenges to, such a label. In Reading 21, the focus shifts from the patient/client to the practitioner. Drawing again on a qualitative study, Ian Shaw is concerned with how doctors respond to what they see as the perceived threat to the 'normal' doctor–patient relationship posed by patients with psychiatric problems. The final reading in this part by Billie Hunter (Reading 22) is also concerned with the relationship between a practitioner and a patient, this time the midwife and the birthing woman. Hunter provides a review of the literature on emotional labour and emotion work within healthcare and a review of the literature on the midwife/birthing women relationship and argues for more work that brings these two types of literature together.

The Body, Medicine and Death

Deborah Lupton

In this reading, Deborah Lupton considers the body in medicine from a sociological perspective. She begins by arguing that as our bodies are always with us, it is easy to take the body for granted. As Lupton notes, social scientists – including medical sociologists – have done this also. This means that the biological, human anatomical conception of the body has historically remained unchallenged. Recently though, in relation to social movements, cultural changes and disciplinary changes, social and cultural theorists have become interested in the body and corporality. In the sections of Lupton's chapter from which this reading is taken, the focus is on the relationship between the Michel Foucault's work and the current theoretical interest in the body in medicine and the dead body. The ways in which we represent death, the rituals surrounding the dying person and the dead body and the status and significance of body parts after death have all changed over time. In addition to highlighting how medical advances have contributed to these changes, Lupton considers the changing differential attitudes and feelings that lay people and the medical profession have towards dead bodies.

Although not reproduced here, there is also a reference in the chapter to the gendered body, the sexual body, public health and the disciplined body and the commodified body. You will find all of these sections relevant in beginning your consideration of the relationship between bodies, minds, emotions and health, illness experience and healthcare and we suggest you find the book and read the whole chapter.

SOCIAL THEORY AND THE BODY

It is easy to ignore the existence and importance of bodies, simply because they are so taken-for-granted as parts of ourselves: 'We have bodies, but we are also, in a specific sense, bodies; our embodiment is a necessary requirement of our social identification so that it would be ludicrous to say "I have arrived and I have brought my body with me"' (Turner, 1996: 42). When pain, sickness or discomfort is not felt, one's body is relatively unobtrusive. It is often not until illness or pain is experienced that the body comes into conscious being; illness may then be conceptualized as the body taking over, as an external environment separate to the self.

Until recently, social and political theory and scholarship tended to ignore the human body, placing emphasis upon social structures and individual subjectivity with little discussion of where the corporality of the 'lived' body fitted in (Berthelot, 1986; Turner, 1991a, 1996). For much of the history and development of medical sociology the biological, human anatomy conception of the body has remained unchallenged: 'Sociologists support, criticize, collude with, and conspire against those health professionals whose claim to expertise is their sophisticated knowledge of the body – but rarely if ever question or criticize their biological vision of that body' (Armstrong, 1987: 651). Likewise, social histories of medicine have neglected attention to the body (Gallagher and Laqueur, 1987: vii)....

This turn towards theorizing the body may be explained with reference to modern social movements such as feminism, the growth of consumer culture and the influence of poststructuralist and postmodernist theories (Turner, 1991: 18). These movements, in concert with the release of the translated writings of Foucault, have focused new attention upon the body, its role in human subjectivity and its constitution by both elite and popular discourses....

FOUCAULT, THE BODY AND THE CLINIC

... the writings of Foucault, as well as feminist critiques, have been extremely influential in establishing the current interest in the body in sociological, historical, philosophical and anthropological scholarship. Foucault was interested in establishing an historical 'genealogy' of the discourses surrounding and constituting contemporary medical practices. For Foucault and his followers, the body is the ultimate site of political and ideological control, surveillance and regulation. He argues that since the eighteenth century it has been the focal point for the exercise of disciplinary power. Through the body and its behaviours, state apparatuses such as medicine, the educational system, psychiatry and the law define the limits of behaviour and record activities, punishing those bodies which violate the established boundaries, and thus rendering bodies productive and politically and economically useful.

In his historico-philosophical accounts of the development of medical knowledge in France, Foucault identifies the establishment of the medical clinic and teaching hospital in the late eighteenth century as a pivotal point for ways of conceptualizing the body. He views medicine as a major institution of power in labelling bodies as deviant or normal, as hygienic or unhygienic, as controlled or needful of control (Foucault, 1979: 54). In *The Birth of the Clinic* (1975) Foucault refers to the 'anatomical atlas' that is the human body constituted by the medico-scientific gaze. He argues that in the late twentieth century, this notion of the body was accepted with little recognition that there are other ways of conceiving of the body and its illnesses. According to Foucault, as medical practices changed in the late eighteenth century, the introduction and routine adoption of the physical examination, the post-mortem, the stethoscope, the microscope, the development of the disciplines of anatomy, psychiatry, radiology and surgery, the institutionalization of the hospital and the doctor's surgery, all served to increasingly exert power upon the body. At the same time, bodies were subjected to increased regulation, constant monitoring, discipline and surveillance in other spheres, most notably the prison, the school, the asylum, the military and the workshop. The medical encounter began to demand that patients reveal the secrets of their bodies, both by allowing physical examination and by giving their medical history under questioning by the doctor: 'The patient had to speak, to confess, to reveal; illness was transformed from what is visible to what was heard' (Armstrong, 1983: 25).

For Foucault, the medical encounter is a supreme example of surveillance, whereby the doctor investigates, questions, touches the exposed flesh of the patient, while the patient acquiesces, and confesses, with little knowledge of why the procedures are carried out. In the doctor's surgery the body is rendered an object to be prodded, tested and examined. The owner is expected to give up his or her jurisdiction of the body over to the doctor. In severe cases of illness or physical disability the body is owned by the medical system, while in mental illness the body is the apparatus by which the brain is kept restrained, often against the owner's will....

THE DEAD BODY

The changing meaning of death over the centuries provides an example of the way in which a physical event is constructed through cultural custom. While death would seem to be the ultimate biological essentialism, there is a wide boundary around which death is negotiated, culturally, historically and politically: 'Death is not a thing or event existing independently of human consciousness; it is simply the word given to a certain threshold, interface, space or point of separation' (Armstrong, 1987a: 655). The dead body has changed form and substance in western society over the past few centuries, in concert with notions of what death is and how it should be achieved. Before the advent of medicine, the most potent symbol of death was the grim reaper, a skeletal figure dressed in black and carrying a scythe. In the late twentieth century, death is represented by a biological lesion or a test result; for example, a positive result for the presence of cancer in a Pap smear or biopsy....

Before the emergence of scientific medicine and epidemiology, death was connected with luck and chance, as random, unpredictable and untamed, as an event that could strike anyone at any time. By the end of the eighteenth century, a new image of death became current, where death was not located in the individual, but in the entire population (Prior and Bloor, 1993; Prior, 2000). The development of the life table, used to calculate the length of life spans based on sex and age employing mathematical laws, symbolized this change, for it was an attempt to rationalize death, to subject it to a formalized pattern which could be predicated using statistical methods: 'The life table, then, is one of the most significant representations of life and death that our own culture has produced. It not only expresses a vision of life as a rationally calculable object, but also provides a set of background expectancies of normal, natural lifespans' (Prior and Bloor, 1993: 356). This cultural artefact is currently relied upon by doctors in their judging of what is and what is not a normal, natural death, and is vital in the construction of reasons for death as reported on the death certificate.

The use of the corpse for medical training and research has been a focal point of concepts of death. In medicine today, the corpse is regarded as a necessary teaching tool, but prior to the nineteenth century, dissection was surrounded with moral prohibitions. Dissection of the corpse violated a number of beliefs about the sanctity and mystery of death and the dead body. By the sixteenth century, dissection was recognized in law as a punishment, a fate worse than death, even while it was serving the purposes of medical knowledge (Richardson, 1988: 32–4). While anatomical dissection was undertaken for teaching and research purposes in medieval France from the fourteenth century onwards, general society did not consider it permissible to open up the secrets of the body for such purposes. Dissection was seen as punishment for criminal behaviour, as a prolongation of the suffering inflicted by the executioner, and its disordering of the body's organs was regarded as symbolic of societal chaos (Pouchelle, 1990). The cutting open of bodies, even in the quest for medical knowledge, was subjected to deeply rooted taboos at that time. Such exposure of the internal workings of the human body was deemed an unacceptable invasion of the microcosm which harboured the soul, laying bare the intimate parts of the person: 'The human body was seen not only as a "little world" (microcosm), but also as the reflection and model of human society... If the members and organs of the microcosm were dispersed, disturbing the order of the world, would not the "body politic" fall apart as well?' (1990: 83).

Blood, in particular, was regarded as sacred and poisonous, and to be avoided by surgeons if possible. Surgeons had to follow rituals before an operation which were designed to purify them, preserve their bodily integrity and keep their strength and power intact; for example, when treating a fracture of the skull, one document of the day noted that the surgeon must, the night before, avoid contact with women and speaking with menstruating women, must not eat any garlic, onion or hot sauces on the day, and must clean his hands thoroughly before the operation (Pouchelle, 1990: 87). It was not until the end of the fifteenth century that official dissections were carried out at the Faculty of Medicine in Paris, accompanied by pomp and ceremony, including a banquet, to highlight the unusual nature and symbolic danger of the event (1990: 84).

Despite the strong moral prohibitions surrounding the cutting open of dead bodies, by the eighteenth century the medical gaze had extended into the previously hidden world of the corpse. Because of the prohibitions surrounding dissection, however, the obtaining of corpses for surgeons and anatomists was difficult, and by the seventeenth century corpses had become a commodity (Richardson, 1988). Condemned prisoners were encouraged to barter their bodies for money, and grave-robbing became rife. 'By 1800, in medical circles, market terminology was being applied to human corpses apparently without embarrassment' (1988: 55) and human bodies were 'dismembered and sold in pieces, or measured and sold by the inch' (1988: 72), yet public opinion did not approve. At the time of the British 1832 Anatomy Act which provided for the requisition of the corpses of the poor for anatomical uses, the corpse was viewed with a mixture of solicitude and fear, with ambiguity concerning both the definition of death and the spiritual status of the dead body expressing a mixture of pagan and Christian beliefs (Richardson, 1988).

Funereal practices in the seventeenth and early eighteenth centuries foregrounded the corpse, and demonstrated beliefs that there was a period between death and burial in which the human being was regarded as 'neither alive nor fully dead', including the custom of placing food and wine beside the corpse in case it woke, and watching over it (Richardson, 1988: 15). In the interim before the onset of rigor mortis and putrefaction, death could only be unreliably defined by listening for a heartbeat or testing for breath on a mirror or glass, and thus could not be decreed with certainty. There was also uncertainty about the time of separation of the soul from the body, whether it left the body at death, or slept in the grave with the body (1988: 15–16). While death in the eighteenth century was considered in medical discourse as an absolute fact, the end of life and the end of disease, it was also relative, because examination of the corpse could not reveal the distinction between the cause and the effect of death, especially once decomposition had set in (Foucault, 1975: 140–1). Following the spread of the dissection of corpses, death became not a single moment in time, but a series of 'partial deaths', of small changes in parts of the body at different times (1975: 142).

The above discussion suggests that there is historical evidence of a schism between the conceptualization of the dead body in medicine and that of the lay person; the former viewing the body as a commodity and teaching tool, the latter continuing to invest the corpse with respect and fear. Thus, dissection 'represented a gross assault upon the integrity and identity of the body *and* upon the repose of the soul, each of which – in other circumstances – would have been carefully fostered' (Richardson, 1988: 76, emphasis in the original). When the stealing of corpses from graveyards in Britain became widespread, customs of protecting graves came into being to foil the bodysnatchers, and public opprobrium was high. As a result, British medical schools could not gain access to enough corpses, and the Anatomy Act was drawn up and passed, allowing anatomists to obtain the 'unclaimed' bodies of people who had died in workhouses, hospitals and other charitable institutions as well as prisons, the reasoning being that such people, who had been kept alive by the public purse, had no relatives to protest against their deployment for dissection. The Act thus discriminated between the bodies of the poor, deemed suitable for dissection, and the wealthy, protected from the ravages of the grave-robbers (Richardson, 1988).

It is worthy of note that in contemporary western societies it is generally considered entirely appropriate for individuals to pledge their dead bodies for transplantation purposes. In some western countries this choice is enshrined on drivers' licences, while in others organs are deemed automatically available for donation at death unless individuals or their relatives specifically request they not be. Allowing medical dissection for the purposes of helping another is generally valorized in the popular media rather than being represented as fraught with moral prohibitions; they routinely depict organ donation as saving lives and the 'ultimate sacrifice', as in the headline 'Organ recipients plead for gift of life for others' printed in a national Australian newspaper in January 1993. The possible discourse highlighting the commodification of bodily parts used in transplant surgery is replaced by that of altruism, or the invoking of the ideal of prolonging one's material existence by living after death in another's body. Ironically, at the same time as the western media champion the altruistic ideal of giving one's organs for transplant surgery, an international trade in human organs exists in which impoverished people from developing countries such as India and the Philippines undertake to have their own organs surgically removed while they are still alive, including kidneys, eyes and pieces of skin, and sold to western nations. It seems that among some medical quarters at least, there is no compunction in removing organs from living bodies and treating them as commodities, just as grave-robbers in the nineteenth century sold pieces of human flesh by the inch.

Since the introduction of medical technology that allows the prolonging of the life of people who previously would have been pronounced dead, the issue of defining death has become even more problematic. When can death be said to have occurred if a body is on a life-support machine, the brain shows no sign of functioning, and breathing could not take place if the machine were to be switched off? Muller and Koenig (1988) emphasized the social nature of defining death exploring the processes by which doctors interpret selected information about patients to reach conclusions about whether the patient is 'dying' or 'still has a chance' (and is thus deserving of further medical intervention designed at forestalling death). What is the status of a person's organs which have been taken from a body pronounced to be dead and transplanted into a living person's body? Are these organs 'dead'? The difficulties of defining death in such situations is evidenced by the three categories of death that currently exist in medical discourse relating to the viability of human body organs and tissue for transplantation or other medical use: tissue may be described as 'dead', 'double dead' or 'triple dead' (Clarke, 1993). Due to such conundrums, death has now moved from the province of the clinician to that of the medical ethicist (Armstrong, 1987a: 656)....

Where once death was considered under the auspices of fate or God's will, contemporary understandings tend to suggest that early death is preventable and therefore, in many cases, subject to the individual's control. Public health discourses claim that taking the appropriate measures will protect against premature death: driving safely, eating well (as in 'the anti-cancer' diet), reducing alcohol consumption, taking regular exercise, avoiding smoking, engaging in safer sex practices and so on (Lupton, 1995; Prior, 2000). Ever greater hopes are pinned on biomedical advances in the effort to vanquish early death and prolong lifespans. In the context of an intensified focus on control over death, to succumb to a fatal disease or accident before old age becomes viewed as a loss of control over one's body. Such deaths can no longer be regarded as simply misfortune: instead, someone must be held accountable.

Part of this need for control over death is the sequestration of dying, death and corpses from everyday life, in such places as hospitals, hospices and cemeteries (Prior, 2000). Although images of the dead body are routinely portrayed in the popular media (violent television or cinematic dramas, for example), the material corpse is hidden from view, so that people may go through their lives never viewing a dead body in the flesh....

REFERENCES

Armstrong, D. (1983) *Political Anatomy of the Body: Medical Knowledge in Britain in the Twentieth Century*. Cambridge: Cambridge University Press.

Armstrong, D. (1987a) 'Silence and truth in death and dying', *Social Science & Medicine*, 24 (8), 651–7.

Berthelot, J. (1986) 'Sociological discourse and the body', *Theory, Culture & Society*, 3 (3), 155–64.

Clark, D. (1993) ' "With my body I thee worship": the social construction of marital sex problems', in S. Scott and D. Morgan (eds), *Body Matters: Essays on the Sociology of the Body*. London: Falmer, pp. 22–34.

Foucault, M. (1975) *The Birth of the Clinic: an Archaeology of Medical Perception*. New York, NY: Vintage Books.

Foucault, M. (1979) *The History of Sexuality, Volume One: An Introduction*. London: Penguin.

Gallagher, C. and Laqueur, T. (1987) 'Introduction', in C. Gallagher and T. Laqueur (eds), *The Making of the Modern Body: Sexuality and Society in the Nineteenth Century*. Berkeley, CA: University of California Press, pp. vii–xv.

Lupton, D. (1995) *The Imperative of Health: Public Health and the Regulated Body*. London: Sage.

Pouchelle, M.-C. (1990) *The Body and Surgery in the Middle Ages* (translated by R. Morris). Cambridge: Polity Press.

Prior, L. (2000) 'Reflections on the "mortal" body in late modernity', in S. Williams, J. Gabe and M. Calnan (eds), *Health, Medicine and Society: Key Theories, Future Agendas*. London: Routledge, pp. 186–202.

Prior, L. and Bloor, M. (1993) 'Why people die: social representations of death and its causes', *Science as Culture*, 3 (3), 346–75.

Richardson, R. (1988) *Death, Dissection and the Destitute*. London: Penguin.

Turner, B. (1991) 'Recent developments in the theory of the body', in M. Featherstone, M. Hepworth and B. Turner (eds), *The Body: Social Process and Cultural Theory*. London: Sage, pp. 1–35.

Turner, B. (1996) *The Body and Society: Explorations in Social Theory* (2nd edn). London: Sage.

Source: D. Lupton, *Medicine as Culture: Illness, Disease and the Body in Western Culture* (London: Sage, 2003).

Study Questions and Activities

1. Why, until recently, has the body been ignored by social scientists? What issues and approaches led to the theorising of the body and embodiment?
2. Are bodies born or made?
3. What do you understand by the phrase 'medico-scientific gaze'?
4. From reading this chapter, and drawing on your own experiences, list some of the different values ascribed to dead bodies by different faith groups, by different healthcare professionals, by funeral directors and by the friends and family of the dead person.
5. Reflect on your practice. What parts of people's bodies do you work with? Does your job involve you working beyond discrete body parts to consider the body as a whole and/or the relationship among minds, bodies and emotions? If it does not, should it?

Further Reading

The rest of Deborah Lupton's book is equally interesting and relevant; amongst other things, she considers theoretical perspectives of medicine and sociology, representations of medicine and illness in elite and popular culture, power relations and the medical encounter. Other books that you will find useful include: S. J. Williams, *Medicine and the Body* (London: Sage, 2003); M. Evans and E. Lee, *Real Bodies: A Sociological Introduction* (Houndmills: Palgrave, 2002) and B. S. Turner, *Regulating Bodies: Essays in Medical Sociology* (London: Routledge, 1992). Mariam Fraser and Monica Greco's edited book – *The Body: A Reader* (London: Routledge, 2005) – also contains lots of useful pieces. You will find Part V of this book especially useful as it concentrates on bodies in relation to health and disease. Andrew Bainham, Shelly Day Sclater and Martin Richards' edited book – *Body Lore and Laws* (Portland, Oregon: Hart Publishing, 2002) – is a fascinating read. The book contains chapters on court-ordered Caesarean sections; bodies and end-of-life decision-making; male medical students and the male body, and the position of parents, professionals and the law in relation to the retention of human material (of children) after post-mortem. Even the front cover is relevant as it portrays a pair of feet with a tag around one of the big toes (obviously on a morgue table). A book that focuses specifically on images of the body, this time the pre-birth body, is V. Hartouni, *Cultural Conceptions: On*

Reproduction and the Remaking of Life (Minneapolis, MN: University of Minnesota Press, 1997). This is interesting because of its attention to the relationship between visual image and selfhood. Finally, the following chapter is interesting because it focuses on academic and media representations of the body following mass death and considers implications for public health: C. Komaromy and S. Handsley, 'Death and contagion: contaminating bodies', in J. Douglas, S. Earle, S. Handsley, C. Lloyd and S. Spurr (eds) *Challenge and Controversy in Promoting Public Health* (London: Sage in association with the Open University, 2007).

'Enhancing' the Body

Peter Conrad and Heather T. Jacobson

Having established in Reading 17 that the status and meanings of the body and biology should not be taken for granted, and that meanings vary amongst different groups of people, and at different historical times, in this reading we turn to the issue of body/biology enhancement. Peter Conrad and Heather T. Jacobson, therefore, continue the challenge to the view that bodies and biology are given and unchanging. As Conrad and Jacobson note, body enhancements are a reflection of what is socially valued in a given society at a given time and the history of breast augmentation mirrors societies' view of the meanings and values of breasts with particular reference to the so-called ideal size, shape and function. This analysis shows how social values are often reflected in medical practice in that at different times both 'small' and 'large' breasts have been defined as a medical problem. With specific reference to the United States, Conrad and Jacobson consider the influences prompting women and men to undergo cosmetic surgery on their breasts and other parts of their bodies. These influences include family and friends, the medical profession and the media. Although, arguably, an issue central to contemporary cultural meanings of the body, cosmetic surgery leads us to consider the mind, given that individuals who opt for body modification often report, amongst their reasons, feelings of inadequacy and inferiority.

While we are all born with a certain biological endowment, how it is manifested is a function of the social environment. This is even true about bodies. Biology may appear to set the limits on bodily development (e.g. we cannot fly), but individuals can work to improve body size and shape by working out and/or taking supplements, or through other methods of enhancement.

One avenue for body improvement is through methods of biomedical enhancement. These include drugs, surgery or other medical interventions aimed at improving body, mind or performance. Cosmetic surgery, including liposuctions, face lifts, 'nose jobs' and breast augmentation, has become a common biomedical road to bodily improvement (cf. Sullivan 2001). One observer depicts enhancements as 'interventions designed to improve the human form or functioning beyond what is needed to sustain or restore human health' (Juengst 1998: 29). While it is not always clear what is 'human form or functioning ... beyond health', since health itself is a social construction, it seems clear that a bodily enhancement is one that is additive to the 'given' biological condition. A biomedical enhancement is an intervention to improve the body (or performance) by medical means.

Clearly, what one chooses to enhance and what constitutes improvement are socially constructed and likely to vary by time and place....Enhancements that modify biology and the body are a reflection of what is socially valued in a society....

BREASTS AND BODIES: THE CULTURAL MEANING OF BREASTS

The meaning of breasts and preferences about size or shape vary enormously by culture and historical moment. In some cultures breasts are seen purely as functional organs for feeding children, with no sexual connotation. Bare breasts have no particular erotic meaning here. In other societies, breasts are considered highly sexual, and are often hidden from view except in the most intimate situations. Some cultures ignore naked breasts, others fetishize them. Not all societies prefer the upright, hemispherical breasts that seem to be idealized in modern western society.

When we examine the history of the breast in western society, however, we see that the meaning and ideal size and shape of the breast has changed over time. Even a casual look at the history of the breast reveals different takes on breasts: an emblem of transition from girl to woman, a sign of femininity, a symbol and a means of nurturence (breast feeding), and an object of erotic attraction and pleasure. In western societies breasts have become very critical to women's body image, but the meanings attributed to breasts varies by time and place. Throughout most of human history breasts were certainly defined in terms of their functionality for nursing babies. Breast milk meant life or death to newborns since there was no substitute for it until the late nineteenth century. Thus it isn't surprising to find statues of multi-breasted women or bare bosomed women with large, globular breasts. By the time the Renaissance began, paintings of a nursing Virgin Mary were common and 'from the fourteenth through the sixteenth century, the nursing Madonna was the prototype of female divinity' (Yalom 1997: 48). There was a kind of holiness infused in the depiction of breast-feeding.

In the seventeenth century we begin to see depictions moving towards a more eroticized breast. The breast begins to be more connected to sexual pleasure. Bare breasts become a common feature in art. But even as breasts become eroticized, the ideal remained 'small, white, round like apples, hard, firm and wide apart' (Yalom 1997: 54).

Art did not always reflect the variety of breast preferences, however. In Renaissance society breast idealization mirrored social class and privilege. An elite 10 per cent pampered their breasts and reserved them for their intimate relations, while 90 per cent used their breasts to feed children. Lower class women often functioned as wet nurses for babies of upper class families. While the upper class ideals were compact breasts under tightly laced bodices, lower class women were revered for their large, globular and lactating breasts (Yalom 1997). Gilman (1999) points out how breasts became racialized; even into the nineteenth century large breasts were associated with Jews and blacks.

In the late seventeenth century the eroticized breast was more common, reflecting gendered power in society. As Yalom (1997: 87) notes, 'women's breasts, shorn of religious associations, became blatant emblems of male desire.' The eroticized breast has become part of western culture, only 'the ideal volume, shape and function' have changed over time (Yalom 1997: 89). Breast-feeding went out of fashion and then returned, but the sexual meaning of breasts has trumped the maternal meaning, perhaps especially in the USA.

In the twentieth century breasts became increasingly commodified, especially through the media, such as films, mass market advertising, and most recently pornography. While women in the 1920s sported a flat-chested look, preferred breast size has grown. With the rise of such stars as Jane Russell and Marilyn Monroe in the 1950s, full and large breasts became a cultural ideal. One indicator of this is measurements of Miss America contestants: in the 1920s the bust measurement averaged 32 inches, by the 1950s it had increased to 36 inches (cited in Latteier 1998). Despite an upsurge in the acceptance of smaller breasts in the wake of the feminist and fitness revolutions, large breasts appear to prevail as the American cultural preference; they are still deemed more feminine and more attractive.

THE RISE OF BREAST AUGMENTATION

'The modern history of aesthetic surgery of the breast begins with breast reduction' (Gilman 1999: 219). In the nineteenth century surgeons began to offer procedures that could reshape parts of the human body. In the 1880s and 1890s they developed procedures that could reduce the size of the nose; parallel to that, 'aesthetic surgeons' began developing techniques to create a more perfect breast, which in this case focused on making large or pendulous breasts smaller. While there was a stated concern with the stress on back muscles and the strain on the body, physicians also saw the reduction of breasts as a way of reducing women's self-consciousness and boosting self-esteem. By the early twentieth century, breast reduction was a going medical concern (Gilman 1999). In the 1930s there was an active medical debate about whether breast reduction was cosmetic or reconstructive surgery. The main issue seems to be the stigma and psychological affect of 'overlarge, pendulous breasts', although both physical discomfort (e.g. excessive weight) and embarrassment were seen as rationales for treatment. These operations fundamentally reshaped breasts, allowing surgeons 'to pay more attention to the aesthetics of the breast' (Jacobson 2000: 51).

Until the 1950s, there was only limited medical interest in enlarging small breasts. There were some efforts at breast augmentation, however. Most of the early attempts could be called reconstruction rather than augmentation. Whatever work was done towards breast enhancement was done primarily as an attempt to restore surgically removed or scarred breasts. In the 1930s, Charles Willi began to experiment with 'aesthetic' breast augmentation in London. His patients wanted larger (and presumably more erotic) breasts. Willi's technique of fat transplantation ultimately failed, providing only a temporary relief from the woe of small breasts (Gilman 1999: 249–51).

While most physicians did not define small breasts as a medical problem, a few surgeons continued to look for materials for the reconstruction of injured or amputated breasts, which of course could also be used to augment small breasts. A wide range of techniques were tried including fat grafts, paraffin injections, sponge rubber prostheses, oestrogen and silicone injections. Concerns were often raised about whether the implant materials were natural or artificial and what impact this would have on the aesthetics of the breast. Eventually all these techniques failed, leaving uneven or lumpy breasts or worse, discomfort and illness.

Medical and surgical interests in breast enhancement increased after the Second World War. Before then, small breasts (rather than breasts that had been surgically removed) were not deemed a serious medical problem. But that was to change shortly. In a 1942 textbook, Max Thorek, a plastic surgeon, devoted a short chapter to the problem of small breasts, what he called 'hypomastia'. In the 1950s small breasts became more widely medicalized (cf. Conrad 1992). In an article published in *Plastic and Reconstructive Surgery* in 1950, H.O. Barnes, a cosmetic surgeon, called attention to the new disease, known equally as hypomastia or micromastia. 'Hypomastia causes psychological rather than physical distress. Its correction has been receiving increased attention only since our "cult of the body beautiful" has revealed its existence in rather large numbers' (quoted in Haiken, 1997: 236). In his article, Barnes proposed 'reshaping' the breast to create 'firmness, conical contours and fullness of the bosom directly above the breast', and a couple of years later published another article that promoted 'fat grafts' for actually enlarging the breast (quoted in Haiken 1997: 236). Robert Alan Franklyn, a somewhat disreputable physician, claimed that 'Four million women suffered from micromastia', and described 'a simple, 25 minute operation' implanting a substance called Surgifoam as a treatment (quoted in Jacobson 2000: 66). Franklyn was severely criticized by the AMA for his claims but by the 1960s there were any number of mainstream plastic surgeons offering new forms of surgical breast enhancement. The woe of small breasts, whether termed hypomastia or just unhappiness or low self-esteem, had been legitimated as a psychological syndrome that could be treated with surgical procedures. At first surgeons resisted the notion that vanity rather than discomfort underlay the demand for breast augmentation. As one surgeon wrote: 'Vanity is the desire to outdo others, while patients who seek cosmetic surgery are not trying to outdo anyone. They simply want to look normal .... The woman who has micromastia has a deformity that is difficult to live with' (quoted in Jacobson 2000: 119). But within a few years, vanity was no longer considered a problem, and cosmetic surgeons welcomed patients who wanted to improve their breast size and shape for any reason.

Many people seem to have bought into the cultural preference that small breasts are inferior. The 'falsies' industry became a multimillion enterprise as women sought to give the appearance of larger breasts (Gilman 1999), but surgery promised to be a better solution. One study found that 'wearing padded bras or falsies was "phony", "cheating" and made the feeling of inadequacy even worse' (Haiken 1997: 244), while women tended to be pleased (at least initially) with breast enhancements. For many women, breast augmentation is a kind of 'self improvement', enriching their distinctly female attributes, and making their bodies more like their ideal images. For others, it is an attempt to overcome the 'disability' of small breasts and to look 'normal' in their own eyes. With the help of surgeons, women could now pursue 'the body I was meant to have' (Gimlin 2000), aligning a perceived disjunction between internal identity and external body. There is considerable evidence that when successful, breast implants increase some women's self-esteem, sexual appeal, and self-fulfilment (Jacobson 2000).

SILICONE BREAST IMPLANTS SINCE THE 1960s

Silicone breast implants were introduced in the early 1960s and soon after their introduction became the most popular choice for augmentation (Jacobson 2000). The connection between silicone and breasts itself was not new, however; injectable silicone had been used to increase breast size since the Second World War. Silicone is a synthetic polymer developed for commercial use by Dow Corning Corporation in the early 1940s. Reports locate the first use of injectable silicone to increase breast size in post-war Japan (Haiken 1997; Zimmerman 1998; Jacobson 2000). Injecting silicon into breasts was introduced into the US in the late 1940s and quickly became popular among physicians, many of whom used the substance illicitly as it had not been approved for breast augmentation (Jacobson 2000). Physiciand liked silicone as they believed it to be 'biologically inert and an ideal soft-tissue substitute' (Zimmerman 1998: 22).

Although silicone injections were for a time popular, with some reports estimating upwards of fifty thousand US women having had their breasts enlarged with the substance, injectable silicone presented serious complications (Zimmerman 1998; Jacobson 2000). Some women experienced pain, scarring, infections, and migrating silicone lumps in their breasts that masked breast cancer and prevented adequate screening. Breasts would often become misshapen and uncomfortable. At times, these complications resulted in amputation of the breasts. By 1971 at least four women had died due to embolisms resulting from silicone injections (Haiken 1997; Zimmerman 1998).

As a result of these complications, negative publicity about injectable silicone increased. In 1965 the Federal Drug Administration (FDA) reclassified liquid silicone as a drug, restricting its use to investigational studies (Haiken 1997; Jacobson 2000). Despite the new monitoring, physicians continued to inject silicone, some receiving the substance through illicit means (Zimmerman 1998). In 1971 the American Medical Association (AMA) declared that 'the injection of silicon fluid to increase the size of the female breast is an unapproved surgical technique and is dangerous' (quoted in Jacobson 2000: 83).

Women 'continued to clamor for a solution [to small breasts] and surgeons continued to search for one' (Haiken 1997: 255). Despite the horror stories emerging around injectable silicon the demand for surgical breast augmentation was still high. Work on the silicone-filled implant had been well underway since the early 1960s. In 1962 the first device was implanted in a women and by 1970 Dow Corning had sold an estimated 50,000 implants. Neither the concerns nor the new regulations of inject-able silicone were applied to silicone implants. At the time, the FDA still did not have the authority to regulate medical devices. Because of this, 'manufacturers were free to develop variations of the original breast implant with few studies to demonstrate their safety and efficacy' (Zimmerman 1998: 29). Analysts suggest that manufacturers and plastic surgeons often were more concerned with the 'naturalness' of the implants (i.e. the look and feel of real breasts) rather than product safety (Zimmerman 1998). It wasn't until 1988 that the jurisdiction of the FDA was expanded to require safety and effectiveness data on breast implants (Jacobson 2000).

In the meantime, from the early 1960s through to 1990 an estimated *two million women* received silicone implants (Jacobson 2000; Yalom 1997: 237). Of these, 20 per cent were for reconstructive purposes following mastectomy, while 80 per cent were for cosmetic purposes (Zimmerman 1998). While plastic surgeons reported high levels of patient satisfaction, negative publicity about silicone implants was increasing. Articles appeared in the popular press and journals questioning the safety of the devices. Women began to become vocal about various medical problems they had been experiencing since implantation of the devices. Among the main complications and risks articulated were capsular contracture (when breasts harden), silicone gel leakage and migration, carcinogenicity, interference with detection of tumours, and autoimmune disease. Some women took legal action to seek compensation for pain and suffering which they claimed was caused by silicone implants. Beginning in 1984 a number of women received multimillion dollar damage awards following rulings that silicone implants caused serious medical conditions. Throughout the 1990s, as the implant controversy exploded, tens of thousands of women joined legal suits, resulting in several global settlements against implant manufacturers.

The controversy surrounding silicone implants included the safety concerns but primarily focused on the efficacy of manufacturers and plastic surgeons in sharing and communicating the potential or known risks associated with silicone. What was at stake then, adcovates argued, was not only women's health but the right to be informed consumers. Consumer groups maintained that manufacturers had misled women about the safety of silicone implants by withholding information, including the results of manufacturing studies. A congressional hearing in 1990 found that information had indeed been withheld, in part due to a court order from an early lawsuit. In 1992 the FDA called for a voluntary moratorium on the distribution and implantation of the devices to which the manufacturers agreed. From 1992 onward silicone breast implants were only made available to women who had or will have breast reconstruction surgery, or have complications from existing implants, and only if they agree to participate in a scientific protocol or study. While many women believe that their implants caused connective tissue disease, the medical evidence is more equivocal (Haiken 1997: 232). The medical community has maintained that the scientific evidence linking breast implants and debilitating medical conditions is insufficient. Several medical associations, including the American Medical Association and the American Society of Plastic and Reconstructive Surgeons, issued position statements opposing the 1992 FDA restriction on silicone implants in which they argued the benefits of the devices outweighed the risks (Zimmerman 1998).

In view of this almost exclusive ban on silicone breast implants, manufacturers and plastic surgeons have turned to saline implants, which were marketed as a safe alternative to silicone. These newer implants are lined with silicone but filled with salt water. Directly following the peak of the controversy and the 1992 ban, breast augmentation figures plunged. In 1990 there were 120,000 implants performed, while in 1992 there were only 30,000 (Jacobson 2000). For a few years in the early 1990s, surgeons were removing silicone implants from as many women as they were implanting. However, over the course of a decade, more and more women were seeking breast enhancements. From 1990 to 2000 there was a 92.6 per cent increase in the numbers of breast augmentations. According to the American Academy of Cosmetic Surgery, in 2000 there were 203,310 breast augmentations in the US, making this procedure the third most popular cosmetic surgery following liposuction and cosmetic eyelid procedures. The widespread promotion and utilization of breast enhancements has become a concern for feminist scholars and activists.

CONTEXTUALIZING BREAST AUGMENTATION

A main project of much feminist scholarship on cosmetic surgery is understanding beauty practices within a broader social, cultural and political context (Wolf 1991).

At the forefront of these discussions is the process through which women come to choose cosmetic surgery. A traditional feminist perspective contends that oppressive beauty practices, which produce and maintain women's inferiority, propel women to seek cosmetic surgery (Bordo 1998; Zimmerman 1998). This framework argues women are influenced by cultural images of the idealized body (slenderness, eternal youth, voluptuous breasts), seeing anything outside of that vision as abnormality. Cosmetic surgery represents the extreme end of the wide spectrum of beauty practices meant to deal with 'abnormality'. Women pluck their eyebrows, wax their legs, put on make-up, colour their hair, get breast implants, tummy tucks, and face-lifts in an attempt to achieve this idealized beauty norm.

Susan Bordo points out the existence of a 'consumer system' tied to ideologies of beauty which 'depends on our perceiving ourselves as defective' (Bordo 1998: 201). Cosmetic surgery is part of this consumer system as it offers a seemingly 'quick-fix' to aesthetic 'abnormalities' such as small breasts, large 'ethnic' noses, and wrinkles. With the ability to manipulate and sculpt the body into the ideal, 'the surgically perfected body (perfect according to certain standards, of course) has become the model of "normal", [and] even the ordinary body becomes the defective body' (Bordo 1998: 212). Women therefore engage in cosmetic surgery, the traditional feminist perspective argues, for the same reasons they engage in other beauty practices: because they have internalized the cultural understanding that their value is to be found in their looks (Davis 1995; Bordo 1998). This idea is supported by a web of interlocking social, cultural and political systems. Beauty therefore becomes 'an essential ingredient of the social subordination of women – an ideal way to keep women in line by lulling them into believing that they could gain control over their lives through continued vigilance over their bodies' (Davis 1995: 24). This traditional feminist perspective therefore sees women – and increasingly men – as victims of these oppressive beauty practices.

More recent scholarship argues that while women are influenced by media norms they do not make decisions to undergo cosmetic surgery blindly (Davis 1995; Bordo 1998; Zimmerman 1998). Rather than victims of beauty standards, women negotiate various systems of meaning and actively participate in the cosmetic surgery decision-making process. Kathy Davis emphasizes the agency of women choosing cosmetic surgery. Cosmetic surgery, she argues, represents control and autonomy for women. It is something women 'do for [themselves]', something that 'takes courage' (Davis 1995: 127–8). She contends that the process can be liberating for women as they make choices perceived to increase quality of life, self-determination, and gratification despite opposition they may face from people in their lives. The women she spoke to felt pressure from husbands, lovers, family, friends, and medical professionals *not* to undergo surgery. They had to overcome this resistance in order to receive surgery they themselves felt was entirely necessary to alleviate psychological suffering or an impediment to their self-esteem. In this sense, breast augmentation is a king of self-improvement available to women.

It is on this point of agency and empowerment that feminist philosopher Susan Bordo disagrees with Davis. While Bordo maintains that both she and Davis support the desire not to cast women as victims, as 'passive sponges', she feels Davis goes too far in the opposite direction, equating cosmetic surgery 'with a state of liberation' (Bordo 1998: 197–9). She does not disagree with Davis in that a woman can feel a perceived 'imperfection' to 'cast a shadow over her entire life, influencing how she [feels] about herself, her relationships, her sexuality, her work, and more' (Davis 1995: 72). Rather, Bordo emphasizes that the idealized body images in the media and the accompanying consumer system lead women to 'believe they are nothing (and are frequently treated as nothing) unless they are trim, tight, lineless, bulgeless, and sagless' (Bordo 1993: 45). While individual women may deny the influence of idealized images in their decisions to seek cosmetic surgery, Bordo maintains 'it's hard to account for most of the choices ... outside the context of current cultural norms' (1998: 193). Susan Zimmerman (1998: 44) concurs: 'although women may actively and knowledgeably participate in the medicalization of femininity by choosing to alter their bodies with breast implants, their decisions are, nevertheless, rooted in a complex web of contexts that shape and perpetuate the objectification of their own bodies.'

While Davis found women had few friends and family who supported their desire to have cosmetic surgery, other scholars point to the strong influence of family members, friends, lovers, and medical professionals (Dull and West 1991; Zimmerman 1998). In her study of women who had received breast implants, Zimmerman found that the majority of her respondents (70 per cent) 'who had implants for "cosmetic" purposes perceived this decision as an action taken under specific interpersonal pressure'. Women were encouraged by spouses, intimates and friends to undergo breast augmentation. She found these women to be less than enthusiastic about breast implants but rather 'reluctantly succumbing to ideal beauty standards to please significant others in their lives' (1998: 49). At the moment, it is debatable how much the motivation for larger breasts is located in women's social network and how much breast augmentation is an act of self-expression and personal liberation.

Primary to the feminist discussions on breast augmentation and cosmetic surgery are issues of agency, control and cultural ideologies of the idealized body. Feminist perspectives on cosmetic surgery range from viewing these surgical procedures as self-determining and empowering for women to bodily alterations rooted in cultural and consumer systems that depend upon women seeing themselves as intrinsically defective. Feminists agree, however, on the influence of cultural images on the ideal body and the need to understand breast augmentation in the particular cultural, social, and historical context.

Feelings of inadequacy and inferiority over breast size do not occur in a vacuum. Nor do technological advancements in biomedical enhancement. The popularity of breast augmentation, despite the seeming failure of technology to give women what they want (safe, 'natural' looking, permanent breasts of a certain size), attests to the power of the cultural meaning of breasts in the contemporary American society....

REFERENCES

Bordo, Susan (1993) *Unbearable Weight: Feminism, Western Culture and the Body*, Berkeley, CA: University of California Press.

Bordo, Susan (1998) 'Braveheart, babe, and the contemporary Body', in Erik Parens (ed.) *Enhancing Human Traits: Ethical and Social Implications*, Washington: Georgetown University Press, pp. 189–221.

Conrad, Peter (1992) 'Medicalization and Social Control', *Annual Review of Sociology*: 209–32.

Davis, Kathy (1995) *Reshaping the Female Body: The Dilemma of Cosmetic Surgery*, New York, NY: Routledge.

Dull, Diana and West, Candace (1991) 'Accounting for cosmetic surgery: the accomplishment of gender', *Social Problems*, 38: 54–70.

Gilman, Sander L. (1999) *Making the Body Beautiful: A Cultural History of Aesthetic Surgery*, Princeton, NJ: Princeton University Press.

Gimlin, Debra (2000) 'Cosmetic surgery: beauty as a commodity', *Qualitative Sociology*, **23**: 77–98.

Haiken, Elizabeth (1997) *Venus Envy: A History of Cosmetic Surgery*, Baltimore, MD: The Johns Hopkins University Press.

Jacobson, Nora (2000) *Cleavage: Technology, Controversy, and the Ironies of the Man-Made Breast*, New Brunswick, NJ: Rutgers University Press.

Juengst, Eric T. (1998) 'What does enhancement mean?', in Erik Parens (ed.) *Enhancing Human Traits: Ethical and Social Implications*. Washington DC: Georgetown University Press, pp. 29–48.

Latteier, Carolyn (1998) Breasts: *The Women's Perspective on an American Obsession*, New York: Haworth Press.

Sullivan, Deborah H. (2001) *Cosmetic Surgery: The Cutting Edge of Medicine in America*, New Brunswick, NJ: Rutgers University Press.

Wolf, Naomi (1991) *The Beauty Myth: How Images of Beauty are Used Against Women*, New York: Morrow.

Yalom, Marilyn (1997) *A History of the Breast*, New York: Knopf.

Zimmerman, Susan (1998) *Silicone Survivors: Women's Experiences with Breast Implants*, Philadelphia, PA: Temple University Pres.

Source: P. Conrad and H. Jacobson, 'Enhancing biology: cosmetic surgery and breast augmentation', in S. J. Williams, L. Birke and G. Bendelow (eds) *Debating Biology: Sociological Reflections on Health, Medicine and Society* (London: Routledge, 2003).

Study Questions and Activities

1. Do you think that medicine created the demand for breast augmentation?
2. What twenty-first-century influences affect our view of the 'normal' and the 'ideal' body?
3. With reference to your own professional and personal life, consider your own experiences of body modification or enhancement. What is the difference between therapeutic and cosmetic surgery? Should people visit the dentist for cosmetic reasons? Is there any social or moral difference between leg waxing, toenail painting or rib removal in order to appear more 'attractive'?

——————————————— **Further Reading** ———————————————

For reading focusing on breasts for breastfeeding, as apposed to breasts for aestheticism, see, for example: R. Shaw, 'Performing breastfeeding: embodiment, ethics and the maternal subject', *Feminist Review*, 78 (2004) 96–116 and S. Earle, 'Is breast best?: breastfeeding, motherhood and identity', in S. Earle and G. Letherby (eds) *Gender, Identity and Reproduction: Social Perspectives* (London: Palgrave, 2003). If you are interested more generally in women and body image and body 'enhancement', try to find the book by Kathy Davis, *Reshaping the Female Body: The Dilemma of Cosmetic Surgery* (New York: Routledge, 1995) or that written by Naomi Wolf, *The Beauty Myth: How Images of Beauty are Used Against Women* (New York: Morrow, 1991). For a piece on men, masculinity and body image, see: L. F. Monaghan, 'Body mass index, masculinities and moral worth: men's critical understanding of 'appropriate' weight-for-height', *Sociology of Health and Illness*, 29:4 (2007) 584–609.

Reading 19

Humour and Illness

Alison Chapple and Sue Ziebland

In this reading, we are, again, reminded of the connection between the body and the mind, between feelings and emotional reactions to illness and bodily change. Alison Chapple and Sue Ziebland draw on qualitative data that they collected from 45 men diagnosed with testicular cancer and consider the use of, and reaction to, humour in coping with this experience. Most of the men in the research spoke of using humour in social settings to challenge assumptions about their disease, and in health settings to manage feelings, hide embarrassment, reduce tension, share a sense of solidarity with others, and/or to encourage others to examine themselves for changes to the testes. Chapple and Ziebland's respondents also described their usually positive reactions to jokes made by others, stressing that such jokes helped to dispel tension and reassured men that they were being treated as 'normal'. Occasionally though the men said that they found some humour hurtful, stating that they were sometimes upset by the jokes made by others, particularly if their fertility was affected by their illness and they were unable to father biological children. So although humour can sometimes ease difficult interactions, it can also sometimes lead to further distress.

HUMOR STUDIED AT A SOCIETAL LEVEL

The significance of humor can be studied at two levels, the societal level and the individual, face-to-face, or small-group level (Davies, 1988; Lynch, 2002; Powell & Paton, 1988). At the societal level, humor can be used to question stereotypes, to deflate and denigrate, and to pour scorn on those in power (Dey, 1993). Indeed, Douglas (1975), asserted that all jokes have a "subversive effect on the dominant structure of ideas" (p. 95). Mulkay (1988) suggested that Douglas has oversimplified the relationship between humor and social structure. He pointed out that some jokes are simply "pure humor," in that they are simply meant to amuse (p. 156). He also argued that although much humor is "applied," in the sense that participants treat humor as a vehicle for serious meanings and motives, applied humor can, in principle, have positive as well as negative consequences for the social structure within which it occurs (see, e.g., Radcliffe-Brown, 1952, p. 108). The relationships between humor and social structures, therefore, differ in different kinds of social setting.

At the societal level, the function of jokes has been examined in many areas of social life (Benton, 1988; Holmes & Hay 1997). In the area of disability, Shakespeare (1999) suggested that in some situations, people with a disability might laugh at themselves, at their situation, and at nondisabled people to challenge the prejudice within our culture, to demand acceptance of disability as a respectable dimension of social diversity.

HUMOR STUDIED AT A MICROSOCIOLOGICAL, INDIVIDUAL, OR SMALL-GROUP LEVEL

At a microsociological or small-group level, humor can serve many functions. It can be used to reinforce solidarity between two or more jokers, marking a social boundary between them and other people (Hay, 2000), or to reduce or emphasize a power imbalance between two people (Holmes, 2000). It can also be a device used by individuals as a form of tension management, as a means of coping with uncertainty or adversity, as a way of reducing embarrassment, as a means of exploring ambiguous situations or distancing unpleasantness, as a bid for love and appreciation, or as a means of satisfying exhibitionism (Goffman, 1967; Linstead, 1988; Strean, 1993). People might also use humor to signal to others that their problem should not be taken too seriously (Kelly & Dickinson, 1997).

AMBIGUITY

Sometimes people enjoy deliberately embarrassing others and laugh at them rather than with them (Billig, 2001), and it is not always clear whether those involved in a situation that appears to be humorous actually find it funny. There are occasions when people with a disability or illness might laugh at an incident out of embarrassment or politeness, or to conform to others' apparent opinion that something is comic (Wyer & Collins, 1992). Thus, if an accident or embarrassing situation occurs, people with a disability or problem might laugh with those who, they fear, might be laughing at them, thus "reclaiming the event for farce rather than tragedy" (Stronach & Allan, 1999, p. 34).

ACCOUNTS CAN CHANGE OVER TIME

Sometimes, people who have been seriously ill, and who have been very pessimistic about their situation, later reassess past events. They might see things in a more positive light, reconstructing their identity and interaction with others through humor, and thus producing what has been called a "progressive narrative" (Gergen & Gergen, 1983, p. 259). People might tell a story that once seemed tragic but is now presented as comic, either because the situation has improved or because they realize that their problem or disability is not as serious as they first imagined. Indeed, Mulkay (1988) asserted, "Even the most serious of texts, it seems, can be transformed into humor by means of appropriate interpretative work" (p. 55).

Mulkay (1988) noted that humor helps us deal with problems of multiplicity and contradiction (p. 218). He suggested that the "serious mode" presumes a unitary social reality and that humor occurs because "mundane, serious discourse simply cannot cope with its own interpretive multiplicity" (p. 214)....

HUMOR IN MEDICINE

Doctors and nurses often use "gallows humor" to reduce tension in the operating room, ward, or emergency department (Buxman, 2000; Paquet, 1994; Robinson, 1993). R. Fox (1973), who made an in-depth study of organ transplantation, observed that transplant physicians frequently played "games of chance" (wagering about the possible outcome of risky experiments on human subjects) and that they often made jokes, laughing at their own scientific and therapeutic inadequacies, and aspects of their patients' predicaments that epitomized what medicine does not yet know, and cannot do for them (p. 103). Fox suggested that these jokes allowed expression of a wide range of emotions, including anxiety, guilt, disappointment, anger, and grief, in a way that the group could accept.

Patients also use humor for a variety of reasons. For example, although the relationship between humor and health remains uncertain (Snowden, 2003), some have used humor for its perceived therapeutic effect (Cousins, 1981; Pasquali, 1990). Patients might also use humor to mask feelings or to avoid dealing with serious issues. On the other hand, patients might use jokes to introduce "awkward" topics and to convey messages about taboo subjects, such as death, that might be unacceptable if conveyed seriously (Emerson, 1973), and in some situations, patients or people with disabilities see humor as the only means of making contact with others (Murphy, 1987; Shakespeare, 1999).

TESTICULAR CANCER

Testicular cancer accounts for about 1% of all cancers in males (Power et al., 2001). About 1,400 new cases are diagnosed in the United Kingdom each year, with peak incidence occurring among men aged 25 to 35 years. If diagnosed early, the cure rate is excellent, approaching 100%. Treatment usually involves an orchidectomy (removal of the testicle) and, depending on the type of tumor, might be followed by radiotherapy or chemotherapy to prevent recurrence (Dearnaley, Huddart, & Horwich, 2001).

Testicular cancer usually occurs in one testicle, not both, and although some men might be anxious at times, fearing that cancer will recur (Frank, 1991), quality of life is not much affected. The removal of one testicle does not usually affect sexual performance or the ability to father children (if the other testicle is healthy), and prostheses are available for men whose self-image might be affected by surgery (Chapple & McPherson, in press). However, occasionally surgery to remove abdominal lymph glands can affect a man's ability to ejaculate or, in a more serious situation, cancer might be found in both testicles or in a man born with only one testicle. In these cases, men are usually given testosterone to replace the missing hormones, so sexual intercourse is possible, but children cannot be conceived in the normal manner. However, sperm can be frozen before surgery or chemotherapy for later use. In some circumstances, the side effects of treatment cause serious longterm problems....

METHOD

Participants: The Sample

...we invited participation from men who had had a diagnosis of testicular cancer, recruited mainly through general practitioners (GPs), hospital consultants, and support groups....We had intended to interview about 40 men, but interviewing continued until our sample of 45 included men at different stages of diagnosis, with different types of testicular cancer, and until no new themes emerged from the data....

The Interviews

...

We asked men to tell their whole story, from when they first noticed unusual signs or symptoms. During the very first interview, a man spoke with passion about his experience of other people's jokes. His account made the interviewer listen carefully to other men's experience of "tumor humor" in the narrative section of their interviews....

RESULTS

Almost all the men talked about humor at some stage of the interview, and many raised the subject, recalling jokes made at the time of the diagnosis, in hospital, or later in the work place or among friends. Most of the men recalled verbal jokes, but some described nonverbal humorous situations too. For example, one man remembered that when he returned to work, a colleague mimicked his new body shape, walking round in circles, pretending to be lopsided. This man found this "quite funny," and he said that he preferred it if someone "took the mickey"[1] instead of offering sympathy.

Pure Humor

S. Fox (1990) noted in his study of business school students that sometimes humor tended to oscillate between what Mulkay (1988) called "pure" and "applied" humor (p. 156). This was also evident in our study of men with testicular cancer. This man said that humor helped him "deal" with his illness and, although acknowledging that people deal with it in different ways, reported that he and his predominately male colleagues joked about his condition at every opportunity, as a means of having "office fun."…

Others described genuinely enjoying the funny cards that were sent to them in hospital. Jokes might have helped them to cope but also provided great amusement.

Applied Humor: When Jokes Served Useful Functions

Most of the humor talked about in these interviews seemed to be applied rather than pure (Mulkay, 1988, p. 156). Most men suggested reasons for the jokes made by either themselves or others and explained why humor played such a large part in their lives.

Jokes used to manage feelings in health settings

Men describe how applied humor was used in different health settings to hide feelings and deal with anxiety about the diagnosis and treatment. In our culture, men do not like to appear "weak," because this threatens their masculinity; nor are they expected to show emotion (Kraemer, 2000; Seidler, 1997).… Although some of the men we interviewed said that they broke down and cried when they were told the diagnosis, others used humor to hide their feelings:

> Yeah, um (3.0) I've always been the sort of person that's always fought things, not physically fought, but you know, that's always been the way that I, get on with things and I've always been, you know, wanted to see the funny side of things really. And I actually said to the (1.0)

um to the doctor at the time, when he told me, he said, "[patient's name], you are allowed to show some emotion." And I just said, "Dr, look, I'm a Leeds United supporter,[2] I get worse news than this every Saturday." And he said, "Are you sure you're alright, do you want me to ring people?" I said, "No, no, I'll do it." And he er went out of the room and when he went out the room I burst into tears, and I don't mind admitting it, yeah.

...

It is notable that in some accounts, the men used humor in the interview to divert attention from discussion of sensitive issues. For example, in the following interview, a man says that he uses humor to deal with the situation, but he also appears to divert attention from a difficult issue (the effect on his masculinity) by recalling, and laughing about, his jokes when he was in hospital:

I: Do you ever feel that it's affected your sense of masculinity or being a man only having one testicle?

R: No, I don't think it has, er, I've still got another one. I mean I think it was in the hospital somebody asked me what I was in for and I said "Oh I can only get it twice," [laughs 7.0]

I: So you were making jokes even at that stage?

R: Oh God, yeah [laughs 2.0]. That's just the way I am I'm afraid, yeah that's the way I deal with life in general. I take the piss[3] out of life because it's the only way to get through it. If you take life too seriously you're lost, you might as well just go home and pack your bags right now.

...

Many men asserted that humor helped them cope in hospital....

R: I have a very nice group of friends, all of whom delight in taking the piss and so as a result (2.0) I remember in the hospital the cards I was getting. And one stands out to this very day and I still have it, and it was [laughs 2.0] and it was just simply entitled on the front, "Sorry for the loss of your loved one" [laughs 5.0] and so you can see what sort of friends I had.

I: How did you feel when you got cards like that?

R: Oh I laughed, but that's me you see.

I: Did you genuinely laugh?

R: Absolutely, genuinely laughed.

I: So it didn't upset you when you say they took the piss?

R: Not at all, not at all, because that's the way that I cope really. I like to think I've got a pretty good sense of humor and it has seen me through many, many different situations. And this was certainly one that helped, I mean it really did....

Jokes helped to reassure men that they were being treated as "normal"

As Coates (2003) has noted, "having a laugh" is something that young men value very highly and is central to being accepted as masculine (p. 53). In our interviews, the ability to take a joke is repeatedly presented as an important and valued aspect of self-identity. Men who become ill might fear that they will no longer be treated as an appropriate subject for banter and jokes, which is presented as an important feature of male-dominated environments. They can be reassured if friends and colleagues continue to joke with them. Many respondents emphasized that they did not mind the jokes made by colleagues because they wanted to be treated normally and did not want others to feel sorry for them. Coates's work has demonstrated how men use humor (and many other devices) in their talk to avoid emotional issues. The following excerpt presents one man's impression that among his colleagues the options were limited to humor or pity—a situation he reports managing by telling them to joke about it:

> Because again a lot of people if they've not had it in the family, they don't know nothing about it, as soon as you say you've probably got cancer they think, "Oh blimey, you know, I feel sorry for him, he hasn't got that long left," sort of thing. But once I'd established I knew what testicular cancer was and the survival rate, once I told them all about it they were a lot more chirpy and they all joke about it now as well. Every time I see them they make jokes about it, they laugh about it and that's how I want them to be. I don't want them to be shying away from it and making me to be an example of, "Oh we feel sorry for him," you know, like a charity case. I don't want to be like that at all. I want them just to treat me normally.

Another man also said that he did not mind the jokes because he wanted to be treated normally, because in his view he was not a different person. He interpreted the jokes—which he stresses that he found funny despite being asked about "bad jokes"—as a positive sign:

> *I*: Did you ever have to put up with any bad jokes about the situation?
> *R*: I found them funny.
> *I*: Did you, were there some jokes?
> *R*: Yeah, there were some, but I don't find them anything [laughs 3.0] to be worried about, I really don't. And I find that if you can joke and have a bit of fun about it, that's much better than people skirting round going, "Oh my God he's got cancer." You see I don't really find it a problem. I prefer someone doing that and treating me the same as they always have done, and all my friends did—as opposed to looking at me as if I'm something that's different, because I'm not.

When Humor was Deemed Inappropriate

Emerson (1973), writing about humor in hospital situations, noted that sometimes the listener will not accept a joke, considering a topic too serious to remain in a joking framework (p. 271). Some men were clearly aware of a tension when using humor about their disease. For example, one man commented, "I know it isn't a joking matter but it [joking] made me feel better when I was waiting to find out." The meanings that people attribute to a cancer diagnosis are important here. Men said that their joking sometimes shocked those who did not understand that testicular cancer was not a death sentence:

> Now I was actually a shift leader so I was in charge of my shift of people. I went back for those couple of weeks. I still had my hair, and was feeling okay. Um, people knew what I had and

wouldn't mention it. They assumed, and I found this out later, that people thought I was going to die. Um, so they wouldn't talk about it, either because of the way I made jokes about it, which um upset some people because they wouldn't talk about it. And someone actually said, "How can you joke about it, you know, if you're dying?" Um (3.0) I didn't feel I was dying because I felt at that point I was going to beat it, um, and I felt you had to be positive anyway.

A few men themselves said that they thought that jokes could be "childish," "inappropriate," or "hurtful." One young man said that he welcomed jokes as long as the intention was good but added that he would not be pleased if people joked without having also shown concern:

> But the jokes do come thick and fast (2.0) but if the wrong person said something to me that perhaps (1.0) wasn't so considerate, and just thought, "I'll just take the piss out of him for the sake of it," and perhaps wasn't one little bit concerned when I did have cancer, then I would probably get a little bit upset.

Another man, who recognized that jokes were helpful in some circumstances, said that sometimes the jokes could "dig a bit too deep":

> R: But I think the problem with jokes is sometimes even if you're going through something and someone's making a joke about it, you don't really want to appear hurt. Um, I think jokes can sometimes (1.0) dig a bit too deep or too personally, but um, unless it really goes too deep or too personally then you just go along with the joke.
> I: Did you ever feel slightly hurt but that you felt you had to go along with the jokes?
> R: Um, I, I knew (1.0) everyone telling a joke or making a joke of it, um (2.0) they were all doing it for the right reasons and um, they weren't, they certainly weren't there to hurt me. So, I mean I'd say the jokes were sometimes um (3.0) you know maybe one or two too much too often, but um (2.0) it was something you know you laugh along with. And it helps, it helps you get through it, because initially you're trying to come to terms with who you are now (1.0) because you're you know, the same person but minus a testicle....

The men who feared jokes the most and did not want to talk about their cancer in the work place or among friends were those who were unfortunate enough to lose both testicles and whose fertility had been affected. For example, one young man was born with only one testicle. He developed cancer in the other testicle and had to have it removed. Although he presented a conventional masculine and positive attitude to humor, when he was asked about "bad jokes," he suggested that there were boundaries:

> Well jokes I think humor is (2.0) I think it's great at combating you know pretty much every sort of bad thing, I mean I think there's always a time for humor, you know but (2.0) it's a funny one (2.0). I mean I would like to say that, God I would love to sit around and laugh about it. I think a lot of it depends on who the joke is, who it's told from. If I'm sat in a room with my best and closest friends, then yeah I like jokes, it's cool, I think it can take the (1.0) it can just take the harsh edge off it. I mean I think you should be able to laugh at these things, to make it better you know because laughter is just, laughter I personally believe helps you get better quicker anyway, it just helps you in a lot of ways. But it would definitely only be my

closest friends and family. Um (1.0) jokes, if for example I had a job where, I had a job that I went to and my coworkers who I sort of liked and got on with, they got wind of it and they made jokes about it, that would drive me crazy.

Another man also lost both his testicles, one in 1991 because of cancer and the other in 1993, because it was infected and fibrosed. He also suffered serious side effects of chemotherapy. He recalled his reaction to jokes made by friends and explained why he never discussed his cancer with work colleagues:

R: Er yeah, I've had the bad jokes, but even nowadays people say things, and for a second it strikes a chord and then when people realize er they are so apologetic. You know the number of times you hear "Oh you haven't got the balls to do that," well I don't have.

I: How does that make you feel when you hear that?

R: Inside it makes me feel upset. Friends of mine that know me don't crack the jokes like that any more but it's not a joke er, it is something that is very serious, it is life-threatening. Look you leave testicular cancer all by itself, cooking very, very nicely in your body it will kill you. There is no doubt about that whatsoever, it will kill you (…)

I: Perhaps just one more question, thinking back to when you first discovered you had testicular cancer, did you feel you could talk to other people and tell work about it?

R: No, not at all. I was frightened of the jokes....

DISCUSSION

Our findings show that nearly all of the humor described in the interviews seems to have been applied rather than pure humor (Mulkay, 1988). Men demonstrate the role that humor can have in easing difficult situations, expressing camaraderie, and challenging others' beliefs about testicular cancer. Although humor was widely reported to have a beneficial effect, some men described instances when it had been thought inappropriate by others—particularly those who were unaware of the good prognosis. Men also pointed out that the intention behind the humor is important, though there were very few examples of circumstances where any malevolent intent was suspected. We have looked at humor mainly from the point of view of men who have lost one testicle. Losing both testicles is another matter, and as this article has shown, jokes can be especially hurtful to men who cannot hope to have children of their own....

NOTES

1. Take the mickey/mick (out of something) is U.K. slang meaning to laugh at someone and make them seem silly, by copying their behavior or tricking them in an amusing or unkind way (Woodford & Jackson, 2003).
2. Leeds United is an English football team that achieved great success in the mid-1990s but at the time of this interview had had a disastrous season and was on the brink of financial ruin.

3. Take the piss (out of something) is U.K. slang that means to make a joke about something or make it look silly (Woodford & Jackson, 2003).

REFERENCES

Benton, G. (1988). The origins of the political joke. In C. Powell & G. Paton (Eds.), *Humor in society: Resistance and control* (pp. 33–55). Basingstoke, UK: Macmillan.

Billig, M. (2001). Humor and embarrassment: Limits of "nice-guy" theories of social life. *Theory, Culture and Society*, 18(5), 23–43.

Buxman, K. (2000). Humor in critical care: No joke. *AACN Critical Issues*, 11(1), 120–127.

Coates, J. (2003). *Men talk*. Oxford, UK: Blackwell.

Cousins, N. (1981). *Anatomy of an illness as perceived by the patient: Reflections on healing and regeneration*. New York: Bantam.

Davies, C. (1988). Stupidity and rationality: Jokes from the iron cage. In C. Powell & G. Paton (Eds.), *Humor in society. Resistance and control* (pp. 1–32). London: Macmillan.

Dearnaley, D., Huddart, R., & Horwich, A. (2001). Managing testicular cancer. *British Medical Journal*, 322, 1583–1588.

Dey, I. (1993). *Qualitative data analysis*. London: Routledge.

Douglas, M. (1975). *Implicit meanings: Essays in anthropology*. London: Routledge Kegan Paul.

Emerson, J. (1973). Negotiating the serious import of humor. In A. Birenbaum & E. Sararin (Eds.), *People in places: The sociology of the familiar* (pp. 269–280). London: Nelson.

Fox, R. (1973). *The courage to fail: A social view of organ transplants and dialysis* (2nd ed. rev.). Chicago: University of Chicago Press.

Fox, S. (1990). The ethnography of humor and the problem of social reality. *Sociology*, 24(3), 431–446.

Frank, A. W. (1991). *At the will of the body: Reflections on illness*. New York: Houghton Mifflin.

Gergen, K., & Gergen, M. (1983) Narratives of the self. In T. Sabin & K. Scheibe (Eds.), *Studies in social identity* (pp. 254–273). New York: Praeger.

Goffman, E. (1967). *Interaction ritual*. New York: Pantheon.

Hay J. (2000). Functions of humor in the conversations of men and women. *Journal of Pragmatics*, 32, 709–742.

Holmes, J. (2000). Politeness, power and provocation: How humor functions in the workplace. *Discourse Studies*, 2(2), 159–185.

Holmes, J., & Hay, J. (1997). Humor as an ethnic boundary marker in New Zealand interaction. *Journal of Intercultural Studies*, 18(2), 127–151.

Kelly, M., & Dickinson, H. (1997). The narrative self in autobiographical accounts of illness. *Sociological Review*, 45(2), 254–278.

Kraemer, S. (2000). The fragile male. *British Medical Journal*, 32, 1609–1612.

Linstead, S. (1988). "Jokers wild": Humor in organisational culture. In C. Powell & G. Paton (Eds.), *Humor in society: Resistance and control* (pp. 123–148). London: Macmillan.

Lynch, O. (2002). Humorous communication: Finding a place for humor in communication research. *Communication Theory*, 12(4), 423–445.

Mulkay, M. (1988). *On humor: Its nature and its place in modern society*. Cambridge, UK: Polity.

Murphy, R. (1987). *The body silent*. New York: Henry Holt.

Paquet J. (1994). Managing stress in the OR: Survery results. *Today's OR*, 16(4), 27–31.

Pasquali, E. (1990). Learning to laugh: Humor as therapy. *Journal of Psychosocial Nursing and Mental Health Services*, 28(3), 31–35.

Powell, C., & Paton, G. (1988). Introduction. In C. Powell & G. Paton (Eds.), *Humor in society: Resistance and control* (pp. xiii–xxii) London: Macmillan.

Power, D., Brown, R., Brock, C., Payne, H., Majeed, A., & Babb, P. (2001). Trends in testicular carcinoma in England and Wales 1971–99. *BJU International, 87*, 361–365.

Radcliffe-Brown, A. (1952). *Structure and function in primitive society*. London: Cohen and West.

Robillard, A. (1999). Wild phenomena and disability jokes. *Body and Society, 5*(4), 61–65.

Robinson, V. (1993). The purpose and function of humor in OR nursing. *Today's OR Nurse, 15*(6), 7–12.

Seidler, V. (1997). *Man enough: Embodying masculinities*. London: Sage.

Shakespeare, T. (1999). Joking a part. *Body and Society, 5*(4), 47–52.

Snowden, A. (2003). Humor and health promotion. *Health Education Journal, 62*(2), 143–152.

Strean, H. (1993). *Jokes: Their purpose and meaning*. London: Jason Aronson.

Stronach, I., & Allan, J. (1999). Joking with disability: What's the difference between the comic and the tragic in disability discourses? *Body and Society, 5*(4), 31–45.

Wyer, R, & Collins, J. (1992). A theory of humor elicitation. *Psychological Review, 99*(4), 663–688.

Yus, F. (2003). Humor and the search for relevance. *Journal of Pragmatics, 35*(9), 1295–1331.

Source: A. Chapple and S. Ziebland, 'The role of humour for men with testicular cancer', *Qualitative Health Research*, 14:8 (2004) 1123–39.

Study Questions and Activities

1. What is the difference between pure and applied humour?
2. Is humour gendered? Can you identify other types of emotional display that are considered to be stereotypically female or stereotypically male? Would you challenge these stereotypes?
3. What functions can humour serve?
4. Do you use humour in your own professional practice? Why or why not? What other emotions do you and/or your clients display and/or try to hide?

Further Reading

Other work on humour (some relating to health and illness, some more general) includes: M. Billig, 'Humor and embarrassment. Limit of "nice-guy" theories of social life', *Theory, Culture and Society*, 18:5 (2001) 23–43; C. Powell and G. Paton (eds) *Humour in Society: Resistance and Control* (Houndmills: Macmillan, 1988) and J. Bremmer and H. Roodenburg (eds) *A Cultural History of Humor* (Cambridge: Polity Press, 1997). For further specific reference to the use of humour in relation to issues of health and in healthcare settings, see: K. Buxman, 'Humor in critical care: no joke AACN', *Critical Issues*, 11:1 (2000) 120–7 and C. Exley and G. Letherby, 'Managing a disrupted lifecourse: issues of identity and emotion work', *Health*, 5:1 (2001) 112–32. Exley and Letherby are concerned, as Shaw is, not just with the use of humour and the management of self in healthcare settings but also in familial and friendship relationships. They also consider other emotional responses to the experience of living with a terminal illness and the experience of infertility.

Reading 20

Anorexia as Disability

Stephanie Tierney

Most people would not ordinarily regard anorexia as a disability which, as Stephanie Tierney argues, exposes the narrow social understanding of the term disability. Using the social model of disability, Tierney suggests in this reading that the oppression faced by people labelled 'anorexic' mirrors that which other writers suggest disadvantages disabled people. Tierney outlines the reasons for and against defining anorexia as a disability and the arguments for incorporating the experiences of people labelled 'anorexic' into the Disability Movement. Drawing on data from interviews with nine individuals medically defined or self-defined as 'anorexic', Tierney explores both the reasons against classing anorexia as a disability (including individuals' reluctance to assume this identity and the fact that such a claim is likely to be challenged by others) and the reasons for classing anorexia as a disability (including the fact that this may help individuals to feel more entitled to public support and may lead to a greater understanding of the condition). Towards the end of the reading, Tierney goes on to consider medical reactions to anorexia and the effects of the labelling process upon an individual's identity.

INTRODUCTION

Anorexia is a high profile condition, often associated with 'superwaif' models and other stars. However, it must be remembered that anorexia affects ordinary people in their daily lives, who have to fight against misconceptions that they are going through a teenage fad or have a 'slimmer's disease', misconceptions that influence how these individuals are treated in society. During the 8 years I have been labelled 'anorexic', my situation has been referred to in various ways: madness, female hysteria, illness, attention seeking, brain disorder, hereditary, family problem, media created. However, 'disabled' is one definition society has declined from imposing on me, even though at one point I became reticent to leave the house because of hostile stares and I was sometimes unable to attend school because the 'stairs' there also proved a barrier to my emaciated frame. So can 'anorexics' legitimately class themselves as disabled? Would they wish to be defined as thus? How does their struggle typify that faced by other disabled people?... I found the social model of disability especially illuminating and applicable to anorexia because it moves away from locating 'disability' within the individual towards locating it in society [1]. It is with this belief in mind that I decided to use this model as a tool when examining anorexia.

Whilst collecting data for this research I was interested in interviewees' reluctance to self-define as disabled. This issue is examined below, as are similarities between the oppression faced by people labelled 'anorexic' and that which theorists suggest disadvantages disabled people. In addition, the advantages of incorporating 'anorexics' into the Disability Movement will be discussed.

ANOREXIA

Anorexia emerged as a clinical entity during the late 19th century, in a social milieu preoccupied with nervous disorders (Malson, 1998, p. 59). The two doctors who first took an interest in this phenomenon defined it differently. Charles Lasegue linked it to hysteria, whereas William Gull saw it as a distinct disease (Malson, 1998, p. 66). After these doctors' 'discovered' and defined anorexia, it was regarded primarily as a psycho-medical condition, a mental and behavioural disorder or syndrome [World Health Organisation (WHO), 1992], with distinctive symptoms. Medical discourses continue to dominate social and academic 'understanding' of the condition (Hepworth, 1999, p. 2) and, consequently, a restoration of weight and a reversal of organic complaints are judged to constitute a recovery (MacLeod, 1981, p. 144). However, this fails to account for the fact that people may continue having 'anorexic' thoughts and behaviours around food, whilst no longer possessing an 'anorexic' body.

The use of the term 'anorexic' in this paper would be contested by some theorists, like Hepworth (1999), who argue that using this term positions those who self-starve as medical entities. Yet because 'anorexic' is a recognised term it is adopted throughout, but in inverted commas, indicating that it is not linked to narrow medical definitions. It must be recognised that 'anorexics', like disabled people, cannot be seen as homogenous and, although traditionally perceived as affecting white, middle-class, young women, research shows that both genders and people of all ages, social and ethnic groups experience the condition (Abraham & Llewellyn-Jones, 1997). Such variables are bound to shape how it is encountered and, therefore, consideration should be given to personal experience of the condition, whilst maintaining a social perspective. This is attempted within the paper, which incorporates interviews from individual 'anorexics', but also discusses social issues associated with anorexia. By amalgamating empirical and theoretical enquiries, I hope to demonstrate that anorexia can be seen as an individual experience with social causes and consequences.

DATA COLLECTION

Qualitative data was collected during in-depth, one-to-one, semi-structured interviews with nine participants, referred to by the following pseudonyms: Crissy, Fiona, Heather, Jayne, Kitty, Louise, Marie, Petra and Shauna. These nine participants attend a support group open to individuals who feel they have a problem around food, at which I act as facilitator. Members range in age from 19 to late 20s. During the 3 years this group has been running, no more than four people from ethnic minorities and only two males have attended....

ANOREXIA AS A DISABILITY?

Most people would not ordinarily regard anorexia as a disability, exposing the narrow social understanding of the latter term, which the general public still tends to reserve for people with physical impairments. Yet, for certain bureaucratic and financial purposes, anorexia is classed as a disability. For example, 'anorexics' are entitled to Disability Living Allowance (DLA) and, at university, people with the condition can claim extra financial support as disabled students. Although 'anorexics' may adopt the label in these circumstances, like many other people with impairments, it is done for expediency (Ablon, 1990), it is not a label they would wish to become part of their identity. This section examines some of the reasons behind 'anorexics'' resistance to being called 'disabled' and counteracts these with benefits that may derive from doing thus.

Reasons Against Classing Anorexia as a Disability

A fundamental barrier to classing anorexia as a disability is individuals' reluctance to assume this identity. Only one interviewee felt able to self-define as disabled. Most interviewees adopted a medical/individual paradigm towards disability, locating it within an impairment and linking it primarily to physical conditions and limitations:

> ... even though I am registered disabled, I get DLA, I don't think of myself as disabled ... I think I feel quite capable and I feel that being disabled is ... when you can't do things I suppose, when part of you doesn't work properly. (Jayne)

This impeded participants' ability to think of themselves as disabled, highlighting the social model's failure to penetrate mainstream thinking, an issue that needs addressing if this concept is to be inclusive and influential.

Individuals may be disinclined to self-define as disabled because of the stereotypical portrayal of disabled people as needy, a characteristic 'anorexics' try to eradicate from their persona (Orbach, 1993) and, for some interviewees, the word 'disabled' also intimated that their condition was permanent:

> You say these people are disabled and like it's a chronic condition that they're always going to be disabled. You're labelling them for life. (Petra)

In addition, self-defining as disabled was regarded as limiting one's life opportunities. The contribution disabled people make to society is often demeaned; their views are frequently disregarded because a 'faulty' body or mind comes to define their whole being, bringing negative consequences in their social life or workplace. Interviewees felt that using this term as a form of identity could impinge on their relationships, changing people's view of them, positioning them as weak and vulnerable, or could jeopardise their career, as Petra commented:

> ... on every job application form there is a section on medical problems that asks have you ever had any form of mental illness. I mean do you say yes, do you say no, what do you say? Some of them say have you ever suffered from any serious illness. And there's a part of you that says, yes, anorexia is a very serious illness, but there's a part of you that says I won't get the job if I put that.

Unfortunately, if 'anorexics' do decide to class themselves as disabled, they may find the legitimacy of such a claim is questioned. For example, if a person has a 'normal' body, but 'anorexic' thoughts and behaviours, the condition is invisible and its reality may be doubted. In addition, anorexia is often regarded as self-inflicted because from a cultural perspective it is viewed as an extension of the socially valued slim 'ideal' that the public is encouraged to pursue. Therefore, the oppression and discrimination 'anorexics' face, as a result of their 'abnormal' appearance or behaviour, can tend to be overlooked:

> I think there are people out there who would not see [anorexia] as a proper disability, people who aren't suffering from it, especially when you don't look like a skeleton. And there might be some kind of backlash from that and I don't know whether really anorexic people could cope very well with someone saying, 'well you don't deserve that' ... (Fiona)

This scepticism may be especially strong when 'anorexics' request financial assistance because they are physically and/or mentally unable to work. When applying for public support people with impairments are forced to accentuate their limitations (Morrissey, 1999, p. 101). For 'anorexics', being made to expose their difficulties can cause their already fragile self-esteem to erode even further. Like other disabled people, they do not want to have to assume the role of 'victim' (Peters, 1996, p. 217).

Reasons for Classing Anorexia as a Disability

Conversely, categorising anorexia as a disability, rather than simply an aversion to food, could be beneficial and liberating for those with the condition. As stated above, when an 'anorexic' is at a low point she/he may be unable to work and will have to claim benefits. As a result, strong feelings of guilt can arise, illustrated in the following comment from Jayne:

> ... I get DLA, which means I've got enough money so I don't have to work to support myself, that I can do my studying without having to work ... I feel really guilty for claiming benefits, I feel that I don't deserve them. But I know that without them I'd be able to do nothing and I'd get really ill because I'm not fit enough to work ... So in that sense I feel I do need benefits, but I still feel really guilty.

To regard anorexia as a disability may therefore make these individuals feel less 'fraudulent' when accessing public support.

In addition, if anorexia was regarded as a disability the condition may be treated seriously, with greater understanding, as Fiona outlined:

> Anorexics don't need the actual physical help that a disabled badge or whatever gives you, but it could help mentally to realise ... that it counts as a disability and that would help, because it wouldn't then be dismissed as self-inflicted.

This may promote more openness, and would be especially useful to male and older 'anorexics', who often feel that the term anorexia relates to young women wishing to look like supermodels. As a result, more 'atypical' cases of anorexia might come to light, reversing misconceived notions that it only affects teenage girls.

Seeing anorexia as a disability would also emphasise the fact that, like other conditions such as arthritis, it is in a state of flux:

> ... people expect anorexics to be skeletal, there's no continuum. It tends to be viewed as something that you've got when you look really awful and then when you get to the stage that I'm at you're better. I think at this stage, in some ways, it's harder because you've still got anorexic thoughts and behaviours but without the body to match. People need to be educated that it's not something that just goes away when you put on weight. I think eating disorders are so misunderstood, especially ... I would say by some of the people who are supposed to be dealing with them, like GPs, teachers. (Fiona)

Classing anorexia as a disability highlights its longevity, which, as suggested in the above quote, is not gone once weight is regained. Individuals with 'anorexic' thoughts, but a 'normal' body may still have problems performing simple activities, such as going out for a meal, going on a catered holiday, or even going food shopping because of others' reactions to their behaviour:

> I spend hours in supermarkets, literally. People must think I'm trying to shop lift or something, but really bad at it ... I find it just daunting ... When I'm in the aisles I get confused and find it hard to think about what I need. I was trying to buy some bacon the other day ... The amount of times I've tried to buy it and haven't been able to. I've put it in and out of my basket so many times. The third time I went past it the other day I managed to put it in my basket and brought it home but it's still in my fridge, I haven't touched it. But I suppose being in the fridge is a step closer than it being on the supermarket shelf. (Crissy)

'Anorexics' need to speak out against the discrimination they encounter because of their appearance, behaviour or because of social stereotypes associated with the terms anorexia and eating disorder, stereotypes of young girls vainly pursuing a thin 'ideal'. Adopting the term disabled and incorporating 'anorexics' experiences and words into the social model, as attempted in this article, could go some way to highlighting the oppression they face, outlined in the following section which examines how social model literature relates to and reflects 'anorexics' situation....

Medicine

In the past, disability was associated with mystical and religious discourses. Then, around the seventeenth and eighteenth centuries, it was medicalised, coming under state control (Ryan & Thomas, 1987). Consequently, the medical model dominated understanding of this issue until challenged by the social model. The history of anorexia is similar, regarded as a religious, spiritual practice in medieval times and only relatively recently (the late nineteenth century) as a medical entity (Hepworth, 1999; MacSween, 1993; Malson, 1998). Unfortunately, the medical model still dominates discourses about anorexia, influencing how 'anorexics' are thought of and treated.

Disability theorists declare that doctors take a controlling role in relationships with patients, ignoring what people have to say about their impairments, referred to as 'epistemic invalidation' by Wendell (1996, p. 127). When Gull first wrote about anorexia as a medical condition he argued against patients having any input into treatment, regarding them as being of unsound mind (Hepworth, 1999, p. 35). This remains common practice today, as suggested by Jayne:

> In hospital the idea is that you don't negotiate, you don't bargain. In a way there's this idea that if you get someone to a healthy weight and get them to keep there then eventually they'll be able to live with it. Personally, I don't think it works because I've never ... no one I've met has that happened to.

Many doctors have little training in anorexia (Palmer, 1980, p. 2) and their under-standing of the condition tends to reflect general social beliefs about it being a form of attention seeking or a vanity issue. Doctors frequently treat 'anorexics' (and other disabled people; see Begum, 1996) as stereotypes, failing to take them seriously:

> I'd mentioned it to my GP and had to keep going back … it was the third time I mentioned it that he eventually accepted I wasn't just seeking attention. (Louise)

For disabled people and 'anorexics', the medicalisation of their condition can be oppressive. It means that they are disassociated from the mainstream, a necessary division to justify the inhumane treatment that may sometimes be experienced at the hands of doctors. For instance, 'anorexics' have been threatened with barbaric interventions such as force-feeding, electro-convulsive therapy (ECT) and lobotomies to get them to eat and in some cases these threats have been carried through (Shelley, 1997). In Great Britain, a person who is self-starving can be 'sectioned' under the Mental Health Act if their life is thought to be at risk; yet even if 'anorexics' have not been sectioned, hospital treatment may still be abusive when behavioural modification programmes are exercised (Orbach, 1993, p. 165). Behavioural modification involves a system of rewards and punishment, whereby removal of clothing, privacy and contact with others is used to coerce an individual into following hospital treatment. An 'anorexic' patient may only win back the 'right' to read a book, for example, or telephone relatives, by increasing her/his weight. It is still the preferred way of treating anorexia in many hospitals, even though it often proves ineffective. Patients will 'eat their way out of hospital' only to lose weight after being discharged because underlying social or psychological problems go ignored.

Professionals and relatives often turn their attention towards 'feeding up' the emaciated individual, but what starts as concern can turn to hostility when it appears that she/he is unwilling to forgo what is regarded as 'an unnecessary, self-imposed disease' (Morgan, 1977, p. 1655):

> My family can't understand why I'm doing this to me, why I'm doing it to them and I feel as if they are bullying me for it. They don't really understand however much I try to explain it. It just frustrates me and we end up arguing. They've just grown tired of me because they think I don't do enough to help myself. (Heather)

Once anorexia is diagnosed, individuals are expected to want to get better. Therefore, 'anorexics' are criticised for not working at their recovery, for failing to co-operate with doctors. Their condition is seen as self-inflicted, which reflects the fact that, today, people are called on to control and maintain their own health, through exercise and diet. We are indoctrinated to believe we can achieve well-being by being prudent and disciplined. Impaired bodies, therefore, are depicted as faulty because they expose the inability of man to have complete control over nature and because they stray too far from the 'norm'.…

Labelling/Identity

People may assume a label, like 'disabled', for political or personal gains, such as taking part in the Disability Movement, or to receive financial assistance. However, this is different to having a label imposed on them for diverting from the 'norm', as in the case of individuals being labelled 'anorexic'. In such circumstances, once someone is labelled, she/he has to fight to be seen as an individual, as Marie explained:

> I think one of the worst things now is that even after being at a reasonably normal weight for a couple of years, friends and relatives, especially those who don't see me so often, still come up and tell me ... how well I'm looking and ask me how I'm coping. It's like I'll never escape this thing because other people still associate me with that stick like creature ... I try and push the problem to the back of mind and concentrate on living, but there are always people too ready to remind me of it.

Psychiatrists' power to define mental dysfunction has been criticised by the antipsychiatry movement because it is based on arbitrary social rules and norms (Borsay, 1986, p. 182). This movement, established in the 1960s, argues that the label of insanity involves 'evaluation, judgement and condemnation of human behaviour' (Busfield, 1996, p. 66). People classed as 'mentally ill' can be seen as breaking taken-for-granted rules governing public interaction, for example standing a certain distance from someone when speaking to her/him (Busfield, 1996, p. 67). Consequently, people who adopt an approach to food regarded as 'abnormal' are labelled as having an eating disorder, a label much resisted by those who self-starve because it is 'caught in a web of complex [negative] social meanings' (Bray, 1996, p. 417).

Identity can be conceptualised as a multiplicity of different and shifting, contradictory subjectivities (Malson, 1998, p. 28), but medical and psychiatric labels and discourses accompanying them mean people get 'typed' (Shearer, 1981, p. 47) and associated with their impairment. In addition, identity is something produced through interaction, shaped in part by others' definitions (Jenkins, 1996). Thus, because disabled people spend so much time around non-disabled individuals they may take on the latter's negative conceptions of disability, internalising social prejudices (French, 1996, p. 153). Theorists warn that changes in society can only be advanced once disabled people address their own negative attitudes towards disability gained through social conditioning (Rieser, 1990; Morris, 1991). However, many disabled people have little or no contact with a subculture 'that destigmatises or positively values their difference from the non-disabled' (Wendell, 1996, p. 60), making identification as disabled hard. This is why the Disability Movement is so important in disabled people's fight for equality, a movement that could benefit 'anorexics' in their struggle for self-definition, away from misconceptions of the condition present in society. It is hoped that, eventually, people labelled, thus may come to construct the term for themselves, an example of conscious raising. Associating with others facing similar prejudices and stereotypes from society would enable those individuals defined as 'anorexic' to gain a sense of empowerment and understanding....

NOTE

1. Cooper's article was a key motivation behind this work (see Cooper, 1997).

REFERENCES

ABLON, J. (1990) Ambiguity and difference: families with dwarf children, *Social Science and Medicine*, 30(8), pp. 879–887.

ABRAHAM, S. & LLEWELLYN-JONES, D. (1997) *Eating Disorders: the facts*, 4th edn. (Oxford, Oxford University Press).

BEGUM, N. (1996) General practitioners' role in shaping disabled women's lives, in: C. BARNES & G. MERCER (Eds) *Exploring the Divide: illness and disability* (Leeds, Disability Press).

BORSAY, A. (1986) Personal trouble or public issue? Towards a model of policy for people with physical and mental disabilities, *Disability, Handicap and Society*, 1(2), pp. 179–195.

BRAY, A. (1996) The anorexic body: reading disorders, *Cultural Studies*, 10(3), pp. 413–429.

BUSFIELD, J. (1996) *Men, Women and Madness—understanding gender and mental disorder* (London, Macmillan).

COOPER, C. (1997) Can a fat woman call herself disabled? *Disability & Society*, 12(1), pp. 31–41.

FRENCH, S. (1996) Stimulation exercises in disability awareness training: a critique, in: G. HALES (Ed.) *Beyond Disability: towards an enabling society* (London, Sage and Open University Press).

HEPWORTH, J. (1999) *The Social Construction of Anorexia Nervosa* (London, Sage).

JENKINS, R. (1996) *Social Identity* (London, Routledge).

MACLEOD, S. (1981) *The Art of Starvation* (London, Virago).

MACSWEEN, M. (1993) *Anorexic Bodies: a feminist and sociological perspective on anorexia nervosa* (London, Routledge).

MALSON, H. (1998) *The Thin Woman: feminism, post-structuralism and the social psychology of anorexia nervosa* (London, Routledge).

MASON, M. (1990) Internalised oppression, in: R. RIESER & M. MASON (Eds) *Disability Equality in the Classroom: a human rights issue* (London, Inner London Education Authority).

MORGAN, H.G. (1977) Fasting girls and our attitudes to them, *British Medical Journal*, 2, pp. 1652–1655.

MORRIS, J. (1991) *Pride Against Prejudice: transforming attitudes towards disability* (London, Women's Press).

MORRISSEY, M.C. (1999) Limits and improvisation: liberating aspects of disability, *Disability Studies Quarterly*, 19(2), Spring, pp. 100–104.

ORBACH, S. (1993) *Hunger Strike: the anorexic's struggle as a metaphor for our age*, 2nd edn. (Harmondsworth, Penguin).

PALMER, R.L. (1980) *Anorexia Nervosa: a guide for sufferers and their families* (Harmondsworth, Penguin).

PETERS, S. (1996) The politics of disabled identity, in: L. BARTON (Ed.) *Disability and Society: emerging issues and insight* (London, Longman).

RIESER, R. (1990) Internalised oppression: how it seems to me, in: R. RIeser & M. MASON (Eds) *Disability Equality in the Classroom* (London, Inner London Education Authority).

RYAN, J. & THOMAS, F. (1987) *The Politics of Mental Handicap* (London, Free Association Books).

SHEARER, A. (1981) *Disability: whose Handicap?* (Oxford, Basil Blackwell).

SHELLEY, R. (Ed.) (1997) *Anorexics on Anorexia* (London, Jessica Kingsley Publishers).

SUSMAN, J. (1994) Disability, stigma and deviance, *Social Science and Medicine*, 38(1), pp. 15–22.

WENDELL, S. (1996) *The Rejected Body* (London, Routledge).

WILLIAMS, G. (1996) Representing disability: some questions of phenomenology and politics, in: C. BARNES & G. MERCER (Eds) *Exploring the Divide. Illness and Disability* (Leeds, Disability Press).

WORLD HEALTH ORGANISATION (1992) *ICD-10: classification of mental and behavioural disorders: clinical descriptions and diagnostic guideline* (Geneva, World Health Organisation).

Source: S. Tierney, 'A reluctance to be defined 'disabled':
how can the social model of disability enhance understanding of anorexia?',
Disability and Society, 16:5 (2001) 749–64.

Study Questions and Activities

1. Stephanie Tierney claims that a consideration of anorexia as a disability improves both the understanding of the condition and the experience of anorexia itself, as well as being beneficial to Disability Studies. Do you agree?
2. Looking back at Reading 18, do you think that anorexia is a form of self-induced bodily enhancement as far as the anorexic person is concerned?
3. Go to any health food shop or newsagents and buy a selection of magazines focusing on healthy and healthy living (alternatively, look for these in your local library). What messages on body shape and size do these publications promote? How are these similar (or different) to the messages in (a) celebrity magazines and (b) magazines aimed at teenage girls? Which of these messages would you want to challenge and why?
4. Reflecting on your own professional experiences, how significant do you think that labelling a patient or client as sick/well, as 'normal'/'abnormal', or as disabled/able influences their sense of self?

Further Reading

In her 1997 article, 'Can a fat woman call herself disabled?', *Disability and Society*, 12:1, 31–41, Charlotte Cooper challenges the definition and boundaries of disability, just as Stephanie Tierney does. Tierney's and Cooper's articles are interesting to compare to the political challenge that writers, researchers and activists in the area of Disability Studies engage in. For examples, see Further Reading section of Reading 27 in Part V of this book. Other interesting and useful books in this area include: J. Morris, *Pride against Prejudice: Transforming Attitudes Towards Disability* (London: Women's Press, 1991): M. Oliver, *Understanding Disability: From Theory to Practice* (London: Macmillan, 1994) and J. Campbell and M. Oliver, *Disability Politics* (London: Routledge, 1996). With reference to women and bodily identity, the following provide a valuable critique of the often contradictory, certainly changeable, expectations on women: K. Chernin, *The Hungry Self: Women, Eating and Identity*

(London: Virago, 1986); M. Macsween, *Anorexic Bodies: A Feminist and Sociological Perspective on Anorexia Nervosa* (London: Routledge, 1993) and S. Bordo, *Unbearable Weight: Feminism, Western Culture and the Body* (Berkeley, CA: University of California Press, 1993). If you are interested in thinking further about labelling and the associated stigma that this may cause, look again at the book by Erving Goffman, which we first referred to in Further Reading section of Reading 3: *Stigma: Studies in Spoiled Identity* (London: Penguin, 1963).

Reading 21

'Dirty Work'

Ian Shaw

In this reading, Ian Shaw considers the usefulness of the concept 'dirty work' in relation to the care of people with a variety of psychiatric diagnoses who are repeatedly admitted to hospital, yet not deemed appropriate for long-term institutionalisation. Dirty work draws attention to the moral division of labour where professionals of high standing come to specialise in the most desirable and 'moral' cases and others with less standing are left with the disgusting, degrading or shameful tasks. For the research on which this article is based, 34 patients and 12 general practitioners (GPs) were interviewed and, from this, GP's perceptions of 'good' and 'bad' patients and the consequences of this for patient management were explored. In line with previous studies Shaw argues that the construction of patients as difficult, and the subsequent dynamics of exclusion, lies in the breakdown of the 'normal' doctor–patient relationship, coupled with the doctor's need to get on with the day's workload. Thus, moral judgements form a part of the exclusion process of what Shaw terms 'revolving-door' psychiatric patients.

The genesis of [this reading] lies in a wider study examining the phenomenon of "revolving-door" psychiatric patients. These are people of a variety of diagnoses who are repeatedly admitted to hospital yet are not deemed appropriate for long-term institutional care. Characteristically, such patients are discharged from hospital with a carefully considered package of community care arrangements that break down after a relatively short time, and further admission is considered necessary, only for the cycle to repeat itself. The phenomenon of the revolving-door patient is an important feature of the criticisms made of the practice of caring for people with enduring mental illness away from hospital. It suggests an inadequacy of the arrangements made to support such patients in the community. In the community, the general practitioner (GP) is the central point for support and care. This study of the perceptions of GPs toward these patients revealed, at an early stage, that such patients are regarded by GPs as "difficult" and that this influenced their management of them. Consequently, in this article, I explore the GPs' conceptualization of revolving-door patients as difficult and the ways in which this reflected in their management of them.

PATIENTS AND "DIRTY WORK"

Over several studies, D. Hughes (1971) demonstrated the relevance of the concept of dirty work in analysis of the nature of the worlds of occupation and work. Dirty work directs attention to the moral division of labor within those worlds, in particular to those processes whereby those with high professional standing come to specialize in the most desirable and "moral" cases, shifting the messy and stigmatizing ones to others with less standing. The concept of dirty work also highlights the stresses and strains faced by those whose work involves disgusting, degrading or shameful tasks. As E. C. Hughes (1958) pointed out,

> In professional as in other lines of work, there grows up both inside and outside some conception of what the essential work of the occupation is or should be. In any occupation people perform a variety of tasks, some of them approaching more closely the ideal or symbolic work of that profession than others. Some tasks are considered nuisances and impositions or even dirty work—physically, socially or morally beneath the dignity of the profession. (pp. 21–22)

E. C. Hughes (1971) went on to argue that "dirty work may be an intimate part of the very activity which gives the occupation its charisma, as is the case with the handling of the human body by the physician" (p. 344). More commonly, dirty work can involve the development of "collective pretensions" or "dignifying rationalizations" whereby workers seek to mitigate the degrading implications of their work.

The process by which tasks come to be regarded as dirty work might have significance at several levels:

> At one level the designations of a task as dirty work may be understood as a more or less faithful portrayal of its odious and onerous qualities. Dirty work designations are typically attended to by co-workers and colleagues in this way—as descriptions of a task's real properties. On an analytical level, dirty work designations are appreciable as more than simple reflections of an occupational reality or expressions of personal attitude. (Emerson & Pollner, 1976, p. 243)

Such designations reflect the perspective of the worker as much as it does the quality of the work. After all, one occupation's dirty work might be another occupation's fought-for prerogative (Emerson & Pollner, 1976; Strong, 1980). Furthermore, although dirty-work designations are the product of a particular occupational perspective, they are also the means through which the perspective is enacted and perpetuated (Emerson & Pollner, 1976; May & Kelly, 1982). In the very designation of a particular task as dirty work, the worker declares a moral distance from that dirtiness, much as someone caught in a shameful situation signals through his embarrassment that it was not his real self that was performing (Goffman, 1967). Just as this discomfort shows that the actor is aware of and committed to the moral order that the particular act has just violated, so the designation of dirty work reaffirms the legitimacy of the occupational moral order that has been blemished. In their work, Emerson and Pollner (1976) explored the process by which work becomes regarded as, what they termed, "shit work." They found that the characterization of shit work emerged when care workers felt not only unable to do something for a patient, in a therapeutic sense, but compelled to do something to them in a coercive sense. The likelihood of a dirty-work experience's existing might, consequently, be increased when the professionals concerned honor therapeutic skills as their distinctive competence but when the patient does not respond to those skills.

The focus of this study is the identification of revolving-door patients as dirty work and how this, coupled with moral judgments by GPs, can lead to a process of exclusion. There is also a sense in which this process with respect to revolving-door patients might be linked to moral judgments about patients as bad or otherwise.

CONCEPTUALIZING GOOD AND BAD PATIENTS

Kelly and May (1982) identified a theoretical framework for conceptualizing good and bad patients using an interactionist perspective in their study of the nursing role. They suggested that patients came to be regarded as good or bad, not because of anything inherent in them or in their behavior but as a consequence of the interaction between staff and patients. They pointed out that much of the literature on good and bad patients is not so much about patients as it is about the staff opinions of them. Why staff might have these opinions has been comparatively ignored in the literature. In suggesting an alternative framework, Kelly and May argued that the nature of the professional role must be considered as well as the conflicts and tensions within it.

Patients dispense legitimation of the professional role. Kelly and May (1982) contended that the role of the caring professional is viable only with reference to an appreciative patient. They argued that professionals assume that the patient has control over his or her behavior and attitudes. Moreover, in doctor/patient interaction, doctors take the patients' perceptions of them as a starting point for making sense of their own response. In this process, the doctor ascribes a sense of patient "worthiness" for treatment, and labeling of a patient might then take place. Patients are not passive recipients of care but are active agents in interactions. As such, they have the power to "influence, shape and reject professionals' attempts to impose a definition on their situation, with profound consequences for nurse-patient relations and the professional task" (p. 154).

In short, it is through the process of providing or withholding legitimation that patients come to be regarded as good or bad. The good patient confirms the professional role; the bad patient denies that legitimation. The arguments of Kelly and May (1982) were based on their study of nursing in a hospital. [Here] argue that their framework might be equally useful in exploring the conceptualizations of GPs in a community setting. I explore the process by which revolving-door patients come to be regarded as dirty work but also how moral judgments can be made about them and how this affects their management. Charns and Lockhart (1997) made a useful distinction between work and working. Work, they argued, is the objective and the impersonal, or, put simply, the task to be accomplished. Working, on the other hand, is a worker's affective response to work: "Work affects working, and working affects work" (p. 205). In professionally oriented management systems (GPs in the United Kingdom are independent practitioners who work to contract for the National Health Service [NHS]), they argued, the emphasis is on working rather than work. This would suggest that professionals might have an affective response to a revolving-door patient as bad before they are categorized as dirty work and managed accordingly.

THE REVOLVING-DOOR STUDY

...

For manageability, we focused on identifying those who were admitted on 6 or more occasions during the previous 3 years. Forty-four patients met these criteria....We intended to select 10 GPs randomly for interview from those who stated that they were willing to participate. However, only 12 practitioners, representing 13 patients, agreed to participate in the study. We decided to interview all 12 and obtained patient permission to examine the case notes....

MEDICAL IRRITATION

Almost without exception, the patients in this study break the three broad principles that shape conventional medical practice. As Strong (1980) has argued, these are

1. the assumption of medical expertise in diagnosis and cure,
2. the belief that medical matters fall largely within the "natural" sphere of things, and
3. the assumption that (despite the doctor's inability to intervene directly in the patients self-management) patients are normally motivated to comply with medical instructions.

As Strong (1980) has pointed out, to break one of these principles would make matters difficult, but to break all three renders normal consultations highly problematic....

The frustration of GPs toward their patients came across quite strongly during the interviews, as can be seen in the following quotations:

> She is very demanding ... rarely happy with her treatment. Very demanding. In fact she has been in yet again this morning. (GP5)

> This man seems to be constantly either at the surgery or ringing out of hours ... this disrupts normal routines and impacts on the management of other patients. (GP3)

The GPs were also unanimous in their perceptions of the problems associated with treating these patients. The following quotations represent an emphasis on noncompliance and manipulation of the medical system that was evident in all of the interview data:

> He rarely complies with treatment as prescribed and then complains that it has not worked! His drinking does not help either and his out of hours complaints are usually associated with drunkenness. (GP3)

> She is very manipulative. I recently refused to prescribe further antidepressants and referred her to a counselor. Later the same day she took a nonlethal dose of multi-vitamins and presented herself to A&E demanding a psychiatric assessment. She got her prescription. What do you do? (GP11)

These two representative responses also link strongly to moral judgments about the patient and the vital role of patients in assisting in their own recovery. This can also affect the GP's image and his or her therapeutic credentials. The following quotations illustrate this:

> She asks for help and I have given it to her. She has been on various medications but nothing seems to work. She is a sad case really, and her anxiety seems to stem from a poor home environment. She gets anxious and then gets anxious about being anxious. I prescribe, but I know she will be back again in a short time. It would not be so bad if she tried to help herself. (GP7)

> Medication does not work, counseling has failed and Psychiatry do not want her ... she complains that I am not helping her. Frankly, I do not know what to do that can help. (GP4)

The first patient is seeking help and apparently trusting the GP, but he is unable to provide a solution, and in the second case, the patient is demanding that the GP live up to his therapeutic credentials. This can contribute to moral judgments about the worthiness of the patient and how they could be managed. One GP went so far as to say,

> She is despondent and neglects herself terribly. She is very smelly. To be honest I wish she would just keep away. (GP8)

"Problem Patients": Management Strategies

May and Kelly (1982) noted that a significant proportion of patients diagnosed with a psychiatric illness fell into the category of "problem patients" and that moral judgments were often made about them. Such findings are supported in this study and are very much in line with previous findings (Becker, Geer, Hughes, & Strauss, 1951; D. Hughes, 1981; Jeffrey, 1979; Roth, 1972; Strong, 1980). Such patients have also been described as "heart sink" cases for GPs (O'Dowd, 1992) because of the demoralizing effect they have on the practitioner. A study of very difficult patients also, through psychological contrast, provides insight into the GPs' perceptions of the characteristics of the ideal patient. This is someone who is polite, who takes good care of him- or herself, has an easily diagnosable condition, is strongly motivated to recover, complies with medication, and recovers quickly after treatment. The farther patients are removed from this ideal, the more they are likely to be perceived as problematic. Certainly, very few patients with mental health problems would meet this notion of an ideal patient. As one of the GPs in the study stated, "I cannot regard such patients as good ... they are sometimes disruptive and do not try to help themselves" (GP4). Jeffrey's study of casualty doctors suggested that the terms *problem patients* and *psychiatric patients* were virtually synonymous. He found that staff frustration over the lack of therapeutic success is often vented as hostility toward those patients. Furthermore, he found that if patients can be held responsible for creating "inconvenience," then the staff felt that they had no moral obligation to treat them, though a legal obligation remained. There was certainly evidence that the experiences of these patients at the GPs surgery were not congenial.

> There is a tendency to put her off—to make her wait for a consultation and to be as unfamiliar with her as possible once she is here. (GP4)

Such avoidance is in line with Strong's (1980) findings. Moreover, it could also be argued that a statement such as "I am treating her as humanely as possible in the hope of a better response" (GP11) would not be necessary unless it were placed against a background of less-than-humane practice. A similar situation was also found in the work of Jeffrey (1979), who reported attempts to deter difficult patients from returning to casualty departments. This strategy of exclusion is also reflected in this study.

Although four of the GPs reported a long history of contact with the patient concerned (GPs 6, 7, 9, and 11), there was a desire expressed by four of the other GPs interviewed to get these patients "off their list" as soon as possible (GPs 2, 3, 8, and 10). The extent of this trend was evident when GPs were providing a short history of contact with the patient. For example,

> She has been under the care of various doctors in the practice, not just me. This patient has been dumped by everyone else, she has actually been on the list here before, but I wasn't involved with her at that time .... She was allocated to us in August '97, so I have had more than my stint, haven't I? ... We have to keep patients for at least 3 months before we can move them on. We will send back her notes soon and ask for her to be reallocated. It has happened to her many times in the past, she has had lots of doctors. We have been trying to get Psychiatry to take her over but with little success at the moment. (GP8)

[She] has been removed from various surgery lists several times in the past and had to be allocated to a new doctor. This patient really needs more support than we can provide here. (GP2)

This picture of difficult patients being constantly "moved on" from one practice to another is another indicator that the patient is being regarded at the level of dirty work (Hughes, 1971; Strong, 1980). However, the patients are not being passed to people of "inferior station," as Strong's analysis would suggest, but, rather, to fellow GPs. At the very least, this indicates a poor professional network. The GP, in moving a patient on, does not appear to care which of his colleagues receives that patient and, equally, has no idea of the nature of the patient he or she might be allocated in return. This might be a patient who has been moved on by another practice. This is in line with Strong's findings, that patients might be passed on to others in the vain hope that someone else has a solution. There is also some evidence that such "paranoia and dynamics of exclusion" (Lemert, 1962) also involve a process of deviancy amplification, which might inform understanding of the revolving-door phenomenon.

Responsibility, Blame, and Authority

Unpublished work by Stokes (2000, and personal communication, May 3, 2001) suggests that the decision-making process involved in removing patients from GP lists includes a degree of moralizing or victim blaming by pointing to the poor motivations or moral character of the patient:

> In the transformation of a difficult patient into a removed patient the patient is usually shown, in GPs' accounts, to be culpable. It is not sufficient, with the exception of violence, for the removed patient to have broken unwritten rules of behavior .... Culpability is achieved by the concepts of "failed negotiation" and "absence of mitigating circumstances." (p. 98)

Stokes (2000) also argued that in a "failed negotiation," the GPs saw patients as rational individuals with whom appropriate written or verbal communication should work. Such patients continued, in the GPs' views, to "abuse the service" despite attempts to address the problem. Within this process, mental illness was not regarded as a mitigating circumstance. In his discussion of "dirtball" and "gomer" patients, Dans (2002) illustrated that the use of pejorative terms is widespread in the U.S. medical world and indicated a similar process to that identified by Stokes. However, one of the GP respondents in this study rationalized the removal of difficult patients from his or her list in slightly different terms:

> Removing difficult patients from a practice list can be a legitimate tactic of patient management. It can educate the patient into displaying more appropriate health-seeking behavior and they then get on well in their new practice. (GP3)

This provides an interesting picture of the GP disciplining a patient and trying to inculcate accepted norms of behavior. The notion that a "receiving" GP might benefit from a disciplined patient could appeal to notions of collegiality that would otherwise be sadly injured by such an action. However, this disciplinary argument cannot be made with respect to some of these patients, who continue to be regarded as difficult after successive moves between practices and GPs. However, this does fit with the findings in Emerson and Pollner's (1975) study (p. 243) that shit work is characterized not only when professional carers are unable to do something for a patient but when they then feel compelled to do something to them in a coercive sense. This trend should be of concern for health services, not least because of the implications it has for continuity of care. Four of the other GPs interviewed (1, 7, 9, and 11) had in place alternative forms of patient management. The following quotations sum up their strategy and hopes of success.

> This patient is trouble, she is very demanding, phones all hours .... We are trying to do something with difficult patients, with the view that if they are continually moved on it does not really benefit anyone .... We sort of enter into informal contracts with patients like her in order to try and improve their behavior. She is not really ill, but has a personality disorder and sometimes harms herself to seek attention. The contract is concerned with limiting such behavior. (GP11)

> It would be easy to "write off" such people and push them away, as they are not an easy group to help, they are not good at helping themselves, and not easy to help. And it is easy to get frustrated by that, just feel, you know, "what's the point"? And you think that time after time and I—I suppose, you know I can understand why colleagues get very frustrated and feel they are not achieving anything and "what's the point"? Then moving the patient on. We do try to help where we can here, but medication does not work, counseling has failed—it is not easy .... (GP7)

CONCLUSIONS

The dislike felt by these GPs for dealing with revolving-door patients was based, in part at least, on rational grounds. The patients did not satisfy the basic assumptions on which an ordinary doctor–patient relationship is premised. The GPs had neither cures nor special knowledge of the problem. This fundamental disjunction with the standard role relationship was reported by all the GPs interviewed and, together with the need to get through the day's workload, was a plausible factor in regarding patients as dirty work. The social nature of their distress contributed to the moral judgments that were made about them.

Another feature of this study was a tendency for older practitioners to have a more authoritarian approach than those who qualified more recently. This supports the hypothesis that intolerance of difficult patients might be associated with the number of years of practice in the community. Perhaps, this is understandable. In less than 50 years, the treatment of mental illness has made a radical shift from providing for those excluded from society by reason of madness (humane segregation) to a more determined therapeutic endeavor. It could be argued that this is a short time for cultural expectations to shift. It is, consequently, not surprising that authoritarian attitudes continue to find expression in the medical world, perhaps particularly among older practitioners.

… The patients' conditions described by the GPs were difficult, perhaps impossible, to treat using a solely medical model, and none of these patients fitted within the traditional doctor–patient role relationship. It is these factors, coupled with high work pressures—and little primary care support for the management of psychosocial distress—that lead GPs to regard revolving-door patients as difficult, attach moral judgments, and manage them accordingly (as dirty work). However, the point must be made that in medicalizing distress, and in excluding difficult patients, doctors might be helping to create the very behavior that they find so distasteful.

REFERENCES

Becker, H. S., Geer, B. G., Hughes, E. C., & Strauss, A. L. (1961). *Boys in white*. Chicago: University of Chicago Press.

Charns, M. P., & Lockhart, C. A. (1997). Work design. In S. M. Shortell & A. D. Kaluzny, *Essentials of health care management* (pp. 198–219). Albany, NY: Delmar.

Dans, P. E. (2002). The use of pejorative terms to describe patients: "Dirtball" revisited. *Baylor University Medical Center (BUMC) Proceedings, 15*, 26–30.

Emerson, R. M., & Pollner, M. (1976). Dirty work designations: Their features and consequences in a psychiatric setting. *Social Problems, 23*, 243–254.

Goffman, E. (1967). Embarrassment and social organization. In E. Goffman, *Interaction ritual: Essays on face to face behavior* (pp. 97–112). Chicago: Aldine.

Hughes, D. (1981). *Lay assessment of clinical seriousness: Practical decision-making by non-medical staff in a hospital casualty department*. Unpublished doctoral dissertation, University of Wales, Swansea, United Kingdom.

Hughes, E. C. (1958). *Men and their work*. Toronto, Canada: Free Press of Glencoe.

Hughes, E. C. (1971). *The sociological eye: Selected papers*. Chicago: Aldine.

Jeffrey, R. (1979). Normal rubbish: Deviant patients in casualty departments. *Sociology of Health and Illness, 1*(1), 1979.

Kelly, M. P., & May, D. (1982). Good and bad patients: A review of the literature and a theoretical critique. *Journal of Advanced Nursing, 7*, 147–156.

May, D., & Kelly, M. P. (1982). Chancers, pests and poor wee souls: Problems of legitimation in psychiatric nursing. *Sociology of Health and Illness, 4*(3), 279–301.

O'Dowd, T. (1992). Heartsink patient: Optimising care. *Practitioner, 236*(1519), 941–942.

Roth, J. (1972). Some contingencies of the moral evaluation and control of clients: The case of the hospital emergency service. *American Journal of Sociology, 77*, 893–856.

Stokes, T. N. (2000, September). *Breaking up is never easy: GPs' accounts of removing patients from their lists*. Paper presented at the British Sociological Association Medical Sociology Conference "Health in Transition: European Perspectives," University of York, United Kingdom.

Strong, P. M. (1980). Doctors and dirty work. *Sociology of Health and Illness, 2*(1), 24–46.

Source: I. Shaw, ' "Dirty work" patients, and "revolving doors" ',
Qualitative Health Research, 14:8 (2004) 1032–1045.

Study Questions and Activities

1. Define 'dirty work', 'shit work' and 'good' and 'bad' patients. Do you do 'dirty work'?
2. Looking back to Readings 3 and 4 you will see that Ian Shaw draws on a specific example of the doctor–patient relationship. What impact do the moral judgements of the doctors have in these particular encounters? What behavioural norms are the patients challenging?
3. Is distress an illness?
4. Many of the articles in this part of the reader draw on/report qualitative data. Why do you think the researchers chose qualitative methods? Would it have been more appropriate/as appropriate to use quantitative methods for any of the studies reported here? You may find it useful to refer to Reading 6.

Further Reading

Look at P. M. Strong, 'Doctors and dirty work', *Sociology of Health and Illness*, 2:1 (1980) 24–46; P. Atkinson and C. Heath (eds) *Medical Work: Realities and Routines* (London: Sage, 1981) and P. Godin, 'A dirty business: caring for people who are a nuisance or a danger', *Journal of Advanced Nursing*, 32:6 (2000) 1396–1402 for more on what Shaw calls 'dirty work'. For further reading specifically in relation to the sociology of mental illness and/or psychiatric care, look for E. Goffman, *Asylums: Essays on the Social Situation of Mental Patients and Other Inmates* (Harmondsworth: Penguin; 1961); J. Busfield, 'Disordered minds: women, men and unreason in thought, emotion and behaviour', in G. Boswell and F. Poland (eds) *Women's Minds, Women's Bodies: Interdisciplinary Approaches to Women's Health* (Houndmills: Palgrave, 2003) and the chapter entitled 'Madness and psychiatry' by C. Samson in Bryan S. Turner's *Medical Power and Social Knowledge*, 2nd edn (London: Sage, 1995). In addition to the stigma surrounding mental illness, many authors have written about the stigma associated with other conditions, for example, see: K. Wilson and K. Luker, 'At home in hospital? Interaction and stigma in people affected by cancer', *Social Science and Medicine*, 62 (2006) 1616–27. There has been much sociological debate on the management and experience of chronic illness. For a classic piece, see: M. Bury, 'Chronic illness as biographical disruption', *Sociology of Health & Illness*, 4:2(1982) 167–82. For more recent discussions, see the journal *Chronic Illness*.

Emotion Work in Midwifery

Billie Hunter

As Billie Hunter notes, at the beginning of this reading, 'pregnancy and child-birth have the potential for being intimate and emotionally charged experiences for all involved'. So it is surprising that there has not been more attention given to emotion within midwifery work. In this reading, Hunter provides a review of the literature relating to emotional labour in the workplace and considers its significance to the midwife/birthing woman relationship. The reading includes an overview of the nursing and sociological literature on emotional labour with reference to the theoretical perspectives relating to the management of emotion at work and a consideration of their application to an analysis of midwifery work. The concept of emotional labour is relevant to most, if not all, occupations. With specific reference to midwives, Hunter notes that midwifery work has the potential for creating high levels of emotion work and there is a significant amount of evidence to indicate that the quality of the relationship between the midwife and the pregnant/birthing woman is significant in determining the quality of the childbirth experience for women. Yet, as Hunter points out, despite this there is a notable lack of research regarding midwives' experiences of participating in the midwife/birthing woman relationship, and even less regarding the emotional issues involved. With reference to the changes in the organisation of UK maternity care, the intimacy of midwifery work, working with women in pain, and division of labour at work, Hunter argues for more work focusing on emotional labour within the midwifery environment.

INTRODUCTION

Pregnancy and childbirth have the potential for being intimate and emotionally charged experiences for all involved. Whether the experience is positive or negative, midwives are involved in providing support for women and their families, and in dealing with the feelings that arise. There is, however, little published research regarding emotion in midwifery....

This lack of research based evidence is surprising, given the nature of the midwife's day-to-day work. Contemporary textbooks for student midwives emphasize the significance of the psychosocial aspects of care (e.g. Sweet & Tiran 1997), but little is known about the implications of providing such care for the midwives involved. This is in contrast to nursing, where the emotional content of work has received growing attention from researchers....

This knowledge deficit is particularly significant given the current recommendations for changes in the British maternity services. These acknowledge the importance of holistic care, and in particular emphasize the significance of the relationship between the woman and her midwife (Department of Health (DOH) 1993). The changes proposed, for example, the introduction of caseload carrying and continuity of the carer, have the potential to increase the emotional content of the midwife's work. It would thus appear to be essential that midwives develop a greater understanding of emotion at work in order both to enhance this aspect of their practice, and also to manage their emotions more effectively.

THINKING ABOUT EMOTION IN THE WORKPLACE

The key thinker in the field remains the American author Hochschild (1979, 1983, 1989). Her ground breaking publication in 1983: *The Managed Heart: Commercialization of Human Feeling*, is significant for naming a previously invisible aspect of work. She proposed that dealing with emotions is an important and demanding component of working with people, entailing management of feelings and the expression of emotion. This is described as 'emotional labour', where workers strive to 'create and maintain a relationship, a mood, or a feeling.' (Hochschild 1983, p. 440).

Hochschild's (1983) empirical research with airline attendants led her to conclude that they are trained to suppress their 'real' feelings in order to maintain an atmosphere that is pleasant and reassuring. This emotion management is underpinned by 'feeling rules' (Hochschild 1979, p. 563) social rules regarding the expression of emotion of which most individuals are not consciously aware (unless there is dissonance between what is felt, and what the individual assumes they should feel).

Hochschild (1983, p. 36) draws on theories of theatre acting techniques to explain how emotions may be controlled or self-induced. She suggests that 'Surface acting' is used when workers change how they appear to others by adapting their body language. The worker is aware that their behaviour lacks sincerity. 'Deep acting', however, a concept derived from Method Acting, proposes that workers induce feelings in themselves by drawing on emotion memories. In this case, the emotions are actually felt by the worker. This is a rather obscure concept, and it could be argued that Hochschild's study lacks substantive evidence to support this claim.

The ultimate outcome of deep acting, Hochschild (1983) suggests, is that these feelings become internalized, and the worker is estranged from their 'real' feelings. Central to Hochschild's (1983) argument is the contention that emotional labour is performed at a personal cost to the worker, and that this is a direct result of the 'commercialization' of emotions. She argues that emotional labour is part of the package that companies are selling to customers, so that in effect, workers are selling their smiles to management (Hochschild 1983). From this perspective, heavily influenced by Marxist theory, control over emotions is no longer voluntary. Ultimately, Hochschild argues, this suppression of authentic feelings has a personal cost to the worker, with a spectrum of negative outcomes from loss of role boundaries and burnout to cynicism and alienation. However, these arguments assume the existence of an 'authenric' self, itself a debatable concept (Lupton 1998).

Being a flight attendant for a huge commercial organization is obviously very different from being a midwife within the United Kingdom (UK) National Health Service (NHS). There are issues of corporate image and profit making that, as yet, thankfully do not feature in our healthcare system. The focus on the exploitation of workers in commercial settings appears to have led to some rather limited thinking on Hochschild's part. Only a small sector of workers are identified as emotion workers when it could be argued that there are many other 'people' workers who undertake just as much, if not more, emotion work. Even within commercial settings, Hochschild's findings may lack relevance. James (1989) points out that airline companies are a very specific type of organization, which explicitly acknowledge emotional labour. She argues that such a scenario is not common, and in fact most emotional labour occurs where 'its centrality and value are not recognized' (James 1989, p. 30). James's (1989, 1992) analysis of emotional labour with the British NHS provides an important alternative perspective, which will be considered in more detail later....

Other critiques of Hochschild's work suggest that her analysis may be too simplistic (Wouters 1989a, 1989b, Tolich 1993, Wharton 1993), and that there is much more to discover. Wouters (1989a, p. 116) questions Hochschild's 'one-sided and moralistic' focus on the 'costs' of emotional labour and proposes that work that involves emotional labour also has the potential to bring joy. Studies undertaken by Stenross and Kleinman (1989) and Tolich (1993) indicate that emotion labour is complex and likely to include both positive and negative emotions. This may well also be true for midwifery.

Nevertheless, Hochschild's thinking continues to underpin the debate related to emotion in the workplace ... [and] the insights offered by her important work remain integral to an understanding of emotion management. For example, Hochschild (1983) suggests that workplace change may impact upon emotional labour resulting in an impossible situation for the worker. If procedures are sped up in the name of cost efficiency, the worker will no longer be able to deliver the same quality of emotional labour. This may lead to purely surface acting or to a situation where the worker may not even attempt to provide emotional labour at all.

There is evidence of this emotional exhaustion in the descriptions of 'burnout' in midwifery research (Beaver *et al.* 1986, Sandall 1997). Given the changes currently recommended within British maternity care (DOH 1993, 1998), and their likely impact upon midwifery practice, it would appear that Hochschild's theories of emotional labour remain worthy of consideration. It is important, however, to acknowledge the contribution of more recent thinking, particularly within healthcare research.

EMOTIONAL LABOUR WITHIN THE BRITISH HEALTH SERVICE

The concept of emotional labour has been embraced and developed by healthcare researchers, in particular James (1989, 1992) and Smith (1992). James (1989, 1992) extends the concept to include management of both personal feelings and those of others. She suggests that, although emotional labour is a key aspect of working with healthcare clients, it is, paradoxically, largely invisible and unacknowledged. As with Hochschild (1983), the focus is on the negative aspects of emotional labour, which James describes as often 'sorrowful and difficult' (James 1989, p. 19). James identifies the ambiguous nature of providing emotional labour in the context of a health service where management focuses on the physical aspects of care and the provision of an efficient and cost effective service. The concept of working with people's emotional needs is at odds with this 'technical–rational' paradigm. The nurses in her study, although working in a hospice environment that espoused a philosophy of holistic care, provided the emotional aspects of care as an add-on after the physical care was finished.

The dominance of physical care is an interesting issue, that has also been noted within British midwifery. Davies and Atkinson (1991) and Hunr and Symonds (1995) observed how midwives 'get through the work' by focusing on task orientated aspects of care, particularly in response to stress and uncertainty. Explanations for task orientated dominance are varied. Early work by Menzies (1970) proposes that it is a coping mechanism that serves to keep health workers at a safe distance from the uncomfortable emotions that may be generated by caring. In contrast, Davies (1990, p. 107) suggests that it is a result of the all-pervasive 'technical-economic rationality' of health service administrators and the 'scientific rationality' of the doctors. The 'nurturing rationality' of nurses and midwives is not quantifiable, and hence its value is obscured.

Both James (1989, 1992) and Smith (1992) suggest that emotional labour is skilled work, that has to be learned in the same way that physical skills are learned. Smith's

(1992) research into how student nurses learn to perform emotional labour suggests that the skills are mostly learnt informally in the workplace, rather than formally in the classroom. James (1989) argues that this is because emotional labour is perceived as a 'natural' female skill. The gendered nature of emotion work results in its invisibility and undervaluing within the workplace (Smith & Gray 2000). This discussion of the significance of gender in emotional work is an important contribution, as it is an issue that Hochschild fails to develop in any depth. It is particularly relevant to midwifery, where the majority of practitioners and clients are female.

Much of the learning of midwifery and nursing students still takes place 'on-the-job', as opposed to the more formal learning of flight attendants described by Hochschild (1983). It is no wonder then that both James (1992) and Smith (1992) noted that learning how to deal with emotion was strongly influenced by social context. Smith (1992) observed that wards had different feeling rules and that the emotional tone of the ward was set by the ward sister. The mentorship system currently utilized in midwifery education is likely to create a similar 'feeling climate' to which students must adapt. In fact, the one-to-one nature of this contact may have more impact than the more removed influence of the ward sister (see also Smith & Gray 2000).

Smith (1992) argues that the demands of nursing work may lead to a 'caring trajectory', whereby students learn to manage emotion by adopting a task-orientated approach to care. She found evidence of the acting techniques described by Hochschild (1983), although is sceptical regarding the possibility of 'deep acting' during prolonged periods of patient contact. Rather, she suggested, when nurses feel under extreme stress, they withdraw emotionally from their patients. Sandall (1997) observed a similar phenomenon; midwives who were concerned about feelings of 'burnout' reported a sense of personal distance and disillusionment when caring for women.

It appears that healthcare research has made valuable contributions to the understanding of emotional labour. In particular, the significance of gender and social context has been highlighted (James 1989, 1992, Davies 1995). As James (1989) observes, acknowledging the emotional component of working within healthcare is an important step towards increasing its visibility, in the eyes of practitioners, clients and managers.

THE SIGNIFICANCE OF EMOTIONAL LABOUR IN MIDWIFERY WORK

The studies described above offer some insights, particularly related to the gendered nature of emotion work and the experience of providing emotional labour within the British healthcare system. However, to date, nursing research into emotional labour has focused on illness settings.... Midwifery work, in contrast, is predominantly concerned with the care of well women and babies, thus the findings are of limited relevance.

Nevertheless, it is argued that emotional labour is potentially highly significant in midwifery practice, although the evidence for this is, as yet, anecdotal and hence tenuous (Gaskin 1977, Davis 1987). No midwifery literature deals explicitly with the emotional aspects of midwifery work. This is a surprising anomaly, as reference to any contemporary textbook for student midwives indicates the current emphasis on the psychosocial aspects of midwifery care (Sweet & Tiran 1997), which is likely to entail emotion work on the part of the midwife.

The evidence that is available comes from the consumer's perspective. Numerous studies demonstrate that the quality of emotional support given by midwives impacts on women's childbirth experiences.... Interactions where emotional labour is used effectively appear to have therapeutic potential (Berg *et al.* 1996, Phillips 1996), whereas negative encounters may lead to fear and anxiety (Berg *et al.* 1996). A recent study by McCrea *et al.* (1998) indicates that the personal 'style' of the midwife is a crucial aspect of practice, and that there is an urgent need to investigate this further so that the quality of care can be improved. Emotional labour would appear to be an essential ingredient of 'style'.

The significance of the midwife in determining the quality of childbirth experiences cannot be overstated. Increasingly, women are being diagnosed as suffering from posttraumatic stress disorder following negative experiences (Allott 1996, Menage 1996). Although this implies that serious consideration is now being given to these issues, it could be argued that acknowledging their seriousness will be of little value if the focus is on pathology and treatment. Rather, it is important that the causes of negative experiences, which may well relate to the quality of the emotion work of midwives, are investigated further.

Midwives' perceptions of their work are largely undocumented. There is little published research based evidence, and British literature has focused historically mainly on issues of stress and burnout (Sandall 1997, Mackin & Sinclair 1998). Recent papers by Kirkham (1999) and Kirkham and Stapleton (2000), however, provide new and thought-provoking insights. Evidence from their study of the supervision of midwives in England suggests that midwives' experiences are strongly influenced, often negatively, by the culture of midwifery within the NHS.

Evidence relating to midwives' perceptions of their relationships with women is also scanty (McCrea & Crute 1991, McCrea 1993), although the recent publication of an edired text by Kirkham (2000) is a significant attempt to rectify this situation.

It is only within anecdotal accounts such as that provided by the British author Flint (1989) or by the American traditional midwives Gaskin (1977) and Davis (1987) that there is explicit discussion of the emotional impact of practice. Interestingly, all three authors work outside of conventional, institution-based maternity care settings. It may be that the issue of context is significant here: perhaps working within an alternative environment legitimizes discussion of the emotionality of care?

On even a casual consideration it would seem to be apparent that midwifery work involves emotion. In particular, there are issues relating to the nature of childbirth and the role of the midwife that have the potential to generate strong feelings....

REFERENCES

Allott H. (1996) Picking up the pieces: the post-delivery stress clinic. *British Journal of Midwifery* 4, 534–536.

Beaver R.C., Sharp E.S. & Corsonis G.A. (1986) Burnout experienced by nurse-midwives. *Journal of Nurse-Midwifery* 31, 3–15.

Berg M., Lundgren I., Hetmansson E. & Wahlberg V. (1996) Women's experience of the encounter with the midwife during childbirth. *Midwifery* 12, 11–15.

Davies K. (1990) *Women, Time and the Weavings of Everyday Life*. Avebury, Aldershot.

Davies C. (1995) *Gender and the Professional Predicament in Nursing*. OU Press, Buckingham.

Davis E. (1987) *Heart and Hands: A Midwife's Guide to Pregnancy and Birth*, 2nd edn. Celestial Arts, California.

Department of Health (1993) *Changing Childbirth: Part 1: Report of the Expert Maternity Group*. HMSO, London.

Department of Health (1998) *Midwifery: Delivering our Future. Report by the Standing Nursing and Midwifery Advisory Committee*. Department of Health, London.

Flint C. (1989) *Sensitive Midwifery*. Heinemann Nursing, Oxford.

Froggarr K. (1998) The place of metaphor and language in exploring nurses' emorional work. *Journal of Advanced Nursing* 28, 332–338.

Gaskin I.M. (1977) *Spiritual Midwifery*. The Book Publishing Company, Summertown, USA.

Hochschild A.R. (1979) Emotion work, feeling rules and social structure. *American Journal of Sociology* 85, 551–575.

Hochschild A.R. (1983) *The Managed Heart. Commercialisation of Human Feeling*. University of California Press, Berkeley, California.

Hochschild A.R. (1989) Reply to Cas Wouter's essay on the managed heart. *Theory, Culture and Society* 6, 439–445.

Hunt S. & Symonds A. (1995) *The Social Meaning of Midwifery*. Macmillan, London.

James N. (1989) Emotional labour: skill and work in the social regulation of feelings. *Sociological Review* 37, 15–42.

James N. (1992) Care = organisation + physical labour + emotional labour. *Sociology of Health and Illness* 14, 489–509.

Kirkham M. (1999) The culture of midwifery in the NHS in England. *Journal of Advanced Nursing* 30, 732–739.

Kirkham M. (ed.) (2000) *The Midwife-Mother Relationship*. Macmillan, London.

Kirkham M. & Stapleton H. (2000) Midwives' support needs as childbirth changes. *Journal of Advanced Nursing* 32, 465–472.

Lupton D. (1998) *The Emotional Self*. Sage, London.

Mackin P. & Sinclair M. (1998) Labour ward midwives' perceptions of stress. *Journal of Advanced Nursing* 27, 986–991.

McCrea H. (1993) Valuing the midwife's role in the midwife/client relationship. *Journal of Clinical Nursing* 2, 47–52.

McCrea H. & Cruce V. (1991) Midwife/client relationship: midwives' perspectives. *Midwifery* 7, 183–192.

McCrea H., Wright M. & Murphy-Black T. (1998) Differences in midwives' approaches to pain relief in labour. *Midwifery* 14, 174–180.

Menage J. (1996) Post-traumatic stress disorder following obstetric/gynaecological procedures. *British Journal of Midwifery* 4, 532–533.

Phillips S. (1996) Labouring the emotions: expanding the remit of nursing work? *Journal of Advanced Nursing* 24, 139–143.

Sandall J. (1997) Midwives' burnout and continuity of care. *British Journal of Midwifery* **5**, 106–111.

Smith P. (1992) *The Emotional Labour of Nursing*. Macmillan, London.

Smith P. & Gray B. (2000) *The Emotional Labour of Nursing: How Student and Qualified Nurses Learn to Care. Report on Nurse Education, Nursing Practice and Emotional Labour in the Contemporary NHS*. South Bank University, London.

Sweet B. & Tiran D. (1997) *Mayes' Midwifery: a Textbook for Midwives*, 12th edn. Bailliere Tindall, London.

Tolich M. (1993) Alienating and liberating emotions at work. *Journal of Contemporary Ethnography* 22, 61–381.

Wharton A.S. (1993) The affective consequences of service work: managing emotions on the job. *Work and Occupations* 20, 205–232.

Wouters C. (1989a) The sociology of emotions and flight attendants: Hochschild's 'Managed Heart'. *Theory, Culture and Society* 6, 95–123.

Wouters C. (1989b) Response to Hochschild's reply. *Theory, Culture and Society* 6, 447–450.

Source: B. Hunter, 'Emotion work in midwifery: a review of current knowledge', *Journal of Advanced Nursing*, 34:4 (2001) 436–44.

Study Questions and Activities

1. What do you understand by the terms 'emotional labour' and 'emotional management'? Try and find some other articles focusing on emotional labour in other healthcare settings. Which healthcare occupations do you think are most likely to contain elements of emotional labour?
2. Is the management of emotions gendered?
3. Re-read Reading 19. Is the use of humour in healthcare settings a form of emotional labour? Who is doing the most 'work': patients or carers?
4. Reflecting on our own practice, how much of your job is devoted to emotional work?

Further Reading

Arlie Hochschild's book, *The Managed Heart: Commercialisation of Human Feeling*, 20th anniversary edn (Berkeley, CA: University of California Press, 2003), has been, as Billie Hunter notes, extremely influential in this area and is also an extremely interesting read. For a key piece specifically concerned with emotions in healthcare settings, see N. James, 'Emotional labour: skill and work in the social regulation of feelings', *Sociological Review*, 37 (1989) 15–42. Also see: H. Staden, 'Alertness to the needs of others: a study of the emotional labour of caring', *Journal of Advanced Nursing*, 27:1 (1998) 147 and N. Daykin and B. Clarke,' "They'll still get the bodily care": discourses of care and relationships between nurses and healthcare assistants in the NHS', *Sociology of Health and Illness*, 22:3 (2000) 349–64 (also referred to in Further Reading section of Reading 26). Somewhat different is Stephen Fineman's book – *Emotion in Organisations*, 2nd edn (London: Sage, 2000) – as he considers the place of emotion in the world of work more broadly. Gillian Bendelow and Simon

J. Williams, as editors of *Emotions in Social Life: Critical Themes and Contemporary Issues* (London: Routledge, 1997), on the other hand, look at emotion more broadly, drawing together a series of pieces concerned with the sociological significance of emotion and emotional management.

For more on the midwife–birthing woman relationship, look at M. Kirkman (ed.) *The Midwife–Mother Relationship* (London: Macmillan, 2000); S. Robinson and A. M. Thomson (eds) *Midwives, Research and Childbirth*, Vol. 3 (London: Chapman and Hall, 1995) and R. Debries, C. Benoit, E. R. Van Teijlingen and S. Wrede, *Birth by Design: Pregnancy, Maternity Care and Midwifery in North America and Europe* (London: Routledge, 2001).

Part V

Power, Professions and Practice in Health and Healthcare

Introduction

This part of the book focuses on the power relations of professional practice. It begins by examining the defining characteristics of the healthcare professions, exploring how they might differ from other professions and from other occupational groups. Part V also considers the power relations between healthcare professions, as well as between healthcare professionals and other groups of healthcare workers. In this part of the book, the relationships between professionals and lay people are also considered. All the six readings contained in this part of the book explore the boundaries of professional practice and the changing relationships between those who give and receive healthcare.

This section begins with Reading 23 and the work of Eliot Friedson on the profession of medicine. In this classic reading, he explores the characteristics of a profession and the distinction between this and the characteristics of other occupational groups. He argues that whilst medicine, and similar consulting professions, might be legitimately regarded as a profession, what he calls the 'paraprofessional occupations' (or professions allied to medicine) cannot. For Eliot Friedson, professional autonomy is the single most important defining feature of a professional occupation. In Reading 24, the focus is on the practitioners of complementary and allied medicine (CAM) in Ontario, Canada. In this reading, Merrijoy Kelner and her colleagues explore the attitudes of formal leaders of the health professions to the professionalisation of a range of CAM groups. Kelner and colleagues conclude by arguing that the majority of healthcare professions are unsympathetic to the professionalisation of CAM groups and are particularly sceptical of the evidence-base for such a move. In the next reading (Reading 25), Tracey Adams writes about the feminisation of professions with specific reference to the case of women in dentistry. She argues that whilst the feminisation of professional employment has occurred over recent decades, little is known about how such feminisation impacts on either patient care or professional issues. In the fourth reading in this section (Reading 26), the emphasis is on occupational boundaries. Here the focus is on the relationship between operating theatre nurses and operating department practitioners. In contrast to what is being described by Tracey Adams in Reading 25, this reading focuses on men's movement into an area of practice traditionally dominated by women. Drawing on both observation and interview data, in this reading Stephen Timmons and Judith Tanner examine how and why boundaries are drawn between these two groups of theatre staff. In the next reading, attention turns away from relationships between professionals to those between healthcare professionals and their patients. In Reading 27, Annily Campbell draws on her research on childfree sterilised women to examine the ways in which doctors, in particular, gatekeep access to healthcare services. In particular, she explores the medical and social disapproval of women who choose to be childfree and considers the impact of this on health and lifestyle. Continuing with the theme of patient–professional relations, in Reading 28, Alex Broom discusses the impact of the Internet on the doctor–patient relationship. In this piece, he explores the Internet use of Australian men with prostate cancer, arguing that the Internet can play an important role in empowering men and changing their experiences of disease.

The Characteristics of a Profession

Eliot Friedson

In this classic piece, Eliot Friedson explores the formal characteristics of a profession by exploring the profession of medicine in relation to what he calls the paraprofessional occupations (for example, dentistry or nursing). He begins by arguing that a profession is essentially a group of workers organised into an occupational group, but that a profession is a special kind of group with particular characteristics. According to Eliot Friedson, one of the key defining characteristics of any profession is the possession of legitimate, organised autonomy. He argues that, in the case of medicine, this autonomy derived from two core defining characteristics: prolonged and specialised training in a body of abstract knowledge and a service orientation. He argues that whilst medicine possesses all of the characteristics that define a profession, paraprofessional occupations are encouraged to take on these professional attributes. He concludes that whatever such occupational groups might wish to claim, they do not stand in the same structural position as the profession on which they model themselves.

What are the formal characteristics of the profession of medicine? In the most elementary sense, the profession is a group of people who perform a set of activities which provide them with the major source of their subsistence–activities which are called "work" rather than "leisure" and "vocation" rather than "avocation." Such activities are performed for compensation, not for their own sake. They are considered to be useful or productive, which is why those who perform them are compensated by others. When a number of people perform the same activity and develop common methods, which are passed on to new recruits and come to be conventional, we may say that workers have been organized into an occupational group, or an occupation. In the most general classification, a profession is an occupation.

However, a profession is usually taken to be a special kind of occupation, so that it is necessary to develop analytically useful distinctions between the profession and other occupations. I have argued that the most strategic distinction lies in legitimate, organized autonomy–that a profession is distinct from other occupations in that it has been given the right to control its own work. Some occupations, like circus jugglers and magicians, possess a de facto autonomy by virtue of the esoteric or isolated character of their work, but their autonomy is more accidental than not and is subject to change should public interest be aroused in it. Unlike other occupations, professions are *deliberately* granted autonomy, including the exclusive right to determine who can legitimately do its work and how the work should be done. Virtually all occupations struggle to obtain both rights, and some manage to seize them, but only the profession is *granted* the right to exercise them legitimately. And while no occupation can prevent employers, customers, clients, and other workers from evaluating its work, only the profession has the recognized right to declare such "outside" evaluation illegitimate and intolerable.

THE SOURCE OF PROFESSIONAL STATUS

Obviously, an occupation does not "naturally" come by so unusual a condition as professional autonomy. The work of one group commonly overlaps, even competes, with that of other occupations. Given the ambiguity of much of reality, and given the role of taste and values in assessing it, it is unlikely that one occupation would be chosen spontaneously over others and granted the singular status of a profession by some kind of a popular vote. Medicine was certainly not so chosen. A profession attains and maintains its position by virtue of the protection and patronage of some elite segment of society which has been persuaded that there is some special value in its work. Its position is thus secured by the political and economic influence of the elite which sponsors it–an influence that drives competing occupations out of the same area of work, that discourages others by virtue of the competitive advantages conferred on the chosen occupation, and that requires still others to be subordinated to the profession. As I have shown, the position of medicine was so established, from the rise of the university to our day.

If the source of the special position of the profession is granted, then it follows that professions are occupations unique to high civilizations, for there it is common to find not only full-time specialists but also elites with organized control over large populations.[1] Further, the work of the chosen occupation is unlikely to have been singled out if it did not represent or express some of the important beliefs or values of that elite–some of the established values and knowledge of the civilization. In the case of medieval medicine, it was its connection with the ancient learning that singled it out. Furthermore, since it is chosen by the elite, the work of the profession need have no necessary relationship to the beliefs or values of the average citizen.

But once a profession is established in its protected position of autonomy, it is likely to have a dynamic of its own, developing new ideas or activities which may only vaguely reflect and which may even contradict those of the dominant elite. The work of the profession may thus eventually diverge from that expected by the elite. If a profession's work comes to have little relationship to the knowledge and values of its society, it may have difficulty surviving. The profession's privileged position is given by, not seized from, society, and it may be allowed to lapse or may even be taken away.[2] It is essential for survival that the dominant elite remain persuaded of the positive value, or at least the harmlessness, of the profession's work, so that it continues to protect it from encroachment.

CONSULTING AND SCHOLARLY PROFESSIONS

Some kinds of work require for their performance the cooperation of laymen and require for their survival some degree of popularity with laymen: they are practicing or consulting occupations which must sustain a direct, continuous relationship with a lay clientele. Work involving a clientele has consequences for occupational organization which are markedly different from work which does not. In the former case the worker must contend with clients who are from *outside* the occupational community and who therefore may not be familiar or sympathetic with his occupation's ideas and practices. In the latter case the worker must contend on a daily basis only with his colleagues and other workers from *within* the occupational community. In the former case the survival of the occupation depends upon bridging the gap between worker and layman. Bridging the gap between worker and lay client is much more of a problem than bridging the gap between workers.

It is in the case of applied work, particularly work involving a broadly based lay clientele, that formal, legal controls are most likely to be imposed.[3] Only applied work is likely to have immediate consequences in human affairs, and some can be serious. When the public is considered too inexpert to be able to evaluate such work, those dominating society may feel that the public needs protection from unqualified or unscrupulous workers. Having been persuaded that one occupation is most qualified by virtue of its formal training and the moral fiber of its members, the state may exclude all others and give the chosen occupation a legal monopoly that may help bridge the gap between it and laymen, if only by restricting the layman's choice. The outcome is support of the profession by licensure or some other formal device of protecting some workers and excluding others. Licensing is much less likely to occur on behalf of the scholar or the scientist, for they are devoted to exploring intellectual systems primarily for the eyes of their colleagues. Nonetheless, in the case of the consulting or practicing professions such a legally exclusive right to work will not assure survival because the work cannot be performed, license or not, without being in some way positively attractive to a lay clientele.

Unlike science and scholarship, which create and elaborate the formal knowledge of a civilization, practicing professions have the task of applying that knowledge to everyday life. Practicing professions are the links between a civilization and its daily life and as such must, unlike science and scholarship, be in some sense joined to everyday life and the average man. Some of this linkage can be politically sustained—as when the legal order permits only one occupation to provide a given service to those seeking it—but some seems to depend upon the attractiveness of the work itself to the average man, upon the direct connection of the work with what the layman considers desirable and appropriate. In the case of medicine I have argued that improvement in the pragmatic results of practice, as well as mass education which brought the average man's ideas, knowledge, and norms closer to that of the profession, led to it becoming a successful consulting profession where before it was primarily an officially supported scholarly or scientific profession with a small practice among the elite....

PROFESSION AND PARAPROFESSION

Just as the analysis of the development of medicine led to the observation of analytical differences between consulting and scholarly professions, so the analysis of the division of labor surrounding the formal organization of healing tasks led to the observation of structural differences in the position of various occupations in that division of labor. In the case of medicine, the division of labor is not simply a functional arrangement of specialists. Some occupations—dentistry, for example—are autonomous professions in their own right, even if they are not as prestigious as medicine.[4] Others, usually called "paramedical," are part of a division of labor organized into a hierarchy of authority, established and enforced by law, and swinging around the dominant authority and responsibility of the medical profession. Some of the occupations which are subordinate members of the medical division of labor, however, call themselves and are frequently called by others, "professions."

These paramedical occupations, of which nursing is perhaps the most prominent example, are clearly in a markedly different position than is medicine, for while it is legitimate for them to take orders from and be evaluated by physicians, it is not legitimate for them to give orders to and to evaluate physicians. Without such reciprocity we can hardly consider them the equals of physicians. And without the autonomy of physicians we can hardly believe it to be useful for them to be classified as the same type of occupations as the physician. They are specifically and generically occupations organized around a profession—paraprofessional occupations. This in itself makes a distinct species of occupation, particularly when people in such an occupation, given their proximity to a profession, are encouraged to take on professional attributes and to claim to be a profession. But whatever the claim, they do not stand in the same structural position as the profession on which they model themselves.

It might be noted that paraprofessional occupations usually seek professional status by creating many of the same institutions as those which possess professional status. They develop a formal standard curriculum of training, hopefully at a university. They create or find abstract theory to teach recruits. They write codes of ethics. They are prone to seek support for licensing or registration so as to be able to exercise some control over who is allowed to do their work. But what they persistently fail to attain is full autonomy in formulating their training and licensing standards and in actually performing their work. Their autonomy is only partial, being second-hand and limited by a dominant profession. This is the irreducible criterion which keeps such occupations paraprofessions in spite of their success at attaining many of the institutional attributes of professions. And the discriminatory power of full autonomy belies the value of using instead such institutional arrangements as training and licensing. That such arrangements are useful conditions for the development of an autonomous occupation is certain; that they are necessary conditions is moot; that they are sufficient conditions is plainly false.

THE FORMAL CRITERIA OF PROFESSION

In analyzing the position of medicine and its associated occupations I have deliberately avoided adopting most of the criteria of profession used by many writers. Indeed, I have just explicitly denied the importance of training and licensing. This is not the place for a detailed examination and analysis of the many definitions which have been published before and after Cogan's review.[5] It does seem necessary, however, to address the issue, even if briefly. Brevity is facilitated by the fact that no new criteria seem to have been added since Cogan's review, though various commentators, like me, emphasize one rather than another of the old. Furthermore, the parsimonious arrangement of those criteria by the most sophisticated and careful of recent analysts, William J. Goode, allows concentration on essentially two "core characteristics" of professions, from which ten other frequently cited characteristics are said to be derived.[6] These two core characteristics are "a prolonged specialized training in a body of abstract knowledge, and a collectivity or service orientation."[7] Among the "derived characteristics," which are presumably "caused" by the core characteristics, are five which refer to autonomy: "(1) The profession determines its own standards of education and training.... (3) Professional practice is often legally recognized by some form of licensure. (4) Licensing and admission boards are manned by members of the profession. (5) Most legislation concerned with the profession is shaped by that profession.... (7) The practitioner is relatively free of lay evaluation and control."[8] Obviously, in Goode's analysis, the core characteristics are critical criteria for professions insofar as they are said to be causal in producing professional autonomy as I have defined it, and many of the attributes others have specified. Let us look at them closely to see if this is so.

What precisely are the empirical referents of those core characteristics? In the first, training, are concealed at least three problems of specification—"prolonged," "specialized," "abstract." Since all training takes some time, how prolonged must training be to qualify? Since all training is somewhat specialized, how does one determine whether it is specialized enough to qualify? Since "abstract" is a relative rather than absolute term, how does one determine whether training is abstract or theoretical enough? It is difficult if not impossible to answer these questions with any reasonable degree of precision. Furthermore, I suggest that any answer one makes will fail to include all occupations clearly agreed to be professions or exclude all occupations clearly agreed not to be professions. Taking the three traditional professions of medicine, law, and the ministry, the range of variation in length of training (particularly in the ministry), the degree of specialization, and the amount and type of theory and abstract knowledge (particularly in the case of law) is in each case sufficiently wide that many other occupations not recognized as professions would fall within it. Nursing, for example, which is specifically excluded from the professions by Goode on the basis of training, falls within the range manifested by the three established professions.

Significantly, however, Goode excludes nursing because he feels its training is no more than "a lower-level medical education,"[9] which implies more the lack of autonomy it is supposed to produce than the specific attributes of nurse training. That is, it is not what nurses learn or how long it takes, but the fact that the bulk of what they learn is ultimately specified by physicians which is important. The objective content and duration of training is considerably less critical than occupational *control* over training. Indeed, in his analysis of the training of the librarian in another paper, Goode's comments rely most heavily on the issue of control—specifying that the occupation must help create the knowledge, "must be the final arbiter in any dispute about what is or is not valid knowledge," and must "largely [control] access to it through control over school admissions, school curriculums, and examinations."[10]

Thus, not training as such, but only the issue of autonomy and control over training granted the occupation by an elite or public persuaded of its importance seems to be able to distinguish clearly among occupations. Pharmacy and optometry, for example, have the same minimum period of training and probably the same degree of specialization and abstract knowledge (so far as one can specify proportion and quantity for such terms). However, in most states the trained optometrist may legally diagnose (e.g., do refractions) and prescribe (order, make, and fit corrective lenses), while the trained pharmacist may not; the optometrist is clearly moving much closer to professional autonomy while the pharmacist is firmly subordinated to medicine.[11] It does not seem to be the actual content of training that explains or produces the differences. As I suggested in my analysis of the medical division of labor, the possibilities for functional autonomy and the relation of the work of an occupation to that of dominant professions seem critical. And the process determining the outcome is essentially political and social rather than technical in character – a process in which power and persuasive rhetoric are of greater importance than the objective character of knowledge, training, and work.

Consonant with the political character of the process, I might point out that the leaders of all aspiring occupations, including nursing, pharmacy, and optometry, insist that their occupations do provide prolonged training in a set of special skills, including training in theory or abstract knowledge which is generic to their field. And they can point to required courses in theory to buttress their assertions. These are institutional facts whose truth cannot be denied, but their meaning is suspect because the content and length of training of an occupation, including abstract knowledge or theory, is frequently a product of the deliberate action of those who are trying to show that their occupation is a profession and should therefore be given autonomy.[12] If there is no systematic body of theory, it is created for the purpose of being able to say there is. The nature of an occupation's training, therefore, can constitute part of an ideology, a deliberate rhetoric in a political process of lobbying, public relations, and other forms of persuasion to attain a desirable end—full control over its work.

It does not seem to be the objective character of the training that leads to success in some cases and failure in others. A neutral observer like Goode cannot determine whether training is "really" abstract, prolonged, and specialized enough to push the occupation to professional status. It is rather the evaluation of such involved observers as legislators, the public, and representatives of other occupations that is critical to success, and the criteria used by each of these may differ from the other's. The legislator may calculate votes; the public, fears; and other occupations, jobs. While the characteristics of training frequently serve as criteria for licensing and otherwise identifying the members of an occupation, professional and otherwise, then, there seem to be no really definite and objective attributes of content and length of training which inevitably or even mostly precede professional status or distinguish professions from all other occupations.

Problematic as training is as a criterion, it has the virtue of empirical substance. The characteristics of an occupation's training refer to the formal rules and regulations embodied in the laws, regulations, and resolutions connected with political institutions, occupational associations, and educational organizations. The second "core characteristic" specified by Goode, however, and very commonly cited in other definitions, is much more problematic. The "collectivity or service orientation" usually refers to the orientation of the *individual* members of an occupation rather than to organizations. But clearly, the attitudes of individuals constitute an entirely different kind of criterion than the attributes of occupational institutions. Unlike the latter, which can be determined empirically by the examination of legislation, administrative regulations, and other formal documents including prescribed curricula, the attitudes of individuals must be determined by the direct study of individuals.

The actual existence of professional training institutions, the number of years and the nature of the courses required for a degree, and the nature of examinations required for a license are certainly established as facts. But curiously enough, there appears to be no reliable information which actually demonstrates that a service orientation is in fact strong and widespread among professionals. The three kinds of data needed for such demonstration are missing: we do not know what proportion of professionals manifests a service orientation and with what intensity; we do not have information on the degree to which a service orientation is more intense and more widely distributed among professionals than other orientations; and we do not know whether the distribution and intensity of a service orientation among professionals is greater than that among other types of workers. Even when one is quite willing to stretch the points of the scanty and inelastic data available, the blunt fact is that discussions of professions assume or assert *by definition* and without supporting empirical evidence that "service orientation" is especially common among professionals. As I shall indicate in a later chapter, I do not deny the reality of a service orientation as such (though it would be good to demonstrate it empirically) so much as I deny its distinct, exclusive, or predominant possession by professional occupations. I have already pointed out that, as part of "professionalism," it can be fairly widespread among occupations which are not autonomous and which are not likely to be so in the future. Goode, in fact, agrees that while nursing has not become a profession, it does have nevertheless a service orientation. As a criterion of "profession," it is therefore of little value.

But a service orientation need not be considered to be an attribute of individual workers. On a different level of abstraction it can be considered to be an *institutional* attribute of an occupation. As a formal characteristic of an occupation, it is a claim about the membership as a body. The claim, of course, is also made by para-professions and by many other kinds of occupational organizations including trade unions and trade associations. As a property of occupational institutions, it too, like training, can be deliberately created so as to attempt to persuade politically important figures of the virtues of the occupation. Perhaps even more than curriculum, it can be created out of whole cloth, to improve the public image of the occupation. Like training, all that may be distinct to professions about a service orientation is *general acceptance of their claim*, acceptance that is fruit of their earlier success at persuasion. As Goode put it, "Only to the extent that the society believes the profession is regulated by this collectivity orientation will it grant the profession much autonomy or freedom from lay supervision and control."[13] Other occupations may actually have as great a proportion of members with such an orientation—that is not the issue. They may have codes of ethics, oaths, and other institutional attributes reflecting such an orientation—that, too, is not the issue. *The profession's service orientation is a public imputation it has successfully won in a process by which its leaders have persuaded society to grant and support its autonomy.* Such imputation does not mean that its members more commonly or more intensely subscribe to a service orientation than members of other occupations.

FORMAL INSTITUTIONS AND PROFESSIONAL PERFORMANCE

... I have been arguing that the only truly important and uniform criterion for distinguishing professions from other occupations is the fact of autonomy—a position of legitimate control over work. That autonomy is not absolute, depending for its existence upon the toleration and even protection by the state and not necessarily including all zones of occupational activity. As I have shown in my comparison of the profession in three different nations, the single zone of activity in which autonomy *must* exist in order for professional status to exist is in the content of the work itself. Autonomy is the critical outcome of the interaction between political and economic power and occupational representation, interaction sometimes facilitated by educational institutions and other devices which successfully persuade the state that the occupation's work is reliable and valuable.

Furthermore, I have argued that there is no stable institutional attribute which inevitably leads to such a position of autonomy. In one way or another, through a process of political negotiation and persuasion, society is led to believe that it is desirable to grant an occupation the professional status of self-regulative autonomy. The occupation's training institutions, code of ethics, and work are attributes which frequently figure prominently in the process of persuasion but are not individually or in concert, invariably, or even mostly, persuasive as *objectively determinable attributes*. It may be true that the public and/or a strategic elite always come to believe that the training, ethics, and work of the occupation they favor have some exclusive qualities, but this is a consequence of the process of persuasion rather than of the attributes themselves, and the attributes may not be said to be either "causes" of professional status or objectively unique to professions.[14]

With few exceptions, my discussion in this chapter has restricted itself almost entirely to the institutional, or formal, level of analysis, dealing with the profession as an organization, part of the larger organization of the state and of the social division of labor. If any individual men figured in the discussion, it was as spokesmen for the profession, leaders in negotiation and persuasion and in the creation and administration of professional associations, training institutions, and work organizations, not as men doing the characteristic everyday work of the profession. This level of analysis is perfectly appropriate for understanding the development of an occupation and its present-day organization, for it specifies the political, legal, and interoccupational structure which sets the general limits within which practitioners may work.

Formal criteria of profession thus establish the framework within which the behavior of all professional individuals takes place. But they are not able to specify whether or not individuals differ in their work performance, whether or not there are systematic differences, and, if so, what is the nature and source of systematic difference. On the formal level, all individuals are the same in that they have all met minimal standards in being recruited and trained, and so in being allowed to practice protected from some kinds of competition, and from the direction and evaluation of others. By such formal criteria, only variation in the ability, character, or other personal characteristics of individuals explains variation in performance. Essentially, such formal criteria do not really carry us over to performance or behavior as such. Such a connection, I believe, is provided only by the concrete and organized settings in which work and performance takes place. The broad limits to those work settings are dictated by the formal characteristics of the profession and its position in the polity and the economy, but their concrete structure is something to be analyzed in and of itself. Once the structure of work settings can be specified, I suggest, it becomes possible to understand and predict systematic variation in the work performance of professionals....

NOTES

1. For an important attempt to conceptualize "the patterned distribution and control of knowledge in a society," see Burkart Holzner, *Reality Construction in Society* (Cambridge: Schenkman Publishing Co., 1968).
2. It can be argued that *as an occupation* the ministry has lost its professional position, particularly in countries where there is no state religion. In the United States the occupation controls ordination in individual churches but neither entrance into the occupation as such nor access to the legal privileges of the occupation (e.g., to perform a marriage ceremony). It is as if doctors could control entrance into and work in particular hospitals but not the development of competing hospitals or entrance into the occupation by those working at such hospitals.
3. See Holzner, *op. cit.*, for the distinction between specialized knowledge and ideological knowledge.
4. Cf. Basil J. Sherlock, "The Second Profession: Parallel Mobilities of the Dental Profession and its Recruits," *Journal of Health and Social Behavior*, X (1969), 41–51.
5. Morris I. Cogan, "Toward a Definition of Profession," *Harvard Educational Review*, XXIII (1953), 33–50.
6. William J. Goode, "Encroachment, Charlatanism, and the Emerging Profession: Psychology, Medicine, and Sociology," *American Sociological Review*, XXV (1960), 902–14.
7. *Ibid.*, p. 903.
8. *Ibid.*, p. 903.
9. *Ibid.*, p. 903.
10. William J. Goode, "The Librarian: From Occupation to Profession?" in Howard M. Vollmer and Donald L. Mills, eds., *Professionalization* (Englewood Cliffs, New Jersey: Prentice-Hall, Inc., 1966), p. 36.
11. Cf. Norman R. Denzin and C. J. Mettlin, "Incomplete Professionalization: The Case of Pharmacy," *Social Forces*, XLVI (1968), 375–82.
12. A number of attempts have been made to outline the natural history of occupations aspiring to professional status. See, for example, Everett C. Hughes, *Men and Their Work* (New York: The Free Press of Glencoe, 1958); Theodore Caplow, *The Sociology of Work* (Minneapolis: University of Minnesota Press, 1954); Harold L. Wilensky, "The Professionalization of Everyone?" *American Journal of Sociology*, LXX (1964), 137–58. See also Corinne Lathrop Gilb, *Hidden Hierarchies, The Professions and Government* (New York: Harper & Row, 1966) for a number of comments on the way political status is developed by professions.
13. Goode, "The Librarian," *op. cit.*, p. 37.

14. It may be noted that this argument is similar to, and in any case indebted to, that in Howard S. Becker, "The Nature of a Profession," National Society for the Study of Education, *Education for the Professions* (Chicago: National Society for the Study of Education, 1962), pp. 24–46.

Source: E. Freidson, *Profession of Medicine: A Study of the Sociology of Applied Knowledge* (London: University of Chicago Press, 1988 [1970]).

Study Questions and Activities

1. To what extent do you have professional autonomy?
2. Do you think that the distinction made by Eliot Friedson between medicine and 'paraprofessions' still holds true today?
3. What criteria would you use to define your own profession? Make a list of these.
4. Make some notes on how your profession attains and maintains its status.

Further Reading

Discussion of professionalisation can be found in most sociological books written for, or about, the healthcare professions. Early discussions focused on the social-isation of medical students; see, for example: R. Fox, 'Training for uncertainty', in R. Merton, G. Reader and P. Kendall (eds) *The Student–Physician* (Cambridge, MA: Harvard University Press, 1957) and H. Becker, B. Greer, E. Hughes and A. Strauss, *Boys in White: A Study of Student Culture in Medical School* (Chicago, IL: University of Chicago Press, 1961). For more recent work on professionalisation in health-care more generally, see: I. R. Jones, 'Health professions', in G. Scambler and D. L. Patrick (eds) *Sociology as Applied to Medicine*, 5th edn (Oxford: Saunders, 2003); R. J. Jones and A. Stewart, 'The sociology of the health professions', in D. Jones, S. E. E. Blaire, T. Hartery and R. K. Jones (eds) *Sociology and Occupational Therapy* (London: Churchill Livingstoke, 1988) and E. Denny, 'Nursing as an occu-pation', in E. Denny and S. Earle (eds) *Sociology for Nurses* (Oxford: Polity Press, 2005). Occupational struggles between medicine and nursing have been especially discussed in the literature, for example, see C. Simon, 'Healthcare practices, profes-sions and perspectives: a case study in intensive care', *Social Science and Medicine*, 62:8 (2006) 2079–90. Recently, considerable attention has been paid to the impact of interprofessional education on identity and practice. Useful further reading in this area includes: H. Priest, A. Sawyer, P. Roberts and S. Rhodes, 'A survey of interpro-fessional education in communication skills in healthcare programmes in the UK', *Journal of Interprofessional Care*, 19:3 (2005) 236–50 and K. Whelan, J. E. Thomas, S. Cooper, R. Hilton, S. C. Jones, T. Newton, B. O'Neill and E. E. Gill (2005) 'Interpro-fessional education in undergraduate healthcare programmes: the reaction of student dieticians', *Journal of Human Nutrition and Dietetics*, 18:6 (2005) 461–66.

Reading 24

The Professionalisation of Complementary and Alternative Medicine

Merrijoy Kelner, Beverly Wellman, Heather Boon and Sandy Welsh

In the previous reading, Eliot Friedson argued that medicine's special status is derived from its legitimate autonomy to practice. In this reading, Merrijoy Kelner and her colleagues argue that this status is being eroded both by a better-informed public and by the efforts of complementary and alternative medicine (CAM) practitioners. Drawing on 10 interviews with formal leaders of the established health professions in Ontario, Canada (medicine, nursing, physiotherapy, clinical nutrition and public health), this reading examines their reactions to the efforts of selected CAM groups (chiropractors, naturopaths, acupuncturists, traditional Chinese doctors, homeopaths and Reiki practitioners). Kelner *et al.* draw on stakeholder theory to show how interested groups often act together to promote their common interest. In the case of response to CAMs, they show that stakeholder groups react differently to CAMS depending on the role they play within the healthcare system. This reading shows how most of the stakeholders were unsympathetic to the potential for professionalisation of CAMs and, in particular, focuses on the role of evidence-based education and practice.

INTRODUCTION

Healthcare is always in the midst of change and crises. In the current environment, this is being fueled by high costs, primary care restructuring and inadequate numbers of medical and nursing personnel. These conditions are influencing the ways in which healthcare is currently being delivered (Mechanic, 1996). At the same time, several groups of complementary and alternative medicine (CAM) practitioners are striving to work their way into the formal healthcare system. Their efforts are bringing about a variety of responses from the established healthcare professions. These responses will have a significant impact on the distribution of power within the system.

In addition, the medical profession is being confronted by increasing directives concerning both the context, and more indirectly, the content of the care they deliver (Coburn, Rappolt, & Bourgeault, 1997; McKinlay & Arches, 1985). Medicine's previously established superior status and authority are being questioned both by CAM practitioners and a more informed public (Haug & Lavin, 1983; Fox & Fallows, 2003). Furthermore, some segments of the population are comparing medicine to the more holistic and individualized approach to care reputed to be employed by most CAM practitioners (Goldstein, 1999; Kelner & Wellman, 1997; Kelner, 2000). The autonomy of medicine is being questioned at the same time that consumer demand for CAM has grown (Berger, 1999; Ramsay, Walker, & Alexander, 1999; Angus Reid Group, 2000), the number of CAM practitioners has increased (Gilmour, Kelner, & Wellman, 2002), courses on CAM are being included in the curricula of most North American medical schools (Ruedy, Kaufman, & MacLeod, 1999; Wetzel, Eisenberg, & Kaptchuk, 1998) and consumers are searching the Web for reliable information on CAM (Landro, 2003). While there is certainly no consensus among all CAM groups about the desire to achieve professional status (Cant & Sharma, 1995; Saks, 2000; Kelner, Boon, Wellman, & Welsh, 2002), a number of the better organized groups are now working to attain statutory self-regulation, with hopes of ultimately becoming fully integrated into the formal healthcare system (Boon, Welsh, Kelner, & Wellman, 2003; Gilmour *et al.*, 2002; Welsh, Kelner, Wellman, & Boon, 2004). It is the reactions of the medical stakeholders to these challenges that constitute the focus of this paper.

The literature on stakeholders has typically been used to analyze the dynamics of large organizations such as business corporations and governments (see for example Hendry, 2001; Jawahar & McLaughlin, 2001; Bryson, Cunningham, & Lokkesmoe, 2002). It has only rarely been applied to the analysis of health policy or healthcare systems (Dymond, Nix, Rotarius, & Savage, 1995; Eyles *et al.*, 2001) .... We view the medical profession and its allied professions as a major stakeholder group in the system of healthcare, and the CAM groups as challengers to their position at the apex of the healing hierarchy. Although it seems obvious that stakeholders in any system would seek to preserve the "status quo" and even to enhance their position, in the field of healthcare it is more complicated than it would at first appear.

Stakeholder theory is based on the concept of "stake" or "interest", and stakeholders act in a strategic fashion to influence the system (Freeman, 1984). A stakeholder group can be understood as any group whose members act together in order to promote their common interest (Pross, 1986). They strive to influence those in power to protect or advance their position within a larger, interacting system (Rowley, 1997). In this case, the system is the healthcare system in Ontario which is currently being restructured (Boase, 1994; O'Reilly, 2000). Stakeholder analysis focuses on the interrelations of groups and their impact on policy (Brugha & Varvasovsky, 2000). Faced with a challenge, stakeholders can: (1) facilitate change; (2) work to maintain the "status quo"; or (3) put constraints on change. Which kinds of influence they attempt to exert depends on how they believe their interests will best be served. While the established health professions seek to regulate market conditions to their advantage against competition, the CAM practitioners, who have been working outside the system, are taking steps to gain legitimation by the state and the relevant publics (Boon *et al.*, 2003; Gilmour *et al.*, 2002; Kelner *et al.*, 2002)....

FINDINGS

Stakeholder Strategies in Response to the Challenge of CAM

The data emanating from interviews with this stakeholder group revealed several differences in attitudes. Some of these differences can be explained by the fact that in spite of sharing in the status of allopathic medicine, the roles they play and the authority they enjoy in the healthcare system are not identical (Wolfe & Puttler, 2002) .... The allied health professions share in the high status that medicine enjoys, but not in the power that medicine exerts. They are auxiliary to medicine, and need its protection in order to maintain their position and protect their jurisdictions. The profession of nursing has been subordinated to medicine throughout its history, due to factors such as social class, gender and institutional arrangements (Carpenter, 1993; Coburn, 1988). Today, organized nursing in Ontario has become openly antagonistic to medical interests, demanding an expanded role for nurses in both the hospitals and the community (Coburn *et al.*, 1999). Differences of opinion were evident in the views that the nursing leaders expressed concerning the various CAM groups we asked about. They were more prepared to consider the claims of the chiropractors and the acupuncturists than the others. While they often answered as if they regarded all CAM groups as one category, they clearly did not see them as a homogeneous entity....

Number One—Insistence on "Scientific" Evidence of Efficacy and Safety

Standards of evidence

Most of the stakeholders were unsympathetic to the potential for professionalization of CAM groups. At best, they gave qualified acceptance to the idea that some CAM groups might have a legitimate role to play in the formal healthcare system. They justified their reservations on the basis of the lack of sufficient evidence. They argued that unless a CAM group had a body of knowledge based on "scientific" evidence and a way of delivering care in an objective, standardized fashion, it was unsafe to allow them to treat patients: "Our role is to assure the public that they have achieved a certain standard" (HP5). This leader indicated his skepticism by adding: "I have not seen any evidence to support that what they do makes a difference—nor have I looked" (HP5). The insistence on valid and reliable evidence of the efficacy and safety of CAM practices and therapies can be viewed as "the line in the sand" for professional status.

These stakeholders considered higher standards of evidence essential for CAM to gain formal recognition and a place within the formal healthcare system: "I would like to see much higher standards of education based on scientific evidence. The lower standards somewhat diminish the respect we should have for the providers" (HP1). Another leader said: "We would be sympathetic if the way they gained acceptance was based on science—Show me the science that is science as we know it; peer reviewed designs that show it works" (HP8). She believed that some CAM therapies are closer to having convincing evidence than others: "Naturopaths, homeopaths and Reiki, we would have real trouble with; chiropractors and acupuncturists are closer to it—Show me the science, and so far I have not seen the science that has convinced me" (HP8). Another said: "These are new and emerging groups with often little more than anecdotal evidence behind them. That makes it hard for the existing professionals to accept them" (HP7).

Part of the problem is the difference in paradigms between medicine and CAM. Conventional medicine aims to diagnose illness and treat, cure, or alleviate symptoms whereas most CAM disciplines are geared not only to relieve symptoms and restore wellness, but also to help individuals to heal themselves within a holistic approach to health (Zollman & Vickers, 1999). A stakeholder put it this way: "the core of these particular practices, the historical background to them, is quite different than traditional Western medicine and there is significant skepticism and doubt as to whether the claims are valid and approaches that are taken are appropriate and the scopes of practice are legitimate in any sense" (HP3). These stakeholders were reluctant to recognize the value of CAM approaches, arguing that they are grounded in beliefs and traditions that fall outside of the Western scientific model.

These responses show how Alford's "professional monopolizers" can use the argument of unsatisfactory and insufficient evidence to maintain their boundaries and strengthen their superior position. Gieryn (1983) refers to these kinds of arguments as "ideologies" which serve to justify boundary-work. He cites the example of the sciences, in which efforts to demarcate science from other intellectual activities (non-science) often take the form of attributing selected characteristics to the institution of science. These sorts of statements construct a social boundary that excludes rivals by defining them as outsiders with labels such as "pseudo", "deviant" or "amateur".

Spokespersons for the nursing associations were more aware of and more sympathetic to CAM versions of evidence than were the other stakeholders:

> I think that when we talk about demonstrating safety and standards and proof, we have to realize that there will be different ways of knowing, different ways of testing the efficacy of these many different practices—not everything can be demonstrated through a randomized clinical trial (HP2).

This belief was shared by a second nursing spokesperson who commented that "There is too much that is unexplained to always look for a scientific rationale for everything" (HP9).

Nurses are more accustomed to using CAM therapies as part of their work. They do this without "scientific proof" of efficacy, but rather base their use on clinical evidence and experience. This approach is reflected in the mission statement of one of their main associations which acknowledges the value of "diversity and creativity" in an evolving system of healthcare (ONA Web site, 2003).

Standards of education and practice

According to a majority of the stakeholders, the current attempts of CAM groups to upgrade their standards of education and practice must be based on solid evidence. They emphasized that in order for CAM practitioners to be credentialed, their therapies and practices would have to be evidence-based.

> There is a place for the areas of knowledge and skill they represent. Both the disciplines and those who practice the disciplines have to be credentialed following appropriate training, and their practices have to be approved based on evidence that meets the standards that our society expects (HP1).

One leader admitted that medicine might be imposing a double standard on CAM practitioners: "We are holding them up to different standards than we hold ourselves" (HP10). Another leader pointed out: "We are all struggling with the need to demonstrate safety in an increasingly evidence-based world" (HP3). Even when the established health professions are not able to summon all the necessary clinical evidence for a particular course of treatment, they nevertheless continue to insist that CAM education and practices must be held to the highest standards of evidence.

Self-regulation

The ability to marshall credible evidence of efficacy and safety was also seen by these stakeholders as an essential step in achieving statutory self-regulation for CAM groups.

> If they progress to the point that they meet the standards that we have for our society—and show that they have something beneficial to add and that they are not harmful, then we would agree that they should be self-regulating professions (HP5).

The leaders of the established professions believed that achieving statutory self-regulation would be an important step in the professionalization process, but emphasized that it was a status that had to be earned: "If there is an evidence-based measurement of positive outcome then it would be helpful to patients if they were to become self-regulated" (HP4).

Once again, the question of a double standard for CAM came up. A leader commented: "I suppose one of the things that challenges these new groups is that their organizations will be held to a higher standard of accountability than the traditional groups were when they were first organized" (HP6). Yet, the acknowledgment that this might be the case did not alter their stance.

The nursing professionals more often emphasized the need for public safety and protection, rather than evidence, as a justification for regulating the CAM practitioners: "There has to be assurances that the public is being protected. That is the whole basis of regulation" (HP9). These nursing officials saw possible risks to safety as presenting barriers to professional acceptance. As one said: "If the public is choosing this type of practitioner, they need to know what they are getting—I am very conscious of the public needing to be informed about who their provider is and what they offer and what their limits are" (HP9). For the nursing profession, ensuring patient safety seemed to be more critical than adequate evidence of efficacy. This stance is understandable in view of the fact that nurses spend much of their time with patients and that their mandate emphasizes caring for them.

The leaders of the other allied health professions felt strongly that regulation should not be granted to CAM groups unless they were able to demonstrate in a scientific manner that their therapies were safe and effective and also that their scope of practice was suitable.

> Regulation would have to be based on science. We would certainly also look at whether or not we felt that the scope of practice requested by a group was really appropriate from our perspective. For example, there are lots of groups that claim they can do spinal manipulation but there are only three that are regulated to do so.—That is the kind of thing that if it was in the scope of practice we would have a concern about (HP3).

The issue of scope of practice clearly evoked tensions and concerns about maintaining jurisdictional boundaries and protecting turf among these particular stakeholders.

These findings show the reluctance of the established healthcare professions to encourage the CAM groups in their quest for statutory self-regulation; a critical step in professionalization. The nursing leaders, while more concerned about issues of safety and public protection than "scientific" evidence, were also unwilling to support self-regulation for CAM....

DISCUSSION

The stakeholders in this study were unwilling to say that CAM groups could not or should not become professionalized. But the requirements they spelled out in order for this process to be completed were exacting, rigorous and comprehensive. Their responses implied that since medicine had previously been required to satisfy the highest standards, newcomers would now have to "jump through the same hoops". The difficulty here is in deciding who will make the judgment that CAM standards are sufficiently high to warrant professional legitimacy. If the decisions are made by, or heavily influenced by, the established professions, then the same people are both competitors and judges. They have the resources to powerfully advance their own interests. This can create significant areas of contention. For example, how much, and what areas of biomedical education would satisfy these stakeholders that CAM practitioners are sufficiently knowledgeable to deliver safe and effective healthcare?

In particular, who is to decide what kinds of evidence will be credible when it comes to issues of efficacy and safety? And how much is enough? Exponents of the biomedical view argue that any explanatory systems that fall short of what biomedicine defines as evidence can not be valid and are only pseudo sciences (Barrett & Jarvis, 1993; Beyerstein, 1997). For the medical community, controlled trials remain the sole arbiter of a therapy's efficacy and safety (Ernst, 2000). This is in spite of the fact that many medical interventions have not been subjected to randomized clinical trials (Leape, 1994; Sanders, 2003). For example, in the field of psychiatry, few of the cognitive therapies employed have ever been tested by controlled trials (Pelletier, 2003). It is still unclear how these interventions work and if they really make a difference beyond the placebo effect.

Yet, the medical profession has gained social authority as the arbiter of truth in healthcare. The fact that the medical approach to healing and the CAM approach are operating from different paradigms, creates serious difficulties when it comes to medical assessments of the evidence of efficacy and safety for CAM practices. While medicine is rooted in biomedical science, CAM healing practices are founded on other forms of evidence, some of which have extensive formal and substantive theoretical structures and practice traditions (Thorne, Best, Balon, Kelner, & Rickhi, 2002). Complementary and alternative healing practices emphasize the uniqueness of each individual, integration of body, mind and spirit, the flow of energy as a source of healing, and disease as having dimensions beyond the purely biological (Berliner & Salmon, 1979; Kelner & Wellman, 2000; Oberbaum, Vithoulkas, & Haselen, 2003; Bell, Koithan, Gorman, & Baldwin, 2003). The two models point to different ways of knowing and understanding reality and judging knowledge (Quah, 2003). Currently, the medical profession, as the dominant structural interest, is in the prime position to impose its version of evidence on others (Coburn et al., 1999). This requirement for "scientific" evidence creates a major barrier for CAM groups wishing to gain professional status.

The leaders of the allied health professions were in general agreement with these views, with the exception of some of the nursing leaders. They expressed some understanding of the difficulties that CAM has in meeting the standards of evidence posed by biomedicine and recognized that there are different approaches to demonstrating efficacy and safety. The nursing leaders also suggested that CAM practices would be held to higher standards than some medical therapies such as aspirin have been in the past. The ties that bind the allied health professions to medicine create a uniformity of view among the professional monopolizers. The nurses, however, are more independent of medicine and thus can be more flexible in their views and alliances.

It is important to recognize that times have changed in regard to standards of evidence and that these changes are not particularly related to CAM. In recent years there has been a widespread move to evidence-based medicine and development of clinical practice guidelines (Sackett, 1998). The era of unfettered, individualized decision-making about treatment is fast disappearing for all forms of healthcare. The established healthcare professions are able to take advantage of these new developments to maintain the boundaries around their own professional authority....

REFERENCES

Alford, R. R. (1975). *Healthcare politics—ideological and interest group barriers to reform*. Chicago: University of Chicago Press.

Angus Reid Group Poll. (2000). *National Angus Reid Poll: Canadian adults views and usage of alternative medicines and practices*. Toronto: Angus Reid Group Poll.

Barrett, S., & Jarvis, W. T. (1993). In *The health robbers: A close look at quackery in America*. Buffalo: Prometheus Books.

Bell, I., Koithan, M., Gorman, M., & Baldwin, C. (2003). Homeopathic practitioner views of changes in patients undergoing constitutional treatment for chronic disease. *Journal of Alternative and Complementary Medicine*, 9(1), 39–50.

Berger, E. (1999). *Social overview report*. Toronto: The Berger Monitor and Hay Consulting Group.

Berliner, H. S., & Salmon, J. W. (1979). The Holistic movement and scientific medicine: The naked and the dead. *Socialist Review*, 43, 31–52.

Beyerstein, B. (1997). Alternative medicine: Where's the evidence? *Canadian Journal of Public Health*, 88(3), 149–150.

Boase, J. P. (1994). *Shifting sands: Government–group relationships in the healthcare sector*. Montreal & Kingston: McGill-Queens University Press.

Boon, H., Welsh, S., Kelner, M., & Wellman, B. (2003). Complementary/alternative practitioners and the professionalization process: A Canadian comparative case study. In P. Tovey, G. Easthope, & J. Adams (Eds.), *Mainstreaming of complementary and alternative medicine in social context: An international perspective*. London: Routledge.

Brugha, R., & Varvasovszky, Z. (2000). Stakeholder analysis: A review. *Health Policy and Planning*, 15(3), 239–246.

Bryson, J. M., Cunningham, G. L., & Lokkesmoe, K. J. (2002). What to do when stakeholders matter: The case of problem formulation for the African American men project of Hennepin county Minnesota. *Public Administration Review*, 62(5), 568–584.

Cant, S., & Sharma, U. (1995). The reluctant profession—homeopathy and the search for legitimacy. *Work, Employment and Society*, 9(4), 743–762.

Carpenter, M. (1993). The subordination of nurses in health care: Towards a social divisions approach. In E. Riska, & K. Wegar (Eds.), *Gender, work and medicine* (pp. 95–130). London: Sage.

Coburn, D. (1988). The development of Canadian nursing: Professionalization and proletarianization. *International Journal of Health Services*, 18(3), 437–456.

Coburn, D., Rappolt, S., & Bourgeault, I. (1997). Decline vs. retention of medical power through restratification: An examination of the Ontario case. *Sociology of Health & Illness*, 19(1), 1–22.

Coburn, D., Rappolt, S., Bourgeault, I., & Angus, J. (1999). *Medicine, nursing and the state*. Aurora, ON: Garamond Press.

Dymond, S., Nix, T. W., Rotarius, T. M., & Savage, G. T. (1995). Why do key integrated delivery stakeholders really matter? Assessing control, coalitions, resources and power. *Medical Group Management Journal, 42*(6), 26–38.

Ernst, E. (2000). Assessing the evidence base for CAM. In M. Kelner, B. Wellman, B. Pescosolido, & M. Saks (Eds.), *Complementary and alternative medicine: Challenge and change*. Amsterdam: Harwood Academic Publishers.

Eyles, J., Brimacombe, M., Chaulk, P., Stoddart, G., Pranger, T., & Moase, O. (2001). What determines health? To where should we shift resources? Attitudes towards the determinants of health among multiple stakeholder groups in prince Edward Island, Canada. *Social Science & Medicine*, 53(2), 1611–1619.

Fox, S., & Fallows, D. (2003). *Internet health resources*. Washington: Pew Internet & American Life Project.

Freeman, R. E. (1984). *Strategic management: A stakeholder approach*. Boston: Pitman/Ballinger (Harper Collins).

Gieryn, T. F. (1983). Boundary-work and the demarcation of science from non-science: Strains and interests in professional ideologies of scientists. *American Sociological Review, 48*, 781–795.

Gilmour, J. M., Kelner, M., & Wellman, B. (2002). Opening the door to complementary and alternative medicine: Self-regulation in Ontario. *Law & Policy, 24*(2), 150–174.

Goldstein, M. S. (1999). *Alternative healthcare: Medicine, miracle, or mirage?* Philadelphia: Temple University Press.

Haug, M. R., & Lavin, B. (1983). *Consumerism in medicine: Challenging physician authority*. Beverly Hills: Sage.

Hendry, J. (2001). Missing the target: Normative stakeholder theory and the corporate governance debate. *Business Ethics Quarterly, 11*(1), 159–176.

http://www.rnao.org/about/mission/asp. (2003). *Mission statement: The Registered Nurses Association of Ontario*. The Registered Nurses Association of Ontario.

Jawahar, I. M., & McLaughlin, G. L. (2001). Toward a descriptive stakeholder theory: An organizational life cycle approach. *Academy of Management Review, 26*(3), 397–414.

Kelner, M. (2000). The therapeutic relationship under fire. In M. Kelner, B. Wellman, B. Pescosolido, & M. Saks (Eds.), *Complementary and alternative medicine: Challenge and change*. Amsterdam: Harwood Academic Publishers.

Kelner, M., Boon, H., Wellman, B., & Welsh, S. (2002). Complementary and alternative groups contemplate the need for effectiveness, safety and cost-effectiveness research. *Complementary Therapies in Medicine, 10*, 235–239.

Kelner, M., & Wellman, B. (1997). Healthcare and consumer choice: Medical and alternative therapies. *Social Science & Medicine, 45*(2), 203–212.

Kelner, M., & Wellman, B. (2000). Introduction in complementary and alternative medicine: Challenge and change. In M. Kelner, B. Wellman, B. Pescosolido, & M. Saks (Eds.), *Complementary and alternative medicine: Challenge and change*. Amsterdam: Harwood Academic Press.

Landro, L. (2003). Personal health (a special report)—net benefits: Where to find reliable sources on alternative medicine. *Wall Street Journal*, R7 October 21, 2003.

Leape, L. L. (1994). Error in medicine. *Journal of the American Medical Association, 272*(23), 1851–1857.

McKinlay, J., & Arches, J. (1985). Towards the proletarianization of physicians. *International Journal of Health Services, 15*(2), 161–195.

Mechanic, D. (1996). Comparative medical systems. *American Review of Sociology, 22*, 239–270.

Oberbaum, M., Vithoulkas, G., & Haselen, R. V. (2003). Clinical trials of classical homeopathy: Reflections on appropriate research designs. *Journal of Alternative and Complementary Medicine*, 9(1), 105–111.

O'Reilly, P. (2000). *Healthcare practitioners: An Ontario case study in policy making*. Toronto: University of Toronto Press.

Pelletier, K. G. E. (2003). Conventional and integrative medicine—evidence based? Sorting fact from fiction. *Journal of Alternative and Complementary Medicine*, 8(1), 3–6.

Pross, P. A. (1986). *Group politics and public policy*. Toronto: Oxford University Press.

Quah, S. R. (2003). Traditional healing systems and the ethos of science. *Social Science & Medicine*, 57, 1997–2012.

Ramsay, C., Walker, M., & Alexander, J. (1999). *Alternative medicine in Canada: Use and public attitudes (public policy sources 21)*. Vancouver, BC: Fraser Institute.

Rowley, T. J. (1997). Moving beyond dyadic ties: A network theory of stakeholder influences. *Academy of Management Review*, 22(4), 887–910.

Ruedy, J., Kaufman, D., & MacLeod, H. (1999). Alternative and complementary medicine in Canadian medical schools: A survey. *Canadian Medical Association Journal*, 160, 816–817.

Sackett, D. L. (1998). Evidence-based medicine. *Spine*, 23, 1085–1086.

Saks, M. (2000). Professionalization, politics and CAM. In M. Kelner, B. Wellman, B. Pescosolido, & M. Saks (Eds.), *Complementary and alternative medicine: Challenge and change*. Amsterdam: Harwood Academic Publishers.

Sanders, L. (2003). Medicine's progress, one setback at a time. *The New York Times Magazine* (pp. 29–43).

Thorne, S., Best, A., Balon, J., Kelner, M., & Rickhi, B. (2002). Ethical dimensions in the borderland between conventional and complementary/alternative medicine. *Journal of Alternative and Complementary Medicine*, 8(6), 907–915.

Welsh, S., Kelner, M., Wellman, B., & Boon, H. (2004). Moving forward? Complementary and alternative practitioners seeking self-regulation. *Sociology of Health & Illness*, 26(2).

Wetzel, M., Eisenberg, D., & Kaptchuk, T. (1998). Courses involving complementary and alternative medicine at US medical schools. *Journal of the American Medical Association*, 280(9), 784–787.

Wolfe, R. A., & Puttler, D. S. (2002). How tight are the ties that bind stakeholder groups? *Organization Science*, 13(1), 64–80.

Zollman, C., & Vickers, A. (1999). ABC of complementary medicine: Users and practitioners of complementary medicine. *British Medical Journal*, 319, 836–838.

Source: M. Kelner, B. Wellman, H. Boon and S. Welsh, 'Responses of established healthcare to the professionalisation of complementary and alternative medicine in Ontario', *Social Science and Medicine*, 59:5 (2004) 915–30.

Study Questions and Activities

1. Think about the way in which CAM impacts on either your professional or personal life.
2. Do you agree that medicine's special status is being eroded by CAMs?
3. Reflect back to your reading in Part II of this book. Why is the debate on 'scientific' evidence so important for the professionalisation of CAM groups?
4. How far does Friedson's discussion of the characteristics of a profession (Reading 23) help you to make sense of the role of CAMs?

──────────────── **Further Reading** ────────────────

You may be interested in exploring further sociological perspectives on CAMs. If you are, then the books by D. Callahan, *The Role of Complementary and Alternative Medicine: Accommodating Pluralism* (Washington, DC: Georgetown University Press, 2002); S. Cant and U. Sharma, *A New Medical Pluralism? Complementary Medicine, Doctors, Patients and the State*, (London: Routledge, 1998) and U. Sharma, *Complementary Medicine Today: Practitioners and Patients* (London: Routledge, 1991) may be useful. Alternatively, the following reader is also very good: G. Lee-Treweek, J. Katz, H. MacQueen, S. Spurr and T. Heller (eds) *Perspectives on Complementary and Alternative Medicine: A Reader* (London/Buckingham: Routledge/Open University Press, 2005). For far shorter discussions on the sociology of CAMs, consider either of the following: P. Tovey, 'On use and purpose in the sociology of CAM', *Complementary Therapies in Medicine*, 9:3 (2001) 134–5 or I. D. Coulter, 'The rise and rise of complementary and alternative medicine: a sociological perspective', *Medical Journal of Australia*, 180:11 (2004) 587–9. To focus specifically on the role of sociological research within CAM, the following article may be useful: J. Chatwin, 'Sociological research and CAM', *Focus on Alternative and Complementary Therapies*, 10:1 (2005) 15–17. The next reading in this part of the book examines the boundaries between two professional groups. To consider boundary issues in CAMs, read the following: N. Mizrachi, J. T. Shuval, and S. Gross, 'Boundary at work: alternative medicine in biomedical settings', *Sociology of Health and Illness*, 27:1 (2005) 20–43.

Reading 25

The Feminisation of Dentistry

Tracey L. Adams

The healthcare professions are not static or bounded, but fluid and constantly moveable. Reading 24 explores some of these issues by examining the tensions between established and 'alternative' healthcare providers. However, occupational changes take place between professional groups as well as within. Reading 25 considers the feminisation of professional employment – that is, the trend of increasing female entrance and employment into particular healthcare professions. In this reading, Tracey Adams examines the feminisation of healthcare, focusing specifically on the case of women in dentistry. Adams questions the impact of women on dentistry and asks: Is feminisation the result of a decline of professional status or the cause of such a decline? Drawing on the examples of medicine, nursing and pharmacy, and professional employment more generally, Adams also explores the potential for women's work to change healthcare practice.

In recent decades, countries like Canada have witnessed a feminization of professional employment. Women have been moving into formerly male-dominated professions in great numbers. According to the 2001 Canadian census, women compose 34 percent of all lawyers, 33 percent of all medical doctors, and 27.6 percent of all dentists. A continuing increase in women's participation is forecast for the next several years as currently women make up roughly half of all new graduates and students in each of these professions (McKenzie Leiper, 2003; McMurray *et al.*, 2002; O'Keefe, 2000). This trend first became an issue of sociological discussion and debate over a decade ago. Many scholars and professional practitioners alike have wondered what the impact of women's participation within male-dominated professions will be (for example, Muzzin *et al.*, 1994; O'Keefe, 2000; Riska, 2001; Frize, 1997). Does the entrance of women signal a decline in professional status? Does it engender change in the nature of professional practice itself? A number of studies have explored these issues, but few concrete answers are evident.

[Here], I explore the impact of feminization within male-dominated professions through a case study of dentistry in Ontario. Dentistry has feminized more slowly than the professions of pharmacy, law and medicine, but it has experienced a greater influx of women than other stubbornly male-dominated professions like engineering and architecture. While a number of studies have explored the movement of women into pharmacy, medicine and law, little attention has been paid to women's entrance into dentistry. Yet, because of the slower rate of women's entrance, and the greater incidence of private practice amongst dentists compared to other professionals, dentistry provides an interesting case for the study of feminization.[1] While determining women's impact on the dental profession is difficult — and inherently somewhat speculative — I contend that an exploration of women's and men's current practice characteristics and attitudes towards dental practise can shed light on the issue. If women currently practise differently, and think differently about professional issues, than male dentists, one would expect that the influx of women into dentistry would provoke professional change....

FEMINIZATION AND PROFESSIONS

In studies of the feminization of professional employment (and of occupational employment more generally), two key sets of questions are evident. The first centres around women's entrance and professional status. Is feminization associated with a loss of professional status? If it is, is feminization the result of a decline in professional status, the cause of such a decline, or both? Historically, the classic case of feminization and declining status is clerical work. In the opening decades of the twentieth century, clerical work was transformed from a moderately-high status, complex, administrative job performed by men, to a more narrow, lower-status, female-dominated occupation (Lowe, 1987). While it seems that it was the rise of corporate capitalism and the accompanying restructuring of clerical work that prompted both feminization and status decline (Lowe, 1987), it is possible that feminization itself contributed to a lowering of occupational status. In the professions literature, the most-examined case of feminization is that of pharmacy. The rapid feminization of pharmacy in the latter half of the twentieth century was associated with occupational change — particularly the rise of large pharmaceutical manufacturers and chain drug stores; this change altered the nature of, and the autonomy associated with, pharmacy practice (Phipps, 1990; Collin, 1992; Muzzin *et al.*, 1994). With these changes, men lost interest in pharmacy and women's participation increased. Phipps (1990) suggests that men's disinterest in pharmacy opened up educational and work opportunities for women. However, Collin (1992) illustrates that occupational change expanded the areas of pharmacy practice (hospital pharmacy) where women were traditionally over-represented, while simultaneously reducing opportunities in the male-dominated area of private pharmacy ownership. Thus, it seems that pharmacy, like clerical work, may have feminized *after* occupational change decreased its status and autonomy.

Nonetheless, the relationship between status decline and feminization is not entirely clear. In fact, as Bottero (1992) argues, there is little evidence that the feminization of professions like pharmacy has been accompanied by a drop in status at all. Pharmacy has recently pursued strategies to increase its professional status, by tinkering with its knowledge base and expanding its educational requirements (Birenbaum, 1982). Thus, one could contend that the feminization of pharmacy has been accompanied by an expansion of the profession's status (Bottero, 1992). Ultimately, there is little convincing evidence that the entrance of women into professions has (in and of itself) led to, or resulted from, a decline in professional status.

The second set of questions evident in the literature on feminization in professions centres around the impact of women on the professions themselves. The central underlying question here is, do women practise professions differently than men? Answers to this question are important for a number of reasons. First, there are implications for service provision: if women work fewer hours than men, and in only some specialties, there may be an under-supply of professional practitioners in the future (Muzzin *et al.*, 1994; Tanner and Cockerill, 1996; Denekens, 2002). Second, the question has implications for the future trajectory of professions. If women truly practise differently than men, then they may alter the nature of professional practice (Riska, 2001; McMurray *et al.*, 2002; Denekens, 2002). For some, this is a goal. For instance, some women have advocated for the recruitment of women into engineering both to maintain the supply of practitioners, and to engender a change in engineering practice; it is believed that women will contribute to a more humane engineering profession and produce more "caring" technologies (discussed in Frize, 1997). Third, whether women practise differently from men has implications for occupational segregation and gender inequality. If women's professional work is associated with ghettoization in a few lower-status specialties, lower-level employment and lower income, gender inequality is perpetuated (Armstrong and Armstrong, 1992; Riska, 2001; Lorber, 1993; Muzzin *et al.*, 1995; Tanner *et al.*, 1999).

There is a substantial body of literature that suggests that women may indeed practise somewhat differently. For instance, women in professions seem to work fewer hours, on average, than men (Tanner and Cockerill, 1996; McMurray *et al.*, 2002). Moreover, there is evidence of internal segregation within professions: women's participation is not evenly spread across specialties, but tends to concentrate in those that are somewhat lower-status and perhaps more easily sex-typed feminine. Thus, women in medicine work disproportionately in general practice, and as obstetricians and gynecologists, while they are under-represented in the high-status specialties of surgery and internal medicine (Hinze, 1999, Armstrong and Armstrong, 1992; Riska, 2001). Similarly, women lawyers are said to be over-represented in family law, but under-represented in the high-status specialty of litigation (Pierce, 1995, Podmore and Spencer, 1986). Women are also less likely than men to be self-employed (Muzzin *et al.*, 1994; Brown and Lazar, 1998; Tanner *et al.*, 1999; Armstrong and Armstrong, 1992). Whether this internal segregation indicates "ghettoization" in professions, or simply a slow-moving integration and uneven trend towards parity, can be debated (Wright and Jacobs, 1994, Chiu and Leicht, 1999; Riska, 2001). However, recent research suggests that the gendering of medical specialties, creates both implicit barriers for women (Hinze, 1999), and explicit structural barriers (Gjerberg, 2002), that prevent women from participating in professions on the same terms as men.

There is also evidence that women professionals earn less than their male counterparts on average (Armstrong and Armstrong, 1992; Wallace and Weeks, 2002; McMurray *et al.*, 2002; Hagan and Kay, 1995). Gender differences in areas outside of working hours, income, and specialty are harder to ascertain. While some studies have debated whether women professionals spend more time with clients/patients, a recent study suggests that women physicians see more patients per office hour than do men (Wallace and Weeks, 2002). It is not clear that either of these proposed differences can be taken as evidence of a distinctly "female" or "more caring" approach to professional practice. There is some evidence that men's and women's motivations for entering professional practice may differ. For instance, female lawyers may be more concerned with justice issues than males (Guinier *et al.*, 1997) and male pharmacists appear to be more concerned with the "business" side of pharmacy practice than are women (Beales, 2002). Nonetheless, it is by no means certain that these differences lead to different practice styles, although they might encourage different work locations and specialties. Overall, when weighing the literature on gender differences and professional practice, it seems clear that some differences between men and women exist. However, the significance of these differences for feminization of professions is not entirely clear.

This opaque picture of feminization is clarified somewhat in a recent study by Chiu and Leicht (1999) who argue that it is the nature of the profession itself, and particularly the context of occupational change in which feminization occurs, that determines its impact — specifically whether it leads to ghettoization and a continuation of gender inequality, or whether the feminization is "successful" and more integrative.[2] Successful feminization is more likely under conditions of occupational job growth and rising wages (due in part to employment demand outstripping supply), and when advanced degrees are required for entry to practise (Chiu and Leicht, 1999: 563). Chiu and Leicht hold that the law profession in the United States experienced successful feminization during the 1980s, because of the above factors and trends. This study is valuable in highlighting the importance of the context in which feminization occurs; however, its framework has not been widely applied. Given the volatile labour market and changes in the regulation of health professions experienced in Ontario over the past fifteen years, it seems unlikely that many professions have been experiencing feminization under such positive conditions. Despite over a decade of research into the topic, the impact of feminization on professions remains unclear.

Dentistry

It is only in the past few decades that women have made inroads into dentistry in significant numbers. In 1991, women composed only 16% of all dentists in Ontario. However, currently women make up almost 28% of dentists in the province — a substantial increase over the past decade, and one that is expected to continue. The feminization of dentistry, however, has not taken place under the favourable conditions of occupational growth and rising wages, outlined by Chiu and Leicht (1999). Rather, dentists have experienced an overall decrease in rates of dental caries (cavities), which combined with other factors including the aging of the population, means that the market for dental services is becoming more competitive, especially in many urban areas. Embarking on a dental career in this climate is further complicated by the fact that students are completing dental degrees later, after obtaining one or more other university degrees, and graduating with high debt loads (Sbaraglia, 1992). Nevertheless, there is little sign that students are turning away from dentistry, and with restricted class sizes, entrance is competitive. Market conditions affect the nature of dental practice, but there is no parallel within dentistry to the broader industrial and organizational changes that seem to have accompanied women's movement into pharmacy and law. While larger dental firms are on the rise, dental practice today is quite similar in organization to practice several decades ago. It seems, then, that "feminization" within dentistry is not taking place under "ideal" conditions.

There have been a few studies on women's entrance into dentistry, and gender differences in dental practice conducted in the United States. These studies indicate that women dentists earn less than men (78% of men's income) and that they are less likely to be self-employed (Brown and Lazar, 1998; Kaldenberg et al., 1996). According to these studies, women dentists may spend more time with patients than men do, but the difference is small, and it appears that women dentists may not work substantially less than male dentists (Kaldenberg et al., 1996). The significance of these few gender differences for the future of dentistry is by no means clear (Kaldenberg et al., 1996: 76–77). More detailed investigation is needed to clarify these gender differences, and to determine how they might shape the future of dental practice....

NOTES

1. Studies of women in pharmacy, law, architecture, and engineering have documented gender differences in employment patterns and rates of promotion (for instance, Devine, 1992; Hagan and Kay, 1995). Organizational barriers to women's advance within male-dominated professions are also evident (Lorber, 1993). However, such barriers should be virtually non-existent in a private practice profession like dentistry, and this may lead to greater gender equality. Approximately 90% of dentists are self-employed (in one form or another).

2. Drawing on Wright and Jacobs (1994), Chiu and Leicht (1999: 561) argue that an integrating occupation is one in which "women's representation is moving towards parity, segregation is decreasing, the gender wage gap is narrowing, and wages are not falling."

REFERENCES

Armstrong, Pat and Hugh Armstrong 1992 "Sex and Professions in Canada." *Journal of Canadian Studies* 27 (1): 118–35.

Beales, Jennifer D. 2002 From Neophyte to professional: investigating pharmacy students' attitudes to their training, future practice and the profession, MA Thesis, Department of Sociology, University of Western Ontario.

Birenbaum, Arnold 1982 "Reprofessionalization in Pharmacy." *Social Science & Medicine* 16 (8): 871–8.

Bottero, Wendy 1992 "The Changing Face of the Professions: Gender and Explanations of Women's Entry into Pharmacy." *Work, Employment and Society* 6 (3): 329–46.

Brown, L. Jackson and Vickie Lazar 1998 "Differences in Net Incomes of Male and Female Owner General Practitioners." *Journal of the American Dental Association* 129 (3): 373–8.

Chiu, Charlotte and Kevin Leicht 1999 "When Does Feminization Increase Equality? The Case of Lawyers." *Law and Society Review* 33 (3): 557–94.

Collin, Johanne 1992 "Les Femmes dans la profession pharmaceutique au Quebec: rupture ou continuite?" *Recherches Feministes* 5 (2): 31–56.

Denekens, Joke P. 2002 "The Impact of Feminisation on General Practice." *Acta Clinica Belgica* 57 (1): 5–10.

Devine, Fiona 1992 "Gender Segregation in the Engineering and Science Professions: A Case of Continuity and Change." *Work, Employment & Society* 6 (4): 557–75.

Frize, Monique 1997 "Missed Opportunities: Women and Technology." Paper presented at the Women and Technology Conference, CASCON97, Toronto, November 1997. www.carleton.ca/cwse-on/missedopur.html. (Date accessed: April 30, 2003.)

Gjerberg, Elisabeth 2002 "Gender Similarities in Doctor's Preferences — and Gender Differences in Final Specialisation." *Social Science & Medicine* 54 (4): 591–605.

Guinier, Lani, Michelle Fine and Jane Balin 1997 *Becoming Gentlemen: Women, Law School and Institutional Change*. Boston: Beacon Press.

Hagan, John and Fiona Kay 1995 *Gender in Practice: A Study of Lawyers Lives*. New York: Oxford University Press.

Hinze, Susan 1999 "Gender and the Body of Medicine or At Least Some Body Parts: Reconstructing the Prestige Hierarchy of Medical Specialties." *The Sociological Quarterly* 40 (2): 217–39.

Kaldenberg, Dennis O., Anisa M. Zvonkovic and Boris W. Becker 1996 "Women Dentists: The Social Construction of a Profession." Pp. 65–85 in *Women and Minorities in American Professions*, edited by J. Tans and E. Smith. New York: SUNY Press.

Lorber, Judith 1993 "Why Women Physicians Will Never be True Equals in the American Medical Profession." Pp. 62–76 in *Gender, Work and Medicine*, edited by E. Riska and K. Wegar. London: Sage Publications.

Lowe, Graham S. 1987 *Women in the Administrative Revolution*. Toronto: University of Toronto Press.

McKenzie Leiper, Jean 2003 "Gender, Class and Legal Education: Standing in the Shadow of The Learned Gentleman." Paper prepared for the Symposium on Professional Education, Halifax Nova Scotia, May 2003.

McMurray, Julie E., Graham Angus, May Cohen, Paul Gavel, John Harding, John Horvath, Elisabeth Paice, Julie Schmittdiel 2002 "Women in Medicine: A Four-Nation Comparison." *Journal of the American Medical Women's Association* 57 (4): 185–90.

Muzzin, Linda., G.P. Brown and Roy W. Hornosty 1994 "Consequences of Feminization of a Profession: The Case of Canadian Pharmacy." *Women & Health* 21 (2/3): 39–56.

Muzzin, Linda., G.P. Brown and Roy W. Hornosty 1995 "Gender, Educational Credentials, Contributions and Career Advancement: Results of a Follow-Up Study in Hospital Pharmacy." *Canadian Review of Sociology and Anthropology* 32 (2): 151–68.

O'Keefe, John 2000 "The Quiet Revolution in Dentistry." *Journal of the Canadian Dental Association* 67(2):67.

Phipps, Pelly 1990 "Industrial and Occupational Change in Pharmacy: Prescriptions for Feminization." Pp. 111–26 in *Job Queues, Gender Queues: Explaining Women's Inroads into Male occupations*, edited by B. Reskin and P. Roos. Philadelphia: Temple University Press.

Pierce, Jennifer 1995 *Gender Trials: Emotional Lives in Contemporary Law Firms*. Berkeley: University of California Press.

Podmore, David and Anne Spencer 1986 "Gender in the Labour Process — the Case of Women and Men Lawyers." Pp. 36–52 in *Gender and the Labour Process*, ed. by D. Knights and H. Willmott. Aldershot: Gower.

Riska, Elianne 2001 "Towards Gender Balance: But Will Women Physicians Have an Impact on Medicine?" *Social Science & Medicine* 52: 179–87.

Sbaraglia, Peter 1992 "The Big Chill: For Today's Dental School Graduates, Life isn't Easy." *Ontario Dentist* 69 (1): 26.

Tanner, Julian and Rhonda Cockerill 1996 "Gender, Social Change and the Professions: The Case of Pharmacy." *Sociological Forum* 11 (4): 643–60.

Tanner, Julian, Rhonda Cockerill, Jan Barnsley and A. Paul Williams 1999 "Gender and Income in Pharmacy: Human Capital and Gender Stratification Theories revisited." *British Journal of Sociology* 50 (1): 97–117.

Wallace, A.E and W.B. Weeks 2002 "Differences in Income between Male and Female Primary Care Physicians." *Journal of the American Medical Women's Association* 57 (4): 180–4.

Wright, Rosemary and Jerry Jacobs 1994 "Male Flight from Computer Work: A New Look at Occupational Re-Segregation and Ghettoization." *American Sociological Review* 59 (4): 511–36.

Source: T. L. Adams, 'Feminization of professions: the case of women in dentistry', *Canadian Journal of Sociology*, 30:1 (2005) 71–94.

Study Questions and Activities

1. Do female practitioners hold different attitudes than men on key professional issues? Do women practice differently than men?
2. Think about some of the different areas of practice within healthcare with which you are familiar. How do you think that feminisation affects issues such as pay, status and working conditions?
3. Can women's work change healthcare practice? What barriers do women face when entering professions dominated by men? Using your own experiences consider the following question: What is the status of men within feminised professions?

--------------------------------- **Further Reading** ---------------------------------

It is worth reading the rest of Tracey Adams' article because it describes her empirical work on the feminisation of dentistry. The subject of feminization in healthcare has also been discussed elsewhere. For example, in the classic text *Professions and Patriarchy* (London: Routledge, 1992), Anne Witz discusses gender segregation and the struggle among medicine, nursing, midwifery and radiography. For a more recent discussion of gender at work, see: S. Halford and P. Leonard, *Negotiating Gendered Identities at Work: Place, Space and Time* (Basingstoke: Palgrave, 2006). There is also some discussion in the literature on the feminization of the physician assistant profession in the United States: S. Lindsay, 'The feminization of the physician assistant profession', *Women and Health*, 41:4 (2005) 37–61 and on the feminization of medicine: A. M. Heru, 'Pink-collar medicine: women and the future of medicine', *Gender Issues*, 22:1 (2004) 20–34. In the latter, the author considers the special place of women in medicine and opportunities for change, as well as the barriers that women face within the profession. There is also considerable discussion of gender, feminization and the nursing profession within the literature – any of the following would be useful: C. Davies, *Gender and the Professional Predicament in Nursing* (Buckingham: Open University Press, 1995); M. Miers, *Gender Issues in Nursing Practice* (Houndmills: Macmillan, 2000) or J. A. Evans, 'Men in nursing: issues of gender segregation and hidden advantage', *Journal of Advanced Nursing*, 26:2 (1997) 226–31. The journals *Gender and Society, Gender, Work and Organization* and the *Journal of Advanced Nursing* also sometimes carry articles on issues relating to work, gender and healthcare.

Occupational Boundaries in the Operating Theatre

Stephen Timmons and Judith Tanner

Sociological analyses of professional boundaries in healthcare have often focused predominantly – though not exclusively – on the relationship between medicine and nursing. However, much of the work that has been conducted on the operating theatre has focused on that between surgeons and anaesthetists. In contrast, in this reading, Stephen Timmons and Judith Tanner focus on the relationship between operating theatre nurses and operating department practitioners. Theatre nursing is an established specialism within nursing and most theatre nurses are women. Operating department practitioners – the majority of whom are men – have a much more recent history, having achieved registration and regulation relatively recently. Historically, theatre nurses have been the most dominant profession although both groups earn roughly comparable salaries. However, as Timmons and Tanner argue, changes in the NHS over the last 20 years, or so, have meant that theatre nurses are concerned that their dominant position may be in decline. This reading draws on a qualitative research study with 17 theatre nurses and 3 operating department practitioners working in five theatre departments in England. The research respondents were observed in practice over the course of their shifts and were then interviewed individually. In this reading, Timmons and Tanner consider the disputed occupational boundaries between operating theatre nurses and operating department practitioners, exploring the way in which this divide is created and maintained.

BOUNDARY WORK AND ATROCITY STORIES

...

The concept of boundary work appears to originate with Gieryn (1983). Analysing how scientists attempt to distinguish their activities (as science) from other activities (which are described as 'technical' or 'unscientific'), he shows how they sought to defend their status and privileges. The strategies that the scientists used included:

■ Expansion of professional expertise into areas contested by rival groups, in order to emphasise the contrast between them.

■ Monopolisation of professional authority, in order to exclude rivals by defining them as, for instance 'amateurs'.

■ Protection of professional autonomy (Gieryn 1999).

However, Gieryn claims that within the workplace (as opposed to with outsiders) boundary disputes of this kind are quite rare. Allen (2001a, 2001b) argues that while boundary disputes of the types analysed by Gieryn may be rare, disputes still occur. This is because within the workplace demarcation is problematic, in that it can be unclear, and varies from setting to setting, while at the public level, occupational boundaries appear to be quite clear. Allen poses the question, 'How does one establish an occupational (moral) identity when the technical lines of demarcation routinely break down?' (Allen 2001a: 79). For Allen, an important part of this process is the telling (and hearing) of 'atrocity stories', building on the work of Dingwall (1977), who shows how difficult it is for professions like nursing and health visiting to establish themselves when there is a 'dominant' profession (medicine) in their environment. Dingwall shows how the health visitors he studied used atrocity stories to demonstrate how they were 'as good as' doctors, or 'better than' social workers, the two groups the health visitors were most keen to distinguish themselves from. These atrocity stories were used as what Sacks (1992a, 1992b) might call a membership categorisation device. As Dingwall says, '[Atrocity] stories are demonstrations by students [of health visiting] to each other of their ability to monitor the social world as competent nurses and to formulate it into appropriate patterns' (Dingwall 1977: 377). The existence and telling of atrocity stories is, in itself, evidence of a boundary dispute. Dingwall (1977) shows how where there are no disputes, there are much less likely to be atrocity stories. 'Where there are more serious problems like those of occupational boundary maintenance, self-defence, or a zero-sum game of status recognition, we need to examine the power relationships involved.' (1977: 393).

Theatre nurses have faced an additional difficulty. Despite being a well-established specialism within nursing (NATN 1989), and, indeed, considered (by themselves at least (Tanner 1996)) to constitute some sort of an elite, they find their status contested by a new 'profession' in the making. Like the health visitors studied by Dingwall, this is particularly problematic because of the similarity of the two professions. It thus becomes an important task for theatre nurses to distinguish themselves from ODPs. This is a problem of exclusion: in order to define yourself as a profession, it is necessary to show how you differ from other professions[1]. Much of what the nurses and the ODPs said can be analysed using the device of the 'atrocity story' (Dingwall 1977, Allen 2001a)....

Doctor–Support versus Caring for Patients

The issue of who ODPs were there to help was of importance to the nurses. ODPs were described as being employed to help and support doctors (anaesthetists and surgeons), by contradistinction with nurses, who were concerned with patient care.

> They are not nurses. With nurses you are there for the patient. They are not accountable, they have no professional body. Nurses are there for the patient. ODPs are there for the anaesthetist (Interviewee A).

> Nurses are there for the patient. ODPs are there for the anaesthetist (Interviewee D).

> *What special skills do you think nurses have that ODPs don't have?*
> Basically caring skills (Interviewee B).

In the light of the history of the ODP profession, this was an easy charge for the nurses to make. It relates to the debate over the status of the two professions, which we will consider in more detail below. Suffice to say at this stage that a profession that cares for patients directly is held to have higher status than one which assists another group of professionals, especially in an organisation like the NHS which professes a rhetoric of being organised around the patient (even if the reality is not all that it might be).

Patient-centred

Developing this theme of being patient-centred, many of the nurses who spoke about this issue used terms like 'caring' or 'holistic' to differentiate themselves and how they worked from ODPs:

> … there, it was an ODP and an anaesthetic nurse, and it was just the little things that the anaesthetic nurse did, like she covered the patient up, she talked to him more than the ODP did. I just felt that there was that little bit of extra care being taken of the patient by one person as opposed to the other (Interviewee A).

> … it sounds awful if I say it – seems to be forgotten, but to a certain extent, if it's an ODA/ODP scrubbing, then the patient does seem to be forgotten. The job in hand is being done – the instruments are being looked after, the sets are being checked, those sort of things are being done, but the little bits of care – making sure that the patient's dignity is maintained (Interviewee A).

These appear to be classic atrocity stories. They have a strong moral component, with the nurse as the 'heroine' who was 'caring for' with the patient, and the ODP as the 'villain'. The nurses present themselves as the actors who were concerned about the patient's dignity and privacy. Surgery necessarily involves the exposure of the body, and managing this so that the patient is not exposed 'unnecessarily' is seen as being the responsibility of the nurse…. Likewise, the 'caring' nurse, who takes time with patients, is contrasted with the 'uncaring' ODP in the following extract:

Nursing is the holistic part – you do everything, holistically, I suppose I've been nursing for a long time, so I know what I'm talking about more – it's natural. A natural rapport, a natural feeling of being with a patient, rather than just whizzing in, seeing a patient for five minutes, sitting them on the trolley, putting them to sleep(Interviewee E).

Perhaps reflecting the possibility that ODPs could be substituted for nurses (as discussed above) the nurses sought to justify their own presence in the theatre by contrasting their training with the ODPs' training to demonstrate how much more 'patient-centred' they were:

The ODP training is good training, but it is entirely focussed on working in theatre and the ODA would say its very technical. Nurse training is three years looking after patients on the ward caring for them, you know after they have been to theatre, I think they have a better whole picture and the whole training is about advocacy and looking after the patients as a whole (Interviewee E).

To start with we all trained as nurses and the basic thing you learn is patient care.... I know that it is going away from nurses in theatre, you are getting ODPs now. Nurses have had that basic hands-on training of looking after people. ODPs they come in, they go to school, they learn about anaesthetics, surgery and recovery but they don't learn about people(Interviewee K).

In addition to this discussion of their training, nurses differentiated themselves from ODPs by claiming to act as an advocate for the patient. This role as advocate is a recurring theme both within nursing in general (for instance UKCC 1989, Gates 1994) as well as in the theatre nursing journals (for instance Mardell 1996, Davis 2003). The only empirical study of theatre nurses (McGarvey 2001) that considered this role suggested that they could not be said to be acting as advocates for patients. However, this does not alter the importance of this as a rhetorical strategy, as deployed here:

Do you think you need nurses in theatre?
Yes I think you need someone to be the patient's advocate. When people come in the department they get put into the anaesthetic room and quite often they get left on their own. Now that's because the ODPs are checking them in and I feel that they haven't had that training on the psychological care of the patient, I don't know what training they've got but I just feel they haven't got it (Interviewee N).

Here the nurses are trying to contrast themselves with the ODPs by reference to other parties in the operating theatre, in this case, patients and doctors. Nurses describe their role as being an advocate, on behalf of the patient (and, by implication, in opposition to the doctor), whereas ODPs are there to work for the doctors. Nurses also sought to differentiate themselves by appealing to more intangible aspects of their practice:

I can't say that [ODPs] actually do anything different [from nurses], it's more just a feeling. I suppose you go into nursing because you want to care for patients.

What do you mean by caring?
Well it's empathy and putting yourself in their place(Interviewee G).

Though the nurses might not have seen it in those terms, it seems that what is going on here is that the nurse is talking about the emotional labour that they perform on behalf of patients (James 1989, 1992, Smith 1992). The nurses also sought to distinguish themselves in terms of their expertise:

> They are not nurses. With nurses you are there for the patient. They are vulnerable. You have experience of nursing models, like Roper, Logan Tierney[2] and a background of training (Interviewee F).

What this interviewee is claiming is that nursing has a distinctive and individual body of knowledge, only available to nurses, and that is being applied here in practice. Intriguingly, this notion of a distinctive body of knowledge was perceived as a defining attribute of a profession in the classical sociology of the professions, thought it has been largely superseded. Drawing all of the above components of the difference together, one interviewee said:

> I can see [ODP training is] more on the technical aspect of surgery rather than we as nurses sort of look at it from a holistic or humanistic approach. Like the nursing term itself, theatre nurse, whereas theirs is more like practitioners.... There are some trainee ODPs who are really excellent but I don't think you see them too much in the caring profession.... Also [ODPs] don't get involved with the spiritual care or proper care of the patient it's more about instrumentation or how the machine is working, what drugs you have to get, but what about the patient? But we are the advocate for the patient, the patient is totally anaesthetised, so we are providing the full care for the patient(Interviewee C).

What is interesting is the rhetoric used to defend nurses' legitimacy as professions. Nurses seek to portray themselves as being 'caring', 'holistic' or 'patient-centred', while at the same contrasting themselves with the 'other' group who are not. They are using the kinds of rhetorical strategies described by Norris (2001). Nurses would criticise ODPs for being insufficiently holistic, claiming that this was something that their training and education enabled them to be, while the training ODPs had was described as 'mechanistic'. Nurses would also claim that they had a repertoire of professional skills and knowledge that ODPs did not possess. This is what Norris (2001) calls 'limitation'.

An issue which cannot be neglected in consideration of issues of 'caring' is division by gender. Up until quite recently, ODPs were almost exclusively male (perhaps unsurprisingly in the light of their historical origins). While this has changed, the majority of ODPs (58%) are male (Department of Health 2000). Theatre nurses, in common with the rest of their profession, are largely (88%) women (Department of Health 2000). Gender seemed to play a part in the divide, though it is striking how rarely it was mentioned:

> [The ODPs'] conversation is more like 'All right sir, we'll get you done, sort you out'. It's more like being down the pub(Interviewee B).

The nurse is suggesting that ODPs have a very 'masculine' way of dealing with patients. This is being contrasted, by implication, with nurses' more 'feminine', and, therefore, more 'caring' ways of interacting with patients. We would not seek to say that nurses are more 'caring' because they are women, though this idea persists, certainly in contemporary British culture (Miers 2000), and it is possibly this resource which is being drawn upon here to emphasise (and account for) the differences between the nurses and the ODPs. However, this was only a minor theme in the explanations given in interviews, and, given an increasing number of both female ODPs and male theatre nurses, it is possible that it will decline even further....

NOTES

1. We wonder whether this problem is particularly acute within the operating theatre environment due to the fact that all staff are dressed identically in theatre suits ('blues' or 'greens'). The signifiers of dress which are so noticeable and carefully observed in the rest of the hospital are not present in the operating theatre.
2. The Roper, Logan and Tierney model of nursing (Roper *et al.* 1980) is a theoretical structure which nurses use to plan, deliver and evaluate care in a structured way. While there are many different models of nursing, this is the one most widely used in the UK.

REFERENCES

Allen, D. (2001a) Narrating nursing jurisdiction: 'atrocity stories' and 'boundary work', *Symbolic Interaction*, 24, 1, 75–103.

Allen, D. (2001b) *The Changing Shape of Nursing Practice: The Role of Nurses in the Hospital Division of Labour*. London: Routledge.

Davis, P. (2003) The essence of peri-operative care, *British Journal of Perioperative Nursing*, 13, 5, 196–208.

Department of Health (2000) *Non-medical Workforce Census 1998–1999*. London: Department of Health.

Dingwall, R. (1977) Atrocity stories and professional relationships, *Sociology of Work and Occupations*, 4, 4, 371–96.

Gates, B. (1994) *Advocacy: a Nurse's Guide*. London: Scutari Press.

Gieryn, T. (1983) Boundary-work and the demarcation of science from non-science: strains and interests in professional ideologies of scientists, *American Sociological Review*, 48, 781–95.

Gieryn, T. (1999) *Cultural Boundaries of Science: Credibility on the Line*. Chicago: University of Chicago Press.

James, N. (1989) Emotional labour: skill and work in the regulation of feelings, *The Sociological Review*, 37, 1, 18–33.

James, N. (1992) Care = organisation + physical labour + emotional labour, *Sociology of Health and Illness*, 14, 4, 488–509.

Mardell, A. (1996) Advocacy; exploring the concept, *British Journal of Theatre Nursing*, 6, 7, 34–6.

McGarvey, H. (2001) *Patient advocacy in the operating department: fact or fantasy? results of a study investigating the role of the nurse*. Paper presented to the RCN nursing research conference, Sheffield.

Miers, M. (2000) *Gender Issues and Nursing Practice (Sociology and Nursing Practice)*. Basingstoke: Palgrave Macmillan.

National Association of Theatre Nurses (NATN) (1989) *National Association of Theatre Nurses: 25 years, a history*. Harrogate: NATN.

Norris, P. (2001) How 'we' are different from 'them': occupational boundary maintenance in the treatment of musculo-skeletal problems, *Sociology of Health and Illness*, 23, 1, 24–43.

Sacks, H. (1992a) *Lectures on Conversation*. Vol. I. Jefferson G. (ed.) with introduction by Schegloff E. A. Oxford: Basil Blackwell.

Sacks, H. (1992b) Lectures on Conversation. Vol. II. Jefferson G. (ed.) with introduction by Schegloff E. A. Oxford: Basil Blackwell.

Smith, P. (1992) *The Emotional Labour of Nursing; Its Impact on Interpersonal Relations, Management and the Educational Environment in Nursing*. London: Macmillan.

Tanner, J. (1996) The appropriateness of nursing models as a basis for operating theatre nursing. Unpublished M.Phil. thesis. University of Glasgow.

United Kingdom Central Council for Nursing, Midwifery and Health Visiting (1989) *Exercising Accountability*. London: UKCC.

Source: S. Timmons and J. Tanner, 'A disputed occupational boundary: operating theatre nurses and Operating Department Practitioners', *Sociology of Health & Illness*, 26:5 (2004) 645–66.

Study Questions and Activities

1. To what extent do you think that gender relations play a part in the disputed occupational boundaries between theatre nurses and operating department practitioners?
2. Think about your own professional role. How do you maintain the divide between your own role and the role of others?
3. What other occupational boundaries exist in your place of work? When you are next at work, observe the interactions between different occupational groups. What evidence is there for disputed occupational boundaries?
4. How does Reading 26 challenge the points made by Atkinson (Reading 4)?

Further Reading

Most sociological analyses have focused on the boundaries between nursing and medicine. To explore some of these in more detail, consider the following: C. May and C. Fleming, 'The professional imagination: narrative and the symbolic boundaries between medicine and nursing', *Journal of Advanced Nursing*, 25:5 (1997) 1094–100. For a discussion of how the boundaries between medicine and nursing can be obscured, read: S. Carmel, 'Boundaries obscured and boundaries reinforced: incorporation as a strategy of occupational enhancement for intensive care', *Sociology of Health & Illness*, 28:2 (2006) 154–77. Of course, other occupational boundaries have also been explored by sociologists. For example, the following considers the relationship between nurses and healthcare assistants: N. Daykin and B. Clarke, ' "They'll still get the bodily care". Discourses of care and relationships between nurses and healthcare assistants in the NHS', *Sociology of Health and Illness*, 22:3 (2000) 349–64 (also referred to in Further Reading section of Reading 22). The next article considers the occupational boundaries between those involved in treating musculo-skeletal problems, in particular, general practitioners, physiotherapists, chiropractors and osteopaths: P. Norris 'How "we" are different from "them": occupational boundary maintenance in the treatment of musculo-skeletal problems', *Sociology of Health & Illness*, 23:1 (2001) 24–43. For a more general discussion of the healthcare workforce within the context of contemporary changes in health service provision, the following article provides a useful overview: S. A. Nancarrow and A. M. Borthwick, 'Dynamic professional boundaries in the healthcare workforce', *Sociology of Health & Illness*, 27:7 (2005) 897–919.

Reading 27

Choosing to be Childfree

Annily Campbell

As noted several times in this reader, sociologists of health, illness and health-care have paid considerable attention to the interaction between patients and professionals, and this reading explores one aspect of this. This reading draws on a qualitative study of 23 white women who choose to be childfree. It explores their accounts of ceasing traditional contraceptive use and their decisions to be sterilised. In this reading, Annily Campbell focuses on their interactions with powerful medical gatekeepers who dismiss and refuse women's requests for sterilisation. Women who choose to be childfree and make the decision to be sterilised, Campbell argues, do not do so on a whim. Most of the women studied insist that they have 'always known' that they did not want children and used all conventional methods of contraception prior to making the decision to be sterilised. Campbell describes the way in which health professionals disem-power and infantilise women, leaving them vulnerable to the continuing threat of unwanted pregnancies. However, this reading maps women's dogged refusal to accept this vulnerability and describes their quest for sterilisation.

WOMEN'S CHOICES, DECISIONS AND MEDICAL RESPONSES

Choosing to be Childfree ...

I have always been quite sure that I never wanted children even as a child myself. I have never given myself the choice between having and not having a child as I have never had the slightest interest in having one. I didn't particularly think, 'Oh, I couldn't do all these things if I had children'. It's not something I put off, or even made a choice about.

(Sally)

The reasons for remaining childfree, presented by the sterilized women in my study, have much in common with childfree women in previous studies. Lifestyle choices, particularly of the younger women, are rated highly although there was little of the hedonism so frequently portrayed (especially in the media) as a negative feature of living childfree. Some childfree women in other studies identified that being childfree emerged as one of many of the important choices that they made in contemplating their future and became a part of other decisions in a lifestyle which developed as a result of remaining childfree (Dowrick and Grundberg 1980; Bartlett 1994; Morell 1994). They appeared not to have made a childfree decision early in life, but lived in ways that made having children unthinkable to them: thus, not having children is not understood to be a 'choice' but a consequence of choosing to live their present lives:

> Seeing women as 'childless by choice' may be accurate at a simple descriptive level. But it misplaces the emphasis and misstates what was chosen. Women are expected to explain a negative occurrence, a negative choice. The absence of motherhood becomes the point of focus, rather than the many prior positive choices.
>
> (Morell 1994:50)

However, in my study, most of the childfree women who opted for sterilization were very clear that they had 'always known' that they did not want children. They planned their lives from a starting point of being and intending to remain childfree, although, at that point, all were using conventional contraceptive methods and had not begun to consider sterilization. Several women insisted that they did not go through any process in deciding not to have children and Sally was quite definite that there was no one point at which she made a choice: '*I just never saw myself as having children therefore I didn't decide not to have them*'. Anne T. was aware of wanting something different for her future life and foresaw restraints on any future ambitions she might have – even those which had not yet become clear – because of what seemed to be very negative aspects of motherhood:

> I didn't have a particular life ambition and if there was one, children weren't part of it! The very strong message when I was a girl was that if you got pregnant it was the end of your life. When I got married I realized it was possible to work and have children, but I just never wanted to – although I never told my mother!
>
> (Anne T.)

A few women recalled that they had taken some time to consider their reasons for making the choice and rather than saying that they had 'always known' the women acknowledged that their decision emerged over a period of time. Sandy had dreams of having loads of kids when she was a child but '… *as soon as I hit maturity at about 18, I was aware that I did not want kids. I remember dreaming that I was pregnant when I was in my early twenties and I was terrified. That was when the feeling I didn't want kids really gelled*' (Linda R.); and her husband made life plans based on their income. There was no definite plan not to have children but they did not allow the issue to just drift on: ' *…periodically we reviewed the situation and decided we were happy as we were*'. The urge to have a child had been quite strong for Heather and she wrote that she couldn't pin-point exactly when she made the decision not to have children as the change was so gradual: ' *… as a youngster I was crazy about babies and little kids. I was always borrowing babies to wheel out in big shiny prams and baby-sitting for all the neighbours. As I got older the urge just sort of faded*'.

An expectation that women will experience such a 'maternal urge' featured in the women's relationships with family and friends and discussions with medical professionals. So 'natural' is this seen to be that even the very youngest women are perceived as behaving 'normally' whilst the childfree wishes of an older woman results in astonishment and resistance, indicating that women without children are not considered to be mature adults:

> If I had gone along to my doctor at the age of sixteen, or even thirty, and said 'I want a baby but don't seem to be getting anywhere', he wouldn't have said 'Are you old enough to know what you are doing? Do you realize that being a mother is irreversible?' Medical people don't seem to take the trouble to check out why people want to have babies because that's just considered normal. But they think it's odd that I don't want any and bizarre that I've been sterilized.
>
> (Sally)

… and Deciding to be Sterilized

Despite deep suspicion within the medical profession about motivation and concerned opinion about future regrets, childfree women who choose sterilization consider that retaining their fertility and the potential for having a child is a negative aspect of their lives. Thus, being sterilized is regarded as a positive statement that safeguards their childfree future. However, once childfree women emerge from the relative privacy of using traditional methods of contraception they find that their choices and decisions about controlling their own fertility in this way is, itself, subject to powerful controlling factors within the medical profession.

The ways in which interventionist and often surgical treatments for infertility are viewed and dealt with by the medical profession have significant similarities with the applications for sterilization by childfree women. Although doctors will assume that it is a 'normal' request to seek to become fertile and 'abnormal' to decide to remain without children, both types of requests are firmly within the discourse of medical power and control. Childfree women and infertile women must demonstrate a single-mindedness that will be acceptable to medics and they may have to negotiate an 'obstacle course' in order to achieve their goal. The 'desperation' of an infertile woman and the 'determination' of a childfree woman are both problematized and may affect the way that the woman is viewed and dealt with (Campbell 1999; Letherby 2002).

The growth of gynaecology as a medical speciality is overwhelmingly seen to be the domain of male doctors and consultants and also provides the context for the increasing medicalization of women's reproductive health (Homans 1985; Doyal 1995). The diversity of women's experiences with medics, and the whole process leading to the operation was perceived by many of the women as an issue of medical power and control. Contrary to what appeared to be the belief of some doctors, women do not choose to be sterilized on the 'spur of the moment' and the women in the study emphasized that they had known for many years that they did not want children. Their decision was not a recent or whimsical thought but a well-considered opportunity to be free of anxieties of unwanted pregnancy and be free of using by-the-month contraception.

Their decision disturbed a number of medics who questioned whether conventional methods had been given a fair try: without exception all of the women had used at least one type of contraceptive and, in a number of cases, had tried a wide variety. Many GPs and consultants tried to insist on a return to the very methods that had been the cause of the application for sterilization, even when it was made clear that there were health risks, discomfort or actual risks of an unwanted pregnancy. Both Pauline's and Helen's comments typify the dissatisfaction that childfree women expressed with currently available methods:

> Before sterilization I had tried the pill, (it made me depressed and I put on a stone in weight). The cap, (I persevered but found the cream gave me cystitis). The rhythm method (I had an unplanned pregnancy and later miscarried) ... lastly the coil (which got lost within the first three weeks and I had to attend hospital for a scan to locate it and have it removed). I did ask to try the pill again but was refused on the grounds of my age and that I smoked half a dozen cigarettes a day ...
>
> (Pauline)

and:

> Prior to sterilization I was on the pill, then the coil, then I got that out, but before I'd decided what to do next I had unprotected intercourse, so I got another coil fitted, then I went back on the pill. I got fitted for a cap, but it was uncomfortable enough just wearing it never mind having sex with it! I think I may have asked for sterilization again at that point. I was sterilized because I never wanted children in my life and didn't see the point in using contraceptives for the rest of my fertile life, particularly as nothing is one hundred percent ...
>
> (Helen)

Those who managed to get as far as a consultant found further refusals. A regular medical response to requests from childfree women for sterilization is that one in ten women will inevitably regret being sterilized. Sandy was amazed that this was thought to be a 'good enough' reason for being turned down:

My GP totally supported my decision having known me since my teens. The gynaecologist didn't and I ended up telling him I would have an abortion if I ever became pregnant (I had been told that this was the thing to say). He said that one woman in ten who comes for the op. changes their minds (meaning that nine in ten don't!). He tried his best to dissuade me despite my arguments … After two years a different consultant saw that I was totally adamant and moved me up the list.

(Sandy)

Apart from the few women who went directly to clinics, all of the other women in the study had been refused by a GP at least once, some several times: one phrase used many times during the interviews and also written about was '*I was laughed out of the surgery* … '. By this they meant that their GP did not take them seriously or would not make the necessary referral to a consultant. They described a constant struggle to assert their personal reproductive choices and anger at the necessity of having to seek 'permission' for the sterilization. Many of the women gauged and rehearsed the 'correct' story to tell the consultant and felt that some of their replies were dishonest: from previous experiences they realized that telling 'the truth' about not wantting a child was not sufficient:

After my previous refusals I spent a long time getting my arguments and reasons ready as I expected to have to put my case very strongly this time to persuade the consultant. He asked me 'What if at thirty-five the urge hits?' I said 'Well, I would adopt' then felt angry and disappointed with myself. I wanted to get him off my back, I knew that I definitely never wanted children, wouldn't adopt, but was aware all the time that he had the power to refuse. I was frightened that my response wasn't good enough and I just kept thinking 'Oh, god, don't take this away from me now … '

(Jude)

The women expressed exasperation and indignation when told repeatedly by doctors and consultants that they would inevitably come to regret their childfree choice and decision to be sterilized. Some spoke of having been infantilized when their first application was rejected. They felt that their right to choose sterilization was denied and they experienced negative and undermining emotions such as humiliation, frustration, helplessness, and anger and rage. Most continued to reapply until their application was successful although, for some, the initial refusal had traumatic consequences. After Gillian's application was refused she became pregnant and then had to face undergoing the sterilization and termination together. There were no regrets but she feels angry that the pregnancy was the result of her application being ignored.

I was sterilized in 1976 (aged 26) three months after we got married. My tubes were tied in case I wanted the procedure reversed due to my age and the fact that I had no children. I had the operation through the BPAS – I got pregnant so had a termination at the same time. I was waiting for an appointment for the NHS and failed contraception led to this.

(Gillian)

Being Childfree and Sterilized

> Other women spoke about babies and milk and feeding and burping – it was all blood, sweat and milk! – but at least they taught me to speak that language so I could pass a 'real' woman. I'm afraid that if a childfree woman doesn't talk the language, then she doesn't pass among other women as real. If I hadn't learned to speak that language then I would have been a reject.
>
> (Vicky)

It is possible to draw a parallel between the feelings of involuntarily childless women and voluntarily childfree women, both of whom may experience and internalize cultural norms about the nature of womanhood and motherhood, and also express negative feelings about being unable to fulfil personal and social expectations of being a 'real' woman. For childfree women, sterilization destroys any illusion that they may eventually come round to the idea of motherhood and become 'real'.

A childfree choice effectively creates barriers and some women who are unable to conceive resent the decision by (seemingly) fertile women to choose sterilization. Childfree women are astonished at such attitudes and resent such unwarranted interest and unwelcome interference in what they thought of as a personal and private decision, commenting that they felt themselves to be the target for veiled or openly insulting comments regarding their 'selfish' nature and other negative qualities. Sally encountered attitudes which were distinctly hostile saying that '...*women generally act quite aggressively particularly if they have children themselves*' and a number of women spoke of feeling the need to defend the decision:

> Since the operation I've tripped over people unable to have children (including my oldest friend for 20 years). It's incomprehensible to them that I should so 'capriciously' give up what they so desperately want. I continually have to justify my choice.
>
> (Helen)

Judith was painfully aware of the way that she may appear to other women who wanted to have children and her successful application for sterilization resulted in a hospital experience in which she felt isolated by her childfree status and choice:

> I tried to avoid getting into conversations in the hospital as there were also women in there who were desperate to have children, or were having infertility treatment or trying to get sterilization reversed. I think one woman was recovering from a miscarriage. I kept my head in a book or was knitting most of the time, but had to mingle at lunch-time. I had made a choice that most felt incomprehensible and a couple of women were really not able to talk to me once they knew why I was there. Most seemed to respect my decision even if they thought I was crazy!
>
> (Judith)

When they described the aftermath of the operation and reflected how it had changed them, the women in the study expressed overwhelming relief at having made a significant life-course transition. Each one felt that she had moved from being a woman who had chosen not to have children but who potentially could do so, to being a woman who was sterilized and would never have children. There was no expression of regret from 22 of the women nor any desire to return for reversal of the procedure, and they recorded their relief in strong and positive terms.

I could not find any data accessible and available for non-medical research purposes that would have provided a breakdown of the sterilization of voluntarily childfree women, compared with the sterilization of women who had children. I concluded that any available figures on reversals, used by doctors to support the 'regrets' argument, relate over-whelmingly to women who have been sterilized after completing their family and who later return for reversal to try to have another child or children.

REFERENCES

J. Bartlett, *Will You Be Mother?: Women Who Choose to Say No* (London: Virago, 1994).

A. Campbell, *Childfree and Sterilized: Women's Decisions and Medical Responses* (London: Cassell, 1999).

S. Dowrick and S. Grundberg (eds), *Why Children?* (London: Women's Press, 1980).

L. Doyal, *What Makes Women Sick?: Gender and the Political Economy of Health* (Basingstoke: Macmillan, 1995).

G. Letherby, 'Challenging dominant discourses: Identity and change and the experience of "infertility" and "involuntary childlessness" ', *Journal of Gender Studies*, 11:3 (2002) 278–287.

C. Morell, *Unwomanly Conduct: The Challenges of Intentional Childlessness* (London: Routledge, 1994).

Source: A. Campbell, 'Cutting out motherhood: childfree sterilized women', in S. Earle and G. Letherby (eds) *Gender, Identity & Reproduction: Social Perspectives* (London: Palgrave, 2003).

Study Questions and Activities

1. In Annily Campbell's study, women reported negative and undermining emotions such as humiliation, frustration, helplessness, anger and rage. How might these negative emotions have been avoided?

2. Are some patients' needs more likely to be dismissed than the needs of others? Whose needs are most likely to be dismissed and why?

3. Reading 27 has highlighted the importance of power relations between patients and healthcare professionals. How aware are you of power relations in your interactions with patients or clients? To what extent might the level of your awareness impact on your interactions?

4. Is Atkinson's (see Reading 4) critique of the sociological consideration of the doctor–patient relationship relevant to Campbell's work. Think back to the readings in Part II – how would you go about researching interactions between patients and professionals? What methods would you use? What can be learned by researching patient–professional interaction? What ethical issues would you need to consider?

——————————————— **Further Reading** ———————————————

There is a considerable body of literature on the sociology of patient–professional interaction (see also Readings 3, 4 and 21). If you enjoyed the reading by Annily Campbell, it may be worth dipping into some of the other chapters in the same book, in particular, the chapter by A. Bowes and T. M. Domokos: 'Your dignity is hung up at the door: Pakistani and White women's experiences of childbirth' (pp. 87–102) and G. Letherby's: '"I didn't think much of his bedside manner but he was very skilled at his job": medical encounters in relation to infertility' (pp. 174–90). Campbell's study of childfree sterilised women is published in full in: *Childfree and Sterilized: Women's Decisions and Medical Responses* (London: Cassell, 1999). Experiences of medical dismissal and infantilisation – similar to those described in Reading 27 – have also been written about by disabled writers and activists. For example, in N. Begum, 'General practitioners' role in shaping disabled women's lives', in C. Barnes and G. Mercer (eds) *Exploring the Divide: Illness and Disability* (Leeds: The Disability Press, 1996), the author describes the power and authority wielded by the health-care profession over disabled people. For a more general discussion of power and interpersonal relations between healthcare professionals and patients/clients, try the following: C. May, 'Individual care? Power and subjectivity in therapeutic relation-ships', *Sociology*, 26:4 (1992) 589–602.

The Internet and the Doctor–Patient Relationship

Alex Broom

In this reading, Alex Broom draws on a study of interviews with 33 Australian men who have prostate cancer. The purpose of this study was to explore men's Internet use and the effects of this on disease experiences. Broom recruited his research respondents through face-to-face support groups and via an article he had written on the subject in a personal computer magazine. All of the respondents were interviewed in their own homes. For many commentators, the Internet is seen as potentially transformative, informative and empowering. They argue that the Internet can transgress traditional boundaries, opening up global opportunities for knowledge sharing and support giving. For others, the Internet harbours potential harm. In Reading 28, Alex Broom presents some of the data from his study and argues that, although there is no one type of Internet experience, it does have the potential to transform the disease experience. As you read this extract, though, consider the impact of the Internet on the patient–professional relationship: What is the role of the Internet in health education? Does the Internet empower patients to question medical knowledge and expertise? How are healthcare professionals coping with the Internet-informed patient?

Drawing on 33 interviews with Australian men who have prostate cancer, I argue in this article that by providing patients with knowledge and support, the Internet has the potential to empower patients and increase their sense of control over their disease....

[However] patient empowerment and the impact of the Internet are inextricably tied to the doctor-patient relationship. Moreover, discussion of the effects of the Internet must involve consideration of the responses of medical professionals to the Internet-informed patient within the context of the medical consultation. There has been considerable discussion concerning the changing role of the medical professional over the past few decades and implications for how patients are interacting with doctors (see Charavel, Bremond, Moumjid-Ferdjaoui, Mignotte, & Carrere, 2001; Freedman, 2002; Ishikawa, Takayama, Yamazaki, Seki, & Katsumata, 2002; Lang, 2000; Lupton, 1997; Zadoroznyj, 2001). In recent years, researchers have speculated about the impact of Internet-informed patients in the medical encounter and the challenge they pose to traditional medical authority (see Anderson et al., 2003; Friedewald, 2000; Hardey, 1999; Pemberton & Goldblatt, 1998). Some commentators have suggested (although little evidence has thus far been presented) that the Internet is changing doctor-patient dynamics (Anderson et al., 2003) and breaking down traditional power imbalances based on previous exclusive access to expert medical knowledge (see Hardey, 1999). Hardey has suggested that by breaking down hierarchical models of information giving (i.e., doctor to patient), the Internet has contributed to clinicians' loss of control over medical knowledge or deprofessionalization, contributing to a decline in awe of and trust in doctors (p. 832). Some clinicians might also feel threatened by patients' seeking information and react negatively in the consultation (Anderson et al., 2003; Crocco et al., 2002; S. Fox & Rainie, 2002). In their study of American Internet users, S. Fox and Rainie found that 13% of respondents had "got the cold shoulder" when presenting Internet material to their doctor (p. 7). Although effects vary between individual patients and individual doctors, there seems to be an increase in concern from doctors that neither they nor the patient can cope with the amount of information patients are bringing into the medical consultation (McLellan, 1998).

The doctor-patient relationship is a vitally important facet of medical care, as, in the large part, it determines the quality of care a patient receives within the medical system. More specifically, effective doctor-patient communication is related to patient satisfaction with medical care, favorable attitudes toward physicians, recall and understanding of information, improved emotional state, and overall health status (see Bennett & Alison, 1996; Frederickson, 1995; Ong, De Haes, & Lammes, 1995; C. Roberts, Cox, Reintgen, Baile, & Gibertini, 1994). With the amount of information now available to patients on the Internet, some might feel they know as much about a certain condition as a doctor does (Anderson et al., 2003; Dudley, Falvo, Podell, & Renner, 1996). This, according to some commentators, poses a new and real challenge to the medical profession (Dudley et al., 1996). Patients are able to become informed about their disease but also to evaluate the performance of their medical specialist as compared to those that other patients talk about online.

I argue [here] that the potential of the Internet to empower patients is, in part, dependent on the responses of the medical professional to changes in the way patients approach decision-making processes and, in particular, the medical consultation. This is not to suggest that doctors are the barrier to the Internet's empowerment of patients. On the contrary, this study illustrates important reasons, unrelated to their clinicians, why men do not access the Internet or find it problematic and unhelpful for making treatment decisions. Conflicting narratives concerning the effects of the Internet illustrate that although it can be empowering for many patients, in other cases it has little or no impact on patients' disease experience. I argue that retaining the complexity and contradictory nature of the effects of the Internet is important to avoid romanticizing its impact on disease experience (i.e., as purely a source of power and liberation) and, second, to provide indications of how to improve it as a source of information and support for patients....

RESULTS

... there is no one archetypal effect of the Internet on disease experience. Experiences and attitudes differed for each patient and were influenced by many factors, such as disease stage, age, literacy level, socioeconomic status, and social support networks. However, although embracing the complexity of effects and perspectives within such a heterogeneous group of men, one is able to identify certain themes within their narratives that provide an idea of the effects the Internet can have on patients' experiences of disease.

The Internet and Control

The role of the Internet in enhancing these respondents' power and control over their disease and decision making processes were prominent themes within the interviews. One respondent talked about this in relation to an online community:

> I found [the online community] extremely useful. I'm one of these people who has a high need for information and knowledge. Knowledge is power. I like to be in control of my situation and the way I want to do that is by knowing what is going to happen ... That need for knowledge or need for control means I really need that information to feel ok. There are some people who are really quite happy just to not have that information. I'm not one of those. (Internet user, 6 months posttreatment, organ-confined disease)

Another patient recalled his experience of using the Internet:

> In terms of the actual outcome it [the Internet] probably doesn't make any difference. In terms of people's need to feel that they are in control of the situation ... if people have confidence in their treatment they're more likely to have a positive outcome. I wasn't stressed out by the information I gained, I just thought I was in greater control ... that's what I thought. (Internet user, 1 year posttreatment, organ-confined disease)

Several of the men who had used the Internet stated that online information sources (and, in some cases, online communities) provided an invaluable method of seeking knowledge and thus control over their treatment process. As the above respondent notes, the information provided by online forums provided clarity in terms of treatments options and, as a result, diminished his reliance on his specialists, allowing him to "take control of my treatment instead of having to rely on my specialist." Although several of the respondents reported that their Internet usage did not necessarily influence the decisions made, and certainly not the physiological outcome of treatment, it was seen as greatly improving the decision-making process by reducing the uncertainties involved in making a treatment decision.

Some members of the medical community have suggested that the Internet is problematic, or even harmful, because of its tendency to either sway patients away from conventional cancer treatments or mislead them in relation to their efficacy (Kiley, 2002; Whiting, 2000). Moreover, fear of increased consumer access to alternative knowledges has contributed to the labeling of Internet usage as an activity that represents dissatisfaction with conventional medicine. Three respondents talked about alternative treatments and the Internet:

> I fairly quickly decided that I didn't want to take these alternative treatments so I didn't really search for them. It was better to get rid of cancer, particularly if it was contained. (Internet user, 3 years posttreatment, organ-confined disease)

> Well, if you went into a site that was telling you to eat green peas six days a week and that will help you [laughs], I wouldn't be eating green peas six days a week. I've made a decision, I've had the operation, so, I look for a particular type of information now and I don't think alternative medicine was much of an option. (Internet user, 1 year posttreatment, organ-confined disease)

> [The Internet] is quite good for people who might be trying alternative treatments who say, no, I don't want the knife. I didn't go down that path. I was happy that my urologist had advised me correctly and that I had made the right decision too so I wasn't really seeking alternative information. I had made up my mind that I wanted to have surgery and then it was a matter of concentrating on achieving fitness to be able to have it happen. So I wasn't really looking around on the Internet for information other than stuff on surgery. (Internet user, 1½ years posttreatment, organconfined disease)

Contrary to the fears of the medical community, for the majority of the men interviewed here, accessing support and information online did not increase their negativity or skepticism toward biomedical cancer treatments. Rather, the result was clarification of the subtleties involved in particular biomedical treatments, enabling a significant proportion of the respondents to experience a heightened sense of control and therefore enter into a comprehensive negotiation with their specialist and make what they perceived to be an informed choice. This ability of patients to negotiate with specialists once informed by the Internet was also observed by Hardey (1999, p. 829).

The reaction of medical specialists to Internet-informed patients was of particular interest in this study. One respondent's response to the question of what effect information seeking had on his encounters with medical professionals was

A lot of the medical community basically see it as loss of control. The standard advice is if you want information about your condition ask your doctor. They don't like it when you seek information from other sources ... it [is] the standard, well, you're not medically trained, you're not competent to understand this, we will interpret it for you. This is back to we have exclusive control over this area of knowledge-type mind-set. I felt that particularly in contact with the urologist I saw. (Internet user, 6 months posttreatment, organ-confined disease)

Like this respondent, the majority of the men who had used the Internet felt that their information seeking was effective and that they were competent to decipher the "good" from the "bad." Despite this, they were acutely aware that their specialists might view this as outside the patient's role, or, as the above respondent suggests, as a challenge to his or her authority. This same respondent states later in the interview, "I don't feel completely comfortable sharing the information that I have found with my specialist," reflecting a pattern in the men interviewed here of being disapproved of in terms of his Internet usage and information seeking. Another respondent explained his specialist's reaction when he disclosed his use of the Internet in the consultation:

I asked him questions and he answered them and I said, "Well, listen, I was on the Internet last night and I've got all these questions for you." And he goes, "Oh, look you've got to be careful when you go on the Internet," and he's telling me, "Keep away, steer away, because information overload is just no good for you." And I thought to myself, hmm, that's thick, for me, and I like the Internet, I like reading, I'm right into it and this bloke is telling me to keep away from it. "That means I leave it up to you and I rely totally on you for information"—he goes, "yes." And I said, "Well, how do I know what to ask you?" He said, "Oh, you just do." I said, "Hmmm." ... And he didn't like that. (Internet user, pretreatment, organ-confined disease)

This perception of feeling disapproved of is a significant barrier to patient-clinician communication that inevitably results in higher levels of anxiety, confusion, and frustration. As Beisecker (1990) has suggested, the behaviors of specialists might discourage patients from asking questions and entering into an open dialogue with them about their treatment preferences and concerns. The reaction of some specialists to the apparent threat of a disruption to the lay-expert divide within the consultation is to create a relationship dynamic whereby the patient feels "bad" for attempting to understand or question the information being provided by the specialist. This produces a complex process of contesting, redefining, and, in some cases, reinforcing the dominance of the passive patient role in the treatment process.

As was the case for several of the respondents, there is clearly a discrepancy between what the above respondent viewed as his role in the treatment process and his specialist's expectations of the patient's role. Thus, increased access to information and support online does not necessarily result in better doctor-patient communication. Being well informed, and attempting to engage in a comprehensive dialogue in treatment decisions might, in fact, result in hostility, irritation, and a less satisfactory level of care. This has the effect of reducing patient control and power in decision making, thus complicating claims of the liberating nature and positive effect of the Internet on disease experience. The narratives of several of the respondents reveal that patients might feel their level of knowledge seeking creates a barrier to receiving effective care from their specialist. Control or power, then, cannot be seen as confined to any one particular facet of a patient's experience, as feelings of power and control are, in part, determined by the reception of patients's Internet usage by medical specialists.

The Internet and Empowerment

In the current study, I asked respondents how their Internet usage affecred their decision-making ability. One man talked about his and his wife's use of the Internet:

> The information available on the Internet was a revelation. It was a real revelation to us. We were reading reports and information about different treatments right up to the minute—material that just wasn't available anywhere else. We picked the bones out of each particular subject. We could log on to brachytherapy and a new world opened up to us. We were able to then sort out statistical information about cure rates, and define centres of excellence. We finally felt as if we had some control over things. (Internet user, midtreatment, extracapsular disease)

The Internet allowed this respondent to "do something" rather than just being "told what to do by our specialist." It provided him with a sense of purpose and control, having a profound effect on his ability to deal with his cancer. Being a very active person, this respondent strove to be able to "throw my energy into getting better," and the Internet, he suggested, provided a vehicle for him to feel as though there was something he could do. Furthermore, it provided him with the resources to help other men with prostate cancer by explaining to them what was happening to them based on the information he retrieved from the Internet. The Internet gave him the knowledge and skills to counsel his friends and take a leadership role in the face-to-face support group he attends, dramatically improving the quality of his life. As he put it, "It made me feel like I had some power over this disease, I could understand it, so I could fight it."

Despite the powerful and liberating effect of the Internet for several of the respondents, findings from the current study indicate that for others, it was a case of too much information too late. Although several of the men found important information on the Internet, by the time they began searching and became computer literate enough to find useful information, they had either already begun a particular treatment regimen or had already gone through surgery. As a result, for several of the respondents, searching the Internet became more a matter of discovering information they felt they should have known before making a treatment decision. Several expressed regret regarding how much more useful the Internet would have been if they had been exposed to it immediately after diagnosis and, in particular, before making a treatment decision:

> The Internet wasn't really very useful in helping to make the decision but it certainly made a tremendous difference in your background information for either accepting what was decided or regretting the decision. I think that that it was extremely useful in reassuring me that that had been the right decision ... I suppose decisions have to be made in real life before you get all the information. (Internet user, midtreatment, extracapsular disease)

This excerpt captures one of the many the practical limitations of the Internet for patients. Often, the testing, diagnosis, and treatment takes place over a number of weeks or just a couple of months, leaving little time for research, let alone learning to use communication technologies such as the Internet. Moreover, for several of these respondents, there was considerable self-imposed and, sometimes, clinician encouraged pressure to make a quick decision to "get the cancer out" as soon as possible, even in the case of low-grade, nonaggressive tumors that are relatively slow growing. As a result, searching the Internet was about making sense of the treatment process they had been through or exploring alternatives if treatment had been unsuccessful. In particular, they often sought information about side effects and how successful their surgery and/or radiation treatment was compared with others (whether their situation was typical or whether something "went wrong").

The Internet and the Patient's Role

As Hardey (1999) has argued, the Internet is, to a certain degree, generating new dynamics between doctors and patients by providing patients with the information and support necessary to understand and, at times, question medical decisions. In the following excerpt, a respondent talks about specialists' attitudes toward patients' seeking information from the Internet and other sources:

> I more than think, I know what their attitude is. We extensively searched the Internet [and] at one urologist's office I was asking about certain information and this went on for some time. I went back to his secretary and we are paying the bill. He was talking into a dictaphone and he was making the referral to somebody else and he said, "[patient's name] is somewhat difficult and over-informed" ... The first urologist that I went to said, "have an operation," he didn't even discuss other forms of treatment. No, they definitely don't really like well-informed people. (Internet user, 1 year posttreatment, organ-confined disease)

As this respondent experienced firsthand, the Internet tests the limits of the "conventional" doctor-patient relationship, having a leveling effect (but not necessarily making them level) in a relationship historically marked by an imbalance of power (McLellan, 1998). However, this can result in specialists' adopting various strategies to discourage this leveling, such as giving patients the impression that they are disapproved of or treating men who ask questions as "problem" patients. Another respondent responds to the question of why specialists are resistant to questioning and informed patients:

> *Participant*: Well, they are probably that busy or whatever that it's all dollars and cents to them. The thing that really disheartened me was that I went away rather shocked like anyone is when they are told they have got cancer and I made a list of things to ask him in the next consultation. I had two foolscap sheets of questions ... I said to him "Could you please tell me what my Gleason score[1] is." He said, "Oh, you've got some questions, have you," and I said yes and he said, "oh, show them to me," and I gave him the two pieces of paper and he just grabbed them like that [shows me] and went [ticking motion] yes, no, yes, no ... not applicable, yes, no, and handed them back to me.
>
> *AB*: Why do you think your urologist reacted like that?
>
> *Participant*: Why ... when you park your car, one parking officer won't even speak and will write out the ticket, but the other bloke will give you a bit of a warning. It's attitudes ... that happens in all professions I guess. (Internet user, 4 years posttreatment, organ-confined disease)

The reaction of this specialist is an example of a strategy to avoid dialogue and reclaim the consultation model whereby it becomes merely a process of, at best, oneway information provision. His response of "yes, no, no" and ticking the questions listed by the respondent disempowers the respondent by not allowing him to initiate a dialogue to work through his concerns. This specialist ignores the respondent's request for his Gleason score, reacting, according to the respondent, as if it was inappropriate and "suspicious for me to want this type of information." This is one example of the various strategies employed by some of the respondents' specialists to limit the successfulness of their attempts to understand and question medical decisions and initiate a dialogue within the consultation.

It is tempting to romanticize the effects of the Internet and the empowering nature of information. However, as a number of the respondents suggested, the empowering nature of the information they retrieved from the Internet and other sources depended on how receptive providers and specialists were to their desire to take part in decision-making processes. Financial constraints combined with a desire to "deal quickly" with their disease meant that several respondents felt that they could not afford to spend a lot of time "shopping around" for sympathetic specialists. One respondent explains the limits to the potential of the Internet:

> You can be empowered to be happier with decisions that are made for you and you also can participate more to a degree in the decision but it's still dependent on finding a consultant or even the hospital which is reactive to this situation or sympathetic. That seems to me to be the difficulty in that, in my case, or in the individual case, you can't go to 4 or 5 specialists. Sooner or later you have to make a choice. (Internet user, midtreatment, suspected extracapsular disease)

The benefits of information are constrained by a number of factors, including an individual's skill in accessing and comprehending it, the amount of time (both perceived by them and prescribed by the specialist) that they have to make a treatment decision, and their access to receptive medical professionals. Several of the men interviewed could not afford to get a second opinion or to choose a specialist. Even though they had access to a substantial amount of information, they either could not afford to see other specialists or opt for limited, costly treatments such as high dose rate (HDR) brachytherapy. Furthermore, their resistance to getting a second opinion was amplified by the fact that they thought it would "slow down" their progress and mean their cancer would be worse when they were eventually treated. The view seemed to be that it would "irritate" their specialists if they sought a second opinion or presented them with information that questioned their advice and possibly result in their receiving less effective care. Thus, information was only one variable in determining whether the respondents were empowered to make an informed decision, with other structural constraints severely limiting their ability to negotiate satisfactory treatment processes.

Trust and Uncertainty

A number of the respondents, particularly the nonusers, were suspicious of the Internet and talked consistently about their reliance on the expertise and advice of their medical specialists. In the following excerpts, two respondents talk about whether patients should seek information and be "active" in making treatment decisions:

> Even now I ask myself: these people, they sit in front of their computers and they search the Internet and they read this but for what reason? Maybe they are chasing something that's not there … I figure if you go to a specialist and you don't follow his advice it's bordering on stupidity—he's the expert and I trust his judgement. (Non–Internet user, 6 years postdiagnosis, hormone treatment for secondary disease)

> I don't think that's my job. I sort of believe you've got to judge your surgeon. I know he goes overseas to conferences. I think you've sort of got to assume that they're up with the latest, um, you've got to hope that they have got a steady hand [laughs] and just go from there. I would be wary of designing me own treatment. (Non–Internet user, 3 years posttreatment, organ-confined disease)

The latter respondent articulates a common feeling of a lack of ability to judge information and a heavy reliance on the expertise of the specialist. This same respondent is then asked why he did not seek information or support from the Internet. He responds, in relation not to the Internet explicitly but, rather, to the futility, in his view, of trying to take control of his treatment process:

> Even though I had been diagnosed with cancer, which is a word everybody fears, I guess I'm fairly accepting of the situation. If I've got little or no control over it … When I went into hospital for this they said, you know, do you want to be a public or a private patient. If you're a private patient you have a doctor of your own choice. Well, I mean, who am I going to pick, I've never had that operation before, obviously, or I wouldn't have a prostate. Am I going to say, well, gee, bring us in the yellow pages and I'll pick one out. So, at the end of they day you sort of go

with something but you've got the stress ... I mean you've got the stress of your own situation and your family is under stress, you're exploring this information and you have got to make good judgments and you can't actually necessarily judge the source. (Non–Internet user, 3 years posttreatment, organ-confined disease)

This respondent vividly articulates the sense of loss of control that a significant proportion of the respondents (not just the nonusers) experienced attempting to make treatment decisions. The provision of options, such as public versus private, gives a perception of choice, whereas clearly this choice almost constricts the previous respondent in the sense that information is not provided for him to make the choice. There are no performance criteria for particular doctors provided. The choice, from the perspective of this respondent, is meaningless, because he has no knowledge and, in his mind, has no way of gaining the knowledge to make a decision that would produce the better outcome.

Three of the non–Internet users considered reliance on their specialist not a negative thing but, rather, the intelligent option. As suggested in one of the earlier excerpts, they considered it "stupid to try and learn what they [specialists] already know." Reliance was viewed as the "safe" option, and using the Internet, as one respondent put it, "is a stupid thing to do. I think they [other men] are probably grasping at straws anyway. Why bother? My specialist knows his stuff." These narratives illustrate the complex needs of men with prostate cancer and the importance of not assuming that all men want to self-educate or develop a sophisticated understanding of the treatment options available....

REFERENCES

Anderson, J., Rainey, M., & Eysenbach, G. (2003). The impact of cyber healthcare on the physician-patient relationship. *Journal of Medical Systems*, 27(1), 67–84.

Beisecker, A. (1990). Patient power in doctor-patient communication: What do we know? *Health Communication*, 2(2), 105–122.

Bennett, M., & Alison, D. (1996). Discussing the diagnosis and prognosis with cancer patients. *Postgraduate Medical Journal*, 72, 25–29.

Charavel, M., Bremond, A., Moumjid-Ferdjaoui, N., Mignotte, H., & Carrere, M. (2001). Shared decision-making in question. *Psychooncology*, 10, 93–102.

Crocco, A., Villasis-Keever, M., & Jadad, A. (2002). Analysis of cases of harm associated with use of health information on the Internet. *Journal of the American Medical Association*, 287(21), 2869–2872.

Dudley, T., Falvo, D., Podell, R., & Renner, J. (1996). The informed patient poses a different challenge. *Patient Care*, 30(19), 128–138.

Fox, S., & Rainie, L. (2002). *Vital decisions: How Internet users decide what information to trust when they or their loved ones are sick*. Washington, DC: Pew Internet & American Life Project.

Frederickson, L. (1995). Exploring information-exchange in consultation: The patients' view of performance and outcomes. *Patient Education and Counselling*, 25, 237–246.

Freedman, T. (2002). "The doctor knows best" revisited: Physician perspectives. *Psychooncology*, 11, 327–335.

Friedewald, V. (2000). The Internet's influence on the doctor-patient relationship. *Health Management Technology*, 21(11), 7980.

Hardey, M. (1999). Doctor in the house: The Internet as a source of health knowledge and a challenge to expertise. *Sociology of Health and Illness, 21*(6), 820–835.

Ishikawa, H., Takayama, T., Yamazaki, Y., Seki, Y., & Katsumata, N. (2002). Physician-patient communication and patient satisfaction in Japanese cancer consultations. *Social Science & Medicine, 55*, 301–311.

Kiley, R. (2002). Does the Internet harm health? *British Medical Journal, 324*, 238.

Lang, F. (2000). The evolving roles of patient and physician. *Archives of Family Medicine, 9*, 65–67.

Lupton, D. (1997). Consumerism, reflexivity and the medical encounter. *Social Science & Medicine, 45*(3), 373–381.

McLellan, F. (1998). Like hunger like thirst: Patients, journals and the Internet. *The Lancet, 352*(2 Suppl. 3), e12.

Ong, L., De Haes, J., & Lammes, F. (1995). Doctor-patient communication: A review of the literature. *Social Science & Medicine, 40*, 903–918.

Pemberton, P., & Goldblatt, J. (1998). The Internet and the changing roles of doctors, patients and families. *Medical Journal of Australia, 169*, 594–595.

Roberts, C., Cox, C., Reintgen, D., Baile, W., & Gibertini, M. (1994). Influence of physician communication on newly diagnosed breast cancer patients' psychological adjustment and decision-making. *Cancer, 74*, 336–341.

Whiting, R. (2000, December 11). A healthy way to learn: The medical community assesses online healthcare. *Information Week*, p. 60. Retrieved October 19, 2004, from http://www.informationweek.com/816/kin4.htm.

Zadoroznyj, M. (2001). Birth and the "reflexive consumer": Trust, risk and medical dominance in obstetric encounters. *Journal of Sociology, 37*(2), 117–141.

Source: A. Broom, 'Virtually he@lthy: the impact of Internet use on disease experience and the doctor–patient relationship', *Qualitative Health Research*, 15:3 (2005) 325–45.

Study Questions and Activities

1. In your capacity as a lay person, do you use the Internet to explore health issues? If yes, why? If no, why not?
2. Does a more informed patient or client challenge professional autonomy and power? How does this challenge the expectations of the sick role (see Reading 3)?
3. Identify one health issue that is relevant to you either professionally or personally. Using the Internet, do some research on this issue – spend not more than one hour doing this. What type of information did you find? How varied was the quality of this information (how would you determine the quality)?
4. Think back to the issue of diversity and inequality in health in Part III of this book. How far might issues of diversity influence the impact of the Internet on disease experience?
5. Having read the pieces in this book and completed the associated questions and activities, reflect on how your view of sociology and your understanding of health and healthcare as social experiences have changed.

─────────────────── **Further Reading** ───────────────────

There is continued and growing interest in the role of the Internet in lay experiences of health and illness and on the impact of this on patient–professional interaction and professional power. Some studies identify the Internet as the source of considerable dissatisfaction and divergence, whereas others show that patients and professionals often agree on the utility of the Internet, e.g. see: S. Nettleton, R. Burrows and L. O'Malley, 'The mundane realities of the everyday lay use of the internet for health, and their consequences for media convergence', *Sociology of Health & Illness*, 27:7 (2005) 972–92. There are also, however, other challenges to professional power. The following article outlines the challenges posed by lay carers: S. Pickard, S. Jacobs and S. Kirk, 'Challenging professional roles: lay carers' involvement in healthcare in the community', *Social Policy and Administration*, 37:1 (2003) 82–96. Considerable attention has also been given to the role of lay experts, e.g.: S. McClean and A. Shaw, 'From schism to continuum? The problematic relationship between expert and lay knowledge – An exploratory conceptual synthesis of two qualitative studies', *Qualitative Health Research*, 15:6 (2005) 729–49 and L. Prior 'Belief, knowledge and expertise: the emergence of the lay expert in medical sociology', *Sociology of Health & Illness*, 25: Special Issue (2003) 41–57. To explore the Internet and cyberspace more generally, consider the following book: M. Dodge and R. Kitchin, *Mapping Cyberspace* (London: Routledge, 2000).

Index